"Psychoanalytic therapies are often assumed to be governed by rigid rules (e.g., one explores the patient's childhood, one tries to be "neutral"). In reality, all analysts create unique integrations of theory, identifications, clinical experience, and their own authentic temperaments. For anyone who wants to know how psychoanalytic therapists really think and behave, this book is indispensable. As we witness seasoned therapists address challenges that have no clear resolution, their individuality comes through vividly, just as it does in actual practice. I recommend this engaging book to anyone who wants to understand what psychoanalysis looks like in real-world clinical situations."
Nancy McWilliams

"This is such a great idea, and the editors have brought together such an all-star cast and keen educational format that it hardly needs my words to support it. I can't think of another book that will so directly grab the curiosity of everyone in the profession. It's irresistible."
Larry Friedman

"Beyond classroom training, supervision, and an analyst's conducted analyses, lies an innovative method of learning involving the presentation of a clinical dilemma in an informal setting to an audience of equals who exchange their reactions from the vantage point of different psychoanalytic schools and cultures. Such a forum, which breaches the confines of formal education and institutionally sanctioned learning, provides a stimulating way for analysts to become increasingly thoughtful about their work. In place of audience participation, this book replicates just such a learning exercise by substituting the voices of master clinicians."
Stefano Bolognini

Conundrums and Predicaments in Psychotherapy and Psychoanalysis

From time to time therapists find themselves in a bind – faced with a challenging situation, unsure how to proceed. Such a conundrum leaves the therapist on edge, concerned that the success of treatment might rest on how he or she responds to the circumstance. The situation seems to call for more than pat clinical protocol, leaving the therapist uncertain as he or she ventures into novel territory wondering, "What do I do now?"

Conundrums and Predicaments in Psychotherapy and Psychoanalysis: The Clinical Moments Project comprises 12 distinct clinical moments during which the treating/presenting analyst feels him- or herself in just such a quandary. The presented moment comes to a head at a point where the therapist feels uncertain what his or her next and best "move" might be – one that balances the protection of the therapeutic alliance with the need to address a clinical development head-on. Space is then left for 25 well-known analysts ("commentators") of varying theoretical persuasions to weigh in, sharing what they think about the situation and how they imagine they might have proceeded.

In the final analysis, the point of this project is not to determine how the moment "should" have been handled given the input of experts; rather, it aims to illuminate the clinical theories that therapists carry with them into sessions where they operate implicitly, directing their attention to select sorts of data that are then used to fashion an intervention. This, then, is the ultimate lesson of the Clinical Moments Project – to learn how to listen to how therapists listen to the unfolding material. This book will be of great interest to psychoanalysts and psychoanalytic psychotherapists of all persuasions.

Richard Tuch is Training and Supervising Analyst at the New Center for Psychoanalysis and the Psychoanalytic Center of California. He is Clinical Professor of Psychiatry at the David Geffen School of Medicine, UCLA.

Lynn S. Kuttnauer is a Training and Supervising Analyst at the New Center for Psychoanalysis. She is the founder of the Clinical Moments Program at the New Center for Psychoanalysis and was one of the founding members of the Clinical Moments Program at the Michigan Psychoanalytic Institute.

Conundrums and Predicaments in Psychotherapy and Psychoanalysis

The Clinical Moments Project

Edited by
Richard Tuch and Lynn S. Kuttnauer

LONDON AND NEW YORK

First published 2018
by Routledge
2 Park Square, Milton Park, Abingdon, Oxon OX14 4RN

and by Routledge
711 Third Avenue, New York, NY 10017

Routledge is an imprint of the Taylor & Francis Group, an informa business

© 2018 selection and editorial matter, Richard Tuch and Lynn S. Kuttnauer; individual chapters, the contributors

The right of the editors to be identified as the authors of the editorial material, and of the authors for their individual chapters, has been asserted in accordance with sections 77 and 78 of the Copyright, Designs and Patents Act 1988.

All rights reserved. No part of this book may be reprinted or reproduced or utilised in any form or by any electronic, mechanical, or other means, now known or hereafter invented, including photocopying and recording, or in any information storage or retrieval system, without permission in writing from the publishers.

Trademark notice: Product or corporate names may be trademarks or registered trademarks, and are used only for identification and explanation without intent to infringe.

British Library Cataloguing in Publication Data
A catalogue record for this book is available from the British Library

Library of Congress Cataloging in Publication Data
Names: Tuch, Richard, editor. | Kuttnauer, Lynn S., editor.
Title: Conundrums and predicaments in psychotherapy and psychoanalysis : the clinical moments project / edited by Richard Tuch and Lynn S. Kuttnauer.
Description: Milton Park, Abingdon, Oxon ; New York, NY : Routledge, 2018. | Includes bibliographical references and index.
Identifiers: LCCN 2017045317| ISBN 9781138079847 (hardback) | ISBN 9781138079854 (pbk.) | ISBN 9781315114217 (ebk.) | ISBN 9781351627030 (ePub) | ISBN 9781351627047 (Web PDF) | ISBN 9781351627023 (Mobipocket/kindle)
Subjects: | MESH: Psychotherapy | Clinical Competence | Countertransference (Psychology) | Professional-Patient Relations
Classification: LCC RC480.5 | NLM WM 21 | DDC 616.89/14–dc23
LC record available at https://lccn.loc.gov/2017045317

ISBN: 978-1-138-07984-7 (hbk)
ISBN: 978-1-138-07985-4 (pbk)
ISBN: 978-1-315-11421-7 (ebk)

Typeset in Times New Roman
by Taylor & Francis Books

This book is dedicated to Marvin Margolis, M.D., Ph.D. who envisioned and created the Clinical Moments Program, reflecting his lifelong passion of welcoming all and nourishing psychoanalytic thinking.

Contents

List of contributors	xi
Acknowledgments	xxii
Introduction: Moments of Waking and Reckoning: "*Now* What Do I Do?"	1

PART I
Taking a Stand — 23

1 Whether to Speak or Let Things Be — 25
   RICHARD TUCH

2 Venturing onto Thin Ice: Tiptoeing in the Wake of Empathic Failures — 48
   LYNN S. KUTTNAUER

3 "If You Keep Talking to Me This Way, I'm Going to Quit!": (You Talk… I Walk) — 72
   ROBERT JAMES PERKINS

PART II
Countertransference Enactments — 87

4 Countertransference Enactments: Three Times Over — 89
   JILL MODEL BARTH

5 Feeling Misunderstood Bilaterally — 112
   SUSAN ORBACH

PART III
What Patients Want; What Therapists Can Provide — 135

6 Patient as Bean Counter — 137
RINA FREEDMAN

7 Withstanding the Patient's Demand for Answers — 159
JANET K. SMITH

8 To Attend or Not to Attend the Exhibit? — 180
NANCY KULISH

PART IV
Having Impact: The Balancing of Power — 199

9 How Far Do We Enter into a Child's Fantasy When We Play? — 201
BERNADETTE KOVACH

10 A Shocking Revelation — 222
DEBORAH HARMS

11 Considering Third Parties: The Question of Allegiance — 242
MICHELE GOMES

12 Worried Sick about a Patient — 284
RICHARD TUCH

Index — 289

List of Contributors

Co-Editors

Richard Tuch, M.D. is a Training and Supervising Analyst at the New Center for Psychoanalysis (NCP) in Los Angeles and at the Psychoanalytic Center of California. He is Clinical Professor of Psychiatry at the David Geffen School of Medicine, University of California Los Angeles, where he has supervised psychiatric residents for almost 40 years. He has published articles in all three of the leading psychoanalytic journals, contributed chapters to a number of books, served as Executive Editor of *The Edinburgh International Encyclopedia of Psychoanalysis*, and most recently released a volume entitled *Psychoanalytic Method in Motion: Controversies and Evolution in Clinical Theory and Practice* (Routledge, 2018). He is the recipient of the Karl A. Menninger Memorial Award for Psychoanalytic Writing and the Edith Sabshin Teaching Award. Dr. Tuch is the former Dean of Training at the New Center for Psychoanalysis and presently serves as Section Head, Scholarship Subcommittee of the Department of Psychoanalytic Education of the American Psychoanalytic Association. Dr. Tuch is in full-time private practice in West Los Angeles.

Lynn S. Kuttnauer, Ph.D. is a Training and Supervising Analyst at the New Center for Psychoanalysis (NCP) in Los Angeles where she is on faculty, teaching in both the core Psychoanalytic Education program and the Psychotherapy program. She serves on many different Institute committees and is the founder of NCP's Clinical Moments Program. Dr. Kuttnauer was also a founding member of the Clinical Moments Program at the Michigan Psychoanalytic Institute, where she did her analytic training. She enjoys supervising interns at both the Wright Institute of Los Angeles and the Maple Center. She is in full-time private practice in West Hollywood.

Other Moment Contributors

Jill Model Barth, Ph.D. is a psychologist and psychoanalyst, Training and Supervising Analyst and senior faculty member at the New Center for

Psychoanalysis, and a member of the Los Angeles Institute and Society for Psychoanalytic Studies. Dr. Barth is an Associate Professor at The Chicago School of Professional Psychology in Los Angeles and is a supervising and teaching faculty member at the Wright Institute. She maintains a private psychoanalytic and psychotherapy practice in Beverly Hills, California, treating adults. She also offers individual and group clinical supervision.

Rina Freedman, Psy.D., LCSW is Senior Faculty at the New Center for Psychoanalysis. She regularly teaches in the Psychoanalytic Training and Psychoanalytic Psychotherapy Programs. Dr. Freedman maintains a private practice in West Los Angeles working with individuals and couples. Cross-cultural phenomena and their relational impact are of great interest to her. Dr. Freedman's fluency in several languages enhances her approach to clinical work.

Michele Gomes, Psy.D. is the Executive Director of Wright Institute Los Angeles, a non-profit psychoanalytic training center and low-fee clinic. She ia a recent graduate of the psychoanalytic training program at the New Center for Psychoanalysis where she also serves as faculty in the Psychoanalytic Psychotherapy Program. She maintains a part-time private practice in West Los Angeles and is passionate about program development and training socially conscious mental health clinicians.

Deborah Harms, Ph.D. is a graduate of the Michigan Psychoanalytic Institute where she has taught classes on trauma, technique, and psychoanalytic writing to candidates and psychotherapy students. She supervises and teaches residents and doctoral students in universities and practices psychotherapy and psychoanalysis in Southfield, Michigan. She has been a frequent presenter locally and nationally at the meetings of the American Psychoanalytic Association. Dr. Harms is Certified in Adult Psychoanalysis by the American Psychoanalytic Association.

Bernadette Kovach, Ph.D. is degreed in both clinical and educational psychology, and is a board-certified child, adolescent, and adult psychoanalyst. In addition to her clinical work with children of all ages she has served as a consultant at Walnut Lake and Allen Creek preschools, provides supervision for graduate students and residents, and is an Associate Faculty at the Michigan Psychoanalytic Institute. Dr. Kovach has been published in *The Psychoanalytic Study of the Child* and presented her research at the American Psychological Association.

Nancy Kulish, Ph.D. is Professor, Department of Psychiatry, Wayne State Medical School and Adjunct Professor of Psychology, University of Detroit/Mercy. She is a Training and Supervising Analyst at the Michigan Psychoanalytic Institute, where she was past president. She was chosen as the National Woman Psychoanalytic Scholar for 2005 of the American

Psychoanalytic Association. Currently she is on the Editorial Boards of the *Psychoanalytic Quarterly* and the *International Journal of Psychoanalysis*. She has published and presented on topics ranging from female sexuality, gender, transference/countertransference, and adolescence to termination. With Deanna Holtzman, she is the co-author of the 2008 book *A Story of Her Own: The Female Oedipus Complex Reexamined and Renamed* and most recently the co-editor of *The Clinical Problem of Masochism*. She is in private practice in Birmingham, Michigan.

Susan L. Orbach, Ph.D. is a clinical psychologist, psychoanalyst, lecturer, and co-chair of the curriculum committee at the Michigan Psychoanalytic Institute. She is on the clinical faculty at Wayne State University Medical School and a clinical supervisor at the University of Detroit Mercy. Dr. Orbach is in full-time private practice in Huntington Woods, Michigan.

Robert James Perkins, M.D. is a board-certified adult and child psychiatrist and psychoanalyst, Training and Supervising Analyst at the New Center for Psychoanalysis, Assistant Clinical Professor of Psychiatry at The David Geffen School of Medicine at the University of California Los Angeles, and past president of the Los Angeles Child Development Center. He is in private practice in Brentwood with particular interest in psychoanalytic treatment and psychotherapy with adults, as well as working with couples, adolescents, and their families.

Janet K. Smith, Ph.D. is a clinical psychologist, psychoanalyst, and active member at the New Center for Psychoanalysis, Los Angeles. She is Senior Faculty in the Psychoanalytic Education Program and teaches in the Psychotherapy Program. She is the author of "The Dynamic Psyche," a column that appeared in *The Therapist*, as well as other articles on borderline and narcissistic disorders. She supervises candidates at the Wright Institute, Los Angeles and has a private practice in West Los Angeles.

Roster of Commentators (25)

Salman Akhtar, M.D. is Professor of Psychiatry at Jefferson Medical College, and Training and Supervising Analyst at the Psychoanalytic Center of Philadelphia. He has served on the Editorial Boards of the *International Journal of Psychoanalysis, Journal of the American Psychoanalytic Association*, and *Psychoanalytic Quarterly*. His 87 books include 18 solo-authored, as well as 58 edited books in psychiatry and psychoanalysis. He received the Best Paper of the Year Award from the *Journal of the American Psychoanalytic Association* (1995), Edith Sabshin Award (2000) from the American Psychoanalytic Association, Sigmund Freud Award from the American Society of Psychoanalytic Physicians (2000), Kun Po Soo Award (2004), Irma Bland Award (2005) from the American Psychiatric

Association, and the prestigious Sigourney Award (2012) for outstanding contributions to psychoanalysis. Dr. Akhtar has delivered lectures around the world in Australia, Belgium, Brazil, Canada, Chile, China, England, France, Germany, India, Italy, Japan, Mexico, New Zealand, Peru, Serbia, and Turkey. His books have been translated into many languages including German, Italian, Korean, Portuguese, Romanian, Serbian, and Turkish. He has also published 11 volumes of poetry and is Scholar-in-Residence at the Inter-Act Theatre Company in Philadelphia.

Anne Alvarez, Ph.D., M.A.C.P. is a Consultant Child and Adolescent Psychotherapist (and retired Co-Convener of the Autism Service, Child and Family Dep't., Tavistock Clinic, London, where she still teaches). She is author of *Live Company: Psychotherapy with Autistic, Borderline, Deprived and Abused Children,* and has edited with Susan Reid *Autism and Personality: Findings from the Tavistock Autism Workshop.* A book in her honor, edited by Judith Edwards, entitled *Being Alive: Building on the Work of Anne Alvarez*, was published in 2002. She was Visiting Professor at the San Francisco Psychoanalytic Society in November 2005 and is an Honorary Member of the Psychoanalytic Center of California. Her latest book, *The Thinking Heart: Three Levels of Psychoanalytic Therapy with Disturbed Children,* was published in April 2012 by Routledge.

Rosemary H. Balsam, F.R.C.Psych. (Lond.), M.R.C.P. (Edin.) is an Associate Clinical Professor of Psychiatry in the Yale Medical School, staff psychiatrist in the Yale Department of Student Mental Health and Counseling, and a Training and Supervising Analyst at the Western New England Institute for Psychoanalysis, New Haven, Connecticut. Her special interests are gender development, and the place of the body in psychic life. She is on the Editorial Boards of *Psychoanalytic Quarterly* and *Imago*, and co-editor of the Book Review Section of the *Journal of the American Psychoanalytic Association.* Her most recent book is *Women's Bodies in Psychoanalysis* (2012, Routledge); and her most recent paper is (2017) "Freud, The Birthing Body and Modern Life," *Journal of the American Psychoanalytic Association,* 65(1), 61–90.

Rachel Blass, Ph.D. is Training Analyst at the Israel Psychoanalytic Society, a member of the British Psychoanalytical Society, Professor of Psychoanalysis at Heythrop College, the University of London, and editor of the "Controversies" section of the *International Journal of Psychoanalysis.* She has published a book and over 70 articles which deal mainly with the close study and elucidation of Freud's texts and Kleinian thinking and practice. Her writings have been translated into 15 languages. Rachel Blass lectures, teaches, and offers clinical seminars in many countries. Having spent eight years in London, she has recently returned to Jerusalem where she maintains her analytic practice.

Stefano Bolognini, M.D. is a psychiatrist and Training and Supervising Analyst in Bologna (Italy), where he has worked for 30 years also as supervisor at the Mental Health Services. He is Past President of the Italian Psychoanalytic Society (SPI) and the International Psychoanalytical Association (IPA). Dr. Bolognini has authored 220 papers and several of his books have been translated into other languages, including *Psychoanalytic Empathy* (2004), *Secret Passages: The Theory and Technique of the Interpsychic Relations* (2010), and *Like Wind, Like Wave* (2006 – a collection of short stories). He is also founder and current chairperson of the *IPA Inter-Regional Encyclopedic Dictionary of Psychoanalysis*.

Fred Busch, Ph.D. is a Training and Supervising Analyst at the Boston Psychoanalytic Society and Institute. He has published over 90 articles in the psychoanalytic literature, and 3 books, primarily on the method and theory of treatment. His work has been translated into 8 languages, and he has been invited to present over 160 papers and clinical workshops nationally and internationally. His third book, *Creating a Psychoanalytic Mind: A Method and Theory of Psychoanalysis*, was a finalist for the Gradiva prize. He was the Editor of *JAPA Books*, and has been on numerous editorial boards.

Andrea Celenza, Ph.D. is a Training and Supervising Analyst at the Boston Psychoanalytic Society and Institute, Faculty at the Massachusetts Institute for Psychoanalysis, and an Assistant Clinical Professor at Harvard Medical School. She is Co-Director (with Martha Stark, MD) of a blended, online program in Psychoanalytic Psychotherapy sponsored by William James College. As part of this program, she offers an online course, "What, Where is Psychoanalysis? Classic Concepts, New Meanings," tracing a trajectory of psychoanalytic theorizing from the intrapsychic to the intersubjective. Dr. Celenza is the recipient of several awards and has authored two books. *Sexual Boundary Violations: Therapeutic, Supervisory and Academic Contexts* was published by Jason Aronson in 2007. She has recently produced an online video-recorded lecture on sexual boundary violations designed for ethics seminars, group viewing, or individual use. Her new book, *Erotic Revelations: Clinical Applications and Perverse Scenarios*, is published by Routledge. She is in private practice in Lexington, Massachusetts.

Susan Donner, M.D. is a child, adolescent, and adult psychiatrist and psychoanalyst, graduate of the adult and child psychoanalytic programs at The New Center for Psychoanalysis where she is now Training and Supervising Analyst, Child and Adolescent Supervising Analyst, and the Chair of the Child Psychoanalytic Program at the New Center for Psychoanalysis in Los Angeles. She also serves as a Senior Teaching Faculty member. A graduate of Harvard University and University of California at San

Francisco School of Medicine, she is an Assistant Clinical Professor in Psychiatry at David Geffen School of Medicine at the University of California Los Angeles, where she teaches medical students and psychiatry residents and supervises child psychiatry fellows. She has contributed a number of chapters and articles in the psychoanalytic literature and has presented at IPA, APsaA, APA, AACAP, and Western Regional conferences on such topics as child development, attachment disorders, psychodynamic formulation, psychoanalytic perspectives on the use of medications, and clinical aspects of child, adolescent, and adult psychoanalytic treatment. Dr. Donner is in full-time private practice in Woodland Hills, California.

Morris Eagle, Ph.D. is Professor Emeritus, Derner Institute of Advanced Psychological Studies, Adelphi University and Distinguished-Educator-in-Residence, California Lutheran University. Dr. Eagle is a recipient of the Sigourney Award (in 2009) and he has authored 150 journal articles and given 150 presentations. His most recent books are *Volume 1: Core Concepts of Classical Psychoanalytic Theory: Evidence and Critique*; and *Volume 2: Core Concepts of Contemporary Psychoanalytic Theory: Evidence and Critique*. Dr. Eagle is in private practice in Los Angeles.

Darlene Bregman Ehrenberg, Ph.D., ABPP has been writing about working at the "intimate edge" of the psychoanalytic relationship since 1974. Her book *The Intimate Edge: Extending The Reach Of Psychoanalytic Interaction* (W. W. Norton and Company) was published in 1992. Dr. Ehrenberg is Training and Supervising Analyst, and on the teaching Faculty at the William Alanson White Institute, New York City; Supervising Analyst and Adjunct Clinical Associate Professor at The New York University Postdoctoral Program in Psychoanalysis; Faculty, Mitchell Center for Psychoanalysis, New York City; Supervising Analyst at the Institute for Contemporary Psychoanalysis, Los Angeles, California; as well as working for other institutes. She is also on the Editorial Board of *Contemporary Psychoanalysis,* Associate Editor for *Psychoanalytic Dialogues*, consulting editor for *Psychoanalytic Inquiry*, on the Editorial Board of *Journal of Psychohistory*, and on the affiliate teaching faculty for the Erikson Institute Fellowship Program, Austen Riggs Center, Stockbridge, Massachusetts. She lectures widely around the world and is currently working on two new books: one on intergenerational transmission of trauma, and the other focusing on issues of desire and therapeutic inter-action and on intimacy and capacity for loving. Dr. Ehrenberg is in private practice in New York City working with individuals and couples.

James L. Fosshage, Ph.D. is Past President of the International Association for Psychoanalytic Self Psychology (IAPSP). He is Co-founder, Board Director, and Faculty member of the National Institute for the

Psychotherapies (NYC), Founding Faculty Member, Institute for the Psychoanalytic Study of Subjectivity (NYC), and Clinical Professor of Psychology of the New York University Postdoctoral Program in Psychotherapy and Psychoanalysis (Co-Founder of the Relational Track). Dr. Fosshage has authored over 125 psychoanalytic publications, including 9 books, focusing on the implicit/explicit motivational and organizing processes traversing dreams, transference, countertransference, listening perspectives, and therapeutic action. His last book, co-edited with Joseph Lichtenberg and Frank Lachmann, is entitled *Narrative and Meaning* (2017). His website is www.jamesfosshage.net.

Robert Alan Glick, M.D. is Professor of Clinical Psychiatry, Columbia University College of Physicians and Surgeons, and former Director of the Columbia University Center for Psychoanalytic Training and Research (1997–2007). Dr. Glick is Training and Supervising Psychoanalyst at the Columbia University Center, and former Associate Editor for Education of the *Journal of the American Psychoanalytic Association*. He has taught and supervised extensively in both the Columbia Psychoanalytic Center curriculum and the New York State Psychiatric Institute Residency Program. Dr. Glick has edited a series of volumes on the Psychoanalytic Theory of Affects, and published numerous chapters and articles on psychoanalytic and psychiatric education, masochism, application of theory in clinical work, and recently with Dr. Gloria Stern *Entering Analysis*, a primer for psychoanalytic clinicians.

Jay Greenberg, Ph.D. is Training and Supervising Analyst, William Alanson White Institute; Editor of *The Psychoanalytic Quarterly*; former Editor for North America of the *International Journal of Psychoanalysis*; former Editor of *Contemporary Psychoanalysis*; co-author (with Stephen Mitchell) of *Object Relations in Psychoanalytic Theory*; author of *Oedipus and Beyond: A Clinical Theory*; and recipient of the 2015 Mary S. Sigourney Award for Outstanding Achievement in the Advancement of Psychoanalysis.

Theodore Jacobs, M.D. is Training and Supervising Analyst at the New York Psychoanalytic Institute and the New York University Psychoanalytic Institute; Child Supervising Analyst at New York University Psychoanalytic Institute and at Columbia University Center for Psychoanalytic Medicine; and Clinical Professor of Psychiatry at Albert Einstein College of Medicine and at New York University School of Medicine. He serves on the editorial boards of a number of psychoanalytic journals and has published over 60 papers and book reviews on a variety of psychoanalytic topics. He is credited with introducing the concept of countertransference enactments (in 1986) and is known for his work on the analyst's use of the self in analysis. In particular, he is an avid baseball fan and penned *The Year of Durocher* in 2013.

Judy L. Kantrowitz, Ph.D. is Training and Supervising Analyst at the Boston Psychoanalytic Institute and a Clinical Associate Professor at Harvard Medical School. She is the author of three books: *The Patient's Impact on the Analyst* (1996); *Writing about Patients: Responsibilities, Risks, and Ramifications* (2006); and *Myths of Termination: What Patients Can Teach Psychoanalysts about Endings* (2014). She has also authored papers on the patient–analyst match and outcome of psychoanalysis and others on impasses in analysis. She has served three times on the Editorial Boards of the *Journal of the American Psychoanalytic Association* and is currently on the board of *The Psychoanalytic Quarterly*. She is in private practice of psychoanalysis and psychoanalytic psychotherapy in Brookline, Massachusetts.

Edgar Levenson, M.D. is Fellow Emeritus, Training and Supervisory Analyst, and Faculty Member at the William Alanson White Institute. He is Adjunct Clinical Professor of Psychology, New York University, Graduate Studies Division; Honorary Fellow, Postgraduate Center for Mental Health; and Honorary Member of the American Psychoanalytic Association. He is a Life Fellow of the American Academy of Psychoanalysis and Distinguished Life Fellow of the American Psychiatric Association. He is a recipient of the Mary S. Sigourney Award (2006). His book titles include: *Fallacy of Understanding; The Ambiguity of Change; The Purloined Self;* and *Interpersonal Psychoanalysis and the Enigma of Consciousness*.

Joseph Lichtenberg, M.D. is Editor-in-Chief of *Psychoanalytic Inquiry* and the Psychoanalytic Inquiry Book Series. He is Founder and Director Emeritus of the Institute of Contemporary Psychotherapy and Psychoanalysis. In papers and books, he has reconceptualized motivation as a comprehensive organization of seven systems that are supported by clinical experience, infant studies, and neuroscience. In *Psychoanalysis and Motivation* (1989), *Self and Motivational Systems: Toward a Theory of Psychoanalytic Technique* (1992), *and Psychoanalysis and Motivation: A New Look* (2010) he presents evidence for a theory of systems that self-organize to ensure attachment, affiliation, caregiving, the regulation of physiological requirements, exploration, expressions of aversion, and sensuality and sexuality.

Albert Mason, MB, BS, Psy.D., F. Inst. Psychoanal. trained at The British Institute of Psychoanalysis and practiced in London before immigrating to the United States in 1969 with Wilfred Bion and Susanna Isaacs to further the work of Melanie Klein. Formerly Clinical Professor of Psychiatry at The University of Southern California, Dr. Mason is a Training and Supervising Analyst at The Psychoanalytic Center of California (PCC) and The New Center for Psychoanalysis in Los Angeles. He is a founding member and twice President of PCC, as well as a past member of The

House of Delegates of The International Psychoanalytic Society. He has published and taught extensively both in the United States and abroad. Dr. Mason is in private practice in Beverly Hills. His most recent lectures on psychoanalysis can be viewed on the PCC website.

Nancy McWilliams, Ph.D. teaches at Rutgers University's Graduate School of Applied & Professional Psychology and practices in Lambertville, New Jersey. She is author of *Psychoanalytic Diagnosis* (1994, revised edition 2011), *Psychoanalytic Case Formulation* (1999), *Psychoanalytic Psychotherapy* (2004), and an upcoming book on overall wellness. Her books are available in 20 languages; she lectures widely both nationally and internationally. She is Associate Editor of the *Psychodynamic Diagnostic Manual,* 2nd edition (2017), a former president of Division 39 (Psychoanalysis) of the APA, and an Honorary Member of the American Psychoanalytic Association. She has been featured in three APA videos of master clinicians, the most recent being "Three Approaches to Psychotherapy."

Robert Michels, M.D. is the Walsh McDermott University Professor of Medicine and Psychiatry at Weill-Cornell Medical College. He is also Deputy Editor of *The American Journal of Psychiatry*, and former Joint Editor-in-Chief of *The International Journal of Psychoanalysis.* In the past he served as the Stephen and Suzanne Weiss Dean of Cornell University Medical College and Provost for Medical Affairs of Cornell University. He also served as the Barklie McKee Henry Professor and Chairman of Cornell's Department of Psychiatry, Psychiatrist-in-Chief at The New York Hospital, and is a former Training and Supervising Analyst at the Columbia University Center for Psychoanalytic Training and Research.

Irma Brenman Pick is a Distinguished Fellow, Past President, and Supervising and Training Analyst at the British Psychoanalytic Society. She is an adult and child psychoanalyst and her best-known paper "Working through in the Countertransference" (1985) is widely quoted. She and her late husband, Eric Brenman, taught extensively abroad, and she continues to teach at home and internationally. A book of her Selected Papers is due for publication next year.

Dominique Scarfone, M.D. is Honorary Professor at the Université de Montréal and a Training-Supervising Analyst in the French Montréal branch of the Canadian Psychoanalytic Society and Institute. A former associate editor of the *International Journal of Psychoanalysis,* he is presently on the Editorial Board of *The Psychoanalytic Quarterly.* He has published six books – *Jean Laplanche* (Paris, PUF, 1997); *Oublier Freud? Mémoire pour la psychanalyse* (Montréal, Boréal, 1999); *Les Pulsions* (Paris, PUF, « Que sais-je? », 2004); *Quartiers aux rues sans nom* (Paris, Éditions de l'Olivier, 2012); *Laplanche: An Introduction* (New York, The Unconscious in

Translation, 2015); *The Unpast. The Actual Unconscious* (New York, The Unconscious in Translation, 2015) – and co-edited, with Howard Levine and Gail Reed, *Unrepresented States and the Construction of Meaning* (London, Karnac Books, 2013). Dr. Scarfone has authored many book chapters and numerous articles on psychoanalysis in, among others, *The International Journal of Psychoanalysis, The Psychoanalytic Quarterly, The Journal of the American Psychoanalytic Association, Psychoanalytic Inquiry*, and *Psychoanalytic Dialogues*. Dr. Scarfone regularly gives lectures and seminars across the United States, Canada, and Europe.

Donnel Stern, Ph.D. is Training and Supervising Analyst at the William Alanson White Institute in New York City; Adjunct Clinical Professor and Clinical Consultant at the New York University Postdoctoral Program; and faculty at the New York Psychoanalytic Institute. He is the author of *Unformulated Experience: From Dissociation to Imagination in Psychoanalysis* (1997), *Partners in Thought: Working with Unformulated Experience, Dissociation, and Enactment* (2010), and *Relational Freedom: Emergent Properties of the Interpersonal Field* (2015). He is the Editor of "Psychoanalysis in a New Key," a book series at Routledge. He is the former Editor-in-Chief of *Contemporary Psychoanalysis*. Most recently he has been co-editor of *The Interpersonal Perspective in Psychoanalysis, 1960s–1990s: Rethinking Transference and Countertransference* (Routledge, 2017); and earlier co-edited *The Handbook of Interpersonal Psychoanalysis* (Routledge, 1995) and *Pioneers of Interpersonal Psychoanalysis* (Routledge, 1995). He is an Associate Editor of *Psychoanalytic Dialogues,* and serves on the Editorial Boards of *Psychoanalytic Inquiry, Psychoanalytic Psychology, The Psychoanalytic Quarterly,* and *The Journal of the American Psychoanalytic Association.* Dr. Stern is in private practice in New York City.

Alan Sugarman, Ph.D. is a Training and Supervising Psychoanalyst, and a Supervising Child and Adolescent Psychoanalyst at the San Diego Psychoanalytic Center. He is also a Clinical Professor of Psychiatry at the University of California, San Diego. He serves on the editorial boards of the *Psychoanalytic Quarterly, Journal of the American Psychoanalytic Association*, and *Psychoanalytic Psychology*. His numerous writings revolve around the application of psychoanalytic developmental thinking to diagnosis and treatment. At present, he is serving as the Head of the Department of Psychoanalytic Education of the American Psychoanalytic Association and as a North American representative to the board of the International Psychoanalytic Association. Dr. Sugarman maintains a private practice in La Jolla and Encinitas, California.

Mitchell Wilson, MD is a Training and Supervising Analyst at the San Francisco Center for Psychoanalysis, and a Supervising Analyst at the

Psychoanalytic Institute of Northern California. He has been awarded the Heinz Hartmann Memorial Lectureship at the New York Psychoanalytic Institute in 2002, the Journal of the American Psychoanalytic Association Prize in 2003, and the Karl A. Menninger Memorial Award in 2005. He is an Associate Editor of the *Journal of the American Psychoanalytic Association*, and on the Editorial Board of the *Psychoanalytic Quarterly*. Dr. Wilson has published widely on a variety of topics that cohere around a theory of ethics, desire, and the psychoanalytic process. He is bringing these ideas into a book project, "The Analyst's Desire and the Ethical in Psychoanalysis." He is in private practice in Berkeley, CA.

Acknowledgments

There are so many individuals we wish to acknowledge for their contributions helping to create and sustain Clinical Moment Programs both in Michigan and in Los Angeles. Insofar as this volume grew more directly out of the Program conducted under the aegis of Lynn Kuttnauer in Los Angeles, we begin by acknowledging those at the New Center for Psychoanalysis (NCP) who were instrumental in championing the idea of transplanting the Program, born at the Michigan Psychoanalytic Institute under the tutelage of Dr. Marvin Margolis, until it was actualized as a thriving monthly program, which is now entering its fifth year of operation in L.A. Initial skepticism about the viability of such a program, given the logistics of L.A.'s sprawling expanse and notorious traffic, gave way as the NCP Board of Directors went on to offer Dr. Kuttnauer free rein in implementing a local Clinical Moments Program, offering assistance by suggesting colleagues willing to aid in this endeavor. I (LK) extend my warmest thanks to my initial Clinical Moments Committee, Drs. Beverly Feinstein, Gittelle Sones, and Mary Le Master Thomsen, who trusted in me, volunteering their time and opening their homes as the Program got underway. Sincerest thanks additionally to our current Clinical Moments Committee members – Drs. Jill Model Barth, Cia Foreman, Michele Gomes, and Janet K. Smith – without whom the program could not have functioned. The Clinical Moments Committee is indebted to NCP and its generous Board of Directors who have granted financial support to our analysts who host Clinical Moments in their homes, which has helped our program thrive.

This book and NCP's Clinical Moments Program would not have existed had it not been for the imagination and persuasiveness of Dr. Marvin Margolis and the hard-working Clinical Moments Committee in Michigan. The founding members are Drs. Kehinde Ayeni, David Dietrich, Lynn S. Kuttnauer, Marc Hirsh, and Marc Rosen.

The Editors extend their heartfelt thanks to all of the analysts who have warmly opened their homes and kitchens on a monthly basis[1] to host and feed the Program's attendees (up to 30 at times!) in both Michigan and Los Angeles. These generous supporters include, in Michigan: Kehinde Ayeni,

Melvin Bornstein, Marcy Palmer Broder, Michael Coleman, Deborah Harms, Marc Hirsch, Bernadette Kovach, Steven Nicholoff, Susan Orbach, Patricia Plopa, Marc Rosen, Sally Rosenberg, Don Spivak, Deborah Tucker, and Susan Wainwright; and in Los Angeles: Jill Model Barth, Allan Compton, Daniel Fast, Beverly Feinstein, Cia Foreman, Rina Freedman, Michael Gales, Katharine Gould, Robin Jacobs, Myra Pomerantz, Sherry Siassi, Heather Silverman, Miriam Tasini, and Mary Thomsen.

The Editors are also indebted to, and wholeheartedly give thanks to, all of the analysts who have generously and thoughtfully exposed their own clinical work for discussion, often on a yearly basis, in Michigan: Kehinde Ayeni, Melvin Bornstein, Marcy Palmer Broder, John Gilkey, Deborah Harms, Marc Hirsch, Bernadette Kovach, Susan Orbach, Patricia Plopa, Marc Rosen, and Deborah Tucker; and in Los Angeles: Jill Model Barth, Van DeGolia, Daniel Fast, Beverly Feinstein, Claudia Feldman, Cia Foreman, Rina Freedman, Michael Gales, Michele Gomes, Karen Kay, Ronnie Kaye, James Perkins, Myra Pomerantz, Dahlia Nissan Russ, Sherry Siassi, Janet K. Smith, Julie Tepper, Scott Tommey, and Shirah Vollmer. We apologize in advance if there is anyone whom we regretfully and inadvertently did not mention.

Many, many thanks to our dedicated administrative staff, Jean Lewis, Monica Simmons Evans (in Michigan), and Cecilia Peck (in Los Angeles), who tediously update the listserv and send out our monthly Clinical Moments invitations, always paying careful attention to the details.

We are particularly indebted to those who shared their own clinical experiences – our "Clinical Moment Contributors" – hailing both from the New Center for Psychoanalysis in Los Angeles: J. Model Barth, Rina Freedman, Michele Gomes, Lynn S. Kuttnauer, Robert James Perkins, Janet K. Smith, and Richard Tuch – two moments); and from the Michigan Psychoanalytic Institute (Deborah Harms, Bernadette Kovach, and Susan L. Orbach). We are equally indebted to our "Clinical Moment Commentators" (who are, in alphabetical order): Salman Akhtar, Anne Alvarez, Rosemary H. Balsam, Rachel Blass, Stefano Bolognini, Fred Busch, Andrea Celenza, Susan Donner, Morris Eagle, Darlene Bregman Ehrenberg, James L. Fosshage, Robert Alan Glick, Jay Greenberg, Theodore Jacobs, Judy L. Kantrowitz, Edgar Levenson, Joseph Lichtenberg, Albert Mason, Nancy McWilliams, Robert Michels, Irma Brenman Pick, Dominique Scarfone, Donnel Stern, Alan Sugarman, and Mitchell Wilson. Thank you one and all. You did an admirable job!

Special thanks to those at Routledge (notably Kate Hawes and Charles Bath) as well as Kristopher Spring, copy-editor extraordinaire, for helping make this volume a reality. We also wish to express gratitude to all of our patients who have entrusted us with their stories and shared their lives with us – to all of you we are grateful, honored, and humbled. It is a precious gift for which we are immensely appreciative.

To our loved ones, family and friends, nearby and across the miles (you know who you are), a special thanks for your patience and encouragement that have supported us during all the times we had to work rather than play.

Richard Tuch and Lynn S. Kuttnauer

Note

1 Summer months excluded.

Introduction: Moments of Waking and Reckoning

"Now What Do I Do?"

This book is about clinical moments of a certain sort – isolated instances in the course of an ongoing treatment that stand out because they present a clinical conundrum that leaves the therapist in a quandary about how best to proceed. The therapist's training along with his/her own clinical experience fail to provide much guidance about how to respond to what seems like a precarious predicament. Different options spring to mind, and much seems to ride on how he/she decides to respond to the situation at hand: A less than ideal intervention runs the risk of creating an unbridgeable rupture in his/her relationship with the patient; a more ideal intervention stands a chance of furthering the treatment by strengthening the therapist's bond with his/her patient. Under such conditions, anxiety rules the day, blurring the analyst's vision and making it hard for him/her to act in a clear-minded fashion. Maintaining or regaining the ability to think analytically when under fire is, in part, a product of the adequacy of the therapist's own psychotherapy or psychoanalysis, which helps him/her develop the ability to transcend the experience of being single-mindedly immersed in the emotions of the moment in order to think about the situation from a more distant and disciplined perspective.

This book is the outgrowth of the Clinical Moments Program that began in Michigan under the tutelage of Dr. Marvin Margolis, Training and Supervising Analyst at the Michigan Psychoanalytic Institute and Past President of The American Psychoanalytic Association.

When Dr. Lynn Kuttnauer, an analyst at the Michigan Psychoanalytic Institute, moved to Los Angeles, she brought with her the Clinical Moments Program, instituting it at the New Center for Psychoanalysis (NCP), where it is beginning its fifth year of operation. Each month, an NCP analyst hosts the program, inviting into their homes community-based psychotherapists, psychotherapists-in-training, psychiatric residents, and academics (anthropologists, sociologists, etc.) who are curious about psychoanalysis. Attendees are provided a meal, after which they are invited to participate in a discussion triggered by the presentation of a clinical moment in which a dicey situation has come to a head, leaving the treating/presenting analyst in a quandary about how best to proceed. Before sharing what he/she decided to do, the floor is opened for participants to weigh in about their thoughts and reactions in response to the facilitators' instructions: If you were the therapist and found yourself confronted with this situation, how would you feel? How do you think you'd react? What would guide your thinking and your decision? What aspects of the moment did you consider salient? What sort of intervention do you think might best facilitate the unfolding process while also protecting the treatment? The goal of the exercise is to explore the range of ways in which therapists of every ilk think about the situation and think they might go about responding to the situation, revealing the participant's core beliefs about how therapy brings about change. While the presented moment lends itself to theorizing about how best to respond given the circumstances, in the final analysis determining how the treating had best proceed is frankly impossible. Facilitators work hard to help steer the discussion away from abstract theorizing about the case, which is largely considered irrelevant relative to the task at hand.

This volume contains a dozen such moments that had previously been presented either in Michigan or in Los Angeles as part of the Clinical Moments Program. In place of comments provided by the gathering's attendees, this book substitutes the responses of a roster of 25 invited commentators – outstanding, international psychoanalysts, each of whom has contributed substantially to the psychoanalytic literature. We refer to the book as the *Clinical Moments Project* to distinguish it from the *Clinical Moments Program* – the live, attended, monthly, in-home presentations of problematic clinical vignettes. The theoretical orientation of these master clinicians runs the gamut from modern ego psychologists, to Kleinians, to interpersonal psychoanalysts, to self psychologists – with a dash of Lacan, Bion, Green, Gray, Ferro, Winnicott, Fonagy, Ogden, Weiss & Sampson, and Kernberg thrown in for good measure. Half of our commentators serve on the editorial boards of major psychoanalytic journals (some serving as Editor-in-Chief or Associate Editors). Four were awarded the prestigious Mary S. Sigourney Award for Outstanding Achievement in the Advancement of Psychoanalysis. Our commentators are on the faculty at such prestigious universities as Harvard, Yale, Columbia, Rutgers, Cornell, NYU, and the University of London and while most reside in the States, practicing[1] in New York City, Englewood and Flemington (New Jersey), Boston, Brookline, and Lexington (Massachusetts), Bethesda, Philadelphia, New Haven, San Francisco, San Diego, and in Beverly Hills and Woodland Hills (Southern California), some commentators practice in London, Montreal, Bologna, and Jerusalem.

Each clinical moment is commented upon by two different commentators,[2] who were asked to comment on their assigned moment by answering the same sorts of questions listed in the previous paragraph. In most cases,[3] commentators offered their input without knowing how the treating analyst had decided to respond to the presented dilemma. The specific direction for commentators reads as follows:[4]

We are hoping that you will react to the moment by reflecting on the situation at hand: What do you "make" of the situation? What does it bring to mind? What aspect(s) of the presented material strike you as salient, and why? What theories does the moment call forth? Which clinical experiences does it evoke? We are interested, first and foremost, with what the moment stimulates in the way of thoughts, feelings, and behavioral inclinations. Naturally, we are also interested in hearing about how you imagine you might have intervened, but that is secondary. Your chosen intervention does not throw into question the validity of the treating/presenting analyst's intervention, which was based on a somewhat different set of data that was then viewed from a somewhat different perspective vis-à-vis the material. We are also interested in hearing about how your imagined response to the situation is informed by your own theory of therapeutic action – how do you think your response might help further the treatment? In summary, we are interested in how you think and how you listen to the clinical material. What do you pay attention to, given that you can't possibly pay attention to everything? What guides your thinking and train of thought? How you think when you listen?

The roster of commentators includes (in alphabetical order): Salman Akhtar, Anne Alvarez, Rosemary H. Balsam, Rachel Blass, Stefano Bolognini, Fred Busch, Andrea Celenza, Susan Donner, Morris Eagle, Darlene Ehrenberg, Jim L. Fosshage, Robert Alan Glick, Jay Greenberg, Ted Jacobs, Judy Kantrowitz, Edgar Levenson, Joe Lichtenberg, Albert Mason, Nancy McWilliams, Robert Michels, Irma Brenman Pick, Dominique Scarfone, Donnel Stern, Alan Sugarman, and Mitchell Wilson. The Editors made efforts to assign commentators who would rely on different clinical theories to comment on the same clinical moment. We are indebted to these commentators, who've gone out of their way and rolled up their collective sleeves to help us out with this project.

We are equally indebted to those clinicians who generously presented their own clinical work and were subjected to the heavy editorial hand of one of the Editors (R.T.). The clinical moments that appear in this book have been contributed by analysts from both the New Center for Psychoanalysis in Los Angeles (J. Model Barth, R. Freedman, M. Gomes, L. Kuttnauer, J. Perkins, J. Smith, and R. Tuch – two moments) and the Michigan Psychoanalytic Institute (D. Harms, B. Kovach, N. Kulish, and S. Orbach). Presenting one's own clinical work is fraught with the dangers associated with exposing one's work to the potential critique of both readers and commentators, who – from the comfort of their armchairs – might imagine themselves responding to the moment at hand in a better way than did the treating/presenting analyst, which is a dubious claim to the extent that no one can know for sure how they'd respond if they were in the moment themselves. The advantage afforded the treating/presenting analyst by virtue of his/her having a first-hand experience of the patient cannot be discounted nor replicated by those observing the process from a distance.

It is important that readers understand the influence that the Editors had in the preparation of this book. Dr. Kuttnauer, who heads up the Clinical Moments Program in Los Angeles, chose which moments would be included in this volume from among those that had been presented both in Los Angeles and in Michigan. The Editors collaborated in writing the *Editors' Introduction* that appears like an abstract before each moment. Furthermore, in certain cases, one of the Editors (R.T.) also penned some of the brief essays – *The Moment in Context* – which preface the moments themselves. Other than being provided help with editing what they had written, moment contributors had a relatively free hand fashioning the presentation of their work. The same applies to commentators who likewise had a free hand fashioning how they responded to the moment assigned to them save for the fact that some were asked to shorten their contributions, to conform to a strict word count limit.

Commentators' responses

One of the directions given to each of our commentators was to comment about how they imagine they might have *intervened* had they been in the treating/presenting analyst's shoes, which – admittedly – is a hypothetical proposition. The Editors recognized that such a request was unreasonable given the fact that commentators would be lacking the requisite experience of being viscerally in the room with the patient and, accordingly, would not be privy to the full expanse of potential data needed to know, with any degree of certainty, how they might have intervened had they been in the room. Accordingly, thinking that commentators are in a position to comment about how treatment *should* have been conducted, relative to how the treating/presenting analyst had handled matters, grants commentators undue authority. Despite this nagging limitation, we pressed on believing that our commentators' responses would still be of interest and might well prove valuable.

Our commentators' responses to the question "What do you think you would have done?" reflect the diversity of how psychoanalysts in general think about the task of conducting psychoanalysis. We had assumed from the outset that a significant number of commentators would continue to prioritize the *offering of interpretations* as their chief tool, with insight seen as the most efficacious method of bringing about psychoanalytically induced psychic change (making the unconscious conscious). This is epitomized in the comments offered by Rachel Blass (Chapter 2):

> The analyst's task is a limited one ... It is not to respond to needs, to help attain designated life goals, or to improve the patient's feelings about herself or her coping capacities. Rather, it is to understand the

unconscious dynamics of the patient's mind, the phantasies that determine how she sees the world and especially how she distorts it, including herself. It is to grasp what she doesn't want to know, the parts of herself that she has denied and split off because she has found them unbearable. And it is to convey these understandings to the patient in a way that allows the split-off parts to be reintegrated. In other words, coming to know unconscious truth is what is curative analytically.

Blass goes on to underscore that such insight is not meant to be gained didactically or to exist merely intellectually, writing: "It is because what's curative is not knowing *about* what's going on unconsciously, but coming to live it in an integrated way, that transference interpretation is, to my mind, the only possible analytic intervention."

There is general agreement that a patient's issues had best become actualized in the here and now – through enactments, transference reactions, and the like – bringing the patient face-to-face with his/her complexes on a gut level, thus ensuring that treatment is more than just an intellectualized exercise. Susan Donner (Chapter 9), writing in response to a clinical moment involving a 5-year-old boy named Adam who'd been treated in analytic play therapy, notes how the analyst's participation in play "was absolutely necessary for the meanings of the actions, symbols, roles, and affects to *come alive* and to help give meaning to previously unrepresented or sequestered ... memories, fantasies, and internal states" (italics added).

Donner speculates that a play sequence might:

> allow Adam's terrors and traumas to be elaborated and re-experienced in a separate and different form, potentially less terrifying and toxic to Adam's experience of himself and his object ... In an effort to master trauma, play sequences and enactments can operate as an opportunity to have a "do-over," as children call it on the playground.

The commentators' responses make clear just how hard it can be to demarcate related clinical phenomena: analytic methods (clinical approaches), theories of action (the mechanisms thought to account for psychoanalytically facilitated psychic change), and therapeutic goals (what is thought to result from successful analytic treatment). Our commentators' responses run the gamut, as would be expected of analysts chosen to represent a cross-section of analysts. Some prioritize certain sorts of interventions over others and they envision treatment resulting in different sorts of outcomes brought about as the result of an array of hypothesized therapeutic actions.

Some commentators think chiefly *intrapsychically* (Busch, Chapter 1; Celenza, Chapter 5; Scarfone, Chapter 7; Sugarman, Chapter 9), envisioning treatment – first and foremost – as resolving internal conflicts that had kept certain affects, memories, impulses, or split-off aspects of the self out of conscious awareness. In this vein, Rachel Blass (Chapter 2) addresses the therapy-propelling effect that ensues when the analyst frustrates certain of the patient's needs, which the patient may interpret as indicating that they are bad or unlovable. This, in turn, unleashes murderous impulses toward the analyst, which – in turn – may trigger guilt, fear, and conflict over one's destructiveness. Blass goes further by offering an interesting perspective on the concept of empathic failures (the subject of Chapter 2): that the tendency to hold the analyst singularly accountable for behaving in ways that become designated as empathic failures *arguably reflects a short-sighted, one-person psychological perspective*; alternately, considering the same phenomena from a two-person, intersubjective perspective redistributes responsibility by envisioning the phenomena as coconstructed. This thought-provoking perspective on empathic failures places self psychology and the broader relational school in direct conflict.

Many of our commentators do not agree with the proposition that transference interpretations and insight are the quintessential curative agents in psychoanalysis. In Chapter 11, Edgar Levenson notes:

> Of dynamic formulations, there is no end. There is never a clear priority amongst often mutually exclusive perspectives on events. The mutative impact may come more from the expansion of the narrative and the patient's subsequent tolerance of multiple viewpoints and ambiguity than from the achievement of some superordinate view that make it all clear at last; or, even, some superordinate experience with the therapist that makes healing possible.

Darlene Ehrenberg, working from an interpersonal theoretic perspective, notes "I do not make 'interpretations' … I agree with Winnicott (1969) that this often prevents the patients from being able to come to things on their own." Some "classically oriented" analysts will likely argue that by offering *tentative rather than conclusive* (saturated) interpretations, they signal to the patient their openness to a patient's saying it isn't so, but Ehrenberg is likely to retort that this does not go far enough to mitigate the chance patients will hear interpretation as if spoken by an oracle, no matter how humble his/her delivery may be.

Fred Busch (Chapter 1), working in the tradition of a modern ego psychologist, somewhat surprisingly (given his more classic-seeming approach to treatment), also eschews the direct offering of interpretations and favors "working at the surface" by, first, drawing a patient's attention to behaviors that he believes are indicative of the fact that underlying psychological factors are at work behind the scenes – factors he wishes to explore with the patient as the two collaborate to understand what such behaviors might mean. Busch eschews doing the patient's work for him/her by spoon-feeding him/her interpretations; rather, he works to make clear to the patient the identified evidence (e.g., manifest behaviors) that is leading him to form certain conclusions. Busch tends to share his observations of the patient with the patient rather than cutting to the chase by telling the patient what his/her behavior means. He takes care, in particular, to avoid "saturated interpretations" that proclaim, in no uncertain terms, what an identified bit of manifest behavior means, which leaves the patient no opening to entertain alternate possibilities or disagree with the analyst's interpretation. Writing about the patient presented in this first chapter, Busch writes:

> Notice I'm not telling [the patient] what's making him uncomfortable, but leaving it open for exploration ... if he's able. Why is this important? Mainly because I believe we can only explore with the patient what he's ready to explore. Prematurely suggesting ideas to a patient usually closes thinking rather than opening it.

These ideas are in line with those offered by James L. Fosshage, who references his work with co-workers Lichtenberg and Lachmann (Lichtenberg, Lachmann, & Fosshage, 2003) in their description of how an empathic listening stance helps create a "spirit of inquiry" – which they believe to be the most efficacious prevailing psychoanalytic stance an analyst can assume.

Some of our commentators believe that certain patients can tolerate neither interpretations themselves nor the experience of being interpreted because they have yet to sufficiently formulate (symbolize) their experiences to then be able to retrieve those experiences from the recesses of their minds in a *fully formed format*, as is thought to be the case when it comes to psychic content that has been repressed and is, accordingly, formatted and hence ultimately reportable by the patient once the need to repress recedes. Donnel Stern (Chapter 5) writes that "Interpretation just doesn't work when you're dealing with psychic states that haven't been symbolized, because while there's 'something' there, the something is not recognizable." He further argues that one needn't make the unconscious conscious in order to foster psychoanalytically induced change; rather, all an analyst need do with certain sorts of patients is transcend inclinations to see the patient in a limiting way, which then frees the analyst to begin to interact with the patient in a somewhat different fashion, from the vantage point of a more expanded view of who the patient is. Stern concludes by noting: "because I see him differently I will now treat the patient differently than before, and in response he will feel differently than before."

Some of our commentators theorize that treatment exerts its effect by providing the patient with developmentally needed experiences (e.g., selfobject needs) that the patient hadn't been provided during his/her formative years. Controversy is particularly intense when it comes to the question of whether such a provisional model of therapeutic action (framed by Janet Smith in Chapter 7) can adequately account for the sorts of changes that come about as a result of an analysis. In Chapter 4, Anne Alvarez opines that analysis can repair deficits leading to a patient's potentially experiencing the transference as healing. Referring specifically to the patient presented in the moment she was assigned for comment, Alvarez notes how the analyst had acted in ways that encouraged the patient to feel that she had "finally been welcomed into the analytic family" – that the analyst was going to "stick with her" and would not be driven away by the patient as past experiences had primed her to anticipate would always be her fate. By contrast, in Chapter 7, Greenberg questions the wisdom and utility of trying to assume the role, as analyst, of "the good object" – a better object "who is more empathic and/or compassionate than her family members" – and in Chapter 11, Levenson echoes these same sentiments:

> In actuality psychoanalysis is a game, play, circumscribed and defined by rules – the containment of the frame – and would be otherwise impossible to sustain. One would be asking the therapist to be the one thing therapists aren't – wonderfully superior people able to undo the vicissitudes of their patients' lives ... I do not believe that therapy proceeds by the therapist providing some restorative love or empathy experience for the patient. I believe the cure comes via the working through, the traditional arduous replay of show and tell that epitomizes psychoanalytic psychotherapies.

Our commentators hold a wide array of theories about therapeutic action. Some think in terms of the "containment" (Celenza, Chapter 5) – the analyst's successfully surviving (without withdrawing, retaliating, or de-compensating) in the face of a patient's projections or expressions of intense affects or powerful (aggressive or libidinal) impulses. Patients may express hostile aggression toward the analyst then wait to see whether the analyst will "pass the test" (per Control-Mastery theory;[5] Weiss et al., 1986) by not reacting as the original object had or as they themselves had reacted in their formative years when treated comparably at the hands of careless caregivers. In Chapter 6, Glick notes how:

> The therapist is saying, wisely and generously, we have lived through versions of this before, we are in this together, nothing truly bad has happened, we both survived the upset and we are continuing on together. This is an excellent example of how a therapist "self-rights" and effectively rebounds from an intense attack on her as an uncaring, failing person. This goes to the heart of the clinical reality in our work. We are unleashing powerful, primitive forces that are real for the patient and become real for us.

In Chapter 9, Donner, writing comparably about the treatment of a 5-year-old boy, notes:

> [The analyst's] test, over time, would be for her to not only bear the affects, tolerate his aggressive and erotic attempts to engage her without rejecting him or withdrawing from him, and survive his real and fantasied

attacks in a way that his parents couldn't, but to turn the unspeakable into words.

Another way in which some of our contributors see therapy working is either by helping patients retrieve and integrate formerly split-off, dissociated "not me" aspects of the self (a more interpersonal or relational perspective) or by helping patients cease to rely upon defenses that not only require energy and effort to maintain but which preclude the patient's access to the breadth of potentially available ego functions (from a more mainstream, North American, modern ego-psychological perspective). Patients are also thought to improve when they have words with which they then can think about, and outwardly express, their emotions (increased affective vocabulary – Busch, Chapter 1). Sugarman (Chapter 9) addresses the use of play therapy to help patients overcome their fear of knowing their feelings, and he also sees treatment as aimed at helping patients better understand how their mind works.

One group of commentators conceptualize certain sorts of patients as suffering from unrepresented, "unformulated" (Celenza, Chapter 5; Stern, Chapter 5), un-symbolized, or dissociated experiences that – if given form and provided voice – can help facilitate psychic change. In Chapter 5, Andrea Celenza describes how therapy provides a "pathway to becoming whole" when unrepresented self states are helped to gain acceptance and expression:

> What is actualized in enactments are those selves or potential selves that are forbidden to be realized, "bad" aspects of a self *not yet represented or formed* for fear of its potential strength, aggression (or other passions) that are the basis of its expression. This sense of oneself ... is dangerous, prohibited, or desires something threatening ... These parts of the self [...] are] walled off or left unpotentiated in some unformulated haze.
>
> (italics added)

Analysts who rely upon an intersubjective perspective, which views patients' manifest behaviors as mightily influenced – to the point of being chiefly determined – by the particulars of the analyst's personality and reactivity (also known as a two-person perspective), tend to reconsider phenomena that other analysts deem to be "defensive" alternately as reflective of self-protective and/or self-promoting motives (Fosshage, Chapter 1).

Some contributors see therapy facilitating a patient's capacity to differentiate self from other – resulting in the analytic couple swimming to shore after floating adrift in an enactment or an instance of projective identification. For example, Celenza (Chapter 5) notes: "The analyst's first task is to sort out what belongs to whom and to own what is ours ... [in] a deft retribution of introjections and projections (from both the analyst's and patient's perspectives)," which is in line with Stern's (Chapter 5) observation that when patients are on the verge of having to accept dissociated ("not me") aspects of themselves in the context of treatment, they "treat the other person as if *they* are whatever it is that I must not be."

Commentators note how certain patients are on the lookout for evidence indicating that they are having, or have had, a powerful, demonstrable effect (impact) on the analyst (Chapter 6, Chapter 9, Chapter 12), illustrated dramatically in the final chapter of the book, in which the analyst becomes worried sick about the whereabouts of his patient. In response to the patient presented in Chapter 6, Glick writes:

> The patient's underlying rage and vulnerability demanded that she test the therapist's resilience and reliability in order to free herself from her narcissistic emotional bunker. The patient needed to feel she had *real* impact on the therapist "where she lived." She had to knock the wind out of her, to attack her moral core as a therapist. She had to find out that the therapist, unlike the internal representations of her primary objects, was truly strong enough, real enough, concerned and caring enough, to survive the test, and that they would both continue together.

In Chapter 5, Celenza refers to a previously published case study (Celenza, 2014) in which her patient, Michael, harbored a fantasy "to stab me repeatedly with a knife ... [out of need] to see me overwhelmed." Celenza concluded that therapeutic progress wasn't furthered by her ability to handle the situation "*expertly,* as one would in retrospect," but – rather – was a function of her finding ways to have one's "authentic, experiencing affective self converge with your asymmetric analytic stance."

Some commentators appreciated the *power of exceptionality* (e.g., "now moments," "moments of meeting"; Stern et al., 1998) – instances in the course of the treatment that stand out in bold relief insofar as they aren't at all what the patient had expected from the analyst and, as such, have a powerfully disruptive effect on the patient's view of himself and of his relationship with others. In Chapter 10, Wilson writes:

> If we are too interested in "connecting the dots," then moments of newness, surprise, oddity, confusion, contradiction, and repetition tend to get ignored. "[T]he unconscious is what closes up again as soon as it has opened, in accordance with a *temporal pulsation,*" Lacan stressed repeatedly in Seminar 11 (Lacan, 1981, p. 143, my emphasis).

In response to the patient presented in Chapter 6, Glick notes how:

> The therapist calls the patient by her name: "Oh Roberta." I find this a very powerful and crucial personalizing action. It says: "This is us, affectively stepping outside the constraining roles as therapist and patient (and into an authentic, affectively real interaction). We are talking to

each other; I take you into account. I am not speaking as a disembodied, objective judgmental voice. You are making me feel what you felt with your mother, that crushing, isolating cancellation. I am living in your shoes. I get it; I feel it; I am truly here for you."

Commentators also talk about the importance of the patient feeling "known," "seen," "recognized for who they are," or "heard" by the analyst – particularly insofar as the patient felt deprived of such experiences when young. The patient may struggle with his/her sense of identity, and may respond well to the recognition/confirmation of an alternate self relative to the particular self that they had been presenting in session, which is a more pathologic or limited iteration of the self that they seek to have disconfirmed, in the Weiss and Sampson sense, because it fails to represent the fullness of him- or herself. The patient may expose and express this alternate self in relatively unconventional ways relative to the fundamental rule that dictates communication ought strictly to be limited to the use of words. For example, in response to Ms. B. presented in Chapter 8, Joseph Lichtenberg writes:

> Ms. B brings into the consulting room not only her associations and dreams but her artwork. I regard Ms. B as saying, "If you want to know me, to really get who I am, you have to see what is central to my sense of self, my identity. Much of my heart and soul is in my creativity – and here it is. Look, share, react, respond. My narrative comes in two forms – verbal and visual."

And it isn't just the analyst who needs to wake up, listen, and learn who the patient is. Patients themselves are often limited by their own self-conceptions that fail to take into account hidden, unrecognized aspects of the self. Levenson (Chapter 11) writes:

> The mutative impact [of psychoanalysis] may come more from the expansion of the narrative and the patient's subsequent tolerance of multiple viewpoints and ambiguity than from the achievement of some superordinate view that makes it all clear at last, or even some superordinate experience with the therapist that makes healing possible. Patients refuse new experience and insight; that is what resistance is about. Mutative change depends more on the patient's grasp of what is happening around and to him than any explanatory set.

A final note before we launch into a description of the sorts of clinical moments we have in mind. We might ask the following question: "If commentators' reactions to these presented moments cannot realistically be translated into concrete recommendations about how the case might have been better handled, what is the relevance of their feedback and how is this

Clinical Moments Project a legitimate exercise?" To this, we respond by answering: What this project does achieve is the illumination of theories that each of these 25 commentators carries with them into session where they implicitly operate to organize the material, shaping the way in which these analysts listen to the material, serving to determine what aspects of the observable data will be deemed salient – prioritizing certain classes of data over others (Tuch, 2018). Based on such selective perception of the clinical material, the analyst reaches a conclusion about what is troubling the patient and what needs to happen for these issues to be worked through psychoanalytically. This, then, is the ultimate lesson of the Clinical Moments Project – to learn how to listen to how the treating/presenting analyst, the commentator, and the reader of this book each listen to the unfolding material.

Examples of clinical moments appearing in the literature

Let's consider some examples that illustrate just such moments. The first example is notoriously historic (though factually mythic) – a dramatic construction invented by Sigmund Freud decades after the incident that he was describing had occurred. In a letter to his friend Arnold Zweig (E. Freud, 1970), Freud describes how Josef Breuer's treatment of his patient Anna O. (Breuer & Freud, 1895) ended abruptly when Breuer happened upon his patient writhing in abdominal pain, declaring, "Now Dr. Breuer's child is coming!" Freud claims this incident so unnerved Breuer that he ran from the room in a cold sweat, transferring the patient's care to another physician. While Freud's tale has now been roundly debunked (Hirschmuller, 1978) and persists merely as myth, his claim that Breuer fumbled the ball at the precise moment when a timely interpretation of Anna O.'s "transference love" was clinically indicated *still stands*, since that claim doesn't require one to place stock in the pseudo-pregnancy myth.[6] The fact that Freud's construction turns out to be nothing more than myth doesn't disqualify it as an example of the sort of moment likely to challenge a therapist's clinical acumen and his ability to muster a response under duress.

Let's now turn to an actual clinical moment that is no less shocking in the degree to which it represents an extreme form of acting out. This is the case of Mr. A., a gay man I'd (R.T.) been treating who behaved in the most challenging and outrageous fashion (Tuch, 2007). The patient would physically trespass upon me in every imaginable way, acting as if I had no privilege or say in the matter. He would rifle through my desk drawer against my protestation and took extraordinary license by touching me whenever and wherever he chose. Efforts to engage the patient in a process aimed at understanding the meaning of these behaviors were dismissed by him out of hand as a colossal waste of time – as something that served my need, not his. Each instance of just such boundary-violating behavior constituted a clinical moment, taxing my capacity to conduct analytic treatment as I saw fit. The one moment that stands out is the time Mr. A. disrobed before me, largely, I suspect, to completely unnerve me – which it indeed did. Had I kept my wits about me, the situation would not have thrown me to the degree it did. But this was not how the situation played out: I'd been temporarily psychically disabled, which kept me from considering the possibility that the patient was "asking" me to contain his own feeling of being completely unnerved by aspects of our relationship (an instance of projective identification) so that he might be relieved of having to feel such feelings. That realization only occurred to me *after the fact* once I'd come to my senses and regained the ability to think.[7] How I handled the incident isn't nearly as important at this juncture as is the illustration of the sort of challenging clinical moments that can arise during the course of a treatment that seriously challenge the analyst's ability to find ways to therapeutically manage the situation.

Let's consider another example that demonstrates how the impact of a patient's behavior can move the analyst to react *unthinkingly*. Jody Davies (1999) presents the case of Daniel that illustrates how a patient's behavior may so affect the analyst that she finds herself acting in a highly uncharacteristic fashion in accordance with pressures arising from her unique countertransference reaction. The incident in question occurred as the patient was relaying a story from his seventh year of life when his father had treated him in an abusive fashion in response to the patient's crying over not having been adequately tended to by his yet again heavily sedated and depressed mother. The drunken father berated his son, calling him a "sissy" and a "weakling," and set about teaching his son a lesson about how hard life could *really* be by ordering him to strip naked and stand outside in the freezing snow for an extended period of time. The patient, who'd subsequently grown to see himself as someone who was literally inured to the cold (arriving to this first session in thin socks and sandals on a bitterly cold day), was suddenly shaking violently and uncontrollably as he relayed this story in session.[8] Davies writes:

> The next thing I knew, I was standing next to Daniel's chair wrapping a blanket around his shoulders, *not quite sure how I ended up there*. I remembered reaching with a disembodied arm into the cabinet where I kept the blanket for my own occasional use, and then getting up out of my chair, *but these were not considered actions*.
>
> (p. 193, italics added)

While analysts typically like to think of themselves as being in better control than Dr. Davies found herself to be, we have little doubt that many analysts from time to time react just as unthinkingly as Dr. Davies had when confronted with a clinical moment that triggers an intense countertransference reaction. Davies goes on to explain how she and her patient came to terms with this event, making clear the extent to which this incident constitutes the sort of clinical moment we'll be referring to in this book. At such times, the intensity of the analyst's countertransference reaction may be so overwhelming as to move her from her typical stance of "considered reflection" to one of immediate action, which can be a feature of clinical moments of a certain sort.

Clinical moments that appear in this volume

Few if any of the clinical moments presented in this book are instances of clinical extremity. No patient is writhing in pain as they prepare to give birth to their analyst's child; no patient disrobes before the analyst. Only a few of the moments presented in this book are so extreme as to reduce the analyst to the point of acting in an unconsidered manner, as was the case with Jody Davies. But while the examples in this book aren't so extreme, they nevertheless are bona fide examples of clinical instances when the analyst found him- or herself in a state of not knowing – a state of uncertainty about how best to proceed given the unusual and challenging nature of what was happening in the room at the time.

Different circumstances give rise to the condition we refer to in this book as a clinical moment. What these moments share in common is the degree to which the analyst feels challenged by uncertainty as to how to proceed, which contrasts with the more usual level of comfort and confidence he/she had previously felt up to this point in time with this given patient. His/her level of confidence, along with a sense of how he/she and the patient traditionally "got along," suddenly lessens as the analyst's deliberations become more labored – as he/she finds him- or herself working harder than usually to figure out his/her next move. Calling it "a move" gives the wrong impression – this is no game! But moments like these are ones that strike the analyst as potentially "dicey" to the extent he/she comes to believe that more seems to be riding on how he/she responds at this precise moment than is usually the case. At this point in the treatment, the analyst may be struck by the thought that his/her particular response – how and whether he/she chooses to act, whether he/she will interpret or let things be, whether he/she will share an observation or allow the patient to proceed without interruption, and so on – will likely have greater consequences than most other times in treatment when his/her way of being on the whole seems to seamlessly facilitate the unfolding process. Because of how critical things now seem, the analyst is a bit on edge, more vigilant about what's about to happen, more careful in his/her consideration of alternatives, and more inclined to employ the rational, decision-making part of his/her brain rather than rely on intuition or a gut feeling about what he/she should do next. In particular, the analyst wonders to him- or herself, "*Now* what do I do?" – which he/she is much less inclined to wonder during the rest of treatment that operates more automatically.

Sooner or later, most analyses arrive at a point when the immediacy of the moment captures the analytic couple's attention, awakened by the glare of the moment that seems pregnant with possibility. Such moments have been referred to alternately as "now moments" (Stern, 2004; Stern et al., 1998), as the sudden emergence of a striking resistance (e.g., a sudden rupture in the patient's ability to freely associate), an acute countertransference enactment (Jacobs, 1986), a powerfully felt and expressed transference, a "disjunction" (Ogden, 2016), and the like.

Stern et al. (1998) describe a "now moment" as an instance:

> That gets lit up subjectively and affectively, pulling one more fully into the present ... [requiring] a response that is *too specific and personal to be a known technical manoeuvre*. Now moments ... demand an intensified attention and some kind of choice of whether or not to remain in the established habitual framework. And if not, what to do? They force the therapist into some kind of "action," be it an interpretation or a response *that is novel relative to the habitual framework*, or a silence ... These "now moments" are often accompanied by expectancy or anxiety because the necessity of choice is pressing, yet there is no immediately available prior plan of action or explanation. The application of habitual technical moves will not suffice. The analyst intuitively recognizes that a window of opportunity for some kind of therapeutic reorganization or derailment is present, and the patient may recognize that he has arrived at a watershed in the therapeutic relationship.
>
> (pp. 909–911)

Note that we are not suggesting that each of the clinical moments presented in this book constitutes a "now moment," though we are quite sure a number are similar to this concept.

The advent of a clinical moment of the sort presented in this volume can be set in motion either by the therapist's actions or reactions, or by the patient's actions or reactions, though it can sometimes prove hard to tell from a chicken-or-egg perspective who was reacting to whom – whose action got the ball rolling in the first place. The analyst's chosen intervention sometimes appears to be the apparent trigger for a given moment. So too might his/her unwitting participation in a countertransference enactment, which hadn't been the product of conscious choice but, rather, turns out to be something he/she finds him- or herself doing unwittingly, as had been the case with Jody Davies. Extricating oneself from an ongoing enactment often requires the analyst to gather his/her wits about him/her in order to, first, recognize that he/she has become drawn into an enactment so that he/she might, then, begin to make sense of why he/she has reacted as he/she did, so that he/she – ultimately – comes to an understanding about what his/her reaction says about the dynamics about the case, using his/her countertransference to make his/her way back to the patient's situation.

Sometimes, it appears clear that the patient was largely responsible for initiating the moment under discussion. For example, powerful transference reactions can constitute a significant and memorable moment in the course of one's analysis. The intensity of affects that are felt and expressed heightens the immediacy of the moment, which many analysts believe is necessary in order for the transference to become animated rather than being appreciated intellectually as a reconstruction of "what must have been back when" – driving home the point Freud was making by noting how one cannot hope to work through problematic interactions of yesteryear without their first becoming tangible and immediate in the form of the manifest transference ("when all is said and done, it is impossible to destroy anyone in absentia or in effigie"; Freud, 1912, p. 108).

Other such moments involve what Ogden (2016) refers to as "disjunctions" – points in time when there is a "seemingly incomprehensible gap between what one person says and how the other responds," creating an emotional climate:

> in which both participants experience some degree of feeling lost, confused, perplexed, at sea, and almost mystified … The analytic pair can no longer rely on what they thought they knew, for what they have known no longer feels sufficient to meaningfully contain the elements of experience now in play.
>
> (p. 413)

Feeling lost, confused, perplexed, and at sea defines the features of an immediate moment that stand out in ways that require the analytic couple's immediate attention.

The immediacy of all of these sorts of clinical moments can be likened to an awakening when business as usual is suddenly dispensed with as the analytic couple begin to relate to one another in a somewhat different fashion. Such moments are lively, filled with spontaneity, and ripe with possibility. Helping patients experience such moments so that they may go on, more of the time, to live life in the moment can be considered an important though unrecognized goal of psychoanalysis.

A somewhat flawed experimental design

The task outlined in this book represents an experiment of sorts: The same clinical vignette is presented to two commentators, who are then asked to weigh in on *what they think about the moment* and *how they believe they might have responded* were they to have been in the analyst's shoes. Many of our commentators address the near impossibility of knowing with any degree of certainty how they themselves would have responded given the circumstances. Naturally, these analysts speak at arm's length from the gravitational pull of the affective to-and-fro taking place in the consulting room. In his response to Dr. Smith's presented moment (clinical moment #7), Jay Greenberg notes:[9]

> I have not seen the patient. I have seen only the analytic dyad, and I have ineradicable impressions of the interaction between the two participants and, perhaps most important, of the analyst's countertransference ... If I were the treating analyst, of course, everything would be different. The analytic conversation would not have gotten exactly to this point, I would have my own countertransference, my own vision of where I would want the conversation to go would be my own. So when I am invited to think about what I would say in a given moment, what I would say is as much about the dyad as it is about the patient.

When Greenberg speaks about his perception of the dyad at work, and his belief that he would have conducted himself differently, he is addressing the limits of a commentator's ability to imagine "substituting in" for the treating/presenting analyst. Accordingly, the question "What would you do if you were in the analyst's shoes?" may amount to one that no commentator can honestly answer.

Echoing these same sentiments, Irma Brenman Pick responds to Dr. Perkins' dicey face-off with a patient who threatened to quit treatment if Perkins didn't back off (clinical moment #3):

> It is interesting to be invited to consider how I might orientate myself to thinking about what might be my reactions, as analyst, faced with this ultimatum; of course, anything I write now may have little bearing on what might have been my actual reaction in this situation. And reading the account of this treatment I am bound to say – like the Irish joke of the man asking for directions from X to Y – that X wouldn't have been the place to start from in the first place.

As mentioned earlier, the Editors of this volume recognized at the outset that it is somewhat unrealistic to ask commentators what they imagine they might have done given the circumstances and expect them to be able to speak authoritatively about the treatment itself. Several commentators note as much. In clinical moment #7, for example, Dominique Scarfone writes:

> A preliminary warning. Since I am not the analyst in the room and am therefore not exposed to the affective load that the patient's words, both in content and tone, would have put on me, I can only try and imagine what I would do or say.

In response to the patient presented in the first clinical moment (Chapter 1), Fred Busch writes:

> there is so much a respondent does not have access to, like the affective coloring of words, the multitude of observations that leads the clinician to

think this or that, the subtle mood shifts in both participants, the analyst's reveries, and so on. Given this sizeable handicap, in order to fill my role as respondent I will proceed as if *I really* knew what was going on.

Reiterating what was mentioned previously, we must acknowledge that the experimental design of this clinical moment exercise is somewhat flawed to the extent it is unrealistic to believe that commentators who have no experience with the patient in question, who lack a first-hand, visceral sense of what it is like to be in the room with such a patient, and who haven't been exposed to the affective interchange that inevitably tugs on the treating analyst's innards – generating countertransferences or evoking reveries of whatever sort – can seriously opine about how they think they would handle matters had they been in the analyst's shoes. The entire experiment reeks of what Greenberg[10] (Chapter 7) refers to as the *illusion of expert advice* – the idea that the supervisor/commentator is in any position to speak authoritatively, in retrospect, about how a clinical moment should have been handled. Writing about the process of supervision (Tuch, 2018), I assert that "supervisors are better situated to make out what is going on between the candidate and his patient, *yet poorly positioned to precisely know what to do with this knowledge*":

> Supervisors oftentimes see the case more clearly because they are unencumbered by the sorts of distractions that can interfere with the treating analyst's (supervisee's) ability to devote his/her full attention to a reflective consideration of the unfolding material. The supervisee's need to be available to the patient by being fully present in the room, in combination with the distractions created by a multitude of subtle interactions and varied affects flying about the room, takes a toll on the supervisee's ability to maintain sufficient presence of mind to be able to fully dedicate himself to the task of figuring out what is going on in the room on multiple levels – to see the forest for the trees [… Hence] the supervisor is better situated than the supervisee to be able to make out the dynamics of the case and to ascertain the nature of what is going on between the supervisee and his/her patient; on the other hand, the supervisor is poorly positioned to know how to make the best use of this knowledge in the actual treatment setting … The supervisor may think he substantially grasps the nuances of the case – and well he might – but that does not translate into his/her knowing how the supervisee should proceed, since the supervisor lacks essential knowledge that he would need to be able to claim authority to direct the treatment from where he sits. When a supervisor comes to believe that an interpretation he's fashioned is precisely what the supervisee "ought to have said," that supervisor has ventured on to shaky ground and may, furthermore, be oblivious to the fact that he is claiming greater authority than circumstances allow.
>
> (pp. 217–227)

There is one other problem with the experimental design of this project that has to do with the myth that analysts give due consideration to most everything they do, which makes their interventions seem more consciously calculated than they often turn out to be. Since one of the main topics of this book has to do with the question of how and why analysts "choose" to intervene in the way they do in treatment, it is important to keep in mind the extent to which "choice" isn't always evident, as was illustrated in the previously mentioned vignette involving Jody Davies. The myth of the carefully crafted intervention involves the belief that the analyst's interventions are by and large the result of conscious deliberation. After all, one thing that psychoanalysis arguably "stands for" is the refinement of the ego's capacity to gain more and more say over one's actions, resulting in a lessening of the tendency to "act out" and a heightened proclivity to think before one speaks. While psychoanalysts tend to go to great lengths to carefully weigh the potential consequences of a considered intervention, this does not mean the analysts' activity is rarely the result of unintended and unconscious psychic processes. As we consider clinical moments of a certain sort, it is important to keep in mind the extent to which the analyst may be intervening unthinkingly before regaining his/her momentarily absent capacity to think analytically.

Having owned the limitations of this particular experimental design, we nevertheless believe there is considerable value reflected in what our commentators have crafted, which can be appreciated just so long as the reader doesn't succumb to the misguided belief that there are those who know better about how a clinical conundrum had best be handled. We encourage the reader to consider the commentators' comments in this spirit – not so much as having specifically to do with the case at hand but, rather, as valuable clinical ideas stimulated by the consideration of a given case, whether or not those ideas meaningfully can be translated into clinical recommendations about how the presented case itself might best be handled. These moments create a springboard for some very interesting thinking, which is why the Editors emphasized in their instructions to commentators, first and foremost, the task of discovering what the moment brings to mind and, only secondarily, what the commentator thinks he might have done given the circumstances.

Clinical moments presented in this book

This volume contains a dozen clinical moments, each of which addresses a somewhat different sort of clinical situation or dilemma. These 12 clinical moments are grouped according to the predominant clinical dilemma illustrated in each. The first group of three moments (CM #1–3) illustrates instances when the analyst finds him- or herself grappling with the question of whether to speak up, in the hope that doing so will deepen the treatment, or whether it is best to keep his/her thoughts to him- or herself for the time being, out of concern that the current state of the therapeutic alliance won't permit him/her to intervene in the way he/she is considering doing. The second group of two moments demonstrates the handling of *countertransference enactments* – in one case (CM #4), a series of three enactments, the last of which lands the patient face-to-face with the analyst's mother; in the other case (CM #5) we are presented with an enactment that leaves the analyst defensively insisting that she *does* in fact understand the patient's position in opposition to the patient's claim to the contrary. The third grouping of three moments involves the matter of provision – what the patient seeks to receive, or demands he/she must receive from the analyst in order for the treatment to work. In the first moment (CM #6), a patient who felt she'd been shortchanged by the analyst takes her to task for not providing the agreed-upon allotment of time. In the second moment (CM #7), a patient demands that the analyst provide her with guidance, answers, and solutions that she steadfastly insists she must receive if she is to improve. In the third moment (CM #8), a patient hopes the analyst will accept an invitation to attend an event that is personally meaningful, and would be made more so by the analyst's attendance. The final grouping of four moments involves the issue of the degree of impact the patient is having, or is trying to have, on the analyst – touching on the issue of interpersonal power. In the first instance (CM #9), a 5-year-old boy invites his analyst to participate in a game that assigns her a role that would leave her in a precarious position – with a bag over her head, blinded from witnessing what is about to happen. In the second instance (CM #10), a family secret defines the patient's life, which he enacts by leaving his analyst in the dark, pulling the wool over her eyes about an essential truth of his life, about which she only comes to learn years into the treatment. In the third instance (CM #11), the patient sadistically plays with the analyst in a cat-and-mouse fashion, toying with what he knows to be a soft spot in her heart, and positioning her to have to decide where her allegiance lies – with him or with the helpless kitten he has brought to treatment whose well-being – he suggests – might be in jeopardy if the analyst doesn't wisely intervene. Finally, in the fourth instance (CM #12), the analyst is greatly affected by a patient's sudden disappearance, resulting in him worrying himself sick over the patient's whereabouts.

The goal of this volume is threefold: to stimulate readers' thinking about clinical dilemmas, to introduce psychoanalytic societies and institutes to the value of conducting their own Clinical Moment Programs, and – finally – to set the stage for another such book containing a series of other clinical moments, submitted by analysts throughout the country (and beyond) who believe they have just such a moment in mind that might be fruitful to present and discuss. Those wishing to submit moments of their own for inclusion in *Volume 2* may do so by sending vignettes either to Richard Tuch at rtuch@aol.com or to Lynn Kuttnauer at lynn.kuttnauer@gmail.com. Moments should be no longer than 4,000 words.

A few final notes before we proceed: one having to do with experimental design, the other with the use of pronouns when referring to analysts. For the most part, commentators had no idea how the treating/presenting analyst would choose to proceed after the moment in question arose. The only exceptions are moments that are presented as a series – where commentators were asked to weigh in at different points along the way as a series of moments unfolded. Commentators did not know the identity of the other commentator with whom they were "paired" in writing about the same moment, nor did they know what that other commentator had written about the situation at hand. Furthermore, those who contributed moments had no access to the commentators' comments until they had finished writing their moments – with no modifications permitted after they had read the commentators' comments. Undoubtedly, some moment contributors would have relished a chance to respond to the commentaries by offering clarifications or even a rebuttal, but space does not allow for such activities. As for the matter of pronouns, the clear majority of moment contributors are female analysts – 9 of the 11 (two moments are written by Richard Tuch). In chapters where the analyst is male, references to "the analyst" in the "moment in context" will use masculine pronouns. In all other instances (the majority), when the moment has been written by a female analyst, the associated "moment in context" will refer to analysts using feminine pronouns. In this Introduction, we chose to use the convention of "he/she" or "his/her."

Notes

1 Shamelessly organized in NYC-centric fashion.
2 In the case of Chapter 7, there are *three* commentators – the result of a simple error on the part of the Editors who erred in assigning the Moments.
3 Save for those clinical moments that contained more than a single designated moment and are presented as a string of moments.
4 Unfortunately, a few commentators who were first invited to participate weren't provided with such a list of specific instructions.
5 Both Morris Eagle (Chapter 8) and Nancy McWilliams (Chapter 11) address Weiss and Sampson's Control-Mastery theory in greater detail.
6 Though Anna O.'s transference didn't in fact play out as Freud later claimed, that doesn't negate the fact that she likely experienced a powerful transference reaction in response to the extraordinary attentiveness of Dr. Breuer, which was relatively unheard of at the time.
7 An alternate interpretation is suggested by Ehrenberg (2003), who writes: "Some patients have described how important it was to them to know they could frighten me, unnerve me, even tyrannize me, by 'regressing.' The regressing was therefore not 'innocent' at all. Regressive behavior actually can be manipulative to the extent that the intention is to upset the analyst. It can be a weapon in a kind of psychic battle" (p. 590).
8 Which might well have represented a reliving of the event in the analyst's presence.
9 Taken from a segment of Dr. Greenberg's comments that have not been included in his formal comments that appear in this book.

10 Taken from a segment of Dr. Greenberg's comments that have not been included in his formal comments that appear in this book.

References

Breuer, J., & Freud, S. (1895). Studies on hysteria. In J. Strachey (Ed. & Trans.), *The standard edition of the complete psychological works of Sigmund Freud* (Vol. 2, pp. 1–321). London: Hogarth Press.

Celenza, A. (2014). *Erotic revelations: Clinical applications and perverse scenarios.* London: Routledge.

Davies, J. (1999). Getting cold feet, defining "safe-enough" borders: Dissociation, multiplicity, and integration in the analyst's experience. *Psychoanalytic Quarterly,* 68 (2), 184–208.

Ehrenberg, D. (2003). A radical shift in thinking about the process of change: Commentary on paper by Gerhardt, Sweetnam, and Borton. *Psychoanalytic Dialogues,* 13(4), 579–603.

Freud, E. L. (1970). Note on Arnold Zweig. In E. L. Freud (Ed.), *The letters of Sigmund Freud and Arnold Zweig* (p. 84). New York: International Psychoanalytic Library.

Freud, S. (1912). The dynamics of transference. In J. Strachey (Ed. & Trans.), *The standard edition of the complete psychological works of Sigmund Freud* (Vol. 12, pp. 99–108). London: Hogarth Press.

Hirschmuller, A. (1978). *The life and work of Joseph Breuer.* New York: New York University Press.

Jacobs, T. (1986). On countertransference enactments. *Journal of the American Psychoanalytic Association,* 34(2), 289–307.

Lacan, J. (1981). *The four fundamental concepts of psycho-analysis.* New York: Norton.

Lichtenberg, J., Lachmann, F., & Fosshage, J. (2003). *A spirit of inquiry: Communications in psychoanalysis.* Hillsdale, NJ: The Analytic Press.

Ogden, T. (2016). On language and truth in psychoanalysis. *Psychoanalytic Quarterly,* 85(2), 411–426.

Stern, D. N. (2004). *The present moment in psychotherapy and everyday life.* New York: W. W. Norton.

Stern, D. N., Sander, L., Nahum, J., Harrison, A., Lyons-Ruth, K., Morgan, A., Bruschweiler-Stern, N., & Tronick, E. (1998). Non-interpretive mechanisms in psychoanalytic therapy: The "something more" than interpretation. *International Journal of Psychoanalysis,* 79(5), 903–921.

Tuch, R. (2007). Thinking with, and about, patients too scared to think: Can non-interpretive maneuvers stimulate reflective thought? *International Journal of Psychoanalysis,* 88(1), 91–111.

Tuch, R. (2018). *Psychoanalytic method in motion: Controversies and evolution in clinical theory and practice.* London: Routledge.

Weiss, J., Sampson, H., & the Mount Zion Psychotherapy Research Group. (1986). *The psychoanalytic process: Theory, clinical observation and empirical research.* New York: Guilford Press.

Winnicott, D. W. (1969). The use of an object and relating through identification. In *Playing and reality* (pp. 86–94). London: Tavistock, 1971.

Part I

Taking a Stand

Chapter 1

Whether to Speak or Let Things Be

Richard Tuch

Editors' introduction

Early in the course of a patient's treatment, the analyst works hard to forge a therapeutic alliance by demonstrating his capacity not only to be caring, trustworthy, and empathic but also to make useful observations and provide worthwhile insights that encourage the patient's hope that change is possible, which goes a way toward ensuring his continuing involvement in treatment. Whether the analyst's interpretation and interventions are seen as helpful or, alternately, are experienced by the patient as shaming or as a narcissistic display of the analyst's cleverness can make a world of difference in terms of the quality and viability of the treatment. This first clinical moment involves an intensely anxious man in his late 20s who'd sought treatment for the very first time complaining, in part, of a dread of acting decisively out of fear he could be proven wrong – a devastating fear that plagued him. Once treatment was underway, the patient developed an interesting behavioral pattern of "showing his hand" by inadvertently revealing aspects of his underlying psychology through slips of the tongue, which he found unnerving to the extent these disclosures left him feeling not only exposed but in error. Early manifestations of resistance to the treatment left the analyst wondering whether he should try to heighten the patient's investment in the treatment by demonstrating how much could be learned by analyzing these slips. The analyst felt he needed to weigh such a maneuver with concern that addressing these slips might shame the patient for his failure to have said what he'd meant to say rather than slipping up by leaking something he'd consciously meant to keep hidden.

The moment in context (Richard Tuch)

What drives a patient into treatment and what keeps him coming once treatment is underway are not always the same. Patients come to treatment for a host of reasons. They may experience the presence of an absence or they may seek to absence a presence. Patients may sense that something is missing from their lives that should be present – a sense of purpose, the capacity to strive toward success in an unfettered fashion, success itself, "get up and go," a reasonable modicum of satisfaction, a significant other, and the like. Alternately, patients may be plagued by something in them that leaves them feeling miserable. They may be filled with self-hatred, wracked with guilt, seized with envy, plagued by random and taunting thoughts, and so on and so forth.

Somewhat surprisingly, a patient's stated reasons for originally seeking help may only obliquely relate to why he keeps coming. Naturally, patients stay in treatment anticipating that doing so will lead to a cure for the conditions that drove them to treatment in the first place. But once therapy is underway, additional factors stimulate the patient to stay involved in treatment, oftentimes for an extended period of time – which benefits the patient in accordance with the research-documented "dose effect": The longer the patient is in treatment, the more probable it is he'll improve (Hansen et al., 2002; Howard et al., 1986; Kordy et al., 1988).

While patients new to treatment are typically oblivious to the fact that their problems – to some extent – reflect the vestiges of unmet childhood needs, once treatment is underway, such needs may make their way to the surface with the help of an analytically oriented therapist who is alert to the manifestations of such early ("infantile") unmet needs. Such needs persist because they weren't met – or weren't adequately met – when the patient was a child, such needs as: a need to be loved, praised, noticed, cherished, contained, admired, mirrored, adored – the list goes on and on. Patients don't tend to directly complain, at the outset of treatment, about having received an insufficient quantity of these development-promoting supplies, but as the treatment progresses and the transference intensifies, patients often become more acutely aware about what they wish to get but have not yet gotten from the therapist. Even when patients have yet to receive what they wish to receive, they may still – consciously or unconsciously – hold out hope that the analyst will gratify their fervent wishes before treatment ends. And while the analyst has every intention of making such yearnings explicit so that they can be worked through, much of what patients wish for never comes to pass to the degree they hoped it might. Analysis wasn't designed to be a tease, and claiming as much would be the height of cynicism. But there is no getting around the fact that analysis capitalizes on, for example, a patients' narcissistic desires that become stimulated in the course of treatment by the analyst's undivided attention, affect attunement, empathy, as well as his devotion to the patient's treatment and – ideally – his palpable care and concern. These factors combine to help stimulate the impression that a payday of sorts is in a patient's future so long as he keeps coming, keeps working, and keeps hoping. Friedman (1997) refers to this as "seduction" – a problematic word, he admits, which he works to clarify by noting he is referring to:

> An arrangement whereby the patient is led to expect love while the analyst, in Freud's words, plans to provide a substitute for it. Admittedly the

love-substitute is something very special, with secrets we have yet to fathom, but it is not the love the patient is imagining ... [the analyst plans to] offer the truth rather than his own love or approval.

The injunction to confront objective truth [gives] the patient an endless task by which he could endeavor to win the analyst's favor.

(pp. 26–29)

There are other factors beside the wish to be cured, the narcissistic gratification of the analyst's undivided attention, and the hoped-for satisfaction of a host of infantile needs that combine to keep patients engaged in treatment. How the analyst conducts him- or herself is one of the first things that captures the patient's attention at the outset of treatment. Patients are often intrigued by the analyst's extraordinary level of thoughtfulness – made apparent in his refusal to accept quick and easy answers, the exquisite care he takes when fashioning his interventions, and his dedication to leave no stone unturned as he conducts a thorough, open-minded exploration for the factors that lie at the heart of what ails the patient. This way of going about analyzing differs markedly from how other individuals in the patient's life might have behaved, and it models a wait-and-see, reflective attitude that facilitates deeper explorations and self-exploration into the patient's psyche.

Another aspect of the analyst's behavior that alerts the patient to the fact he's about to experience something somewhat unexpected and unique from treatment has to do with the way in which the analyst listens and observes – his keenly attuned antennae that have him noticing nuances in what the patient says or does, which others had either failed to notice or – if they had – had failed to mention. The patient himself may not have noticed things the analyst now brings to his attention for their joint consideration. Patients typically find this highly attuned style of listening and observing quite alluring – dare we say "seductive." It may feel at first like the analyst is speaking a different tongue – one that views behavior from a different vantage point – but many patients are quick to note this foreign-seeming way of thinking and speaking resonates with something deep within them, causing them to recognize something familiar that they'd previously tended to gloss over – like recognizing a language that one had spoken when young but hadn't spoken for quite some time. The patient senses that the analyst is "on" to something – that much the patient knows. Taken together, the analyst's exquisite thoughtfulness combined with his capacity to listen and observe engenders confidence in how the analyst goes about "finding out" and, ultimately, in what he reports having found out.

One of the first tasks of analytic treatment is to forge a positive, collaborative, mature, reality-based working relationship with the patient, referred to alternately as the "therapeutic alliance" or "working alliance" (Friedman, 1969; Gitelson, 1962; Greenson, 1965, 1967; Greenson & Wexler, 1969; Zetzel, 1956). This alliance is more or less *conflict-free*[1] to the extent early infantile needs ("transference") are kept from interfering with the patient's understanding of what's required of him for the treatment to work and what the analyst will be trying to accomplish when he offers his observations or interpretations. On the surface, the requirements of treatment merely involve coming, paying, and obeying the fundamental rule to free associate. This short list of basic requirements is oftentimes elaborated by the patient's transference-based fantasies and/or the analyst's covertly communicated needs that have the patient believing that the analyst personally requires much more of the patient than the analyst lets on. Furthermore, patients who are prone to experience persecutory fantasies may interpret the analyst's efforts as other than benign, with the patient imagining the therapist's interventions as attacking, criticizing, demeaning, demoting, and the like – in other words, doing anything but trying to help the patient.

A therapeutic alliance is facilitated by the analyst's capacity to conduct himself in ways that establish his trustworthiness, his respectfulness, his acceptance of the patient, his capacity for empathy, his genuine concern and commitment, his ability to contain the patient's internal processes, and his ability to provide a safe environment,[2] as well as his non-defensive ability to accept responsibility for his role in helping shape the events taking place in the consulting room. Research demonstrates that the therapeutic alliance is more than a theoretic construct and has practical implications to the extent the development of a therapeutic alliance is correlated with treatment outcome: Treatments characterized by the establishment of a positive therapeutic alliance stand a much higher chance of succeeding (Baldwin et al., 2007; Horvath & Symonds, 1991; Krupnick et al., 1996; Martin et al., 2000), and the stronger the alliance, the greater the change observed (Klein et al., 2003). Whether a strong enough therapeutic alliance must first exist before the analyst risks offering his interpretations to the patient (Hausner, 2000) or, conversely, such an alliance *comes about* as a result of the analyst's offering interpretations that demonstrate he understands the patient on a very deep level (Adler, 2000; Hanly, 1994) is a matter of considerable debate. Freud (1913) himself was abundantly clear on the matter of what must first be accomplished before the analyst ventures to interpret. Freud argues that an analyst cannot begin to work interpretively with patients until the analyst has established that a level of "rapport" has been established between analyst and analysand:

> It remains the first aim of the treatment to attach [the patient] ... to the person of the doctor. To ensure this, nothing need be done but to give him time. If one exhibits a serious interest in him, carefully clears away the resistances that crop up at the beginning and avoids making certain mistakes, he will of himself form such an attachment and link the doctor up with one of the imagos of the people by whom he was to be treated with affection. It is certainly possible to forfeit this first success if from

the start one takes up any standpoint other than one of sympathetic understanding, such as a moralizing one, or if one behaves like a representative or advocate of some contending party.

(pp. 139–140)

To a greater or lesser extent, resistance is an ever-present factor in every analysis, and the factors outlined so far help tilt the balance in favor of the patient's continued involvement in treatment. Patients stay in treatment because they hope that continued treatment will relieve them of their symptoms, provide for their unmet psychological needs, satisfy their wish to have another's complete and undivided attention, provide a window into the deeper parts of their psyches, develop a heightened capacity to be self-reflective, engage them in a relationship that ultimately proves that not everyone is like the patient's earliest caregivers, and so on and so forth. When one stands back and thinks about it, psychoanalytic treatment accomplishes more than most neophytes might imagine.

The clinical moment

This case involves a 28-year-old single man, Jeff, who's just begun treatment but has only come a handful of times ostensibly due to circumstances beyond his control – travelling for work and the intervening holiday season spent with his family in Mexico. Beneath these seemingly valid reasons offered by the patient to explain his difficulty getting in to see me lay resistance that I felt was needing to be addressed lest it cause the patient to run from treatment. I wondered how addressing the resistance might be achieved seeing that the patient and I had yet to establish a mutual understanding that therapy would involve our joint commitment to explore such matters analytically. I imagined that if the patient came to treatment more consistently or more often, that might provide me the necessary leverage – but how was I going to get the patient to appreciate that therapy required more from him if it was to work?

My wish that Jeff come at least twice weekly – and, ideally, enter analysis – is very much on my mind as we enter the session I'm about to present. Admittedly, I'm a tad frustrated that we haven't yet settled into a regular schedule of treatment, but I remain hopeful that we'll be able to do so soon. The patient reassures me as much – knowing his irregular attendance is not ideal and sensing that I am hankering for us to meet more regularly and more often.

I am awaiting Jeff's arrival to our first session since his three-week absence from treatment following the holiday break. I have in mind something he'd mentioned the last time we met that has me a bit concerned. He'd been travelling back and forth to the East Coast for work and had met a young woman who piqued his interest. Most of his friends lived on the East Coast, and he was entertaining the idea that he might move there, which his work would permit. Jeff had not been able to maintain a successful long-term relationship with a woman, so he was open to the possibility of moving to see whether this new love interest might pan out.

The possibility of Jeff's moving back east left hanging the question of his ability to continue his treatment with me. While the proposed plan to relocate was limited to a period of three months, such a break often spells the end to treatment. To a greater or lesser extent, resistance is a factor in every treatment, and interruptions offer the patient a chance to run. Yes, we could try to keep the treatment going by Skyping, but that was not my preferred way of working. At any rate, the patient had had a decision to make in the weeks he'd been away from treatment, and I was left sitting and waiting to see what he'd decide to do without any opportunity to interpret signs of resistance to treatment or to advocate on behalf of the treatment.

I felt strongly that Jeff would make an ideal analytic patient: He was young, motivated, psychologically minded, intelligent, and... troubled. Jeff was open – he listened and considered what I had to say rather than fending off my input and clinging to his own ways of thinking to explain why he did the things he did and felt the way he felt. It was surprising that he'd never before been in treatment given that he is one of the most anxious patients I'd ever met. Jeff was naive about therapy and did something when he arrived for his first session that no other patient has ever done before or since: Instead of coming into the waiting room, sitting down, and waiting, I was surprised to find him standing in the hallway outside the front door of my office looking flustered and perplexed, as if he hadn't a clue as to where he was to be. Getting himself through the front door is the first move a patient must make to declare his acceptance of "patienthood."

After finding him outside my office door, I invited Jeff in, noting that he looked more anxious than most new patients who are confronted with the issue of where to sit. Once seated, Jeff's anxiety did not abate. His anxiety was palpable, and – frankly – a bit hard to witness, manifesting as a breathlessness and a restlessness that immediately evoked my sympathy for his suffering, as well as my curiosity about why it had taken him so long to seek help.

Once we'd settled in I inquired about what had just happened – what he'd been experiencing and thinking as he stood outside my door waiting for me to show. In response, Jeff explained that he'd gone into the waiting room but was immediately seized with worry that he'd erred and was acting inappropriately, so he went back out and stood in the hallway. He apologized just in case I considered him to have acted in a "wrong" fashion. This was the opening line to his story about how terrified he was about ever erring in life. The patient explained: "I can't stand to be wrong... it drives me insane," which – to my way of thinking – presented a host of possibilities. What does it mean to be wrong? Wrong in what way? After all, no one can avoid being wrong at one time or another – it's inevitable. Furthermore, what does he mean by "insane?" That is quite a statement to make to a psychiatrist. Does he mean that he feels intolerable shame when he is proven wrong? I assumed he was concerned with being proven wrong in the eyes of others. But... maybe not. Maybe having to privately come to terms with being wrong was what he'd meant. Clearly, I needed to know more.

Jeff continued, "In order to avoid being proven wrong I tend to stick with decisions I ought not to stay with," which was a lead-in to the patient's explaining about his most recent error – a relationship with a young and troubled woman named Susie, which had just ended. Jeff explained that he'd precipitously invited her to move in with him – seeing that she had no place to stay – and he just as quickly realized it was foolhardy to have done so – though he hadn't the nerve to face the fact that the relationship was "wrong" and ought to be brought to a swift end. He'd known Susie when they were students at an Ivy League college, and he had had a crush on her back then, though he'd failed to make a move. Later, when he met up with her in Hollywood, she was a struggling actress and wasn't able to make ends meet; he, on the other hand, was successfully employed at a film production company. He relished the idea of providing for her, and provide he did, only to discover how unstable she was – downing countless numbers of pills to help manage her emotionality. "We couldn't have been more different," Jeff explained. He'd been wrong to choose her as a lover, Jeff said in retrospect, and wrong to have allowed her to move in so precipitously. But admitting as much came hard for Jeff. Besides, he hadn't a clue about how to break it off. He was deeply disappointed in his inability to take the bull by the horns by doing what he knew he needed to do – to end the relationship as quickly as possible. He berated himself for having made a colossal mistake and took no comfort realizing such things happen in the course of dating – that one cannot always know as much as one wishes to know or needs to know to know whether a love interest will make an appropriate long-term mate. Yes, he'd acted in haste and we could fruitfully explore why that had been, but first we'd need to get him past his self-loathing. Yes, he'd been rash deciding to invite her to live with him, but she was in need and he particularly liked being in a position to offer her a place to stay, thus proving his worth.

Jeff's failed relationship with Susie was but one of the two precipitating factors that drove him to treatment. He'd recently been back east for work when his grandmother choked on some food, went into a coma, and died. This threw Jeff for a loop emotionally, and he was highly critical of the fact he had reacted as strongly as he had to the eventful loss. He argued that most others his age had already lost a grandparent... so... what was his problem? Why had he overreacted to the degree that he had? Another instance of his judging himself wrong, I wondered?

Days after the funeral, Jeff got a text from Susie suggesting that they break off their relationship. Since he'd been unable to terminate the relationship himself, it fell to Susie to have to act. Jeff felt relieved, though he faulted himself for having "chickened out" – for not taking charge, for not having acted decisively by doing what he knew he needed to do. At any rate, it was over. Susie moved out, and Jeff was left grieving for his beloved grandmother and for a relationship that never turned out the way he hoped it might.

Jeff opened his first session by telling me how "insane" it made him feel to be proven wrong. In the second session, he elaborated on that theme by presenting an example of something he'd done when he was 12 years old that still haunted him to this day – something he felt he'd never been able, and would never be able, to live down. While at summer camp, he got into a heated debate with a girl about two actors who'd played the same role in two particular movies. He was insistent that one actor had played the part much better than the other – hands down! This girl begged to differ. Jeff dug in his heels, becoming ever more insistent. Years later, he came to "realize" he'd been mistaken, and he couldn't stand the fact he'd erred in so egregious a fashion.

I was curious about how long it had taken Jeff to seek help and inquired as to what he knew of his difficulty getting himself into treatment. The patient wasn't sure he knew, though he was quick to credit his neurotic tendencies – his perfectionism and his tendency to give himself a hard time whenever he'd err – for getting him as far as he'd gotten professionally. Given his successes, he did not want to risk the chance of relaxing the pressure he put on himself to always be "right," since it was this precise tendency that he credited for his success. What if treatment got him to relax? Might he then be less successful? That worry concerned him – the possibility that the therapy might screw with the tools he relied upon to be a high achiever.

As treatment progressed, I noted a striking pattern in how the patient would act. Jeff couldn't seem to help himself from "spilling the beans" by inadvertently divulging aspects of his unconscious that made their way in to treatment on a regular basis through his many slips of the tongue. His tendency to let the cat out of the bag flustered and embarrassed Jeff, who was constantly trying to backtrack and "take back" things he appeared to be saying, if only obliquely. He'd say he hadn't meant to choose that particular word, which he knew had given me the wrong impression of what it was he was trying to say. Still, his unconscious seemed to persist in demanding to be heard, seemingly against the patient's better judgment and much to his chagrin. This pattern was like something I'd never seen before – a pattern that might be equated with a sort of psychic incontinence that very much embarrassed the patient, resulting in seemingly inadvertent admissions that he was constantly working to undo. These tendencies helped show his hand – helped reveal all sorts of things about his psychology. But while such tendencies benefited the treatment insofar as these revelations furthered the work, the patient was deeply disturbed by such tendencies – by the very behavior that made him an ideal candidate for analysis – which brings us to the session under consideration.

It was the patient's first session of the New Year following his three-week hiatus from treatment. I entered the session wondering about the fate of his treatment – whether he'd decided to move back east, whether cancelling our last scheduled session was a sign of a mounting resistance. The patient began the session by providing an update about his time away, after which he posed the question: "How are we doing here?" We had met fewer than a dozen times, and the question didn't seem out of order. Jeff seemed anxious to know how he was performing as a patient – was he conducting himself properly as a patient? He'd noted the random nature of the topics we discussed in session, in line with my recommendation that he try to free associate, but this did not comport with how he imagined therapy would progress – in a step-by-step fashion, which he saw as ideally suited to facilitate his progress. I assured the patient that he was doing what he needed to do when in session, but I took the opportunity to express my belief that I felt he'd feel more satisfied with the progress of treatment if we met on a more frequent basis.

In response, Jeff said he'd realized as much himself, adding that he no longer had to travel as much for work as he had in the past, so meeting more often and more regularly was a definite possibility, but – he added – I needed to know how hard it was to tear himself away from work to come. His father had recently expressed a desire that they go away together for a five-day trip later in the month, leading to the patient's explaining how hard it was for him to take time off from work. The patient talked about how important he felt it was to "give his all" to work otherwise his contributions might be judged wanting. I told the patient that I wondered whether he felt he had to demonstrate his complete commitment to work because otherwise his boss might discover that he's "an imposter" – building on something the patient had told me in a previous session. The patient protested that this was not the whole story – he was equally driven by his passion for the work he did. I clarified my remark by stating that I hadn't intended to suggest the entire reason he worked as hard as he did was fear-based, nor did I mean to imply that I was saying: "You think you do x for y reason, when, in fact you do it for z reason." Such interventions can lead the patient to feel corrected and/or shamed, which is the last thing I wanted Jeff to feel, given how shame-sensitive he was.

Elaborating on the subject of giving "his all" at work, Jeff launched into describing his habit, in his capacity as "one amongst many" of the show's producers, of showing up on set the very first day of the shoot to establish his influence and imbed himself in the decision-making process. Were he to show up days later, Jeff argued, he'd not be able to position himself to ensure his input would be taken seriously. Working overtime – working extra-hard – was his way of maintaining his authority and ensuring his influence. The patient then said: "*I get in there and grab all I can.*"

Jeff's phrasing struck me – it seemed to be yet another example of a statement Jeff would quickly realize, after making it, would give me the wrong impression of what he was really trying to say – that he hadn't, in fact, meant to suggest he was "grabby," even though that was pretty much what he had said and realized he had said. But now he was insisting he meant nothing of the sort, and should be excused for yet again misspeaking. So here we were, face-to-face, with yet another of his now famous unconscious slips that seemed to reveal something about Jeff that Jeff had not consciously intended to say about himself. He scrambled to correct what he'd just said, begging for a chance to set the record straight. Then, having set the record straight, Jeff continued on his way... but I don't quite remember what he said next because I was struck by what had just happened, which left me wondering about the meaning of his statement as well as his correction. Should I speak up and address the issue or let it slide? Would my bringing the patient back to the subject of his slip highlight what he clearly saw as a faux pas proving unnecessarily shaming, or might there be some clinical utility in such a maneuver? Might my highlighting his statement heighten his already substantial self-consciousness, which seemed like a distinct possibility given what I'd learned about him thus far? And, were I to address the slip – if it could be considered as such – what might be accomplished by bringing the patient's attention back to that event?

It struck me that the patient had, in fact, inadvertently admitted to something he now wished to take back. Had he unwittingly "copped" to the impulse of *greedily* grabbing all he could for himself? That seemed possible, though I wondered if our relationship could withstand the stress of my suggesting as much. Besides, I wasn't entirely sure whether that was what his statement had revealed. Maybe getting the patient to focus on the slip would help acquaint him with the voice of his unconscious. Maybe our working together on the slip might demonstrate to Jeff how he and I might work together to deepen the treatment. Maybe I wanted to show him the value of the sort of work he and I could do, which – I hoped – might lessen his resistance. But I also wondered whether my activity might serve a more personal agenda: Was I trying to show how closely I was attending to the patient's associations? Was I showing off by demonstrating my capacity to think more deeply about such matters? Maybe I was just being clever, against Sullivan's admonition: "God keep me from a clever therapist" (Levenson, 1996, p. 643). Maybe I should avoid making a big deal of what the patient might regard as something that didn't matter in the least. Besides, there was the ever-present danger that the patient might become hung up on the idea that he'd erred, rather than appreciating how such "errors" are gifts insofar as they expose aspects of the unconscious so that we might together learn more about his underlying psychology. What do you think you'd do?

Invited commentator responses: Fred Busch and James L. Fosshage

Fred Busch

The author's introduction captures well the various factors that play a role in beginning a treatment, and the special problems in working with those who are narcissistically vulnerable. Mindful of their difficulties, he reflects on how to integrate the intrapsychic and interpersonal components of the psychoanalytic process, a position many of us struggle to maintain. In my comments, I will focus on the intrapsychic perspective, as I think it offers, in this case, the potential to both further the treatment and not narcissistically injure the patient. Having said this, I believe that commenting on the work of another clinician is a task to be approached with humility. Although the author has done an admirable job of bringing the reader into the room with him, there is so much a respondent does not have access to, like the affective coloring of words, the multitude of observations that leads the clinician to think this or that, the subtle mood shifts in both participants, the analyst's reveries, and so on. Given this sizeable handicap, in order to fill my role as respondent I will proceed as if *I really* knew what was going on.

In 1938, in a review of Anna Freud's book on defense analysis, Ernst Kris (1938) warned that the subtle but significant changes in technique emphasized by Miss Freud might go unnoticed. "Somehow or other, many analysts conceived the idea that, in analysis, the value of the scientific and therapeutic work was in direct proportion to the depth of the psychic strata upon which attention was focused" (p. 3). It is the issue of *defense analysis* that is central to my response to the clinical dilemma as presented, "whether to speak or let things be."[3] I see defense analysis as one component of what I call *creating a psychoanalytic mind* (Busch, 2014), whereby one primary goal of analysis is the analysand's increased capacity to think and feel what was previously unthinkable and unknowable.

In the moment under consideration in this sensitive, highly readable portrayal of the beginning (or not) of an analysis, Jeff brings into the open that he wants to "grab all he can" and then beats a hasty retreat, feeling his words were not what they seemed. The analyst then struggles with the question of whether to bring Jeff back to what he (Jeff) saw as a faux pas, or leave it alone because of Jeff's already heightened self-consciousness, and raises a series of important issues with regards to whether to say something or not. The question we are asked to consider is, "What would you do?" in such a situation.

I will begin the discussion with my observation that what we see in Jeff's response to his "grabbing" thought is a typical defense of *undoing*. Jeff's response (i.e., I didn't mean that) has a desperate quality to it, indicating there is something very frightening to him about this idea that slipped out. How did this idea slip out? I see two possibilities. The first is that a defense has been briefly loosened so that Jeff wants to communicate his hidden self to the analyst, but this feels very dangerous to him and thus the immediate cover-up. A second possibility is that the drive to grab is so strong it couldn't be contained. In either case, we see a weakened ego. I agree with the analyst that just bringing Jeff back to the slip wouldn't make sense as he's indicated that's not what he meant, and all the signs are that slip made him extremely uncomfortable. Yet saying nothing would bypass a chance to begin the analysis of the defense, which could help the patient understand more about his need for this seemingly panicky defense. Thus, a basic question becomes: Why should this thought – he'd like to "grab all he can" – make him so uncomfortable?

I feel we get a hint of what may lie behind Jeff's extreme discomfort around showing his *grabbing* feelings in his uneasiness about entering the waiting room in the first session. As reported by the analyst:

> The patient explained that he'd gone into the waiting room but was immediately seized with worry that he was acting *inappropriately*, so he went back out and stood in the hallway. He apologized in case I considered him to have acted in a "wrong" fashion. This was the opening line to his story about how terrified he was about ever erring in life. The patient explained: "I can't stand to be wrong... it drives me insane."
>
> (italics added)

In this moment, one fear that Jeff brings up is over being *inappropriate*. My private musings led me to think that unconsciously, such a word often has sexual meanings. There also seem to be strong feelings of shame associated with being wrong (e.g., the argument when he was 12). That it drives him *insane* is a worry I would take seriously, and could well be a major part of his difficulty committing to treatment (i.e., *it will drive him insane*). It would lead me to be cautious about trying to get him to come more frequently until this was better understood.

So how might I proceed in a way that hopefully would deepen the treatment without increasing Jeff's fear over what he's revealed? I would say something like:

> I can see how having this thought, "I get in there and grab all I can," bothered you. I know you feel this wasn't what you meant, but even so, I wonder if you can let your mind go and see what comes to mind about what was so *disquieting about this thought*.

How do I think this would be useful? First of all, I would be trying to represent in words what just happened. While it may seem obvious, I would assume Jeff would quickly try to bury what occurred and be left with a vague feeling of discomfort, at best, and possibly panic. As suggested by Green (1974, 1975), representations are the first step in building structures that contain affects. Containment of feelings is an important element in the beginning of any treatment, but especially important in this treatment because of how Jeff seems overwhelmed at times (e.g., like in the first session). Further, I would attempt to give recognition and space for Jeff's discomfort while raising the issue, in an unsaturated fashion,[4] of why this statement of "grabbing" made him so uncomfortable. Notice I'm not telling him what's making him uncomfortable, but leaving it open for exploration... if he's able. Why is this important? Mainly because I believe we can only explore with the patient what he's ready to explore. Prematurely suggesting ideas to a patient usually closes thinking rather than opening it. Further, it will be difficult for Jeff to explore these grabbing feelings until he can understand more about what was disquieting about the thought. If, for example, Jeff believes his feelings are *inappropriate*, then exploration of the expected feelings of guilt, shame, and possibly insanity (that drive the defensive reaction) would need to be an important part of the working through process.[5]

Now if the reader (and author) would allow me even greater speculative latitude, I would like to follow a thought that came to me while reading the clinical material – Bion's idea of analyzing without memory or desire. The longer I've practiced psychoanalysis, the more I've understood the importance of trying to maintain this stance for an analytic approach to each session. It is a difficult task, and I more often fail than succeed. Yet I hold it out as an ideal. From this perspective, listen to the analyst's thinking:

> I want to find a way to get Jeff to not only come more consistently but to come more often as well. We'd been meeting on a once-a-week basis and while we were making surprising headway given the infrequency of our meetings, I sensed the pace of treatment would quicken and the work would deepen were we to meet more often. My wish that he come at least twice weekly – and ideally to enter analysis – is very much on my mind as we enter the session I'm about to present. Admittedly, I'm a tad frustrated that we haven't yet settled into regular treatment but I remain hopeful that our being able to do so is just around the corner. The patient reassures me as much – knowing his irregular attendance is not ideal and sensing that I am hankering for us to meet more regularly and more often.

While the analyst's reasons are understandable (i.e., the wish to deepen the treatment for the patient's benefit), it was my impression that the analyst's therapeutic zeal (desire) outpaced his appreciation for the patient's wish to not enter a relationship too precipitously because he feared he couldn't get out of it (like with his girlfriends). Further, his overwhelming anxiety in the first session suggests a weakened ego, unable to contain feelings, which might lead one to proceed cautiously.

The above led me to wonder if, indeed, the analyst was trying to *grab* the patient for an analysis. I saw this as a likely countertransference in response to something unconsciously stimulated in the transference. It's my impression this transference/countertransference is a microcosm of his relationship with Susie, where they grab on to each other quickly, and then Jeff immediately wants out. I also wondered if the retreat from the *grabbing* thoughts might have triggered some fear of something Jeff felt toward the analyst (wanting to be grabbed as much as wanting to grab him), which might have been especially upsetting.

As I wrote the last paragraph, I thought of how attitudes toward countertransference have changed in the decades I've been practicing psychoanalysis. Early in my career, it was something not to be talked about, as it was associated with pathology. However, over time, we've come to realize it is something we all have to grapple with, and if raised to the level of awareness and worked through, it can be an impetus to understanding the patient at a deeper level. Yet I get concerned about the use of countertransference as a direct understanding of the patient's unconscious without first reflecting upon it.

I would like to remind the reader that my thoughts about the clinical question the analyst asked us to ponder were about a *virtual* patient, not necessarily the analyst's patient. I once heard Merton Gill say, if six analysts are discussing a patient, they will come up with at least eight different opinions. We've all experienced this. I've been involved with groups of analysts where we discuss a single patient over a period of time. In general, people with different theoretical backgrounds often can agree on the patient's basic dynamics. Yet when we discuss how we would proceed to treat this same patient, our methods vary considerably. This is why I think the Editors of this book have provided such a rich format for the discussion of important technical questions in that therapists can compare and contrast how analysts from different perspectives approach the same clinical dilemma.

Finally, I would like to thank the analyst for sharing his clinical data with us. While for a variety of reasons, it is difficult to have seasoned analysts present clinical data, the Editors, by making it anonymous, have allowed us to hear a sample of such work. The analyst's thoughtful approach to the multiple factors that play a role in beginning an analysis, along with his willingness to share his private musings, have given us a rich tapestry for us to gaze upon and play with.

James L. Fosshage

Every clinical encounter is uniquely co-created within an intersubjective or relational field. This understanding is based on an ongoing transformation of psychoanalytic theory and clinical practice, over the past 60 years, through the integration of two fundamental changes in paradigms: the epistemological transition from objectivism to constructivism, and the conceptual transition in explaining the formation of psychological organization as primarily generated intrapsychically versus within relational fields (or systems). These paradigm changes have enabled us to shift clinically from a singular focus on the assumed intrapsychically generated world of the patient – that is, making the unconscious conflict conscious primarily through interpretation and insight – to a detailed focus on the patient's experiential world as it emerges within relational contexts, including the patient/analyst co-creation and co-construction of their ongoing intersubjective or relational field. We gain access to the patient/analyst intersubjective field through the close tracking and exploration of both the patient/analyst interaction and their respective subjective experiences.

Contemporary psychoanalysts of all persuasions have been variably affected by these paradigm shifts, and we can view how contemporary clinical practice varies along these two continuous dimensions – that is, objectivism to constructivism and intrapsychically to relationally generated (or systems) emphases. Utilizing these two continua, we can understand a clinical/theoretical formulation and corresponding intervention as emanating from an "objectivist" or "constructivist" position and from an "intrapsychic" or "relational" perspective. I designate my theoretical/clinical model to be *relational self psychology* (for a detailed description, see Fosshage, 2003, 2011).

In his introduction, the analyst describes the patient, Jeff, as "an intensely anxious man" in his late 20s. Jeff spoke of a "dread of acting decisively out of fear he could be proven wrong – a devastating fear that plagued him." As I read this, I begin to conjecture that the patient's fear of being proven wrong is most likely a *primary organizing pattern* (or experiential theme) that took form through repetitive relational experience in which Jeff felt shamefully "proven wrong." The analyst then notices that the patient makes "slips of the tongue that he [Jeff] found unnerving to the extent these disclosures left him feeling not only exposed but in error." The analyst was concerned that to focus on the "slip" might narcissistically injure "this shame-sensitive patient" and increase "resistance" rather than "capture the patient's interest" and demonstrate "the treatment's potential worth."

Emanating from the traditional intrapsychic conflict model, the analyst focuses on unconscious conflictual processes, in this instance, "slips of the tongue" and resistance. The focus on slips (unwanted expressions of repressed wishes or thoughts) and resistances, combined with a declarative tone suggestive of an underlying objectivist perspective, can easily evoke the patient's repetitive experience that he did something "wrong" and feels defensive about it. The analyst senses, correctly I believe, the potential for shaming the patient that, in turn, creates the analyst's dilemma as "whether to speak or let things be." Interestingly, the analyst's sensitive recognition of his potential impact on the patient emanates from a relational perspective. In my view, the analyst's intrapsychic model for explanation and focus, in this instance, potentiates shaming the patient and, thus, creates the analyst's dilemma.

In contrast, from a relational perspective, I would explore what is occurring within the patient/analyst relational field that is creating anxiety for the patient – specifically, what are the patient's, analyst's, and contextual contributions to the patient's experience? I would ask questions like: Were you feeling anxious before you came today? What were your fantasies and expectations about our meeting? Has your anxiety increased or decreased since you have been here? Is there something that is happening here, including what I am doing, that exacerbates your anxiety or alleviates your anxiety? In this close tracking of the patient's feelings and interactive scene, I am inquiring about the patient's experience and the various contributing factors to that experience generated, not just intrapsychically, but by both participants within the context of the analyst/patient relational field. In my view, the patient's anxiety and propensity to feel shamefully "wrong" appear to be a dominant organizing pattern that emerged out of repetitive relational experience and is the patient's contribution to his experience within the patient/analyst intersubjective field. The analyst's contribution is his intrapsychially based model that, more easily than the relational model, evokes shame through placing total responsibility on the patient.

From my perspective, a more consistent use of the empathic listening perspective, combined with a conceptualization of the organizing mind and establishment of patterns of organization, will facilitate tracking Jeff's experience more closely and will contribute to a more open "spirit of inquiry" (Lichtenberg, Lachmann, & Fosshage, 2003). An analyst engages the patient in a mutual exploratory effort to identify, in this instance, a major organizing pattern and illuminate its relational origins as well as other contributing factors within the analyst/patient intersubjective field. With these explorations and explanations, the patient will begin to feel that his fear of being wrong is not something inherently wrong within him, but rather that this is a learned procedural attitude that emerged out of his past and is now operative in current relational experience. Procedural attitudes or organizing patterns, based on learning from previous relational experience, are the patient's current "intrapsychic" component, if you will, that is activated within the current relational context. This exploratory/interpretive process is aimed to increase reflective awareness of how he came to feel so scared of being wrong on the basis of previous relational experience. This relational conceptualization reduces self-blame and simultaneously creates a new non-shaming patient/analyst relational experience for the formation of new self and self-with-other organizations.

Specific responses to the presented moment

Treatment began with a "handful" of sessions and a number of "travel-for-work" and "holiday-travel-with-family" disruptions. While the analyst does not dismiss or invalidate Jeff's explanations of his absences, the analyst anxiously figures that Jeff is also "resisting," a traditional assumption anchored in intrapsychic/unconscious conflict theory, and he is concerned that the patient will end treatment before he begins. To conceptualize and focus on a patient's defensive operations as resistance lends a pejorative cast, for it implies that the patient is in an intrapsychically generated opposition to the analysis. This conceptualization can easily create a patient/analyst oppositional struggle. Eschewing the concept of resistance, Kohut (1977, 1984) reconceptualized defenses as self-protective measures, facilitating the analyst's exploration of what accounts for the emergence of self-protective measures at that moment within the current analyst/patient relational field (what Kohut referred to as the self-selfobject matrix). Viewing these measures as protective of the self reveals their usefulness and elicits a more compassionate and accepting view of them. "Resistance" is not explored here, because the analyst, I suspect once again, correctly senses that the patient could easily feel criticized and shamed. The analyst's focus on his impact on the patient, again, emanates from a relational field perspective, demonstrating the analyst's partial integration of this paradigm shift.

The patient senses that the analyst is "hankering for us to meet more regularly and more often." While the analyst reflectively recognizes his own desires, the analyst, at least in the material provided here, does not directly validate his patient's perception or explore the impact of the analyst's agenda. My hunch is that his predominantly intrapsychic model, which focuses on transferential projections and displacements, interferes with a consistent awareness and exploration of the impact of his formulations and agenda on the patient and the analytic field. In contrast, a relational field model prompts us to explore and understand the mutual reciprocal impact that analyst and patient have on one another.

The patient then offers that he has met a woman in New York, and since he very much wants a long-term romantic relationship, he is contemplating moving. This news is disturbing to the analyst, for the analyst really wants to do analysis with Jeff. As a reader of this material, the analyst's agenda is quite palpable and too much in the foreground, perhaps again the fertile ground for giving rise to the analyst's view of resistance. If Jeff is aversive to treatment, which is unclear to me, might he be, in part, aversively reacting to the analyst and his agenda (again focusing on what is occurring in the intersubjective field)? At these moments, we, in my view, need to reflectively "decenter" from our agenda and ally with Jeff's good news and hopes for a romantic relationship – what in self psychology we call allying with the leading edge[6] (Kohut, 1984; Tolpin, 2002) or the developmental motivation of the patient. Here we would attempt to help him evaluate this potential relationship and the complexities of moving. Feeling supported in his developmental efforts would, most likely, be experienced as vitalizing and further enticing of the analysis, whether to occur now or later, or face-to-face or over FaceTime.

The analyst observes that Jeff is highly anxious. Upon arrival for the first session, Jeff had ended up pacing in the hallway rather than sitting in the waiting room for fear that "he was acting inappropriately." This organizing theme of fearing that he would do something wrong was reactivated when entering a new situation. By now I know that this is a major organizing theme in his life, and I would be exploring with the patient when he first remembered having the experience of being shamed and criticized for being wrong, assuming that such a dominant theme came out of repetitive relational experience (a relational perspective). In contrast, the analyst, using an intrapsychic unconscious conflict model, focuses on what he conceptualizes as unconscious "slips," where the unconscious speaks, blurting out and shaming Jeff. I believe that the intrapsychic model increases the potential for activating this shame-ridden organizing pattern, which the analyst clearly sensed. The analyst could not resolve his dilemma of "whether to speak up or let things be," I reiterate, because of the limitations of his intrapsychic model. In contrast, identification of the dominant organizing theme and exploration of and understanding the relational experiential origins of the theme – that is, how it was learned within the specific family context – tend to diminish the shame-saturated self-blaming and increase reflective awareness of the patient's learned establishment of a primary organizing pattern with which he now understandably (that's the way mind works) constructs his world.

Jeff then describes two situations involving the choice of a woman and reacting to his grandmother's death where he feels he was "wrong," wrong in his choice of a woman and not knowing how to extricate himself, and wrong over the intensity of his upset about his grandmother. This theme of feeling "wrong" is so dominant that it clearly does not require "slips" to trigger it, confirming my earlier conjecture that this dominant organizing pattern, not the slips, is what needs to be addressed.

The analyst becomes quite conflicted as to how to approach Jeff's "slips" and raises this issue as the central question for our discussion. To search for defended-against meanings of the slips will probably serve, as the analyst expects, to further shame the patient. The analyst's intrapsychic model in this situation enhances the analyst's anxiety about losing the patient through shaming him, thus preventing a full exploration and deepening of treatment.

In contrast, I would shift the focus to the process, trying to understand what was happening between us that activated the organizing pattern. On those occasions when Jeff felt especially shamed, I would attempt to explore it in detail to identify the especially painful contributing factors. For example, tell me as best as you can what seemed to trigger the shame? I would also wonder with Jeff if, on occasion, he becomes very anxious, expecting to be shamed for "doing something wrong," and how his anxiety dysregulates and discombobulates him which, in turn, terrifies him for he feels out of control (perhaps when "slips" occur). I would continue to look for and emphasize the relational origins of that narrative. As he understands the source of his anxiety as emerging out of past relational experience, he will gradually be able to use his reflective awareness to free himself more and more from the grips of that pattern and its associated pain. Gradually, the pattern will be activated less and less as he will be able with his new reflective awareness to intercede and silence (deactivate) the old pattern, be able to connect with his new experience of himself in the treatment, and consolidate new more vitalizing organizing themes or attitudes about himself and himself with others.

I wish to add one last note. In my view, exclusively intrapsychically generated formulations tend to leave the analyst out of the interaction and to distance the analyst from the patient. Relational field formulations, in contrast, tend to invite analyst and patient to attend to their reciprocal contributions to each other's relational experience, all good tools for engaging, understanding, and succeeding in relationships.

In summary, with the analyst's intrapsychic focus on repressed, shame-ridden "slips" and "resistance" the analyst's dilemma emerges: "Whether to speak up or let things be." While the analyst does not want to shame the patient (a relational perspective), his theory, an intrapsychic-generated focus on slips of the tongue and resistance, in my view, locks him into a stalemate. In contrast, active exploration and elucidation of the organizing theme of feeling shamefully "wrong" and its relational experiential origins will increase reflective awareness and help the patient gradually to intercede consciously and deactivate the pattern as well as experience himself and the world in new more vitalizing ways.

I thank the analyst for providing the clinical material for this comparative discussion.

My intervention

I chose to comment on the patient's behavior by venturing that he was worried that speaking as he had *might lead me to think* he was admitting to being "greedy." At first, the patient bristled at my use of the word *greedy*, defensively explaining that he thought he'd chosen his words poorly and, as a result, might well have given me the wrong impression that he was now keen to correct. I asked the patient why he felt such a pressing need to set the matter straight – what underlying concern might account for this apparent need to "scramble" to undo the impression he feared he'd created. Might he be worried that I would think less of him given what he'd said?

It was then that I learned something about the patient I'd not known before, which emerged as he further explained his need to show up early to ensure his place vis-à-vis the film crew. His life had been fine up until he was around eight years old, when his family moved from a big city to the suburbs. For the next several years, the patient was unable to find a way to plug into the social world at school. He was late to the party and felt like a social isolate without a clue as to how to change the situation. It was painful to hear how lonely and isolated he'd felt, a condition that persisted unabated for years, until he reached the 11th grade when, somehow, things began to change. Not until the patient was in college did he finally feel "amongst his own," but now that he'd made it to Hollywood, he worried that his continued success depended on his being socially adept, which was not his strong suit. Showing up early on set was his way of compensating for his inability to command respect by the strength of his personality and a way of ensuring he would not have to re-experience showing up late (having moved to the suburbs) without a clue as to how he might successfully insert himself into the social circle. Were he not to be present on day one, he'd be lost establishing a position.

Up until that point, I had known nothing of the patient's social struggles. I suggested to the patient that his belief that he needed to commit substantial energy to the task of forming and maintaining friendships was at work in our relationship as well. I further surmised that a portion of his mind was perennially dedicated to monitoring his actions to ensure he not act in ways that might prove off-putting given how precious relationships could be once formed. Were he to suddenly conclude he'd "slipped up" – as he evidently felt when he spoke of "grabbing all I can get" – he then might work hard to rescue himself from what he deemed to be a serious misstep that could negatively impact his relationship with me. I went on to suggest that this intense level of self-monitoring required an inordinate amount of mental energy, which likely diminished his ability to be comfortably spontaneous – present and in the moment. Lacking the sort of self-confidence and self-assurance that makes one relatively comfortable in social settings, the patient was left having to compensate in this fashion, which paradoxically made matters worse – made it harder for him to win friends and influence people. I suggested that were we to work together in treatment in order to lessen his anxiety, he might then feel less of a need to dedicate inordinate amounts of energy to monitoring his behavior, which could go a ways toward helping him feel comfortable with himself and, hence, with others. In response, the patient reconfirmed my suspicion that he'd become adept at "faking it" – at appearing more spontaneous – to hide risking exposure of his true self with others who were oblivious to how he really felt or who he actually was.

Having finally expressed these feelings to another being, the patient was no longer alone in feeling this way. I knew that he felt this way as well. For the first time since we'd begun to meet, I'd directly addressed the patient's problem as being about his overwhelming anxiety, which I felt we could only address if we met more often. I believe it may well have been the patient's core anxiety – manifesting as it had in a fear of social interaction – which may have contributed to his earlier difficulties approaching others and establishing himself within the social milieu.

As for the premise that Jeff had let the cat out of the bag by inadvertently admitting his feelings of greed – I concluded that such feelings could only be addressed when and if the patient was far enough along in his treatment to be ready to hear and struggle with such feelings. For the time being, I planned to avoid any mention of the matter. We had, for the time being, bigger fish to fry that came with the realization that attending to the solidification of a therapeutic alliance took precedence over our working interpretively together.

Notes

1 It should be noted that some analysts see a conflict-free working relationship as an unachievable ideal (Adler, 2000; Brenner, 1979; Curtis, 1979; Friedman, 1969).

2 Safety arising from the provision of consistency, honesty, authenticity, attention to the frame, the establishment and maintenance of boundaries, and so on.
3 Unfortunately, in spite of attempts to correct it (Busch, 1995; Gray, 1994), defense analysis, if performed at all, has been misunderstood and maligned.
4 Ferro's (2002) introduction of the term *unsaturated interpretations* has led me to consider the many ways the analyst's interventions might best be unsaturated (Busch, 2014). In this case, I am not suggesting I know what the fear is that drives Jeff's defense. Rather, I invite him to explore what aspect, if any, he can allow himself to think about. One of the major problems in defense analysis done at an earlier time was the analyst brought to the patient's attention what the analyst thought he was defending against, rather than allowing the patient to explore what he might be ready to face at the moment.
5 Freud (1914) believed defense analysis was crucial to working through, a position I believe still has merit.
6 "The 'leading edge' addresses what the person is striving to achieve, and the 'trailing edge' addresses the contents and conflicts that are avoided, repressed, or disavowed. Both edges are important in psychoanalytic treatment ..." (Lachmann, 2004, p. 581).

References

Adler, G. (2000). The alliance and the more disturbed patient. In S. T. Levy (Ed.), *The therapeutic alliance* (pp. 75–91). Madison, CT: International Universities Press.

Baldwin, S., Wampold, B., & Imel, Z. (2007). Untangling the alliance-outcome correlation: Exploring the relative importance of therapist and patient variability in the alliance. *Journal of Consulting & Clinical Psychology*, 75(6), 842–852.

Brenner, C. (1979). Working alliance, therapeutic alliance, and transference. *Journal of the American Psychoanalytic Association*, 27, 137–157.

Busch, F. (1995). *The ego at the center of psychoanalytic technique*. Northridge, NJ: Jason Aronson.

Busch, F. (2014). *Creating a psychoanalytic mind*. London: Routledge.

Curtis, H. C. (1979). The concept of therapeutic alliance: Implications for the "widening scope." *Journal of the American Psychoanalytic Association*, 27, 159–192.

Ferro, A. (2002). *In the analyst's consulting room*. Hove: Brunner/Routledge.

Fosshage, J. (2003). Contextualizing self psychology and relational psychoanalysis: Bi-directional influence and proposed syntheses. *Contemporary Psychoanalysis*, 39(3), 411–448.

Fosshage, J. (2011). The use and impact of the analyst's subjectivity with empathic and other listening/experiencing perspectives. *Psychoanalytic Quarterly*, 80(1), 139–160.

Freud, S. (1913). On the beginning of treatment. In J. Strachey (Ed. & Trans.), *The standard edition of the complete psychological works of Sigmund Freud* (Vol. 12, pp. 139–140). London: Hogarth Press, 1958.

Freud, S. (1914). Remembering, repeating and working through. In J. Strachey (Ed. & Trans.), *The standard edition of the complete psychological works of Sigmund Freud* (Vol. 12, pp. 145–156). London: Hogarth Press.

Friedman, L. (1969). The therapeutic alliance. *International Journal of Psychoanalysis*, 50(2), 139–153.

Friedman, L. (1997). Ferrum, ignis, and medicina: Return to the crucible. *Journal of the American Psychoanalytic Association*, 45, 20–36.

Gitelson, M. (1962). The curative factors in psychoanalysis. *International Journal of Psychoanalysis*, 43(4–5), 194–205.
Gray, P. (1994). *The ego and mechanisms of defense*. Northridge, NJ: Jason Aronson.
Green, A. (1974). Surface analysis, deep analysis (The role of the preconscious in psychoanalytical technique). *International Review of Psychoanalysis*, 1, 415–423.
Green, A. (1975). The analyst, symbolization and absence in the analytic setting (on changes in analytic practice and analytic experience): In memory of D. W. Winnicott. *International Journal of Psychoanalysis*, 56(1), 1–22.
Greenson, R. (1965). The working alliance and the transference neurosis. *Psychoanalytic Quarterly*, 34(2), 155–181.
Greenson, R. (1967). *The technique and practice of psychoanalysis*. New York: International Universities Press.
Greenson, R., & Wexler, M. (1969). The non-transference relationship in the psychoanalytic situation. *International Journal of Psychoanalysis*, 50(1), 27–39.
Hanly, C. (1994). Reflections on the place of the therapeutic alliance in psychoanalysis. *International Journal of Psychoanalysis*, 75(3), 457–467.
Hansen, N., Lambert, M., & Forman, E. (2002). The psychotherapy dose-response effect and its implication for treatment delivery systems. *Clinical Psychology: Science and Practice*, 9(3), 329–343.
Hausner, R. S. (2000). The therapeutic and working alliances. *Journal of the American Psychoanalytic Association*, 48(1), 155–187.
Horvath, A., & Symonds, B. (1991). Relation between working alliance and outcome in psychotherapy: A meta-analysis. *Journal of Counseling Psychology*, 38(2), 139–149.
Howard, K., Kopta, S., Krause, M., et al. (1986). The dose-response relationship in psychotherapy. *American Psychologist*, 41(2), 159–164.
Klein, L., Schwartz, L., Santiago, L., Vivian, L., Vocisano, L., Castonguay, L., et al. (2003). Therapeutic alliance in depression treatment: Controlling for prior change and patient characteristics. *Journal of Consulting and Clinical Psychology*, 71(6), 997–1006.
Kohut, H. (1977). *The restoration of the self*. New York: International Universities Press.
Kohut, H. (1984). *How does analysis cure?* Hillsdale, NJ: The Analytic Press.
Kordy, H., von Rad, M., & Senf, W. (1988). Time and its relevance for a successful psychotherapy. *Psychotherapy and Psychosomatics*, 49(3–4), 212–222.
Kris, E. (1938). Review of "The ego and the mechanisms of defense." *International Journal of Psychoanalysis*, 19, 347–348.
Krupnick, J., Sotsky, S., Simmons, S., Moyer, J., Elkin, I., Watkins, J., & Pilkonis, P. A. (1996). The role of the therapeutic alliance in psychotherapy and pharmacotherapy outcome: Findings in the National Institute of Mental Health Treatment of Depression Collaborative Research Program. *Journal of Consulting and Clinical Psychology*, 64(3), 532–539.
Lachmann, F. (2004). Beyond the mainstreams. *Psychoanalytic Inquiry*, 24(4), 576–592.
Levenson, E. (1996). The politics of interpretation. *Contemporary Psychoanalysis*, 32(4), 631–648.
Lichtenberg, J., Lachmann, F., & Fosshage, J. (2003). *A spirit of inquiry: Communications in psychoanalysis*. Hillsdale, NJ: The Analytic Press.
Martin, D., Garske, J., & Davis, M. (2000). Relation of the therapeutic alliance with outcome and other variables: A meta-analytic review. *Journal of Consulting and Clinical Psychology*, 68(3), 438–450.

Tolpin, M. (2002). Doing psychoanalysis of normal development: Forward edge transferences. In A. Goldberg (Ed.), *Progress in self psychology* (Vol. 18, pp. 167–190). New York: Guilford Press.

Zetzel, E. (1956). *The capacity for emotional growth*. New York: International Universities Press.

Chapter 2

Venturing onto Thin Ice
Tiptoeing in the Wake of Empathic Failures

Lynn S. Kuttnauer

Editors' introduction

Analysts are sometimes faced with what feels like an impossible dilemma relative to the question of whether they'd be better off addressing the transference even though they fear that doing so could easily jeopardize the ongoing treatment that has grown precarious. This clinical moment involves a married woman in her early 50s who tended to react to the act of being interpreted by becoming angry, denying the gist of what the analyst had suggested, then withdrawing. While the patient created an initial impression that she was strong, this appearance belied the fact she was, in fact, fragile and brittle – the legacy of an emotionally impoverished and volatile childhood. This particular clinical moment occurred at the end of the first year of the patient's analysis after a period during which the patient had weathered three difficult empathic failures at the hand of the analyst, which left her feeling "adrift, alone and disconnected." The working through of these empathic failures lessened the patient's tendency to idealize the analyst and heightened her capacity to tolerate ambivalent feelings toward the analyst. Still, the therapeutic alliance remained tenuous, leaving the analyst struggling with the question of whether to risk jeopardizing her relationship with the patient by interpreting the transference aspects of a presented dream. On the other hand, failing to offer a transference interpretation risked forgoing an opportunity to address something important that was happening between the patient and her analyst.

The moment in context (Lynn S. Kuttnauer)

This clinical moment raises two interesting issues. The central issue has to do with the advisability of pursuing the transference aspects of a dream with a patient who not only found such interpretations challenging but who was healing from a series of clinically based empathic failures that weakened the strength of the therapeutic alliance. Such conditions left the analyst wondering whether it might be wiser to steer clear of directly addressing the transference aspects of a presented dream in favor of pursuing the less alliance-challenging approach of offering an extra-transference interpretation. The other issue illustrated in this moment addresses an interesting set of questions about the role a patient's religious beliefs may play in analysis and whether facilitating a patient's capacity to have faith, or restoring a patient's faltering sense of connection with God, may be considered a legitimate goal of psychoanalysis.

Some analysts insist that transference interpretations are the mainstay of the psychoanalytic venture. Merton Gill (1982, 1984), chief advocate for the single-minded pursuit of the transference, strongly believed that psychoanalysis hinged on resolving the transference neurosis, which – in Gill's mind – could only be accomplished through the use of transference interpretations. Gill was known to believe "that the transference is everything: that transference meaning, the allusions to the transference, the defenses against the transference is what analysis is about, whether it is five times a week on a couch, or once a week sitting up" (Bulletin of the Anna Freud Centre, 1992, p. 176). Some note that Gill's (1984) call for analysts to "systematically search for implicit references to the transference" (p. 490) flies in the face of Freud's recommendation that analysts employ "evenly suspended attention" (Freud, 1912a) and Bion's (1967) dictum that analysts enter the session "without memory or desire."

The recommendation that analysts exclusively attend to interpreting the transference presents a problem when working with patients who are intolerant of interpretations in general and transference interpretations in particular. Not all patients see the motive behind the analyst's offering of interpretations as benign – as meant to help the patient. On the one hand, we have analysts who insist on the necessity of offering transference interpretations; on the other hand, some analysts remind us that such offerings are beyond the capacity of some patients to tolerate (Britton, 2004; Slochower, 1996; Tuch, 2007). Between these two extremes is a middle ground – extra-analytic interpretations that do not address the here-and-now manifestation of the transference. "Though it is true that extra-transference interpretations are not for the most part mutative, and do not themselves bring about the crucial result," notes Strachey (1934), "they are nonetheless essential" (p. 158), and while "a large majority of our interpretations are outside the transference… it should be added that it often happens that when one is ostensibly giving an extra-transference interpretation one is implicitly giving a transference one" (p. 158). Expanding on this idea, Blum (1983) concludes that the:

> Extratransference interpretation has a position and value which is not simply ancillary, preparatory, and supplementary to transference interpretation. Transference analysis is essential, but extratransference interpretation, including genetic interpretation and reconstruction, is also necessary, complementary, and synergistic.
>
> (p. 615)

Gill (1982) saw danger in extra-transference and genetic interpretations, seeing them as leading to intellectualization and a flight from the intimacy of the transference. However, many analysts (Brenner, 1976; Dewald, 1972; A. Freud, 1954, 1965) saw danger in focusing exclusively on the transference to the extent such a focus ran the risk of isolating the analysis from the patient's life, distorting the analytic process, turning the analysis into an empty ritual, and undermining the reality principle and analytic grandiosity. Couch (2002) references Blum (1983) and Arlow (1993) when he takes a position opposed to an exclusive preoccupation with the transference, warning that the transference should not be torn out of its context or interpreted in isolation. Dewald (1972) and Stone (1967) opine that the transference cannot be understood independent of knowledge about the non-transference reality spheres and their transference implications, with the patient's "extra-analytic life" providing crucial information about the patient's psyche not provided by a sole focus on the analytic relationship. Couch (2002) arrives at the position that combining extra-transference and transference interpretations creates a "more humane analytic atmosphere, in the sense that it accepts the significance of the real life relationships in the past and present" (p. 88).

Turning to the second issue raised in this clinical moment, we are confronted with the question: Do religious beliefs in general, and a belief in a Divinity in particular, have a rightful place in an analysis? Psychoanalysts tend to shy away from clinically addressing religious beliefs. The trend for analysts to be suspicious of, and hostile toward, religious thinking is likely a legacy of Sigmund Freud's own position on the matter. He called such beliefs "patently infantile" (Freud, 1930, p. 74) and considered them indicative of a "weakness of intellect" (Freud, 1927, p. 48), a sign of one's having accepted uncritically the "absurdities" (p. 48) of religion. Furthermore, he pathologized a belief in God, alternately calling it an "illusion" (pp. 30–31) and a "mass delusion" arising from the "ignorant times of the childhood of humanity" (Freud, 1930, p. 81).

While Freud (1927) considered religious belief to be an "illusion" – something the human race had best get over – Meissner (1984) notes: "If Freud wished to rule out illusion and destroy it, Winnicott wished to foster it and to increase man's capacity for creatively experiencing it" (p. 177). Winnicott (1971) accomplished this goal by introducing the concept of "a transitional space," envisioned as "the early stages of the use of illusion" (p. 11). In the transitional space, no regard is paid to the question of what is and is not real – the matter remains forever in question, requiring no resolution whatsoever. "Rather than viewing [illusion] as a flight from reality," writes Sorenson (1994), "Winnicott (1971) saw the child's capacity for illusion as one type of transitional phenomenon that is prerequisite for increasing relatedness toward reality" (p. 233). Though Freud (1927) thought otherwise, "this transitional space *between believing and knowing* then becomes the life-long basis of illusion, which adults can utilize to fend off traumatic realizations [e.g., non-existence everlasting] that are more than they can psychically bear" (Tuch, 2016, p. 54, italics added) – issues for which psychoanalysis has no answers and provides no solace.

Blass (2004) surveyed the current trend that has analysts (Eigen, 1988, 2001; Jones, 2002; Kakar, 1991; Meissner, 1984; Rizzuto, 1979; Spezzano & Gargiulo, 1997; Symington, [1994] 1998) regarding religious belief as a healthy development and a sign of psychic well-being – "an expression of a kind of achievement – emotional, moral, spiritual and cultural – that could be expected to emerge through a successful psychoanalytic process" (p. 615). These analysts see how "religion may allow for the expression, and even reinforcement, of various desirable human capacities for relationship, such as trust, intimacy, care and community" (p. 618). They focus on the spiritual/mystical dimension of religion, downplaying the dogma, ritual, and authority of organized religion and sidestepping the question of whether religious beliefs are to be considered "truths." They see religious beliefs as "merely a kind of fiction accepted as true for their great practical significance, both culturally and in terms of the needs of mankind that cannot be fulfilled by 'cold science'" (p. 623), which Blass notes ignores the fact that many present-day believers "maintain that there is no meaning or value to religion *if its assertions are not true*, not real" (p. 625, italics added).

Current analytic writers who address the role of religious beliefs in treatment (Eigen, 1988, 2001; Jones, 2002; Kakar, 1991; Meissner, 1984; Rizzuto, 1979; Spezzano & Gargiulo, 1997; Symington, [1994] 1998) tend to advocate that analysts adopt an accepting, non-pathologizing attitude, expressing open curiosity no different than what one would have about any relationship patients bring into the treatment. Meissner (2013) views religious beliefs as personal illusions that contribute a vital element to the human capacity to sustain oneself in the face of the harsh limitations of reality. In this regard, he sees religious illusions/beliefs as constituting a valuable form of adaptation and, as such, deserving to be respected as a rich and nuanced opportunity to explore the human psyche rather than being condemned as psychopathology to be interpretively undone. Spero (2004) frames one's relationship with God through the lens of the child's relationship with early caretakers, utilizing Winnicott's (1951) concept of the "unique primary object" and envisioning Mother/God as *the object seemingly created by the infant* even though the object already existed and was there waiting to be found. From this perspective, God is seen as developing within the transitional space – a space where illusion reigns – and not equated with delusion, as was the case for Freud. Along these lines, Winnicott (1963) suggests that "man continues to create and recreate God as a place to put that which is god in himself, and which he might spoil if he left it in himself along with the hate and destructiveness which is [*sic*] also to be found there" (p. 94).

Several analytic writers conceptualize God as an outgrowth of the transitional object that becomes internalized as part of the personality and relationship with the world (Lijtmaer, 2009). In his review of Sorenson (2004), Shaw (2005) cites the author's views about the various ways God functions as representations of both archaic and wished-for compensatory objects, while other analysts (Fauteux, 1995; Kilpatrick & Shaver, 1990; Rizzuto, 1979) address the ways in which God serves as the wished-for perfect object in contrast to the fallible real objects. In this vein, humankind's "creation" of God is seen as an attempt to restore the idealized archaic internal object. From a self-psychological perspective, Bacal (1981) states that God can function as a "phantasy self-object" (p. 36) fostering reparation for love, guidance, and protection where "real" objects failed.

As analysts, we need to create a space in which we can explore with our patients their religious beliefs and practices – appreciating this as rich and fertile ground for understanding aspects of their psychic life, their conflicts, and their self representation and object representations. At the same time, we must not lose track of the fact a patient's religious beliefs are never entirely free from conflicted intrapsychic underpinnings – complicating the question of pathological entanglements embedded within a patient's religious beliefs and the techniques that might be used to address these in analysis. Furthermore, working in the religious arena can be ripe ground for countertransference reactions and enactments. As psychoanalytic therapists, it is crucial to be aware of our own beliefs and disbeliefs and the ways in which these affect how we listen to our patient's relationship with religion.

Taking into consideration these more psychologically nuanced understandings of God, as well as the sorts of complicated relationships individuals have with God and religious beliefs, one wonders whether more constructive questions might be asked by analysts treating patients who hold strong religious beliefs: How do we understand one's religious beliefs – their idiosyncratic meanings and the role they play in one's psychic life? What are the ways in which intrapsychic conflicts become embedded in these beliefs, making use of them in the process? What is the patient's image of God, and what attributes does their God possess? To what degree do one's religious beliefs hinder or foster healthy adaptation to internal and external experiences of life?

The clinical moment

Ms. L, a bright, articulate, and attractive married woman in her 50s, consulted me desiring to improve her relationships with her adult children, wishing to find a way to be more relaxed and playful when interacting with them. Additionally, Ms. L wanted help coping with her complicated feelings of intense, agitated sadness that was coupled with eternal hope that her son, Seth, would awaken from the coma he'd been in for the last several years. A devout and observant Orthodox Jew, Ms. L firmly believed that God – being infinitely good and all-powerful – could and would completely restore Seth's health even though his doctors believed otherwise. Her steadfast religious conviction ("If only I can be good enough in my prayers and beliefs, show God how truly devout and faithful I am, he will bring him back to us") helped alleviate her sense of helplessness, yet it simultaneously interfered with her ability to face her son's grim prognosis in order to begin to mourn his loss.

Ms. L hadn't been raised Orthodox, and it wasn't until she became a parent that she and her husband transitioned to living a religiously observant life. She found this way of life enriching, as it provided her a comforting internal structure, solace from a neglectful, emotionally turbulent childhood, and a solid sense of community.

Ms. L had been in treatment for the better part of her adult life and had even undergone a prior analysis. Over time, I came to learn about her frightening and painful childhood with severely impaired parents who were highly volatile and emotionally unavailable. Ms. L had patched together a very convincing façade of self-assured competence, which I slowly realized concealed profound vulnerability. Her sense of self vacillated between self-loathing and a sense of contemptuous superiority. Her demand for perfection, in herself and others, became manifest in the analysis, leading her to cling to a vision of me as purely benevolent and perennially attuned. Any attempts on my part to interpret what I saw as evidence of her critical or negative thoughts or feelings about me were met with denial, hurt, and anger.

Not surprisingly, Ms. L approached her religious observances with the same fervent perfectionism that characterized every aspect of her internal life and relationships. A rigid stoicism colored all aspects of her daily life, from her eating and exercising habits to the amount of time she dedicated to, and the way she went about practicing, her religious observances.

Initially, Ms. L was reluctant to begin an analysis, so we agreed on twice-weekly meetings face-to-face. Within a very short period of time, Ms. L asked for a third session, and as she considered meeting a fourth time weekly she expressed concern about being in analysis with an analyst she feared might become "cold, silent and distant," making formulaic interpretations that would leave her feeling "alone and adrift, voyaging into dark, murky waters without direction or an anchor of safety." She'd experienced her former analyst as having acted in this fashion, and exploring these concerns helped her transition into a four and then five times weekly, on-the-couch analysis six months after we initially began meeting.

Ms. L easily settled into analysis and quickly developed a solid therapeutic alliance. I enjoyed our work together and looked forward to our sessions. Ms. L was introspective, learned, and she valued the analysis. Her belief in and relationship to God were very much a part of our work. Initially, I struggled to negotiate how to enter her religious world, trying to view God through her eyes. Only after she felt that I had successfully done so was she comfortable joining me in exploring the various ways in which God could additionally be understood as metaphor within a psychoanalytic frame of reference: God as representation of early parental figures and, later, within the transference;

God as a loving presence; God as structure and an anchor to her life. Ms. L was both a passionate student and teacher of Talmud (the body of Jewish civil and ceremonial laws and legends), portions of which became woven into our work. God, rabbis, and analysts frequently formed composite figures in her mind.

This clinical moment occurred a year and a half into the analysis, in the wake of our having weathered three significant empathic ruptures, failures on my part, which occurred in rapid succession over the course of a few months. The first therapy-threatening rupture involved my commenting to Ms. L that I thought she was feeling disappointed with me just as she'd been with her husband for his having tuned her out as he became less emotionally involved with her. After vehemently rejecting my suggestion, incredulous that I could think such a thing – that I could believe she had "anything but wonderful feelings about me" – Ms. L proceeded to describe in exquisite but mind-numbing detail how she was preparing her home for Passover. When she noticed, ten minutes into her recitation, that I had glazed over and emotionally left her, she became understandably hurt and enraged, saying that she didn't know whether she could ever return to treatment. In retrospect, I came to the realization that by tuning her out and disengaging from her in the process, I paradoxically, inadvertently, and unintentionally had enacted the very point I was making when I'd suggested she had previously been upset with me for having *tuned her out*.

The second of my three empathic failures (a misattunement) occurred when Ms. L experienced me as neither appreciating what she was feeling nor matching (through mirroring) the intensity of what she was experiencing. As was her pattern, Ms. L quickly regained her positive transference – her high regard and affection for me – after having become momentarily disappointed and angry with me, without ever allowing her disappointment to modulate the intensity of her idealization of me.

The last in this series of ruptures centered around Ms. L's sense that her son, Seth, had more recently seemed "less responsive and further away," leaving her feeling discouraged about his chance for recovery. Up until this point, Ms. L could not tolerate any questioning of Seth's capacity to fully recover, believing that any expression of doubt could hinder the possibility of his recovery. Seeing Seth as less responsive stirred up a monumental internal conflict within Ms. L regarding her loving relationship with God. For her to feel despair and anger meant that her belief in God's infinite goodness was faltering, and realizing as much shook her world.

Through our previous analytic work, we had created a space in the treatment in which Ms. L could allow herself the freedom to think and feel without the penalty of God's judgment. However, as she began to approach the precipice of considering the possibility that Seth's condition could be permanent, her previous reliance on a more rigid and judgmental conceptualization of God reasserted itself, making it difficult for her to acknowledge her disappointment, confusion, and anger at God. This ushered in a process of intense mourning, not just for her son but also for her sense of closeness with God – feeling bereft and forsaken by Him. She ceased to take comfort in prayer, noting that she was merely going through the motions while feeling a sense of deadness and loss.

Ms. L struggled against acknowledging her discouragement, the implications of which left her adrift vis-à-vis God. In this context, she heard my comments as siding with the recognition and expression of the very feelings that she was trying hard to keep repressed. As the atmosphere in the room became heavy with grief, Ms. L worked all the harder at fending off the possibility that Seth would not fully recover, with fantasies of receiving a phone call from his rehabilitation center conveying that he was smiling and asking to speak to her. I tiptoed gingerly, traversing this fine line between trying to help her mourn her son, who was both alive and gone, and not challenging her religious convictions that an omnipotent God could/would bring him back.

The following day, Ms. L came in feeling happy and greatly relieved after she'd consulted "a very revered rebbe" (rabbi) in another city. He not only gave her permission to verbalize whatever was on her mind, but he also told her to "live her life in a way that made her happy, especially with regard to prayer." He counseled her to "do the most minimum of required prayer" rather than continuing to spend such extreme amounts of time (45-minute praying sessions three times daily) praying and he subsequently sent her a passage from a religious text that supported his recommendation. Ms. L felt a great weight had been lifted and wondered how I felt about this: "I'm worried that you might feel frustrated, that you'd think, 'Here I've worked with this woman so long and one 15-minute phone call with this person has fixed everything.'" I expressed my happiness for her and for her ability to feel relief. I encouraged her to elaborate on her reaction as well as her fantasy of my frustration. As the hour progressed, I had the sense that she was surprised by the rebbe's response, and I inquired about what she had anticipated he would say when she consulted him. She indeed had imagined that he would tell her to keep doing what she had been doing – that she could not give up on God or attempt to understand His ways. She was surprised by his response and commented about how terrible it would have been had he actually said what she had imagined he would say.

The following day, Ms. L entered the consulting room, walked over to the chair, and sat there rather than lying down on the couch, explaining that she had a cold and couldn't breathe lying down. She then commented about how she felt about my reaction the day before. She said she was aware that I had done nothing to warrant her feeling as she did, and thought it best that we explore her feelings in greater depth. She felt that I hadn't expressed enough happiness at her relief. Furthermore, she remained worried that I was frustrated with her for listening to and following the rebbe's suggestion, which helped her to let things go, when she hadn't been nearly as moved or as influenced by my suggestions along these same lines. She said, "You must be thinking to yourself: 'That woman, I've been telling her this for over a year and then, with one phone call, she's all better.' I'd be frustrated if I were you. I thought that you'd be so happy for me. And I think that you were, but you didn't express it strongly enough so I thought maybe you were put out."

I expressed how important and helpful it was that she could come in and explore her thoughts and feelings with me. I told her that I was delighted that she could allow herself to make use of all of her supports, including her rabbis. I wondered aloud about her having called him given her expectation that he would tell her the very things she most wanted *not* to hear. My inquiry piqued her curiosity, leaving her to wonder why she had risked the possibility he would reinforce her over-dedication to pious practice, noting that were he to have done so, it would have been horrible for her. She thanked me for sharing my feelings with her. I said that I thought perhaps, in addition to her cold, she needed to sit face-to-face today – as she had in the past whenever she experienced a rupture in our relationship. I further noted the progress she'd made to the extent she was less inclined to run in response to the momentary ruptures in our relationship and better able to sit and discuss the matter, to take the opportunity to heal the rupture by working it through with me.

While we were able to successfully work through these ruptures and make good use of them as building blocks in our work – helping strengthen her ego in the process – they nevertheless threatened the continuation of our work when they occurred, though less so with each passing rupture. They eventually led to a strengthening of our relationship/work by helping her better tolerate ambivalent feelings towards me, others, and herself, and eventually allowed me to be "good enough" rather than idealized.

Ms. L began the hour relaying how sad she had been feeling, particularly since our last meeting the day before. She had called a friend of hers who solicitously enquired as to how she was doing. She told her friend that she was "okay" but her friend did not accept her answer, responding back: "No, you're *not* okay and it's *okay* that you're *not okay*. No one would be okay with what you're struggling with." Ms. L went on to describe to me how unacceptable it was for her to be "not okay," explaining: "You know what 'not okay' looks like – my mother screaming hysterically: 'they're coming to get me, they're coming to get me!' She's hitting her head with her fists and screaming [as she pantomimes hitting her own head]. *That's* what 'not okay' looks like."

Ms. L then proceeded to describe just how scared she had felt during the previous session, feeling as if she was "floating without any anchoring." She went on to mention that ever since the rebbe had given her permission to cut back on praying and do what made her happy she has "davened" (praying while rhythmically rocking) very little. "I'm so tired all the time. I've been sleeping a lot, I thought it was because I was sick but I don't think that's it. I haven't been *that* sick or sick this whole time. I'm not exercising anymore either and I only pray the smallest amount."

Ms. L's words brought to mind our most recent rupture and the way in which we had come to understand the dynamics involved – her enacting a loyalty conflict between the rebbe and me, paralleling the way in which her mother had tried time and again to turn her against her father. I began to wonder whether she needed to experience me as wounded and angry in response to her seeming to be siding with the rebbe. I also reflected, as a good parent might, on the pleasure and support her religion had provided her up to that point, which led me to wonder to myself about her need to deprive herself of that. I said, "I know it initially felt like such a relief to you to have the rebbe's permission to do only that which makes you happy and to have the freedom of all your thoughts and feelings, yet now you're telling me how scared and unanchored you've been feeling. You've gone from doing far beyond what was required to doing the barest minimum or nothing. In the past the structure that you've created for yourself in prayer and exercise has helped you to feel good, secure. So I'm wondering about you're not doing any of that now. It's almost as though you're depriving yourself of all the things that had previously given you pleasure and comfort as you have in the past, but now in a different way, now depriving yourself of prayer. With what the rebbe told you, you can daven without the pressure of feeling that Seth's recovery rests upon you."

Ms. L responded, "Davening no longer gives me pleasure. When I daven, I thank ha-Shem [God] for all his blessings. Davening is thanking ha-Shem. When I daven now, I just feel mad at Him and then my davening feels like a lie. I don't feel close to Him, I feel further away. I feel like I have lost my faith and feel so removed and distant from Him. So davening is painful. I have been so sad. Seth seems further and further away from me."

I mentioned to Ms. L that she seemed to feel adrift, alone, and disconnected ever since she had allowed herself to consider the possibility that Seth might not recover. She replied that it is an "awful feeling, unanchored and out there floating alone. It is so hard to put into words but helpful to try."

I was reminded of Ms. L's fear that she would end up feeling "left out there all alone and floating unanchored and adrift [from me]," as we transitioned from twice-weekly psychotherapy to five times weekly, on-the-couch analysis, and I shared this thought with her. She replied, "Yes, but that hasn't happened here. You get me. You stay with me."

Our most recent rupture was still with me, and I was speculating in the privacy of my own mind that she was still feeling further away from me and was defending against becoming aware of just how disconnected from me she felt. I had been traversing, in my mind, between the transference and memories of Ms. L's early childhood experiences of being left alone, frightened and sad. I empathized aloud with Ms. L's sense of feeling frighteningly unanchored and disconnected and suggested additionally that it might also be a way of trying to *rise above* what was going on in an effort to manage the terror of what was happening around her and within her. She agreed, remembering the experience of having looked in the mirror when she was much younger only to find no image.[1] Ms. L's thoughts then shifted to Seth, painfully lamenting how full of life Seth was, questioning how God could give him so much life only to then take it all away.

Ms. L then remembered and relayed a dream she'd had the previous night: "I was walking on a campus-like place, walking into a classroom. It was familiar from other dreams. There are chairs around, not like a regular classroom however. There are chairs scattered around and some tables by the chairs. It reminds me of my Shul [a synagogue – a Jewish place of worship]. It makes it easier to daven when you can place your Siddur [Prayer book] down rather than holding it. I'm in class and my old teacher, Professor G, the one with whom I had had an intimate relationship, was lecturing. He made eye contact with me, noticing me. After class I approached him and we spoke. As we were leaving I wrapped my arm in his. At this point he turns into Dr. T [her previous analyst], a composite of both of them. We walk out together. It reminds me of the feeling that I had with Professor G. When he was lecturing he'd make special eye contact with me, making it clear that he was speaking directly *to me*. It was the same with Rabbi H. [a rabbi with whom she shared an especially close relationship] in gatherings where he was speaking, he'd look directly at me and it was like he was talking to me directly. That always made me feel good, warm, noticed. It was a good dream. I felt good, warm, in the midst of feeling so sad and alone. It was interesting how the professor turned into Dr. T and how the classroom was set up like my Shul. It's like the combination of all three men who I've gone to for help, comfort, and learning." She continued associating to how good she felt in the dream and upon awakening, to have these men who were her teachers and guides be there making contact with her when in fact they were no longer in her life in the same way they had been in the past.

As we neared the end of the hour, I was of two minds with regard to which aspect of the material to interpret. I understood her dream represented, in part, a wish fulfillment – to feel connected and close in the midst of feeling so alone with her sadness. I understood her composite figure as both a representation of me as well as that of God and all that is represented within God. I vacillated between making a transference interpretation – drawing her attention to what this dream might be saying about how she was presently feeling about me – and making an extra-transference interpretation that addressed her wishing to feel connected to God. God had sustained her mightily, and her feeling alienated from him was a deep blow to her sense of self and capacity to cope.

I wondered to myself whether it made the most clinical sense to return to the matter of our recent rupture, which had left her feeling frighteningly disconnected from me, in contrast with how she felt with these three important men who had been in her life but were no longer. I was very cognizant of her ongoing need to idealize me, particularly following on the heels of such empathic failures – setting herself up for future failures to the extent she imagined me to be the ideal analyst who was above making such errors.[2] I wondered: Was this the time to continue to work with our recent ruptures and her need to idealize me, or, alternately, might she be needing me to work in the extra-transferential realm by assisting her in reconnecting with ha-Shem? I was also aware of her sense that a loyalty conflict had become manifest in the transference. I wondered whether she might be unconsciously testing me to see whether I was feeling "put-out" (feeling disconnected from her – adrift and angry) from her having both turned to the rebbe and shown herself more receptive to his intervention than to mine.

Invited commentator responses: Rosemary H. Balsam and Rachel Blass

Rosemary H. Balsam

It is easy to have fellow feeling for this emotional and technical predicament between this difficult patient and her analyst. There is no "right way" to proceed. Having identified the stuck repetitive quality of an impasse, I would consider the implications of as many ways to proceed as I could imagine given its over-determined nature – approaching the constellation through defense; object relations and interactional aspects in transference and countertransference; problematic affect issues; and importantly, illumination of underlying traumatic elements – to see how these differing elements might open up the materials judged by the patient's response over time. (Foreclosures would be a harbinger of expectable repetitions ahead.) There is a "chipping away" called forth in the technical approach that is a part of our art that has been analogized to sculpture in Leonardo by Freud and Loewald.

Dr. K admirably describes a signature dilemma that has been repetitive in the course of this analysis. It now reemerges between them in the interpretation of one of the patient's rare dreams. One direction is a direct "transferential" comment about the analyst's exclusion from the Pantheon of "Gods" in the dream – the idealized old professor; Ms. L's previous analyst; a previous religious teacher and indeed G-d himself (as a male transferential role?) – which risks a *negative* response. Alternatively, Dr. K suggests addressing material she views as "extra-transferential" – Ms. L's *positive* feelings about these other figures (thus evading discomforts surrounding the patient's hostile motivations about that exclusion).

The field's attitudes have shifted. Many analysts like this writer – and the many ego psychologists of especially, say, the 1960s, 1970s, and 1980s that she quotes in her introduction – have been very taken with technical questions in analysis that (for them) distinguish clearly between what is "transferential" and what is "extra-transferential." The latter is viewed as the lesser intervention, merely paving the way for mutatively potent "transferential" interpretations (a point of view shared, for example, by classicist teachers like Greenson or Eissler). "Transferential" intervention refers to a direct spoken reference by the analyst about the influence of him- or herself within the patient's emotional problem. From differing traditions, some have passionately represented transferential interpretation as *the* optimal psychoanalytic technique – for example, the contemporary ego psychologist Merton Gill, or Betty Joseph from the contemporary Kleinian tradition. Her "total transference" version places much emphasis on her own countertransference as a method of detecting pressures coming from a patient's internal objects. The field of transference thus expands to the whole internal scenario of the patient – the "total" surround of the child in his environment. She (like others for their own methods) claims the most favorable results. (However, we must alas acknowledge that we have no studies comparing techniques regarding outcome.) "Extra-transferential" phenomena then, in many approaches, are seen as a detour. The patient's so-called "outside" life is compartmentalized from the "inside" life of the session, and to speak of it, at worst, is perhaps not even "analytic"!

Other contemporary trends/schools, however, also seem to question these severe distinctions, without necessarily discussing this topic directly. For example, in post-Bionian field theory, the technique of Ferro (Italy) calls for the analyst taking maximal interest in the patient's language and "metaphor," thus technically he engages *indirect* communication of unconscious materials *indirectly*, even when the manifest materials may seem "transferential." Ferro also is interested in child analysis, where play dominates, and internal dilemmas are tackled indirectly through set-ups with the toys, staying within the child patient's discourse. A Loewaldian approach, which I favor, like Joseph's view, assumes the analytic situation as totally representing the inner world of the patient. But unlike Joseph, Loewald keeps close to all figures *and* events represented from present and past within the associative materials, where the analytic situation is akin to a staged drama in the office, and the analyst is unconsciously included by the patient's psyche as a part of the dramatis personae of the staged play of interactional enactments. For Loewald, then, both transferential and extra-transferential are blended. Nothing need be judged as too trivial to count in the exploratory or therapeutic interaction, where the analyst is assumed to be simultaneously both old and new object.

Dr. K in this case example also works with consideration of "empathic failures," a terminology associated with self psychology. This explains too why she experiences her technical dilemma. Ms. L is manifestly happy in this dream, being accompanied by her past beloved "Gods." By Dr. K's transferentially *directly* alluding to being left out of this fine array of elite men in Ms. L's inner world, she fears she will provoke an empathic failure due to Ms. L taking the comment as a "complaint," evoking terror that Dr. K is angry at her for this lapse – similar to three severe reactions in the past that resulted in her being miserable, "alone and drifting." This would then possibly create yet another "rupture" of their relationship in need of repair before progressing. On the other hand, Dr. K, in assessing this risk or rupture, wonders if Ms. L's ego and sense of self may now be sufficiently tolerant of ambivalence toward her, so that a negative transferential comment, even if painful initially, might push the work forward constructively rather than setting it back.

Trying to grasp the author's theoretical orientation illuminates for me her response to the material. It also provides her ideas about why it is occurring, plus her thoughts about how she may address it with Ms. L, and its timing. Freud's recommendations for "timing and tact" (as we each see them) endure for all our schools. Dr. K looks through the combined lenses of traditional ego psychology and self psychology. In the latter mode, she worries about an interruption in sustaining a selfobject transference for the patient's fragile grandiose self with its (therapeutic) idealization of her (Kohut, 1971); in the former mode, Dr. K invokes a more traditional Freudian idea of maximal therapeutic benefit occurring if and when one works directly in the "the transference," because only then can we assure its psychic liveliness, because it is impossible to "destroy" a person "in absentia or in effigie" (Freud, 1912b, p. 108).

Dr. K's is a fair way of seeing the present dilemma with Ms. L's treatment. She aims for direct transferential intervention, while sensitively keeping a close eye on the patient's fragile sense of "self." In spite of Ms. L's manifest pleasure, the analyst is aware that hidden darkness surrounds the glorious male figures. Indeed, there is a mini-mention of her as a student having been "intimate" with that old Professor, and one can only fantasize how that may have led to some element of disillusionment that belies her present happiness. Dr. K is coping with Ms. L's gradual crumbling idealization and her childlike vision and dependence upon what she deemed the vast wisdom of these glorious male figures and that of her analyst as well. For this 50-year-old, school-child-like, and possibly borderline woman, I agree with Dr. K who sees her task of mourning the loss of idealizations of these "authority" figures as constituting a painful, difficult, but hopefully therapeutic developmental step. (I would be interested in knowing more about the original parental contributions to her internal life. Her dependence on male wisdom is certainly culturally derived, but I think that the recent Rebbe's response to her shows that her craven dependence is much more than he seems to expect culturally. I will elaborate on this later.)

My addition to this analyst's vision of this case foregrounds the trauma of the tragedy of Ms. L's son, which I believe stirs up all her powerful sexed gender issues that are present in this impasse with her female analyst. For Ms. L, I think it would be hard to try to separate out her "religion" (as does Dr. K) from her Orthodox Jewish culture and its longstanding traditions and her female identity. Such conflicts may be especially marked in this postmenopausal period of her life – as they might be for any mother – confronted with the profound trauma of her precious son's loss into a coma. (We are not told of Seth's sibling position or anything about the other children.) This male child could represent some of Ms. L's own ambitions outside home life that may still be invested with him, as long as she maintains a fantasy that he can come back to life. I would be interested in Ms. L's gender and body history prior to becoming Orthodox. We are told she can be self-loathing as well as contemptuous – in adolescence, looking in the mirror "without" a body, a radical if unconscious damnation of her own body, besides not being "seen" by the parents; I suspect that her inner world *could* be close to Freud's vision of females. The birth of the oldest son in Freud's mind was for a woman *the* joy that compensated for life inside an unquestioned, denigrated, and despised female body. (In Orthodox Judaism, as we know, males pray every day that they are glad they are not born as women, even if analytic sophisticates feel conflicted about it!) This deeply ingrained attitude certainly affects a female's view of herself in a culture where male societal privilege is taken for granted, and which she embraced after marriage. We are told Ms. L is an avid Talmud student. This history too has not been without struggle for Jewish females. We do not really know anything about the level of internalization of phallic superiority that Ms. L may struggle with. But because of her activities, the desperately unmourned loss of her son, and her symptomatic religious practices within her tradition, the three major rages at Dr. K could be interpreted as confrontations with Ms. L's inner battles about being female (for example, the put-down of Dr. K's "male" glazed-over eyes at the "female" activities of getting rid of all crumbs in the house pre-Passover).

In the collection of male Gods in the dream – all of whose specifically Jewish identity is emphasized – *why* is the analyst excluded? Rather than leaping instantly to an archaic psychic level, I wonder what left-out (and possibly denigrated) figure in her family life Dr. K represents. Could she represent a denigrated mother, rather than a glowing father-figure in fact? (This is where I might have gone.) Ms. L too often addresses Dr. K as a "woman," which suggests to me that she may be unconsciously registering to the analyst an extreme sharpness of male and female difference for her. To my ear, she almost pleads for an opening to this discussion by taunting Dr. L with materials about the curing magic of men (the Rebbe, even though his magic seems to have lasted about a day!) as diametrically opposed to the ineffectiveness of women (the analyst). Ms. L associates closely among sadness, her burgeoning mourning, and an absolute *terror* of morphing into her own mother, whom she apparently views as too scary to dwell with, and perhaps mentalize. Attempts to flee a frightening internal mother often make bodily and gender development for a woman exceptionally difficult (Balsam, 2012).

The dream may express Ms. L's strong wish to be "at-one" with the glorious men, in fact. Such a position would relieve her of the agony of contacting her womanhood and being the mother of this worshipped but now dead boy, who had briefly given her hope to mitigate the pain of being female, and whose life and gender power are now lost – possibly with a collapse of her own dreams. Ms. L has withstood the pressure to face this awful emotional collapse of her possible *raison d'être*, through her increased worship of the men around her, including G-d who as well as offering generic solace may have been supposed to help her feel more male, through her fusion with her resurrected boy child. If only she could pray enough (more like an Orthodox man), and if she passionately kept the (fantasy) faith in the males' God-given and God-like magical phallic power, this boy would after all prove alive to carry on, uninterrupted, her own phallic dreams. The rationale for this route might be to avoid doing the pained work of slow detachment from her deep unconscious fusion with a denigrated mother, and the uphill psychological toil of trying to recreate a more flexible gender identity, one that is more at ease within her female body.

I would therefore not necessarily see the analyst's potential comment about being "left out" of the Gods as an empathic failure, but perhaps as yet another confrontation in the series of the patient's (unaddressed or less addressed as yet) issues of being forever "left out" as a female and as a male – and the opening up of all her miserable, attendant bad feelings about herself as female, especially in menopause with no reproductive value any more, and with a dead beloved son. I agree therefore that this is a major entrance to a miserable phase. I might use a comment about the dream to start to raise her consciousness about the pained gender issues of her struggle... perhaps by drawing attention to the fact that these are all *males* worthy of being admired, and asking where might the women be for her, in this dream. Are they in the background? Or really just not present at all?... Sounds awkward, but something like that!

Taking the dream as a follow-on from the consultation with the Rebbe, I wonder if the absence of Dr. K in the dream actually signals an advance – that she may be becoming more of a *mother* figure to her, rather than yet another male transferential figure to be worshipped – even as it may signal to Ms. L an inner "precipice" as Dr. K calls it, a severe come-down of being with a "mother." This highlights in her a female mother figure in mourning – far from her favored boy self, the striving "male scholar" who is still compensating for an ambition insistently lived through her ghostly son.

Seen through these family cultural modes of lived out transferences (in the plural), Ms. L is facing huge losses and identity crises that are eroding a possibly long-evolved flight from her womanhood. The road ahead is very, very hard for her, and I predict that it may bring up much more about her early life with her mother. Why did she opt to become an Orthodox Jew later in life? There is a dilemma here for this patient concerning the present and past meaning of her life and roles.

I do not think Dr. K should worry about hurting her feelings in saying the "wrong" thing. I think Ms. L's brittleness has to do with the degree that she has been living in a pretend world, and with her own discomfort and partial knowledge of that possibility, that may lead her (temporarily and repeatedly) to become angry with the female messenger, whom she nevertheless clearly highly values as her companion on this painful journey.

Rachel Blass

The analyst ends the presentation of this clinical moment wondering whether to interpret Ms. L's dream transferentially or extra-transferentially. In the transference, she could relate to Ms. L's "need to idealize" the analyst particularly following her recent "empathic failures," or she could relate to Ms. L's feelings of conflicted loyalty to the analyst and how she imagined that the analyst was reacting to this. Extra-transferentially, she could help Ms. L reconnect with God. This would entail addressing Ms. L's wish to be so connected, how God had sustained her "mightily," and how her sense of alienation from God has harmed her sense of self and capacity to cope. The analyst was uncertain which kind of interpretation Ms. L "needed" of her most.

I see the options differently. Ms. L, like all people, experiences various wishes, needs, and desires; she has set various goals and has preferred ways of attaining them. The analyst's task is a limited one – albeit life-transforming. It is not to respond to needs, to help attain designated life goals, or to improve the patient's feelings about herself or her coping capacities. Rather, it is to understand the unconscious dynamics of the patient's mind, the phantasies that determine how she sees the world and especially how she distorts it, including herself. It is to grasp what she doesn't want to know, the parts of herself that she has denied and split off because she has found them unbearable. And it is to convey these understandings to the patient in a way that allows the split-off parts to be reintegrated. In other words, coming to know unconscious truth is what is curative analytically. It is because what's curative is not knowing *about* what's going on unconsciously but coming to live it in an integrated way, that transference interpretation is, to my mind, the only possible analytic intervention. Through the transference the analyst can come to know how the patient's mind actually works, the phantasies, the unconscious motives and meanings that are at play. And through the interpretation of transference the patient can feel these motives and meanings from within, touch how and why she wants them split them off as well as the self-integrative forces, the life instinct, that oppose the split. Integrating such split-off parts inevitably changes the person, the nature of the motives that come into play, the nature of inner objects, and consequently the person's wishes, desires, and needs may also change.

What does this mean for the work with Ms. L? The author's presentation of Ms. L centers on her perfectionism. Ms. L, we are told, needs to maintain perfection in herself and others, and her need shapes her relationships, both to man and to God. In fact, according to the author, it's her inability to accept imperfection that stands in the way of mourning her son. She maintains that since both she and God are perfect, her son will recover. In her mind, if God will not cure her son, he isn't infinitely good and that cannot be acknowledged. The analyst seems to tie Ms. L's perfectionism to her having had highly volatile and emotionally unavailable parents. The connection is not fully spelled out, but it's suggested that for Ms. L to be imperfect is to be like them (as implied in Ms. L's comments in the clinical moment on "not being OK") or, in line with Kohut's thinking, the perfectionism is a pathological consequence of their deficient parenting in the course of Ms. L's early development. Accordingly, it would seem that the analyst, through interventions that relate either to the analytic relationship or to extra-analytic events, tries to provide better parenting – by way of sympathy, encouraging comments (e.g., on how she is happy for her), and emotional attunement. The analyst also offers a safe environment in which experiencing imperfection could be first practiced and survived. As I see it, it is in this context that the analyst thinks that perhaps supporting the patient's connection to God may be a good thing. He too could be adduced as an ego support.

But in the light of my view of psychoanalysis and the kind of cure that it can offer, what the analyst needs to discover are the unconscious workings of Ms. L's mind, which underlie and meaningfully explain how she feels and acts. Explanations that speak of her need to idealize because she can't accept imperfection, or suggest that she can't accept disappointment or mourn because it means imperfection or that she fears that if she doubts her son's recovery it won't happen – and all this because of her deficient upbringing – do not provide a meaningful psychological account of her unconscious mind. That is, they do not explain *why* she is this way (why, for example, imperfection is so terrible) by turning to her reasons, her wishes, her fears, and so on. Explanations such as "because she can't accept imperfection" may help provide corrective experiences, but such experiences within the limited and contrived framework of analysis can't impact how her mind works. Indeed, through practice, the patient may come to learn that no one dies from imperfection. However, this kind of learning process, in fact adopted by non-analytic approaches, does not work through the meaningful source of the patient's belief that imperfection kills and thus does not really change the truths she lives. For that, we must come to a meaningful psychological understanding of Ms. L as it comes alive in the transference, and we must there interpret it.

Here's how I would see one potential account of what's going on in Ms. L's unconscious mind as it emerges in some of the clinical material associated with what has been referred to as the "first therapy-threatening rupture" leading up to the clinical moment: Ms. L's vehement rejection of the analyst's comment on her being disappointed may be because in Ms. L's mind disappointment is associated with imperfection, but for Ms. L what imperfection means is potential frustration and therefore harm. The frustrating object not only directly hurts her and her sense of being good and loved, but the murderous feelings this object arouses in her are felt to be harmful to the object, to her beloved object. So Ms. L denies her disappointment and forbids the analyst to relate to it. She basically tells the analyst that if she does, she will pull the plug on the analysis. The threat is both a defensive maneuver to prevent acknowledgement of imperfection and an act of destruction following its acknowledgment. That is, the analyst, forbidden to think independently, is in Ms. L's mind wiped out as a person and, forbidden to interpret analytically, is wiped out as analyst. And while this destruction is directed against the analyst, it ultimately harms Ms. L, who is left with a dead and thus ineffective analyst. In this sense, the attack on the analyst is also a self-inflicted punishment.

All is well, according Ms. L, only so long as the analyst adopts her idealized world in which all is only wonderful. But it should be emphasized that all is only *supposedly* well. In the analyst's acquiescence to Ms. L's demands, to her alleged "need for idealization" in order to preserve the relationship, the analyst actually helps make real the patient's phantasy of her death (allowing herself to be wiped out as a separate person). In other words, responding to the patient's demand for perfect attunement is just as much an enactment as the analyst's tuning out. Moreover, it's more dangerous – supported by the analyst's theoretical approach, the destructiveness of the enacted attunement goes unrecognized as such. Similarly, the patient's responsibility for causing the analyst to tune out is denied (despite the fact that it was brought about by reports of home-preparations for Passover in mind-numbing details). Tuning out, the analyst tells us, was an empathic failure (not an understandable reaction to having one's mind numbed). It's the analyst, not the patient, who is supposedly rupturing the analysis. Here we may see how along with enacting Ms. L's phantasy of killing her off, the analyst also enacts Ms. L's phantasy that her guilt can be denied, projected into the analyst, and thus she could be rid of it.

It should be clear that to understand the analytic situation in this way requires a certain kind of listening to what Ms. L says. Not only are her words not taken at face value, as accurate descriptions of what she wants and feels, but they are also considered to be acts of various kinds (e.g., projection of guilt into the analyst).

To interpret within the transference, as I would recommend, is not to invite Ms. L to reflect on what's happening in the relationship; it's not for the analyst to point to patterns and needs and to encourage the patient to join in the exploration (as seems to be the case in some of the material described). Rather, it is to directly touch the phantasy as it's finding expression in the session. For example: "You tell me that when I now saw your frustration with me, your anger with me became real and very terrible. You feel it could tear the analysis apart. But you tell me that I must recognize this as my fault not yours." Or: "You feel that when you describe Passover preparations in sufficient detail you wipe out my mind and I am no longer able to think about what's going on in yours, but then you are left alone without me."[3] Or: "You tell me that I should not see anything you don't; I should be mind-dead, but in a supposedly positive kind of way. We can then both be together in the illusion that I am a wonderful analyst and you a wonderful patient. We can erase the fact that in this way we are going nowhere."

Looking at Ms. L in this light, we can see her predicament in life differently. While having a son in a coma from which there is no hope of recovery is horrible for anyone, our understanding of the patient would not be limited to how her dynamics impede her ability to deal with the tragedy that befell her. Rather, it would include how her dynamics shape the tragedy, how her unconscious phantasies determine the meanings of the horror for her. For example, Ms. L's aggression and her expectation of punishment for it may, in part, lead her to regard her son's coma as part of such punishment and as a constant unconscious reminder of her aggression. Similarly, the fact that Ms. L has, at times, a deadening effect on herself and others may impact her experience of the situation with her son, his death-in-life kind of condition, with which she may feel identified or into which she may project.

Through such processes of understanding, of listening and interpreting, Ms. L's inner world would come into play in a live way. She would more clearly and directly know of her destructiveness towards the frustrating object, her guilt over the destruction, the love behind the guilt both towards the object and from it. In this situation, the hope of making reparation for damage done may take the place of despair, and the desire to encounter the object as it is in its imperfection, the place of insistence on ideal relationships. It is in such an imperfect world, a world in which there is destruction, but nevertheless love and forgiveness, that death can be acknowledged and loss mourned.

From this perspective, it may be clear that any attempt to use the patient's relationship to God as an ego support would be misguided. The analyst tells us that for Ms. L God is sometimes a loving presence, a representation of a good object and strengthening ties with such an object may be adaptive. However, encouraging patients' relationships with objects, no matter how good they may be, is to adopt a directive, superego role that runs counter to the analytic one that I've outlined here. This is especially the case if the analyst encourages a relationship to an object which the analyst considers to be imaginary (as she describes it), a "metaphor" for a real good object.

How then should the analyst deal with the patient's religion in analysis? In a sense, like anything else. Like other aspects of the patient's life and other beliefs held, it contains unconscious meanings, expresses phantasies, which the analyst should strive to understand.[4] To understand such meanings and phantasies is not to see things through the patient's eyes, but rather to see through one's own distinct eyes both what the patient sees and what she doesn't and in some respects does not want to. Understanding in this context is helped by having some basic knowledge about the religious beliefs, concepts, and practices to which the patient refers. This is similar to knowing something about illnesses or political affiliations that patients describe as having significant influences on their lives. One needs to know just enough to make sense of what the patient is saying and doing. If a patient is concerned with having arthritis and speaks of taking morphine to deal with the pain it causes, to understand what's finding expression in this statement it would be helpful to have some idea of what arthritis is, what morphine does, and what the patient thinks the analyst knows or should know about this.

In the present clinical moment, if one is to understand what Ms. L is expressing (beyond her overt assertions) one would need to have some idea what the terms she uses mean, what are the typical religious practices within the community she belongs to, and what these practices usually mean – and all this cannot be based solely on what the patient reports. For example, it would be important to know that any Orthodox layperson would consider the amount of time Ms. L was praying strangely excessive and that *no* rabbi would suggest that this is reasonable practice for a woman, that one usually has only one rabbi with whom one consults and that the line of authority would be especially clear if she belonged to a Hasidic sect (which is implied by the fact that she refers to the person she turned to as a "rebbe" rather than a "rabbi"), and that physical contact with men, even if nonsexual and supportive (as positively described in the dream), would be regarded as forbidden and scandalous. To make sense of the material, it would also be important to know what Ms. L thinks about the analyst's religiosity and knowledge. Does she feel that in this area the analyst accepts whatever she says as authoritative? That she could mislead the analyst, leave her in the dark so that she could make little of what's going on, or alternatively could be her teacher and guide? Does she believe that out of political correctness the analyst would be compelled to be especially empathic to her beliefs even though she doesn't believe in them herself? The special importance of attending to what's going on in the transference applies here as well.

I mentioned that according to my view of the analytic task the analyst wouldn't encourage religious belief or practice. In conclusion, it should be added that the analyst wouldn't discourage them either. Religious belief and practice, like all other life choices, is left to the patient. Hopefully, the curative process of analysis will allow the patient to better see reality as it is in all its depth and richness and from this better position make her choices.

My intervention

I chose to stay in the extra-transferential realm, saying: "It seems as though your dream fulfilled a really important wish. You've been describing these three men with whom you felt very close, men you've experienced as noticing you and talking directly to you, making contact – eye contact and emotional contact – men who listened to you and made you feel cared about and warm. You have been feeling so bereft and forsaken by God, feeling as though He is not paying attention, leaving you to feel as if you are floating out there – alone and adrift. I think that your dream fulfills your wish to be noticed by God, that he will listen to you and you could feel once again comforted by his presence."

Ms. L was silent and covered her face in her hands. After a long pause, she said that what I had said surprised her. "As you started talking I thought that you were going to say that the man represented you, as I had been feeling so close to you on Monday. I thought, 'here she goes again, saying it's about her and my being conflicted about feeling close to you.' Thank you [tearful] for saying what you did, for giving me that space. Thank you for allowing me to have God. You don't know what that means to me. You have always been very respectful of my religion and spirituality but this is beyond that."

I commented that she had a strong reaction to what I had said and wondered with her if this might be connected with her recent concerns that I was feeling frustrated and annoyed with her about her consulting with the rebbe, not just relying on what I said. I linked this with her more recent memories of the loyalty conflicts she experienced when her mother tried to poison her feelings about her father.

Ms. L then mentioned that she felt so relieved that I wasn't annoyed. She ended the hour saying, "I do think that the man in the dream – that composite figure – is also you. I do feel so comforted by you, you listen and notice. But I am feeling so removed from God and I feel so sad. My spirituality and religion have given me the strength I needed – it has helped me survive. You don't just respect that, you allow me to have it and make it a part of what we do. I was so surprised by what you said. Yes, I do feel floating and unanchored from God. I am so mad. Why did he create Seth to be so full of life and then take it away? You anchor me and don't let me float too far away. I feel very much listened to. Thank you."

Notes

1 This was a reference to a repeated experience Ms. L described, mainly during adolescence, in which she could not find her reflection in the mirror. We have come to understand this as her sense of invisibility and not experiencing herself as reflected in her parents' eyes. We have given some thought to the extent that this expressed some form of dissociation, but there have been no indications of any thought disorder.
2 Kohut (1975) called this process "transmuting internalization" (p. 329), by which the patient gradually works through repeated empathic failures with the analyst resulting in a step-wise lessening of the tendency to idealize the analyst with each passing rupture.
3 It should be noted that the main activity of preparing one's home for Passover is cleaning and more particularly of ensuring that the home is cleansed of unleavened bread; not even a crumb should remain. As Judaism has tied this cleansing process to the removal of evil, if Ms. L was actually speaking about cleaning her house for Passover, this may come into the interpretation as well – e.g., how in wiping out my mind, she feels that she can prevent me from seeing any unclean thoughts in hers.
4 The difference between regarding something as a metaphor or as an expression of a phantasy is a notable one. The former implies a gap between the form of expression and the thing expressed, which the latter does not.

References

Arlow, J. (1993). Transference as a compromise defense: Panel. *Psychoanalytic Quarterly*, 62, 702–704.

Bacal, H. (1981). Notes on some therapeutic challenges in the analysis of severely regressed patients. *Psychoanalytic Inquiry*, 1(1), 29–56.

Balsam, R. (2012). *Women's bodies in psychoanalysis*. London: Routledge.

Bion, W. (1967). Notes on memory and desire. *Psychoanalytic Forum*, 2(3), 272–273, 279–280.

Blass, R. (2004). Beyond illusion: Psychoanalysis and the question of religious truth. *International Journal of Psychoanalysis*, 85(3), 615–634.

Blum, H. (1983). The position and value of extratransference interpretation. *Journal of the American Psychoanalytic Association*, 31(3), 587–617.

Brenner, C. (1976). *Psychoanalytic technique and psychic conflict*. New York: International Universities Press.

Britton, R. (2004). Subjectivity, objectivity, and triangular space. *Psychoanalytic Quarterly*, 73(1), 47–61.

Bulletin of the Anna Freud Centre (1992). Final summary statement. *Bulletin of the Anna Freud Centre*, 15(2), 173–182.

Couch, A. (2002). Extra-transference interpretation. *Psychoanalytic Study of the Child*, 57(1), 63–92.

Dewald, P. (1972). *The psychoanalytic process*. New York: Basic Books.

Eigen, M. (1988). *The psychoanalytic mystic*. New York: Free Association Books.

Eigen, M. (2001). *Ecstasy*. Middletown, CT: Wesleyan University Press.

Fauteux, K. (1995). Regression and reparation in religious experience and creativity. *Psychoanalysis and Contemporary Thought*, 18(1), 33–52.

Freud, A. (1954). The widening scope of indications for psychoanalysis: Discussion. *Journal of the American Psychoanalytic Association*, 2(4), 607–620.

Freud, A. (1965). *Normality and pathology in childhood: Assessments of development*. New York: International Universities Press.

Freud, S. (1912a). Recommendations to physicians practising psycho-analysis. In J. Strachey (Ed. & Trans.), *The standard edition of the complete psychological works of Sigmund Freud* (Vol. 12, pp. 109–120). London: Hogarth Press.

Freud, S. (1912b). The dynamics of transference. In J. Strachey (Ed. & Trans.), *The standard edition of the complete psychological works of Sigmund Freud* (Vol. 12, pp. 97–108). London: Hogarth Press.

Freud, S. (1927). The future of an illusion. In J. Strachey (Ed. & Trans.), *The standard edition of the complete psychological works of Sigmund Freud* (Vol. 21, pp. 1–56). London: Hogarth Press.

Freud, S. (1930). Civilization and its discontents. In J. Strachey (Ed. & Trans.), *The standard edition of the complete psychological works of Sigmund Freud* (Vol. 21, pp. 57–146). London: Hogarth Press.

Gill, M. (1982). *Analysis of transference* (Vol. 1). New York: International Universities Press.

Gill, M. (1984). Transference: A change in conception or only in emphasis? A response. *Psychoanalytic Inquiry*, 4(3), 489–524.

Jones, J. (2002). *Terror and transformation: The ambiguity of religion in psychoanalytic perspectives*. New York: Brunner-Routledge.

Kakar, S. (1991). *The analyst and the mystic: Psychoanalytic reflections on religion and mysticism*. Chicago, IL: University of Chicago Press.

Kilpatrick, L., & Shaver, P. (1990). Attachment theory and religion: Childhood attachments, religious beliefs, and conversion. *Journal for the Scientific Study of Religion*, 29(3), 315–334.

Kohut, H. (1971). *The analysis of the self.* New York: International Universities Press.
Kohut, H. (1975). The future of psychoanalysis. *Annual of Psychoanalysis,* 3, 325–340.
Lijtmaer, R. (2009). The patient who believes and the analyst who does not. *Journal of the American Psychoanalytic Association,* 37(1), 99–110.
Meissner, W. (1984). *Psychoanalysis and religious experience.* New Haven, CT: Yale University Press.
Meissner, W. (2013). Winnicott's legacy: On psychoanalyzing religious patients. *Psychoanalytic Inquiry,* 33(1), 21–35.
Rizzuto, A. (1979). *The birth of the living God: A psychoanalytic study.* Chicago, IL: University of Chicago Press.
Shaw, D. (2005). Psychoanalysis, meet religion: And this time, get it right: A review of Minding spirituality by Randall Lehman Sorenson. *Contemporary Psychoanalysis,* 41(2), 352–360.
Slochower, J. (1996). *Holding and psychoanalysis: A relational perspective.* Hillsdale, NJ: The Analytic Press.
Sorenson, R. (1994). Ongoing change in psychoanalytic theory: Implications for analysis of religious experience. *Psychoanalytic Dialogues,* 4(4), 631–660.
Sorenson, R. (2004). *Minding spirituality.* Hillsdale, NJ: The Analytic Press.
Spero, M. (2004). What *con*-verges and what *di*-verges when religious object representations transform? An annotated critique of Cohen (2002). *Journal of the American Academy of Psychoanalysis and Dynamic Psychiatry,* 32(4), 669–708.
Spezzano, C., & Gargiulo, G. (Eds.). (1997). *Souls on the couch: Spirituality, religion and morality in contemporary psychoanalysis.* Hillsdale, NJ: The Analytic Press.
Stone, L. (1967). The psychoanalytic situation and transference: Postscript to an earlier communication. *Journal of the American Psychoanalytic Association,* 15(1), 3–58.
Strachey, J. (1934). The nature of the therapeutic action of psycho-analysis. *International Journal of Psychoanalysis,* 15, 127–159.
Symington, N. ([1994] 1998). *Emotion and spirit: Questioning the claims of psychoanalysis and religion.* London: Karnac Books.
Tuch, R. (2007). Thinking with, and about, patients too scared to think: Can non-interpretive maneuvers stimulate reflective thought? *International Journal of Psychoanalysis,* 88, 91–111.
Tuch, R. (2016). Between knowing and believing: Salvaging illusion's rightful place in psychoanalysis. *Psychoanalytic Quarterly,* 85(1), 35–57.
Winnicott, D. W. (1951). Transitional objects and transitional phenomena. In *Through paediatrics to psycho-analysis* (pp. 229–242). London: Tavistock, 1958.
Winnicott, D. W. (1963). Morals and education. In *The maturational processes and the facilitating environment* (pp. 93–105). New York: International Universities Press, 1965.
Winnicott, D. W. (1971). *Playing and reality.* London: Tavistock Publications.

Chapter 3

"If You Keep Talking to Me This Way, I'm Going to Quit!"

(You Talk... I Walk)

Robert James Perkins

Editors' introduction

While psychoanalysts sense when an interpretive path they are pursuing is beyond a patient's capacity to tolerate, backing off when a patient indicates he can't handle what the analyst is suggesting, there are occasions when an analyst is left to weigh whether it is nevertheless necessary to continue interpreting in spite of the patient's protestation. This was the case with Mr. F, a 50-year-old married attorney who'd been making good strides in treatment until the third year of his analysis when the tide began to turn in a most disconcerting fashion as the patient underwent an alarming regression. While he'd begun treatment insisting he'd had "a very happy childhood," as the treatment progressed, a dramatically different picture emerged that contrasted markedly from the story the patient had been telling, thus turning his life "upside down." Suddenly, the patient became possessed by a fear that "niggers" would invade his home, so he armed himself and took to submitting scathing and racist op-ed pieces aimed at alerting people who "just can't see what's going on." The analyst suggested that this radical shift in the patient's feelings and behavior had to do with rage triggered by realizing the true condition of his childhood, but the patient was having none of it, furiously insisting that the analyst was naive about real dangers and off-base in his interpretation. Anxiety dreams marked a worsening of the patient's condition, leading him to threaten the analyst by claiming "*if you keep talking to me this way, I'm going to quit.*" Aware that the patient had abruptly broken off two previous treatments, the analyst took the patient's threats seriously and struggled with the question of what to do next.

The moment in context (Richard Tuch)

There are times, in the midst of treatment, when the analyst comes to question the wisdom of the approach he's been taking with a given patient. Progress may be lacking or the therapeutic alliance has turned contentious, leaving the analyst to wonder what it is he might do to rectify matters. If a therapist decides to stick to his guns – to hold fast to his chosen clinical approach to the treatment of a given patient – the end result can either prove disastrous, spelling the end of treatment, or it may save the day as the analyst "doubles down" by rededicating himself to stay the course, hold the frame, and insist the patient confront what he is working to convince the analyst is something that is "un-confrontable" – leaving the analyst struggling with doubt about the wisdom of pressing on in the face of warning lights signaling him to back off. In Chapter 7, we will encounter a clinical moment where the analyst decided to alter her approach to treatment because the patient was not responding well, so she backed off and decided to re-approach the situation from a different angle. The clinical moment that follows involves a comparable situation when the analyst is unsure whether to stay the course or alter his present approach to the situation.

The evolution of psychoanalytic technique has involved a series of modifications that were necessitated by the failure of a given approach to yield adequate clinical results. First, Freud relied on the use of hypnosis to slyly circumvent the operations of resistance. When he was unable to induce trances in sufficient numbers of patients, he abandoned hypnosis and began using the "pressure technique" – which involved applying pressure to the patient's forehead and commanding them to remember the details of their traumatic, pathogenic experiences. When Frau Emma von N. suggested Freud stop trying to direct the way in which she was trying to tell her story, free association became the "fundamental rule," which remains in place today. Since then, others have suggested minor or major shifts in technique, typically when they found classic technique failed to produce the hoped-for therapeutic result. Self psychology grew out of a failure to successfully treat patients suffering from narcissistic personality disorders using the prevailing techniques – illustrated in Kohut's (1979) publication of "The Two Analyses of Mr. Z."[1] The same can be said about Fonagy's introduction of a mentalization-based approach to psychoanalysis, which grew out of his treatment of Mr. S., who reacted to Fonagy's efforts to interpret the patient's transference reactions by yelling: "Don't you understand anything? It doesn't matter a damn what you feel. As far as I am concerned you don't exist" (Fonagy, 1991, p. 645). Awakened to the fact that his core assumptions about this patient were flawed, that his reliance on a classical, interpretive approach to treatment was not yielding the desired result in this case, Fonagy felt forced to go back to the drawing board and redesign a theory for this given patient who – he realized – was unable to understand others' minds and found the task of even considering the contents of others' minds unthinkable.

Much of the time, psychoanalysis proceeds with only minor hitches. Yes – the transference may heat up and the intensity of the analysand's transference may become a challenge to contain and address, but many times the analysand is able to keep in mind the "as if" quality of the transference, which keeps him from losing track of the fact that something may be playing out from his past – that the analyst may not, in fact, be precisely as the patient is imagining him to be at the present moment. Such analyses tend not to require a reconsideration of the analyst's approach to treatment. Clinical conditions that can trigger an analyst to rethink his clinical approach may grow out of the analyst's growing concern or alarm about where therapy is heading – or, in the case of an impasse, not heading. The patient may appear to be deteriorating in whatever way. He may be acting in self-destructive ways. Concerned friends and relatives may contact the analyst to express their alarm that the patient is acting very much "out of character." The patient may be getting into trouble because he's acting rashly, whether the patient realizes as much or not. The analyst may express concern and, in response, the analysand may push back by insisting that the analyst is worrying for no good reason. The patient may even liken the analyst's worry to the unwarranted fearfulness of parents who had worried themselves needlessly about the patient. The patient's reality testing may seem impaired, his thinking may border on being delusional, and – if he acts in accordance with such beliefs – the analyst may have cause for concern, leading him to re-evaluate whether his treatment approach may even be contributing to the problem. So long as a florid negative transference hasn't developed and the patient keeps coming, the analyst may feel the situation remains "manageable" – even if the therapeutic alliance seems challenged and the patient had ceased to give due consideration to the analyst's input. Such are the conditions of the clinical moment we are about to discuss.

Let's consider a case report that appears in *Failures in Psychoanalytic Treatment* (Reppen & Schulman, 2002). Ms. P. (Vida, 2002) was a patient who acted in a "tyrannical" manner – carrying out a campaign ("disruptions of terrifying magnitude," p. 29) involving the wholesale devaluation and contemptuous mistreatment of the analyst (scornfully characterizing the analyst's offerings as "trite," "stupid," etc., p. 28), which the patient felt to have been her right given that analysis, by design, was to meet and accommodate her every need. The analyst eventually came to feel as if she was being "held hostage" (p. 30) as her capacity to think gradually waned. This patient reports having chosen her analyst on the grounds that she was known to be a committed self psychologist. She entered treatment claiming to be looking for "empathy" – which turned out to reflect an expectation that the analyst accommodate her every whim without she, herself, having to accommodate the analyst in any way (p. 29). For example, when Ms. P. complained about the analyst's make-up, cologne, or clothes, the analyst was then expected to change to be less objectionable to the patient. The analyst sought consultation, which failed to clarify the matter, and it wasn't until she heard from a colleague, who was seeing the patient in marital therapy, that she regarded the analyst's patient as a "monstrously controlling presence" (p. 30), that she was finally able to "break the spell" she had fallen under. In the process, the analyst came to the realization that she herself had "idealized self psychological theory" (p. 19), which she mistakenly had come to believe dictated that she "privilege the patient's perceptions ahead of my own preconceptions" (which she calls her "mantra," p. 29). Slowly, it dawned on the analyst that "there was going to be no room for me in this analysis" (p. 28). The patient "conceived of the treatment as her being in a boat in which she held the rudder and [the analyst was] the (mute) passenger" (p. 29). This case, I would submit, is an illustrative example of how rigid adherence to theory doomed the treatment to the extent it tied the analyst's hands, keeping her from adopting a more confrontational approach that would have demanded the patient explore her contempt and consider the outrageous and inhuman demands she was making on the analyst.

The clinical moment that follows is interesting in that the analyst rededicates himself to the continuing task of confronting the patient with interpretations that ran counter to how the patient was tending to see things. The patient's frankly paranoid perspective led to his becoming remarkably closed-minded – refusing to even consider the analyst's point of view. This was, in fact, a newly emerging phenomenon in the course of what had otherwise been a treatment characterized by the patient's ability to not only hear what the analyst had to say but to realize the analyst was correctly interpreting what his childhood had been like for him. What a shock it must have been, then, when the analyst discovered their therapeutic alliance had attenuated and the patient was outright hostile toward the analyst, refusing to hear what he had to say. As it turned out, the analyst's continued dedication to stay the course and fight to be heard, when the patient threatened to leave if the analyst continued to pursue his line of thinking, eventually paid off, even though some might consider the analyst's insistence – his belief that he need not change his tack when under fire – to be a sign of his stubbornness and short-sightedness to the extent *flexibility/adaptability* is often celebrated rather than open-mindedly questioned.

Casement (1982) writes about a similar dilemma, arguing persuasively in favor of staying the course after he'd openly considered the possibility of permitting the patient to hold his hand, as she insisted she must in order to be able to relive a traumatic experience from the seventeenth month of her life. At that time, the patient had been undergoing skin surgery conducted under local anesthesia, reassured by the fact that her mother would be holding her hand throughout the procedure. The mother had let go of the patient's hand, fainting away, causing the young girl to panic over the thought that her mother had died. The patient felt certain that she'd be retraumatized if she were to remember the event without, at the same time, altering the event by holding the analyst's (mother's) hand – believing that doing so would mitigate the level of trauma she would re-experience if she couldn't change the original situation in this fashion (as if such a thing is possible). The analyst felt extraordinarily pressured by the patient to accede to her request – heightened by her becoming suicidal and delusional – which left him feeling that he was facing an impossible situation. He came to understand his countertransference reaction as one that the patient unconsciously aimed to evoke in him so that he would then contain the unbearable state that the patient felt she could not contain herself. Understanding as much helped Casement rededicate himself to preserve "*psychoanalytical* holding, in the face of considerable pressures upon me to relinquish it, which eventually enabled my patient to receive her own frightened personality back again in a form that she could tolerate" (p. 285, italics added). Casement reasoned that the patient needed:

> to experience in the present, in relation to a real situation between patient and analyst, the extremes of feeling which belonged to an early traumatic experience but which had been "frozen" because of being too intense for the primitive ego to encompass *at that time*.
>
> (p. 284; italics in the original)

Having the courage to change tack when conditions seem to require as much may prove to be as heroic as mustering the courage to finish up what one set out to accomplish. In the final analysis, blind adherence to accepted technique should not be conflated with a continuing dedication to stay the course, which might prove to be just what the doctor ordered. Having said as much, blind allegiance to a given approach in the face of mounting evidence that strongly suggests the treatment is spiraling downward is a tragedy in the making. Having the wisdom to distinguish between these two alternatives defines the making of a master clinician.

The clinical moment

Mr. F, a 50-year-old married attorney, came to treatment because of depression and complaints from his wife that he was becoming increasingly irritable. He mentioned having undergone two unsatisfactory treatments in the past. He was comfortable financially and described his home life as pleasant but very boring. In fact, he went on about how he missed the high spirits of his mother and the excitement of his childhood with her. His parents divorced when he was a baby, and thereafter he was raised by his single mother, a waitress. True, she had worked evening hours and much of the child care was done by sitters, but what fun they had during the time they did spend together! The patient's wife, by comparison, felt dull and unimaginative. She was content to be a good homemaker and mother to their three children, the sort of person his mother always called a "square."

Mr. F described having had a very happy childhood. His mother and her girlfriends were always looking for a good time, and sometimes he was allowed to come along on their adventures. They would drive to the beach with the top down, singing to the radio and drinking wine and – if it was the sitter's day off – he got to sit in the back seat.

His mother had a series of "gentlemen callers" over the years. They had new cars and fancy clothes. He was allowed to mix them their favorite drinks when they came to take her out. They often had pet names for him, and he would miss them when they no longer came about. He fondly reminisced about this one's cologne or that one's cashmere sport coat. They would take his mother to local resorts, and – because the sitter was off on weekends – he would often go along. He would have his very own room, even at an early age, and he would be allowed to order anything he wanted from room service. "That was living," he declared. True, he didn't have many real friends. But his mother was willing to pay for manicures and tennis lessons for him at an upscale hotel across town. He felt very lucky. When the two of them walked out of their apartment, past little families sitting together on the lawn, she would sneer at them for the losers they were. They would laugh together, and life felt good.

In the early months of his analysis, I heard a lot about his glorious childhood and how his life in the present felt ordinary and depressing by comparison. He complained bitterly that his wife was a huge disappointment, never able to relax and have a really good time. And, what was worse, she claimed that he was the one who couldn't enjoy what he had. "Well can you?" I asked. At this, he flew into a rage. "Oh no you don't," he said, "I can see what you're trying to do, and it won't work! You're trying to brainwash me and get me to like broccoli, and I just don't!"

I began to question aloud if his childhood had indeed been as happy as he claimed. "It sounds to me like a lonely existence," I said, "missing many of the basic ingredients a kid needs." He proved surprisingly open to this revisionism and, after an initial pushback, slowly became interested in this alternate version of his childhood. I began to hear stories about how sad and alone he had felt. He now remembered how little time his mother spent with him, his attempts to connect with the boyfriends who never seemed to hang around for long, and his sense that his mother had felt stuck with him when she really wanted a good time for herself. As he got in touch with these long-buried memories – so at odds with what had been the "official version" – he was also becoming aware of the extent to which he had adopted his mother's attitudes about her life as well as his. "I guess I was in a bubble with her," he said. He hadn't let himself find the comfort of friends or other relationships, instead waiting for his time with her and not complaining in the meantime. "Not even letting yourself know what you really felt," I noted, to which he responded by nodding his head sadly. He began to write out his painful memories and bring them to sessions, reading them to me and crying. The list was long. He was telling his story and finally had someone to tell it to – finally had someone who would take interest and listen.

For some time, I mainly listened to what, for both of us, was a flood of new material. I was struck by how different this version of his childhood was in comparison to the tale he had originally told, and I told him so. For his part, he mainly focused on describing how incredibly bleak it had been. At times, there was a sense of bewilderment in him as he rewrote his own history. I continued to remark on the dramatic difference in how he now felt about his mother and his childhood. He could see that he had "bought into" her ideas about a lot of things, but "no more!"

I began to suggest that he had buried these longstanding feelings of bitterness and sadness, and I raised the question of whether these feelings may have spilled over into his present-day life and his marriage. "Was his day-to-day life really so bad?" I wondered aloud. Was his wife the "square," as his mother would have said? A bit to my surprise, considering his capacity to respond to new ideas, this idea made him furious. "There you go," he said, "trying to make me like broccoli. That's not going to work with me!"

At the time, I attributed this angry volatility to the night-and-day shift in his sense of what his childhood had been like. I commented that he might well be wary that I, like his mother, might be intent on selling him my version of the facts. I asked whether he'd taken note of how vigilant he was being in these moments, and I inquired as to whether we might find a way for him to be open to new ideas without feeling brainwashed in the process. He dismissed the idea, saying that only *he* knew what he knew. I interjected: "But we have both seen how, on some important matters relative to your childhood, you hadn't always known all that you now know." Once again, the patient became very angry and challenging.

It struck me that Mr. F wasn't just disagreeing with me. His stubborn anger covered what I felt was anxiety over the complete collapse of his defensive idealization of what, in fact, had been a thoroughly depressive childhood. I was being experienced as both the messenger and the brainwashing mother. I cautioned myself, believing it best – for the time being – that I proceed cautiously to permit him time to adjust to this newly emerging reality and to regain his waning trust in me. It did not prove to be that simple.

What developed next took me by surprise. The patient began to talk about his fear that "niggers" from the central city would flood into his affluent suburb and invade his house. At this point, we were nearly two years into his treatment, and I had not heard this theme before. Though he had never before sounded racist or fearful, he was now full of anxiety. "They're coming," he insisted, "and will take away everything I have." He read up on the riots that had rocked our city at one time and felt convinced it would all be happening again: "They've been lying back, waiting, but this time they won't be stopped." To prepare for a home invasion, he armed himself. He took to submitting scathing, racist op-ed pieces to the local newspaper, aimed at alerting people who "just can't see what's going on."

His fearful rage was now a preoccupation that filled his sessions, largely replacing his retrieval of childhood memories. When the newspaper didn't print his rants, he became furious. "They make excuses for these people because they supposedly had such hard lives. There will be hell to pay!" At night, he would sit at home checking that the security system was still on, feeling frightened that someone or something was on his property. He became particularly livid when anyone questioned the reality of his concerns, convinced that they weren't letting themselves see the risk posed by the angry, destructive "niggers."

My attempts to recruit his curiosity about these new feelings were met by furious attacks on me. I was a bleeding-heart liberal, he said, blinded by political correctness. I should stick to therapy and leave my world view out of it. When he did speak of other matters, which he did less and less, he tended to calm down and become collaborative again. He brought in a series of repetitive dreams in which he would be in his home, sitting at the top of the stairs, with a shadowy intruder coming up. The hallway was always dark, and he would wake up shaking with fear. Dreams had been a useful part of the analysis, but this one proved not to be. He reacted strongly to my effort to locate the source of his anxiety within him. "You know," he said furiously, "I don't have to come here. I don't have to put up with this. Leave me alone."

I tried to find ways to interpret what I thought was going on without triggering yet another violent reaction on the patient's part. There was no shortage of likely dynamics to choose from. It seemed that although he was now in touch with the desperately sad and empty side of himself that issued from his emotionally deprived childhood, the anger that accompanied it remained split off, threatening to emerge as a furious element that endangered his everyday life. He was afraid of this side of himself – the side he kept buried for so long, the side he no longer could pretend to not know. I told him as much, adding: "We have now seen that you were a sad little boy. But you were also a very angry little guy and that's a big part of what you are afraid will invade you and take over your life. You may have felt that you would lose whatever you were getting from your mother if you got angry and complained. Maybe underneath you feel that the 'niggers' have been deprived and are angry about it, as you were." When I would attempt to get him to consider this perspective about his fear, his push back was immediate. "There you go," he would say, "don't you try to distort things with your psycho-babble. The risk is real. Ask anybody! I don't have to put up with this!"

I tried to remind him about how readily he had been able to revise his memories of a happy childhood to see and accept the underlying truth about how sad his childhood had actually been, adding that the inevitable anger that was associated with that realization was now being experienced as a threat – as if it weren't a part of him as well. I suggested that maybe when he was little he had felt that his anger could burst his bubble if it got out of hand. Maybe that was why it felt off-limits even today. In response, the patient flew into a rage, saying, "I see what you are trying to do and I've had enough of it."

At this juncture, the patient's wife called. The therapy was only making him worse, she told me. His behavior was starting to frighten her – he had gotten into terrible shouting matches with a neighbor. When I told the patient about the call, he was incensed. "She doesn't have the slightest idea what's going on," he insisted, "and that's exactly the kind of bullshit I have to put up with!" He was comforted by reading internet postings written by kindred spirits who shared his views on the coming apocalypse. He complained about the "kind of people" who were moving into his neighborhood and got into a huge row with his local community organization, going so far as to file a lawsuit against them for negligence.

I was now becoming concerned. He was insisting that I not touch upon his paranoid fears, which – in the name of tact and timing – I was willing to do for a time. But these issues were taking over his life, not just his sessions. What had started as a somewhat depressed man who was bored with his marriage – a man who had been psychologically and emotionally amenable and accessible in treatment – had now evolved into a man who was consumed with fear and anger and acting on these concerns. He was no longer open to considering my ideas and saw no reason to question what he knew to be the unquestionable realities of life. The treatment, which had initially seen such a dramatic response, now felt stalled, with his new symptoms declared off-limits as they rapidly gained momentum. It was becoming clear that simply "going slow" and respecting his fragile defenses was not working. He was undergoing a significant regression before my eyes and was getting himself into trouble in the real world.

I shared my concerns about him. "You're losing it," I said, "and you're not letting me help you. You've had the experience of letting yourself change in a big way and found it helpful. But look how hard you are fighting back to avoid another change. You are the one that just can't see what is going on. When you stop me from talking about it – your fears, the 'niggers,' all of it – you shut down your chance to understand what is going on in your mind so that you might then get some peace of mind. Can we work together on this?"

"That's it!" he shouted. "If you keep talking this way, I'm quitting!" I had never seen the patient this angry. I had learned along the way that he had abruptly stopped two earlier therapies, and now he sounded in deadly earnest. A gentle, supportive approach whereby I followed his lead clearly was not working, as he continued his rather profound and escalating regression. I had concerns where this might lead. At the same time, his threat to abruptly quit felt very credible. He had done it before – twice! He and the treatment were rapidly unraveling and I was not sure what to do. It felt as if it hung in the balance. Of course, this analytic showdown took place on a Friday, so that I had the weekend to think about it.

Invited commentator responses: Irma Brenman Pick and Robert Michels

Irma Brenman Pick

It is interesting to be invited to consider how I might orientate myself to thinking about what might be my reactions, as analyst, faced with this ultimatum; of course, anything I write now may have little bearing on what might have been my actual reaction in this situation. And reading the account of this treatment I am bound to say – like the Irish joke of the man asking for directions from X to Y – that X wouldn't have been the place to start from in the first place.

For in this case, the analyst conducts the analysis as an attempt to analyze the patient's early experiences. My own way of working would be to keep what is going on in the here and now (in the transference and also the countertransference) as the central focus of the work.

So supposing my mind was free enough to think constructively – what then? Might I find myself wondering: How frightened am I? And how serious a threat is this? In the tyrannical tone I hear, am I seriously frightened that the patient is breaking down into a psychosis, or is my fear that of losing my patient? And if the latter is the case, why is this frightening – do I depend on him for survival? And if it feels like I am so dependent on him (for survival) – who am I? What part of him have I become?

I recall Melanie Klein saying one should always have one patient too many – suggesting that one would not then feel so dependent on the patient – thus the fear of losing the patient would not be so intense as to get in the way of the work to be done. Interesting, that comment of hers, since she did not have much time for the use of the countertransference in clinical work! While welcoming her ideas on early development, and her focus on what is going on in the transference, I would also be paying close attention to my countertransference experience.

I would be wondering about who I am and who the patient is at this moment. I would think that he is bringing, hopefully also for us to understand, some picture of an early interaction with an internal object. I would assume that the intrusive "niggers" are in part "black" intrusive parts of himself, but I would not think he would be able to hear this now. And I would be mindful that, instead, he is likely to experience whatever I say as me intruding/attacking him.

Is he a child in a temper tantrum? Or, more likely, am I to have the experience of being the child, and knowing what it feels like to be tyrannized over by a dangerous object? I would take seriously the idea that he feels that I do not realize how dangerous the situation is; how I/one will not be tolerated if I do not conform to his demands, but behind that – the demands of a tyrannical object or objects.

I might be inclined to link this with his account of his own childhood: for example, that he will come for his sessions and offer me fees that provide for my needs and wishes, give me a "nice time" only so long as I conform to his demands; that he wants me to understand how it is to depend for survival (now the survival of the treatment) on such an object. I would have in mind Bion's idea that projective identification becomes violent when there is no home for ordinary projective identification; that he, the patient, believes that he is dealing with dangerous objects that threaten when they are not submitted to; and that he believes that this has not been taken seriously by me.

So I might ask myself: What have I failed to take seriously enough? Who are these "niggers" who threaten him – are they, as I said, parts of himself, or are they the men coming into the house to take his mother away? Does he feel tyrannized over by them – or indeed, perhaps earlier yet, by his mother – so that if he is not a good boy she will abandon him? And have I failed to take seriously how frightening the situation is? Has the situation escalated in this way, projective identification becoming violent, because I did not take in his fears? I now have really to know what it is like, to have to take the back seat and shut up or be abandoned.

Thus I might be inclined to think in terms of what John Steiner (1994) has called "analyst centred interpretations" – that he wants me to know what it feels like to feel so threatened by orders coming in from dark, shadowy people, letting me know that if I do not do what I am told, I will be abandoned, and so on… that he really needs me to have that experience, to know what that feels like… I would preface any comment by saying that while he will hear whatever I say as though I am an "intrusive nigger," perhaps we can try to think together about where this is coming from?

He will not see me as an "understanding" analyst speaking about his early experiences, but can I allow myself to have the painful experience of being seen in that way? I think that is a very different way of working – or working through – the experience of feeling so threatened. Many years ago, I worked with a patient who was a scientist – he said that his boss in the lab used to say "treasure your unsuccessful results." That stayed with me as a metaphor for our work too – the "unsuccessful result" in this case would be the fear of being dropped.

If we begin to think about what this means – does it touch my narcissistic self – perhaps I can't bear to lose a patient/fail; if that is so, is that just about me or is it about some aspect of the narcissism of the patient or his mother? Alternately, might it ring bells with a deeper and more threatening fear for survival? And whose fear is this? Is this an early infantile fear for survival, one that requires the infant submit, in which case one may hate the object as well as oneself for submitting? Alternately, might one respond to one's fear by reacting violently, risking the chance of destroying either the object or oneself? This hatred of the object to whom one submits, when projected into the object, would make the patient very fearful of that object – in the transference he would now fear my hatred of him.

I would need then to be thinking about whether I submit and hate – might I really be the child wishing to be rid of him/these parents/and so on? And is that what he hears in my voice?

These are issues I have considered in my paper "Working through in the Countertransference" (Pick, 1985), and this thinking would guide me now!

Robert Michels

We are presented with a clinical crisis. The patient, in the second year of his analysis, becomes enraged, paranoid, and nearly delusional. Before we discuss how to manage this, we must first try to understand it. The analyst describes it in the context of a preceding extensive discussion of the patient's childhood, with a dramatic revision of his original account of a blissful tie to his mother, reconstructed with the active participation of the analyst's challenges and confrontations so that the reconfigured account included a growing recognition of the patient's repressed anger and despair. The analyst's interpretations seem convincing, well-formed, and readily accepted by the patient.

The crisis begins when the analyst questions the patient, "Was his day-to-day life really so bad?" The patient had flown into a rage once before, when he felt that the analyst was accusing him of being unable to enjoy life, and was agreeing with his wife's view that the problem was caused by himself, not by his wife. We are not told that this earlier crisis had been resolved. The patient had shown little opposition to the analyst's enthusiastic participation in reformulating his childhood story, but the analyst's questioning his version of his current life problem was different. The patient dug in his heels and fought back ferociously.

That is one story, a story based upon the explicit content of the sessions preceding the crisis. However, there are hints of possible alternative contexts and alternative stories. The second sentence of the report tells us that the patient "mentioned having undergone two unsatisfactory treatments in the past." The issue is not mentioned again until the final paragraph: "His threat to abruptly quit felt very credible. He had done it before – twice!" So another version of the crisis is of a patient who repeats a pattern – the third time around, of abruptly quitting a therapy. The exploration and understanding of this repeated enactment would seem critical, a pattern of resistance that would have to be anticipated and attended to if the treatment were to be successful. I would give priority to exploring this danger of fleeing therapy rather than to revising the patient's account of his childhood. One can imagine discussion of his turning against previous treatments early in this one, along with consideration of how to manage the situation if he finds himself repeating the pattern in this one.

Yet another context for understanding the crisis can be imagined. There is surprisingly little reference to the transference in this account, although many would describe the critical event as the sudden emergence of a powerful negative transference, perhaps even a transference psychosis. In fact, just as the biographical account is of the patient's experience of a good mother who is turned into a bad mother, the story of the therapy is of the patient's experience of a good therapist who turns into a bad therapist. We could explore whether this plot represents a core fantasy, revealed in his life story, his treatment history, and perhaps even in his relationship with his wife.

All well and good, but what about the crisis? It sounds like things may be too "hot" to continue analysis as usual. We have traditional options – the patient sitting up, the analyst suggesting that it might be useful to explore these other contexts and to emphasize that the goal is not to discover the "truth" of his marriage (or, for that matter, of his childhood relationship with his mother or his earlier treatments). The goal is to understand what is happening in the consultation room, his response to the analyst's interventions, and the relationship of those responses to his experiences in the world.

The analyst tries an interpretation: "He might well be wary that I, like his mother, might be intent on selling him my version of the facts." (I might have speculated further, that in the revision of his childhood, it became clear that he was really a victim, but now he was being asked to relinquish his claim to victimhood in his current life.)

His anxiety focused on his fear of the imagined rage of victims in the community ("niggers"). He feels his own rage as a victim of the analyst and attacks the analyst who questioned his own claim to victimhood and now questions his fear of retaliation from other victims.

The account ends on a Friday session. It is somewhat scary. The patient's enactments have extended into his life in the community, and his anger and mistrust of the analyst make it seem unlikely that he can even listen to him, and even less likely that he might accept his advice.

I would consider "psychiatric" interventions – "parameters" in psychoanalytic jargon. I would have the patient sit up, consider using medication (but be fearful lest it increased his paranoia rather than reduced it), and perhaps suggest that his wife join us for a discussion, all in the hope of limiting his regression and disorganization. However, most important, I would focus our discussion on his transference, avoiding discussion of his childhood, his marriage, and his current near-delusional thinking.

If this plan worked, his anger at me and perhaps his previous therapists would gradually be understood, at least partially, as his response to my trying to convince him that his complaints were inappropriate. He had accepted my challenging his initial view that his childhood was blissful, but rebelled when I challenged his view of his marriage or of the outer world. The goal would not be to have him accept my point of view (indeed I don't think that I should have a "point of view"); the goal would be to reopen channels of communication between us. If that were successful, the analysis might even continue, but with close monitoring of the transference and avoidance of any suggestion that the analyst has privileged knowledge about the "truth" of either the past or the present.

My intervention

I had begun to feel that the state of the treatment called for something more and not less, despite his insistence to the contrary. On the other hand, there was the very real possibility he would leave and the discussion would end. Was an enactment at play, as had been the case years before, where my speaking the truth would be the death of the relationship? Were his striking efforts to silence me a mirror of the implicit constraints of his childhood? I noted that when I avoided addressing certain "inconvenient" truths, the patient would calm down and our shaky therapeutic alliance would be re-established. He had not (or hadn't yet?) become locked into a negative transference on all fronts, so at least he continued to attend sessions. That, of course, was what hung in the balance. It was tempting to try to keep the treatment afloat, play for time, hoping eventually to see things through analytically. I wondered whether, at some level, he might be aware of the conundrum he was creating. Would he in fact quit? He and I both knew that this treatment was one in which great strides had been made. We had worked well together during his dramatic change of view about his childhood. Were my apprehensions part of the enactment? Did I need to stand firm and express my beliefs about his situation even if doing so ran the risk of destroying all that he and I had labored to create in the way of a therapeutic bond? Or, was it essential that I speak the truth in a way he had not been able to do as a child? The difficulty, of course, is that his level of regression made a careful expression and examination of these possibilities problematic.

The patient came to his Monday session with a dream. Once again, he was on the stairway at his home, watching a shadowy intruder, holding his gun. Once again, he could not clearly see who it was. He was terrified. And now, having told his dream, it seemed to me that he was waiting to see what I would do.

"I think these dreams have to do with your fear of a part of yourself that frightens you," I began, "that is your fear of the 'niggers.' It is the hungry, angry part of you, the part that you had to bury, at all costs, fearing you would lose what little you did get from your mother. I can only imagine how hard you worked to silence yourself when you were little, avoiding even the thoughts, for fear you would burst the bubble and realize you had nothing. That's what you have been so afraid of. And you have been trying to silence me about it, as well." I held my breath and waited. The patient was uncharacteristically subdued in this session. He muttered that there was a real threat that I just couldn't see, but there was no threat to quit his treatment.

He came into his next session with a sheepish look on his face. He had had the dream again. This time he had reached the light switch and turned it on. "The guy on the stairs was... me," he said, evenly. "I guess maybe you've been right about this." In this case – which was filled with dramatic twists – I shouldn't have been surprised, but I was.

Now the sessions became less fevered, and we had a chance to think about our "crisis." I shared my thinking about the enactment, how he had tried to silence me, and our standoff. We wondered if he had the revealing dream when he did because we had already turned a corner. It was not the last crisis in our work, which continued on for many years. From then on, however, he was able to engage, most of the time, in a much more thoughtful way. There were no more threats to leave.

Note

1 Setting aside the likely possibility that this case report was in fact Kohut's reconceptualization of how he imagined his own "classical" analysis might have played out in the hands of a self-psychologically oriented analyst (Kohut's "self-analysis" – see Strozier, 2001).

References

Casement, P. J. (1982). Some pressures on the analyst for physical contact during the re-living of an early trauma. *International Review of Psychoanalysis*, 9(3), 279–286.

Fonagy, P. (1991). Thinking about thinking: Some clinical and theoretical considerations in the treatment of a borderline patient. *International Journal of Psychoanalysis*, 72(4), 639–656.

Kohut, H. (1979). The two analyses of Mr. Z. *International Journal of Psychoanalysis*, 60(1), 3–18.

Pick, I. B. (1985). Working through in the countertransference. *International Journal of Psychoanalysis*, 66(2), 157–166.

Reppen, J., & Schulman, M. (2002). *Failures in psychoanalytic treatment*. New York: International University Press.

Steiner, J. (1994). Patient-centered and analyst-centered interpretations: Some implications of containment and countertransference. *Psychoanalytic Inquiry*, 14(3), 406–422.

Strozier, C. (2001). *Heinz Kohut: The making of a psychoanalyst*. New York: Farrar, Strauss and Giroux.

Vida, J. (2002). The indispensable "difficult event." In J. Reppen & M. Schulman (Eds.), *Failures in psychoanalytic treatment* (pp. 17–36). New York: International University Press.

Part II

Countertransference Enactments

Chapter 4

Countertransference Enactments: Three Times Over

Jill Model Barth

Editors' introduction

Analysts who see patients in their home offices are well aware of the possibility that patients may catch a glimpse of an aspect of their outside life, sometimes coming face-to-face with a significant other from the analyst's personal life. This clinical moment takes place four years into an ongoing analysis of a single, middle-aged woman who had previously been married and divorced three times. The gist of the patient's treatment involved her painful conviction that she was unlovable – the vestige of her having been placed for adoption then shunted from one mother to the next. She yearned to be adopted by the analyst and included in her Jewish family, though she would often make off-putting, disparaging remarks about Jews whom she saw as clannish and exclusionary. This clinical moment, which ultimately came to be understood as a countertransference enactment, was prefaced by two other such enactments that demonstrated a mixture of both complementary and concordant type countertransference reactions (Racker, 1968). The clinical moment in question took place over two days, set in motion when the analyst's parents arrived from the airport nearly an hour earlier than expected, positioning the limousine that had transported them behind the patient's car in the analyst's driveway, blocking her exit from the property upon the completion of her session. The analyst heard the commotion and waited to see how the incident would play out. As she awaited the patient's arrival at the next session, the analyst wondered how the patient had reacted to the event and how the two would explore what had taken place. The analyst faulted herself for having been careless – for not having taken greater care to avoid exposing the patient to the extra-analytic encounter. This triggered her to reflect on the nature and meaning of this particular enactment – to consider how it related to the previous two enactments and how the three enactments related to one another. Subsequently, the analyst recognized it as an opportunity to reflect on the nature and meaning of this series of countertransference enactments.

The moment in context (Jill Model Barth)

The following clinical moment brings together two noteworthy clinical features – one, having to do with countertransference enactments; the other, related to the matter of extra-analytic (out-of-the-office) encounters. The clinical moment that follows involves a series of countertransference enactments that culminated in an extra-analytic encounter. What at first had appeared to be an inadvertent extra-analytic encounter involving the patient and the analyst's mother was later recognized by the analyst to have been a countertransference enactment involving her less than careful management of the situation, which she came to recognize could easily have been avoided. While such extra-analytic encounters can throw the analyst off-guard, they may ultimately go on to enlighten the transference-countertransference dynamics once the event has been processed (Jacobs, 2001a; Ogden, 1986).

The term *countertransference enactment* was first introduced by Ted Jacobs (1986) to describe the reliving of unconscious emotional experiences involved in the analytic relationship. Jacobs considers countertransference enactment to be an interactional phenomenon that gets set in motion by the patient's transferences, affective experiences, and behavioral presentations that interact with the personality characteristics, affective frame, and unresolved personal issues of the analyst. Bohleber et al. (2013) offer a serviceable definition of the phenomenon:

> Enactment involves a collapse in the analytic dialogue in which the analyst is drawn into an interaction where he unwittingly acts, thereby actualizing unconscious wishes of both himself and the patient. This collapse implies disturbance of the symbolic function; something emerges that at the moment of enactment is not accessible by language. What follows this moment will determine whether the enactment will have therapeutic value, that is, whether the symbolic function will be restored and integrative work can or cannot happen.
>
> (p. 517)

While not all enactments can be analyzed given that some go on to have a permanently injurious effect, Jacobs (2001a) argues that many such enactments not only prove analyzable but can access aspects of the patient's unconscious that previously had been inaccessible. Typically, lack of awareness about the underlying feelings going on in the analytic relationship leads to collusion and acting-out. The working through of an enactment brings to the foreground these underlying feelings, which can have a positive effect on the analysis, creating greater therapeutic intimacy – as illustrated in the following clinical moment. Jacobs (2001a) highlights that the more obvious forms of countertransference are the ones usually discussed in analytic literature, stressing that it "is precisely those subtle, often scarcely visible countertransference reactions, so easily rationalized as parts of our standard operating procedures and so easily overlooked, that may in the end have the greatest impact on our analytic work" (p. 289).

While it is widely recognized that the awareness of countertransference can have many positive influences on the analytic dyad, the negative impact of unanalyzed countertransference is less often discussed (Jacobs, 2001b). One major consequence of unanalyzed countertransference is the analyst's engagement in an ongoing enactment with her patients. Jacobs (2001b) concludes that these enactments have a wide range of implications for the analytic work. Therefore, it is imperative that the analyst, as much as possible, become aware of the pervasiveness of countertransference throughout the course of the analytic relationship.

Many analysts have concluded that enactments are inevitable (Chused, 1991). Ideally, the analyst should not react outwardly when emotionally triggered by a patient; rather, she should treat those emotions as critical information and should use that data to help form her interpretations. Clinical missteps, or the inevitability of enactments, further intensifies the need to examine countertransference reactions in more depth and with more fervor. While enactments are not therapeutic in and of themselves (Chused, 1991), if addressed and analyzed they can deepen the analysis. One reason enactments can be detrimental as well as powerful is because they are "evocative of relationships with the primary objects" and therefore can greatly increase the "potential for regression [which] exposes the individual to dormant internal conflicts and the possibility of maladaptive compromise formations, laden with transference" (Chused, 1991, p. 617).

Chused (1991) distinguishes enactments from projective identification by stating that *"enactments occur when an attempt to actualize a transference fantasy elicits a countertransference reaction"* (p. 629; italics in the original). She highlights both the active and unconscious participation of the analyst in the dyad – underscoring the fact that the therapist is a full partner in the enactment. The enactment becomes a shared experience between the patient and the analyst and therefore holds less opportunity for "defensive denial, intellectualization, and distortion" (p. 617), which is one reason the analysis of enactments can be so rich. Chused cautions, however, that the analyst will likely resist a full understanding of the enactment because it is so laden with the analyst's own unconscious conflicts and motivations, which increase her anxiety and discomfort. Enactments, and the recognition of enactments, can be highly anxiety provoking for both the patient and the analyst (Chused, 1991; Jacobs, 2001a). Just as using a client's discomfort in a state of transference, rather than dissipating the tension, allows for greater insight (Ogden, 1986), so too exposing oneself and one's patient to the anxiety that comes with analyzing an enactment leads to deeper levels of understanding in analysis (Jacobs, 2001a).

In the clinical moment that follows, a series of countertransference enactments ultimately results in an extra-analytic encounter, with the patient coming face-to-face with the analyst's mother as the patient leaves the analyst's home office at the precise moment the analyst's mother is arriving. This is one of the varied ways in which extra-analytic encounters can take place. Sometimes, such encounters involve an instance when the therapeutic "frame" is *purposively* compromised, for instance, when a clinician accepts a patient's invitation to attend a meaningful life event. (In Chapter 8, the analyst considers the possibility of doing just that with her patient.) Extra-analytic encounters also occur *inadvertently* – chiefly in the form of chance encounters. For example, an analysand may learn something about her analyst in passing from an outside source. Alternately, the patient and the analyst might run into each other when the two are out and about.

In the following clinical moment, what had seemed like a chance encounter between the patient and the analyst's mother came to be understood – upon reflection – to not have been nearly as random nor as unavoidable as it first appeared, having been unconsciously orchestrated by the analyst as part of a string of countertransference enactments that proved messy and difficult to sort out; it was an extra-analytic encounter "with a twist." This extra-analytic contact had been orchestrated by the analyst, who came to retrospectively recognize the role she had played by her collusive participation in the event.

Some analysts fear that such encounters can irreparably damage the transference – rendering it unanalyzable to the extent reality interferes with the patient's ability to maintain her transference fantasies/perceptions. Many who have written about the subject discount this concern, arguing that the transference tends to be so durable, making it more likely that the perception of the analyst will bend to the transference beliefs during the encounter (e.g., due to selective perception) rather than the transference itself becoming substantially altered by the revelation of new data arising from the encounter. Ganzarain (1991) writes that during an extra-analytic encounter, "The analyst actually 'exposes' only a small fraction of the analyst's reality... [accordingly] the patient's transference will prevail and deform the 'real' meaning of such extra-analytic encounters" (p. 138).

Aside from concern about the prospect of disrupting the transference, analysts also worry that such encounters may strenghten the patient's regressive impulses to the extent the extra-analytic encounter heightens a patient's wish to have an outside relationship with the analyst if momentarely actualized when the two see one another outside the consulting norm. Analysis promotes the emergence of regressive feelings and impulses so that they then can be worked through in the process of the analysis. Strict maintenance of the frame reassures the patient that such impulses will be contained rather than gratified, which requires the analyst protect the patient as best she can from experiencing extra-analytic encounters of whatever sort. However, concern that such encounters might contribute to a therapy-endangering regression seems overblown to the extent such dangers are likely limited to patients who are more regression-prone and impulse-ridden – patients who may experience a crescendo of urges that proves difficult to manage clinically once the patient has experienced an extra-analytic encounter.

Patients typically wish to know more about their analyst, though they also fear that their curiosity may kill the cat to the extent that inadvertent disclosures issuing from an extra-analytic encounter prove more than the patient can handle. Beyond disturbing information being gleaned, extra-analytic encounters may either stir up incestuous wishes to metaphorically peep through the proverbial keyhole of the parental bedroom or stimulate the patient's wish to extend the relationship beyond the confines of the consulting room – beyond a relationship between a patient and an analyst. Such encounters can stimulate intense anxiety in patients who not only fear *seeing* the analyst outside the office, but also fear *being seen by* the analyst – seen to be acting in ways that reveal a different side of themselves than the one they had meticulously cultivated in session (e.g., a transferential fear of father's finding out what the patient had been up to when away from the father's watchful eye – Tarnower, 1966).

Extra-analytic encounters can affect the analyst just as much as they can affect the patient. How the analyst reacts when she encounters the patient outside the office, when she learns of an instance when the patient had watched her from afar or had inadvertently learned something about her personal life, must be taken into consideration since the analyst's reaction becomes an important part of the enactment, which cannot be properly managed unless these reactions are also considered. Analysts vary with respect to how uncomfortable they feel when caught off-guard by encountering a patient outside the office. McWilliams (2004), for example, writes that many therapists find out-of-office encounters with patients "very troublesome" (p. 167) – that therapists' worries about such encounters are "a significant unacknowledged stress for therapists" (p. 165) to the extent therapists liken this much dreaded experience to "a near death experience" (p. 165). While certain therapists may feel as McWilliams portrays them to feel, such reactions are unlikely to be as universal as her description makes them out to be. Strean (1981) concludes:

> Whether an extra-analytic contact is viewed as valuable or hazardous depends to a large extent on *how the analyst feels* about meeting his patient outside of the consultation room. If he is anxious that treasured transference and countertransference positions will be altered, if he is worried that he cannot contain regressive wishes in the patient *or in himself*, if he is uncomfortable in departing from his anonymous, unseen role behind the couch, then he will in all probability find reasons to explain why the meeting should be avoided.
>
> (p. 256, italics added)

The regressive wishes about which Strean is referring include "the tension between wish and prohibition" (Tarnower, 1966, p. 399) stimulated by the analyst's natural curiosity to see how her patient functions *outside* the treatment setting (Tarnower, 1966), which the analyst may nevertheless deny – to the detriment of the treatment. And, as with patients, extra-analytic encounters offer a chance not only *to see* but *to be seen*. An analyst may wish to expose the patient to reality aspects of her life, for example, to directly contradict the patient's negative transference beliefs that the analyst finds disquieting and unflattering, leading to the unconscious wish to disabuse the patient of such beliefs by confronting the patient with a reality that "says it isn't so." Naturally, a whole host of other unconscious wishes may also drive the analyst to not only wish for, but *unconsciously arrange for*, just such an encounter. Yet, if the analyst is able to contain the patient's regressive longings, and is able to process her own primitive mental states – which may include sadistic pleasure at exposing her patient to the extra-analytic contact – a rich resolution between patient and analyst can ensue.

The clinical moment

In our first consultation session, Susan – a woman in her late 50s, who is small in stature with childlike mannerisms and gestures – waddled like a duck into my consultation room. As she settled onto my couch, my eyes fixated on her black boots – the significance of which would only become clear as our work progressed. Throughout the first session, Susan maintained a penetrating gaze that I couldn't shake. Susan tearfully revealed that she was adopted and had a fantasy that I would become "like a mother to her." The patient was seeking treatment following the completion of her Doctorate in History after a ten-year course of study. She'd been unable to seek an academic appointment primarily due to symptoms of depression and anxiety, specifically around her "fear of rejection." She added, "Before I can work, I need to study my own history."

Susan's birth mother was a teenager who put her up for adoption shortly after she was born. Her congenital hip dysplasia made Susan initially "unadoptable." For the first several months of her life, the patient was shuffled from one foster placement to the next until she was finally adopted at 18 months of age. Her adoptive parents divorced when Susan was six, after which time she lived with her adoptive father and his newly reconstituted family. She had infrequent and inconsistent contact with her adoptive mother, whose job required extensive travel. She promised the patient that she could come and live with her once she got "settled," but this never materialized. While her adoptive mother remarried and got pregnant when the patient was ten years of age, the patient continued to live with her adoptive father until age 18.

Susan often referred to her "three mothers" (birth mother, adoptive mother, and stepmother) and the five different homes she lived in until age 18. Her experience of having three mothers, all of whom eventually abandoned her, had a "lifelong impact" on the patient. Specifically, her early traumatic history profoundly affected her subsequent object choices. She had been married three times, with her longest marriage lasting 14 years. By and large, her pattern was to choose men either who excited her but would ultimately leave her or, alternately, who would bore her, causing her to leave them.

Three countertransference enactments will be highlighted in the remainder of this chapter, the last of which involved an instance when the patient suddenly encountered a family member of mine, which will serve as the crux of the clinical moment.

Upon first meeting Susan, I noted that she appeared no more than 4'11" in height. Her tiny size was symbolic of her child-like state and narcissistic vulnerability. I wondered about whether she would be able to tolerate intensive treatment, and I further wondered whether she might "dump me" (turn the tables) just as she herself had been "dumped" by her birth mother and, later, by her adoptive mother. Susan seemed to desperately seek a mother who would love her and not abandon her.

The first countertransference enactment occurred upon opening the door for the second session; I could not remember the patient's first name. Perhaps I was in complementary identification (Racker, 1968) with her internalized mother(s) who felt ambivalently attached toward her. Or, perhaps the patient projected her attachment deficits into me, and I acted them out. I was struck by my lack of connection to her, and how early in the treatment I found myself engaging in a countertransference enactment. I later learned that her adoptive parents changed her given name and renamed her Susan at 18 months of age. My initial countertransference reaction to this tiny, odd, demanding, baby-like patient was to feel a strong pressure to take care of her mixed with wondering about whether I would want to keep her as a patient.

In this second session, Susan's profound pain of early object loss and internalized rejection were palpable as she relayed the story of having met her birth mother when she was 50 years old, stating:

> I left our last session feeling there may be a place in the world for me. It goes back to being adopted and feeling I don't belong in this world. There must be a parallel universe and this one was not mine… an unknown world for 50 years. Then I was born. Then I had a mother. As badly as it ended, it was really important to lay eyes on my [birth] mother with my cheekbones and my knees… No one can understand this if they weren't adopted. I did not exist. I was an undeveloped idea. My mother had given me up and my adopted parents "chose me" – the preferred language.

The unfortunate circumstances of her upbringing and her response to those circumstances severely impaired the patient's ego functioning, leaving her to rely upon primitive defense mechanisms. These circumstances predisposed her to experience complex emotional reactions to loss and, furthermore, contributed to her own difficulties establishing and maintaining a sense of identity. Susan's emotional states, cognitive functioning, and biological regulatory patterns were all highly symptomatic.

Susan's dreams in the early phase of the analysis were of maternal and erotic longings and they demonstrated a lack of self-regulation. Susan reported a dream:

> I shared a hotel room with a woman. I slept with her. I was fascinated with her and attracted to her, especially her long dark hair. Then, there was a small ethnic man. He was a bad guy. There was a conflict. I captured the man, and turned the table. I tightly wrapped him up, in a sheet, into a cigar... he got small. I was putting him in and out of the garbage disposal. If I hit the switch, he would die. I pulled him out. I was reminded that he had arms and legs.

The patient revealed her sexual fantasies of me. I understood her erotic transference as a defense against her maternal longings, and I said, "Your sexual longings are disguises for loving feelings. When you make contact with these feelings you wish to make me disappear." The patient was able to acknowledge her longing for a mother who cares for her and does not abandon her. I added, "Perhaps I am also the man (the analytic father) who threatens to penetrate your mind (unconscious) and then you wish to reduce my size." Susan recognized that she alternately needed to either sexualize me or violently destroy me, but found it impossible to see me as a mother who cared for her. Together, we explored her need to represent me as a man in order to dispose of me. Yet, when she recognized the arms and legs – the connection to me – she stopped the violent attack. Upon further reflection of this dream, I considered that perhaps Susan wished to annihilate the moving parts of me so I could not move away from her. At this point in treatment, Susan was becoming increasingly frightened of my autonomous existence because it underscored her fear that I could leave her just as she had been left countless times before – that being left was her self-defining destiny.

While all patients come to sense their analysts' souls, some patients more than others intuit aspects of their analyst's personal beliefs, customs, and core values. In this case, the "soles" of Susan's black boots became a symbol of her tendency to treat me sadistically. Susan "knew" early in the treatment that I am Jewish, and she would make derogatory remarks about, and offer sweeping generalizations about, the Jews, including their materialism, sense of entitlement, and greed. Susan talked about how Jews "stick together," and about how their sense of superiority helps promote their exclusionary ("clannish") practices that insulate them as a "tribe." Breaks in the treatment at the time of the Jewish Holidays prompted a transference neurosis whereby the patient experienced me going off with the tribe, leaving her to fend for herself.

At times, I had fantasies of abandoning my patient as she waddled like an odd duck in and out of my office wearing what I came to see as her black, Nazi-like boots. I was consciously aware that I was not fully able to take in Susan's profoundly impoverished early body-ego trauma, which echoed her previously voiced sentiment that only those who had been through what she had been through could truly understand her experience. Her early trauma of multiple rejections left her with such an overwhelming hunger for me that it often felt devouring – and likely contributed to times when I would slip into enactments characterized by her slipping out of my mind (much like in the first enactment previously addressed). I was not conscious at the time of the intensity of my rage toward her, whom I fantasized as a Nazi who wished to murder me, the Jew. Her *portrayal* of disdain for Jews was something I found personally offensive, stirring up sadistic impulses in me, which became the basis of the next countertransference enactment.

At a point in time when Susan was expressing both her deep longings for me to adopt her as well as her angry attack on the "tribe" that rejects her, I mistakenly left a $1,000 cash payment (from the patient I had just seen) lying on my ottoman in full view. I felt mortified by my carelessness and quickly scooped up the money while saying nothing. I then asked myself: What was the meaning of this unconscious countertransference enactment? I had not kept Susan in mind when I filled up the analytic space with valuable traces of my prior patient, just as her three mothers had also failed to keep her in mind, and as I had previously failed to do when I had not remembered her name. Because my countertransference was not conscious at the time, I was not available to be empathically introspective. It is noteworthy that the patient did not comment about the event, leaving it completely unexplored throughout the length of the session.

I have since thought about that countertransference enactment. I've come to recognize my need to be seen as valuable ("worth it") in order to counteract the patient's unrelenting and pervasive, devaluing assaults on me, the Jew. Her disparaging treatment of me was likely responsible for this *concordant* countertransference reaction[1] whereby her treatment of me effectively caused me to feel just as worthless as she felt. Not only was I trying to graphically retrieve my sense of worth by showing how much other patients valued me, I was also struggling with my impulse to punish her – showing her what I had that she didn't have.

The day following this enactment Susan reported the following dream:

> I am in a station wagon, or hearse. There was an open white casket. Inside the casket was a child wrapped-up. A woman was driving to dump the coffin and the child. I thought, "You cannot drop a live child into a hole and bury it." I gave the woman $1,000 to stop and turn around.

The patient said that she was the child whose hidden parts were trying to come up, but could not. She stated, "There are some things that I have tried to bury." I said, "Perhaps you fear that your deep longings and unwrapped feelings will be 'dumped' by me." Susan cried, and said, "I was dumped from birth." She then associated to the hearse as an ambulance. She said, "No one knew that my 15-year-old birth mother was pregnant until she gave birth to me on the bathroom floor. I came early... I must have been a bloody, tiny mess, anything but the white in my dream."

The secret pregnancy, and this tiny baby, born to a teenage girl, stirred up overwhelming sadness in the patient and in me. Susan identified the driver as her birth mother; she fantasized that her birth mother wished that she could eliminate (deny) this tiny, costly mistake. She told me that she still feared that I (also the driver) would disappear, dump her, and let her die. But, something new appeared: "The casket was open and it was white." Susan believed it was hopeful that she was also an adult, asserting her voice and protecting the baby. For the first time, she considered that I would not let her die, and that the analysis was helping to turn things around. I asked about the $1,000, and nothing came to Susan's mind, which was shocking given what had just occurred in the prior session. I suggested that acting as if she'd not seen the money was analogous to the way in which she keeps *herself* unseen – but, again, this train of thought developed no traction.

From the dream, I more clearly understood that her fear that I would disappear was not only a repetition of her early life, but also a projection of her existence having been kept a secret by her then pregnant birth mother. She needed me to feel her as loveable, adoptable, and not as a tiny, bloody, sick mistake of an infant. This dream and the dream work helped Susan face her traumatic birth history and framed the clinical moment that I will soon present.

The patient also touched something unconscious in me about which I was only dimly aware – the depth of my anger at the patient. Susan's attacks on the Jews (and on me) seemed to be driven by several possible motives: (1) to rail against our differences that kept us apart; (2) to attack her internal rejecting ("bad") object that was projected on to me; (3) an attempt to create a powerful engagement between us by virtue of her capacity to create powerful countertransference reactions in me. As I came to understand my countertransference more deeply, I became increasingly able to tolerate her wish to get inside my internal and external life. Furthermore, what I initially understood superficially to be the patient's racism and prejudice, I came to appreciate more accurately as her longing to be accepted – to be able to be a member of the tribe. This, then, set the stage for the third enactment that constitutes the clinical moment for discussion.

Invited commentator response I: Salman Akhtar

A few things stand out in this section of the write-up. The patient, a short-statured woman with multiple separation traumas in her formative years and with a congenital hip dysplasia (the degree of its "correction" is not revealed), is desperately hungry for attachment (in fact, belonging) and, at the same time, bitter and angry at what has been done to her. I became aware, as I read further, that the patient herself is identified with rejecting objects and quite ambivalent about caring and being cared for. She has been married thrice and divorced thrice; other relationships have also ended up as broken. And she entered treatment soon after finishing ("separating from") her doctoral dissertation. Exclusion and un-belonging are central themes in her anguished life.

I also became aware of the rapidity with which the patient develops transference, and the parallel quickness of the analyst's subjective turmoil. By the second session (!), the analyst has difficulty recalling the patient's name and finds herself reacting with "a strong pressure to take care of her [the patient] mixed with a wondering about whether I would want to keep her as a patient." The ambivalence of the patient has "infected" the analyst.

Soon after this passage, the write-up suddenly turns intellectual and jargon-laden. I found this section boring and unnecessary. Upon further reflection, I found something deeper here. It is as if the emotional intensity of the preceding passages was becoming too much for the analyst/writer and had to be interrupted by a detour into clinical diagnosis and ontogenetic formulation (referring to impaired ego functioning, her reliance on primitive defense mechanisms, and so on). Yet another feature of this experience was *my* disappointment and sense of rupture ("separation") from being raptly absorbed and empathically resonating with the patient–analyst emotional dialectic to being suddenly brought into a well-lit but cold classroom. The game of acceptance-attachment followed by anxiety-rejection thus got extended to include me!

Soon afterwards, the patient attacks the analyst for being a Jew and Jews in general. While this repeats the patient's pattern of seeking acceptance and rejecting it when it is offered, deeper technical issues are involved here. First, am I correct in assuming that the patient knew (could have known or surmised) that the analyst is a Jew *before* calling her for the very first appointment? If so, then the patient's choice of the analyst seems to have a dual agenda: first, a sadomasochistic agenda by which she will have a "suitable" person to rant against (sadism) and one to whom she, being ethnically different, will never "fully" belong (masochism); and second, a hyper-optimistic agenda by which her hate of the analyst and the analyst's "tribe" will be contained and absorbed by the analyst with utter equanimity and she will continue to be loved. These relational scenarios will need to be opened up sooner or later in the course of the treatment.

Another question pertains to how one views the patient's apparent anti-Semitism. Is it a pre-existing character trait, which might have to do with the destructive projection of her rejected and (more or less) deformed self? Is it a manifestation of negative transference (after all, each patient knows how to please and torment his or her analyst), and the anti-Semitic remarks reflect merely a "content of convenience"? Or is this hostility a defense against love (felt by the patient towards the analyst and needed by the patient from the analyst)? Clearly, more thinking is needed here, since this matter seems to be fueling the transference-countertransference fires. The patient makes derogatory remarks about Jews and the analyst experiences her as a Nazi, finds her "personally offensive," and more than once refers to the patient as "odd," as one who "waddle[s] like a duck." Hate is seeping into the relational matrix.

Next, the analyst reports her leaving a cash payment of $1,000 from the day's previous patient in clear sight of the patient under discussion. The analyst is mortified, but the patient makes no mention of it; in the following session, though, she has a dream where she (the patient) pays $1,000 to a woman hearse-driver about to dump a baby wrapped in a coffin. The question of technique that had begun arising in the mind is in a way answered, but allow me to elaborate upon the issue anyway, since it can lead to an interesting discussion of how we work.

What is the "proper" technical stance when a patient does not bring up some aspect of reality (in this case, the $1,000 lying on the analyst's ottoman)? Are all such omissions dynamically significant and therapeutically useful to explore? What if a patient, seen a day or two after 9/11, for instance, does not mention the national tragedy at all? Should the analyst introduce the topic then? I do not know what the "right" thing to do is, and, frankly, what might be right for one clinical dyad might not be so for another. Generally speaking, however, the following guidelines apply: the reality must be a shared one; conjectured reasons for the patient's omission can be linked to aspects of his or her childhood history and/or current transference configurations; the analyst finds himself or herself unable to disregard the omission, in part, due to the patient's unconscious but "non-omitting" sector of ego being split-off and deposited in the analyst; and derivative material (e.g., a parapraxis, strained silence, reversed associations, a dream) gives testimony to the unconscious activity of the omitted material. Since the patient brought up the previous day's omission in the form of a dream, it became possible to clinically deal with that omission.

The session continues

My home office is located in a detached structure on my property, and patients park in a tandem spot in my driveway. At the end of Susan's Wednesday hour, my parents unexpectedly arrived early for Mother's Day weekend in a black limousine, with six pieces of luggage. When my patient left her session, her car was blocked by the limo. I heard commotion in the driveway. I had to sit tight and wait to see how things played out, and it wouldn't be until the following session that I would get a chance to see how this event had unfolded. I felt responsible for the encounter, and I struggled to listen to the material as I worked to manage my anxiety and guilt over assaulting my patient's senses with the intrusion of reality as I had previously done by leaving a cash payment in clear view.

The patient began the hour by talking of her plans to move to a quieter location, with less traffic, 350 miles away. She then shifted to the traumatic dental work she had sustained during the past week. The drilling noises from the construction next door reminded her of the trauma she had endured. She reported numbness in her legs, shakiness, weakness, and light-headedness. We discussed her symptoms as being a somatic expression of the intrusive event that occurred at the end of the prior session, which the patient finds difficult to talk about. She then spoke of how she had felt cold and boxed in by the "limo" that pulled into the driveway behind her, interfering with her attempt to leave the session. I wondered aloud whether her feeling cold and boxed in might also have been a response to being exposed to events that left her feeling trapped. She responded by sarcastically referring to my personal life that she had been exposed to and was not a part of.

Susan went on to describe seeing a suitcase, an older lady, someone's mother, maybe my mother. She struggled to say what was on her mind, and then, in a raised voice, said that the event "left her breathless." She exclaimed, "It is so hard to be vulnerable, to depend on you when you have others in your life, a mother maybe, who you care for more than me." Susan acknowledged that she was also curious about the woman. She said:

> She looked like she comes from the old country, not a modern woman, an immigrant – who would wear a babushka over her head, a hardworking peasant woman. She seemed unwell. She got on your porch and stood in the shadow. She was leaning against the wall – maybe for support, just waiting. She started ringing the bell to the main house. She was just waiting to be let inside.

I found it hard to manage the guilt I felt. I commented, "This frail woman, barely able to hold herself upright. What was witnessing this like for you?" My patient, now angry, turned around and yelled, "You planned poorly! Was this woman your mother? I need to know!" I was silent, though I was very much aware of feeling pressured by her question. I did not want to respond concretely, but I did struggle with how to respond.

What would you have done under the circumstances? Might it have been helpful to clarify the reality, or would that have further traumatized the patient, burdening her with too much reality?

Invited commentator responses 2: Salman Akhtar and Anne Alvarez

Salman Akhtar

This scene involves the patient's seeing a black limo, six pieces of luggage, and "an older lady, someone's mother, maybe [your] mother," who sort of looks like "an immigrant woman." The following session opens with the patient's desire to move to a town some 350 miles away and with her recent "traumatic" dental work. These are clearly derivative references to what the patient had seen and experienced. She wants to leave the analyst; she feels traumatized by what happened the day before. Soon the material becomes naked. The patient asks, "Was this woman your mother? I need to know." This is followed by the analyst's posing two questions, I suppose for me. The analyst asks: "What would you have done under the circumstances?" *and*, "Might it have been helpful to clarify the reality, or would that have further traumatized the patient, burdening her with too much reality?"

Let me take one question at a time. Permit me also to clarify that I have *not* read the literature reviews that the analyst provided before beginning her case presentation. I wanted to experience the latter unbiased, even uninformed. That having been said, I offer the following response to the first question, namely, "What would you have done under the circumstances?"

Psychoanalysts who have home offices know (or should know) that this increases the chances of a patient inadvertently encountering a family member of the analyst. Moreover, the location of the house can itself reveal information about the analyst's financial status, resources, and talent (or lack thereof) for maintaining the exterior of the house, and, at times, even the analyst's ethno-political affiliation. A home office also demands greater psychological flexibility from the analyst, since his or her clinical and living areas are in close proximity to each other. The analyst needs to have stronger internal boundaries, since external boundaries are permeable under such circumstances. And the patient is affected by the sounds, sights, and smells of the home, imputing plausible and implausible meanings to them.

This is what happened here. The patient was exposed to the arrival of the analyst's family. Should the analyst answer the question in a straightforward way? And *then* explore its ramifications and transference implications? Should the analyst remain silent? Should the analyst say that she might (will?) answer the question ("Was that woman your mother?") *after* she and the patient have explored the patient's fantasies? Or should the analyst say, "It is not the actual reality that matters here; in the end, what matters is what you have made of what you saw and how it affects your feelings and attitudes about me and us."

I can see all these ways of responding to be applicable to one or the other patient. However, with this particular patient and with this particular situation, my preference is to respond by saying something like this: "Yes, she is my mother and in telling you this, I am aware that you might be deeply affected by knowing it, since the issue of having and not having a mother is so critical in your life's trajectory and in your feelings about me. I do apologize for having contributed to this intrusion upon our collaboration and feel badly about complicating things for you. But I am here, ready and capable of listening to whatever you have to say about it: good, bad, and ugly."

A look at the components of this intervention reveals that: It is validating a shared reality; recognizing the potential for its causing disturbance;

acknowledging the iatrogenic origins of this crisis; linking the occurrence and its reverberations to the patient's history and transference; and respecting the patient's dignity as an adult human being and therefore apologizing for the "analyst-caused" disruption. Vis-à-vis this last part, it is always important to keep in mind that while the analysis requires clinical "asymmetry," it does not give license to human "inequality."

The second question raised by the analyst is whether telling the "reality" would burden or traumatize the patient? I do not think so at all. I think telling the fact (that it was the analyst's mother) would preclude confusion, avoid "gas-lighting," and make the patient feel respected and not one to be excluded or feared. It is *not* telling that carries greater risk here. Not telling will hurt her where it hurts most: being excluded, not allowed to belong. It also can discourage her from "seeing" things around the analyst's house and asking questions in the future. Now, I am aware that telling the patient that the woman she saw was the analyst's mother will have its own consequences in affect, imagination, and in the patient's relationship to the analyst. The possibility of stirring up envy is great here. But that can be better handled if an act of deprivation (e.g., silence, not telling) is not superimposed upon an iatrogenic trauma.

Anne Alvarez

Dr. Barth asks us what we might have done in the session immediately after the one in which her patient had had her car blocked in the driveway and seen her mother at the door. She felt very pressured by Susan and asks if we would have answered whether it was really our mother. I think it can be a false dichotomy to think that we have only two choices at such moments: either to simply press for the patient's fantasy while making it clear that we aren't confirming or denying, or to go on concretely to clarify the reality. I think there can be a third range of choices to do with taking the fantasy seriously by imagining along with the patient (i.e., alongside the patient as it were) what might have been the case, rather than taking a position that places us on the opposite side of the fence, refusing to reveal something or, for that matter, deciding to reveal it. Nowadays, after the experience of working with neglected children, I probably wouldn't even remind them that I wasn't giving more details. So something along the lines of, "Well, you are assuming it probably was my mother so why don't we go along with that idea and see where it gets us?" Further along Dr. Barth says to the patient: "I didn't protect you and I unwittingly exposed you to something you shouldn't have seen," and that of course was the important thing to understand, and I think it helped. She also used the word "we" in her interpretation, and I think that may have helped Susan to feel invited into the tribe a little.

I have become interested in the issue of how we repair deficits, or to use Balint's term "basic faults," not only in the self, but in the internal object.

Susan really did have rejecting external as well as internal maternal objects, and she did, as Dr. Barth says, certainly have ways of evoking rejecting countertransference enactments. I shall return to that matter later, but for the moment I would like to raise the issue of how we can use a maternal countertransference to repair those deficits without appearing to make false promises of a kind of adoption or without breaking boundaries. The transference experience can be a healing one; the patient can begin to believe she has finally been welcomed into the analytic family, that you are going to stick with her and that she can't after all drive you away. The internal world can end up being different from the external and historical one, as we know. The analyst acknowledged in the second session after the car episode that she had disappointed her patient, the implication being that she wasn't looking after either her mother or her patient properly, and I think this helped. Sometimes, one can add something along the lines of, "It's hard for you to believe that I could care about both of you" (i.e., you [the patient] and my mother). But this of course depends on whether the patient is ready for a bit of hope or still needs more processing of deep disappointments. Another example, however, of possible new developments in feeling or dreaming of being a member of a family might be Susan's dream, after the second enactment (of leaving out the money paid by the previous patient), that she was using $1,000 to buy the safety of the little baby. Dr. Barth thought there was some hope in the attempt to save the baby and the whiteness of the coffin, and I wondered if we might think also of Susan being the one with the $1,000, not just as a competition with other patients, but also as an attempt at an identification with a sibling patient who knew how to fight to protect babies. Donald Meltzer pointed out that introjection and internalization are invisible processes, and you often don't know how they happen until afterwards, when you suddenly realize the patient is more thoughtful, or, I would add in Susan's case, begins to walk more gracefully or to care for her hair.

The session continues

I sheepishly said, "I didn't protect you, and I unwittingly exposed you to something you shouldn't have seen. I believe that to give you more details would not be useful; what is most important is to keep doing what we do."

It was nearing the end of the hour; the patient shifted from lying down to sitting up. She sat in silence. I waited, and then added: "Maybe it feels that you have to pack up and show me how hurt you feel." Tearfully, Susan responded, "It triggered my sense of not being a part of... of not having a mother. I still struggle with what it means to be a part of a family."

How does the analyst's way of handling the matter strike you? Would you be inclined to handle it in a different way? If so, how and why?

Invited commentator responses 3: Salman Akhtar and Anne Alvarez

Salman Akhtar

While the analyst acknowledged her responsibility in exposing the patient to something that she [the patient] should not have seen, she did not apologize, reveal that the woman was her mother, and include a mention of the patient's ontogenetic trauma in her comment. The patient's response to this intervention says it all. It was not in words: "The patient shifted from lying down to sitting up. She sat in silence." The change from words to action is suggestive of the depth of trauma experienced by the patient (remember a baby has only two ways of conveying what it feels: crying and bodily movement). Moreover, just the way one word can stand for another word, or one feeling for another, one action can stand for another action. Giving up the recumbent posture might have more meaning than wanting to leave. It might imply hitting the analyst, "killing" the analysis, competing with the analyst (you sit up, I sit up) in a motoric realm while wanting to compete in a withholding realm, and so on. To be sure, none of this can be interpreted at a time when the patient is so distraught, but keeping such possibilities in mind would enhance the analyst's empathy with the patient.

The patient then expresses that she feels "motherless" by the previous day's exposure *or* more likely as a consequence to the analyst's interpretation. In other words, she felt "un-affirmed," invalidated, and not properly "held." So when the analyst asks *me*, "Would you be inclined to handle it in a different way? If so, how and why?" I would like to refer her to the interpretation I gave above, including the rationale I provided for it. I must note though that I am quite senior in the field and now conduct analysis with more openness of heart and greater spontaneity of praxis. I might have been as "restrained" (which in this instance got translated into "depriving") as this analyst when I was younger and less experienced.

Anne Alvarez

Some of these thoughts refer to the overall picture of the patient's possible personality difficulties deriving from information we are given at the start and considering the fact of the three enactments. I was struck from the beginning by the analyst's description of the patient coming in "waddling like a duck" and by the list of diagnostic features in the initial Clinical Moment section. In an expanded version of her moment, which was subsequently eliminated to shorten the book, Dr. Barth referred to functions that were missing by using such phrases as "lack of," "inability to sustain," "premature," "impulsive," "refusal to assume adult responsibilities," and "unintegrated." My first reaction to this list was that Dr. Barth finds this patient pretty unlikeable: She conveys not much about the patient's suffering. In an earlier version of Dr. Barth's moment, she questioned whether the patient could "withstand the rigors of analytic treatment." My thought was that this is not a neurotic patient, need it be so rigorous? Is work with such patients all about helping them to face loss, or must we also help them to learn how to accept gain? Can this work still be psychoanalytic and true to our roots in searching for the truth? Later, we hear that the analyst is indeed concerned about why she cannot fully take in "Susan's profoundly impoverished early body-ego trauma." And even later, Dr. Barth is appalled by what she suspects is her sadism (not just her countertransference identification with the patient's rejecting maternal object) in exposing Susan to the sight of "the tribe" all together. I wondered if it might not be sadism in the sense of revenge for all the Nazi-like jibes about the Jews, but rather a naturally irritated sadistic response to something masochistic and addictive in the patient's complaints. Betty Joseph has written about the phenomenon she termed "addiction to near death" in a patient who was genuinely depressed and miserable, but could use this to drag others down into a despairing state with him which he then got a sexual kick from. She termed his way of talking at such moments "chuntering" (an English term), but we might in Canada or the US say that a child is whining, and a whining child can really get on people's nerves and does not evoke sympathy – indeed, it evokes its opposite. I am unable to tell from the material, and I might be wrong, but every time Susan spoke about her childhood and birth it was in generalities, and slightly repetitive ones, and we didn't really hear about individual painful episodes, although it sounded as though more of that developed later. In such patients who have real misery together with an addiction to it, we can usually tell the difference between the two in the way their tone of voice changes. It may be worth pointing out that Joseph used the terms "addiction" and "perversion" interchangeably in her paper, but I think there is a difference. We have learned this from autistic patients whose repetitive behaviors can move from being defensive or expressive, to addictive and then even on to perverse gratifications. The addictive stage involves a kind of bad habit where the patient is stuck in a response that need not necessarily lead to perverse excitement. In either case, however, it is helpful to note that the patient is not simply expressing a disturbing state of mind in order to communicate it, but is doing something else with it.

On a similar note, I was struck that Dr. Barth suggested that the sexual dream about her implied a disguise for loving feelings. That would be a relatively healthy response implying some degree of symbolization of the love. Hanna Segal has helpfully distinguished between material that is genuinely symbolic of something more fundamental, and material that is more concretely identified with it. Tustin similarly distinguished between a symbolic object and an autistic one and pointed out that when her little autistic patient constantly turned to his toy Austin car, it was not a symbolic substitute for Tustin, it was instead *of* Tustin. Indeed, it was better than Tustin. Winnicott's previous idea of the nature of transitional objects, halfway between the "me" and the "not-me," helps us to consider the idea of a continuum. In any case, I wondered if the sexual fantasy was not a defensive disguise for love, but rather something which had arisen in her personality more as a substitute for love, as it seemed she hardly knew what love was. However, this is all speculation, and the important thing is that things developed between patient and analyst way beyond these difficult exchanges. It is interesting that Dr. Barth points out that Susan needed her to bear the monotony of her helplessness, her frustration, and her feeling of rejection as it unfolded in the transference. This is an important reminder that not all repetition is perverse or addictive. There are simply years of experiences to process and thank God for psychoanalysis and Dr. Barth's careful work, which are there to enable it. There are no quick fixes for such patients.

My intervention

Susan arrived ten minutes late to her following session and was in a state of agitation. The drilling continued unabated next door. With sarcasm, she said, "Really?!" followed by silence. She continued:

> An intrusive, invasive presence… the woman in the driveway. It tells a story. I am thinking about your cancellation earlier in the month. I got it. Your father died. She may be staying for a while. There was a heaviness; it was not a happy visit. She is in mourning.

After silently reflecting, she continued:

> The driver was lovely. He was kind to her, kind to me. He was taking care of the woman. He asked me if you were in back. He moved his car right away. He was nice. The woman did not speak. She seemed kind of lost, sad. [Susan then blurted out]: Like, there is some family event that is a secret.

I was able to add, "We are back to your birth, a secret. From birth on I think you experienced yourself as an unwanted intrusion, not belonging." After a long pause, she tearfully said:

> That is me, the unwanted intrusion, born to a mother who gave me away. Then a second mother who left me with promises that I could live with her once she got settled. She went on to get pregnant, had two kids, and I never lived with her. And then my stepmother stole my father, the only parent who didn't give me up. It is pathetic. I am a bloody mess [referring again to her birth experience].

I continued:

I think the grieving woman in the driveway is the depressed, foreign part of you – the lost woman, the wandering Jew, who's suffering in a way that you are all too familiar with. Yet, somewhere there is also hope. And I think the hope is in here with me, in the analysis.

Following a brief silence, I asked, "Are you aware that you were ten minutes late to session today?" Susan, exhausted from the high emotion of the hour, said, "Uh huh. If I am gonna be vulnerable, then it is your job to provide a safe environment for that."

These two sessions left me feeling stirred up. "The woman" – as she had referred to her – was, in fact, my mother, and it was difficult to hear her being described as weak and frail through my patient's lens. It took a few moments to remind myself that Susan's transferences and her envy and jealousy of me for having a mother were operating in full force. Interestingly, my father was with her, yet Susan only had eyes for my mother – hardly a coincidence. At first, I had thought of this strictly as an extra-analytic encounter, a mistimed arrival, poor planning, not well thought out, a mistake that happened, grist for the mill – just like other chance occurrence-type extra-analytic encounters. Upon reflection, however – particularly given the history of my having engaged in two previous countertransference enactments – I began to question what role I had unconsciously played in allowing the enactment to take place. I considered whether I was acting out a sadistic attack by "introducing" the patient to another piece of my reality – a woman she likely would recognize as my mother – the mother that I had that she didn't have. Naturally, this was a more painful possibility that I would have to consider. To be caught engaging in a complementary countertransference reaction (acting neglectfully in league with how other rejecting figures in her life had treated her) was one thing; to feel I was striking back in self-defense in response to her attempts to "diddle" with my sense of worth (a concordant countertransference reaction) was another matter entirely – one that is harder for an analyst to "cop" to because it generally feels worse to be cruel than it does to feel neglectful.

Susan's organized state of mind was hiding a more disorganized, primitive state that needed to emerge – to come into full view in order that it could then be understood and worked through in the analysis. Susan initially found the emotional reality of her life too painful to endure, so she interacted with me in ways that effectively stirred up my countertransference reactions, which were strong enough and unconscious enough to go on to become enactments – feelings it took time for me to realize. In this mutual collusion between patient and analyst, I too had to face my own primitive states that contributed to an inclination to engage in not just one but a series of countertransference enactments. I was having some difficulty discerning what role my countertransference played until I became aware that I was recruited into playing the *complementary role of the abandoning mother*, a starring role in the patient's internal drama. I also came to appreciate that I played a concordant role by experiencing worthlessness just as the patient had experienced and had projected into me.

Susan needed me to bear the monotony of her helplessness, her frustration, and her feelings of rejection as it unfolded in the transference. Thankfully, she suffered through these enactments without becoming overly discouraged – without packing her bags, as she had been apt to do when she had been exposed to what was nearly more than she could bear.

Invited commentator's final thoughts: Salman Akhtar

The patient arrives ten minutes late for the following session and is agitated. She links seeing the older woman outside the analyst's home with a recent cancellation by the analyst. She figures out: The analyst's mother was in mourning because the analyst's father has died! She quickly moves on to praise the courteous limo driver (a man) who was very kind. But the older woman certainly appeared "lost" to the patient. The analyst says that sensing that the older woman was in need of care evoked certain feelings in the patient. The patient retorted by saying that some secret is being kept from her; she is being excluded for not being a Jew. The analyst links the "secret" with the circumstances of the patient's birth. *After a long pause*, the patient recalls all the mothers who had abandoned her. Soon afterward, the analyst interprets the "grieving woman in the driveway [as] the depressed, foreign part" of the patient. Meanwhile, drilling noises from the neighboring house (where construction is going on) impinge upon the session. The analyst brings it up, and the patient affirms its impact by associating to something being ripped apart and a sense of loss.

Reading this piece of clinical material made me feel that the analyst overlooked a murder (of her father) by the patient and the subsequent resurrection of the killed object (by invoking the tenderness of the limo driver). Why did the patient think the analyst's father was *dead*? Who arranged his death, if not the patient? After all, she could have imagined the older woman on the porch was sad for reasons other than death (e.g., economic reasons, or because the analyst's house was reminding her of her childhood home, etc.). No! She thought of a death and almost immediately began talking about the liveliness of the driver (undoing). As neither the patient's biological father nor her adoptive father appear at all in the patient's associations nor in the clinical write-up, we can assume her thinking that the analyst's father was dead was related to her own "dead father"! On the other hand, "killing" the father might be a displacement for wanting to kill the analyst's mother (out of envy). To be sure, these are speculations and could only be confirmed or refuted after gentle encouragement to the patient to associate to her thinking that the father was dead. That material is, however, not available to her because that investigative path was not taken by the analyst.

I read further. This led to my discovering that the analyst wonders if she could have been more careful in planning her parents' arrival and made sure that this accidental encounter with the patient could have been avoided. The analyst goes on to link this "neglect" with her earlier forgetting the patient's name and having the patient see the money given by another patient. "Was I being neglectful?" the analyst wonders. Then, in an act of great boldness, the analyst opens up the possibility that she might have been "cruel" rather than neglectful, "striking back in self-defense in response to her [the patient's] attempts to 'diddle' with my sense of worth." This is impressive indeed. What remains unsaid is that the analyst's "striking back" might have been in response to all the anti-Semitic remarks by the patient. One other possibility that the analyst might consider is that the exposure of the patient to the analyst's parents might be a genuine "accident." To trace its causation to the analyst's mind might be an omnipotent defense against the helplessness induced by such a randomly occurring problem. After all, not everything is subject to psychic determinism; the analyst must retain openness to considering *some* things as *not* psychologically caused.

Note

1 Racker (1968) identifies two types of countertransference reactions – "complementary" (whereby the analyst identifies with an internal object within the patient) and "concordant" (whereby the analyst feels as the patient themselves had felt). Of interest is the fact that my countertransference reactions were of both types.

References

Bohleber, W., Fonagy, P., Jiménez, J., Scarfone, D., Varvin, S., & Zysman, S. (2013). Towards a better use of psychoanalytic concepts: A model illustrated using the concept of enactment. *International Journal of Psychoanalysis*, 94(3), 501–530.

Chused, J. (1991). The evocative power of enactments. *Journal of the American Psychoanalytic Association*, 39(3), 615–639.

Ganzarain, R. (1991). Extra-analytic contacts: Fantasy and reality. *International Journal of Psychoanalysis*, 72(1), 131–140.

Jacobs, T. (1986). On countertransference enactments. *Journal of the American Psychoanalytic Association*, 34(2), 289–307.

Jacobs, T. (2001a). On unconscious communications and covert enactments: Some reflections on their role in the analytic situation. *Psychoanalytic Inquiry*, 21(1), 4–23.

Jacobs, T. (2001b). On misreading and misleading patients: Some reflections on communications, miscommunications and countertransference enactments. *International Journal of Psychoanalysis*, 82(6), 653–669.

McWilliams, N. (2004). *Psychoanalytic psychotherapy: A practitioner's guide*. New York: Guilford Press.

Ogden, T. (1986). *The matrix of the mind: Object relations and the psychoanalytic dialogue*. Northvale, NJ: Jason Aronson.

Racker, H. (1968). *Transference and countertransference.* New York: International Universities Press.

Strean, H. (1981). Extra-analytic contacts: Theoretical and clinical considerations. *Psychoanalytic Quarterly,* 50(2), 238–259.

Tarnower, W. (1966). Extra-analytic contacts between the psychoanalyst and the patient. *Psychoanalytic Quarterly,* 35(3), 399–413.

Chapter 5

Feeling Misunderstood Bilaterally

Susan Orbach

Editors' introduction

While countertransference enactments increasingly have come to be appreciated as an important therapeutic tool, their value lies not in the enactments' mere development but, rather, in the process of working through what has transpired – what each partner had contributed to bringing the enactment about. This process is illustrated in the following clinical moment – one in which the patient experiences the analyst as having painfully missed the point, leading the analyst, in turn, to feel misunderstood as if words were being put in her mouth. In the meantime, the patient himself felt that the analyst had misunderstood *him*. This clinical moment takes place midway through the second year of an analysis of a 45-year-old academic. Early in his analysis, the patient's limited capacity for self-reflection, his reliance on intellectualization, his disdain for the analyst's efforts to empathize, his dedication to the stance of reject-or-be-rejected, and his habit of dismissing clinical efforts to connect him with his feelings were experienced by the analyst as off-putting and frustrating. This clinical moment followed a new and notable period in which the patient's attitude appeared to soften and the beginnings of a therapeutic collaboration were emerging. The patient reluctantly told the analyst that he'd been awarded a prestigious grant. In response to the analyst's curiosity and interest, the patient became curt, accusing her of not understanding what the award had meant to him. Caught off-guard by his accusation, the analyst defensively lapsed into an attempt to convince the patient of her good intentions. Both patient and analyst were surprised and struck by the vehemence of this shared interaction. Through the participation in the enactment, the analyst made good use of their mutually shared vulnerability as they collaborated to capitalize on what proved to be a valuable clinical experience.

The moment in context (Richard Tuch and Susan Orbach)

Countertransference enactments offer unique opportunities to help the patient and the analyst learn more about themselves in an *experiential* fashion

(Chused, 1996). While such enactments have been classically conceptualized as resulting from the patient acting in ways designed to stimulate the analyst ` more inclined to think of enactments as arising from the process of dissociation. Dissociated parts are seen by such analysts as unformulated experiences that exist internally as "not me" aspects of the patient. These unformulated aspects can either be *recognized as existing* in the analyst (dissociated aspects of the analyst that can be effectively mobilized in response to the patient's need to externalize dissociated parts) or, alternately, *induced* in the analyst in ways that leave the analyst oblivious – "not knowing what hit her."

Writing from a more classical perspective, Chused (1991) writes about how progress in an analysis is advanced to the extent the analyst successfully resists covert pressure emanating from the patient to engage unwittingly in an enactment:

> When [the analyst] is expected to be prohibiting, threatening, rejecting, provoked, seductive or seducible, and [she] is not, when [her] actions do not fulfill transference expectations, whether [her] behavior pleases or disappoints, it will inform the patient about himself. And that is what analysis is all about.
>
> (Chused, 1996, p. 1070)

Enactments are not considered, in and of themselves, therapeutic until fruits of the enactment are recognized for what they are and translated into an understanding of the transference that, for a time, was relived rather than remembered. When the analyst becomes *unwittingly* caught up in an enactment, both she and the patient are uniquely positioned to capitalize on the opportunity to effect change that reaches beyond one's head and resonates in one's very bones. This, too, is what analysis is sometimes about.

Gabbard and Westin (2003) elaborate the concept of projective identification, thought by some[1] to be the mechanism of underlying enactments, as necessarily involving a "hook" (p. 477) within the analyst upon which the patient's projection can be hung – suggesting that the patient must locate something in the analyst *that is hers*[2] to make the projection "take." Accordingly, factors favoring the analyst's engagement in an enactment have much to do with a given analyst's inherent proclivities. An analyst who is particularly prone to narcissistic injury, for example, will be more inclined than other analysts to assume the assigned role of the patient's injured parent. Donnel Stern (2004) notes that "the patient cannot provoke such a dissociation if the analyst is not vulnerable to it" (p. 216).

The mechanisms thought to account for enactments differ depending on one's psychoanalytic perspective. Most schools of thought see enactments as the product of conflict that results in the repression of psychic content that becomes split off from consciousness in both analyst and analysand. This repressed/split off content gets projected into/attributed to the other. This content is *latently accessible* but remains, for the moment, inaccessible because of processes at work that keep the repressed content repressed, reinforced with the help of projection. Those from the relational school, by contrast, see enactments not as the product of conflict and repression but as the product of dissociation (Bromberg, 1998; Stern, 1997, 2003, 2004), which renders certain psychic content unthinkable – beyond access to the extent it is unformulated (has not been symbolized; Stern, 1997) – and is, accordingly, unknowable in the usual sense of the term. Stern (2004) suggests "that a significant part of the pain of human relatedness occurs because conflicts that might be actualized within us *are not*" (p. 229, italics added).

Donnel Stern (2004) believes that dissociation involves "the experience we never have" (p. 222). Dissociated experiences lead one to recognize one's own dissociated parts as they are *seen to exist in another*, which Stern refers to as "the interpersonalization of dissociation: the conflict that cannot be experienced within one mind is experienced across two minds" (p. 213). When working with patients who dissociate, pressure is brought to bear on the analyst to act in ways that help support the illusion that dissociated aspects of the patient exist in the analyst (and, potentially, vice versa). Stern argues that enactment is never *the result* of intrapsychic conflict; in fact, he sees an absence of internal conflict as one of the defining features of enactments, which results in a depletion of the self. Stern sees the working through of enactments resulting in a growing capacity to tolerate intrapsychic conflict by way of a process that helps formulate previously unformulated, dissociated aspects of one's experience. An *expansion of one's sense of self*, and with it a heightened sense of freedom, is in the offing – the result of a patient's heightened capacity to psychically tolerate and contain a greater portion of his lived experience, which heretofore had been disowned and experienced as belonging to another.

Of critical interest is the matter of how the analyst regains her sense of psychic equilibrium in order to regain her capacity to think psychoanalytically – the requisite experience needed to clinically capitalize on an enactment. Stern (2004) suggests this process is set in motion when the analyst is alerted to the fact that she'd been engaging in an enactment by the experiencing of strange affects – "the snags and affective chafings" (p. 225) – which alert the analyst to the fact that more had been going on at the time than the analyst imagined. "It was my clinical interest in those signs, my everyday devotion to the clinical task," he notes, "that eventually brought my own dissociation to light and allowed me to experience a conflict where none had been before" (p. 225).

Once the analyst begins to emerge from an enactment, resulting ultimately in her regaining her capacity to maintain multiple perspectives, she is on the road to being in a position to help the patient *formulate unformulated experience* so that he can then internally tolerate and contain "not me" parts that had previously been lived interpersonally. Bromberg (1998) believes that the articulation of understanding (interpretation) isn't nearly as powerful in resolving enactments as is the analyst's surviving the enactment by gradually extricating herself from it, which permits her to emerge as a subjective entity *separate and apart* from who the enactment had – for a time – made her seem to be. This requires the patient transcend his reliance upon the analyst as the one who contains the "not me" parts of his experience. Stern (2017) believes the resolution of an enactment does not take place through an articulable (intellectual) understanding of the situation but, rather, through a sudden alteration on either party's part in the way in which they view the other – a development that precludes them from continuing to see the other as they had previously seen them, which – by necessity – alters how they go about relating to the other. Put in other terms, an enactment yields to the widening scope of a patient's potential responses and capacities to connect at different levels with others as a result of alterations in the patient's view of others and his relationship with others. Stern makes clear that this is not a matter of an individual's purposely attempting to see things in a different manner; rather, it is something that "just happens" without intention or conscious, willful effort. A change in perception begets changes in the way in which one relates to the other, which, in turn, changes how that other responds in kind. We would say that a change in perception involves one's becoming open to seeing the other in an entirely different light – one that is less limiting.

Having outlined the topic of enactments, we now turn to a consideration of a particular type of enactment. While enactments typically involve the analyst's adopting and playing out a role in concert with the patient's transference expectations (in the classical model) or in keeping with the patient's need to locate disowned aspects of his experience in the person of the analyst (the interpersonal perspective), enactments can also come about when the analyst steadfastly refuses to play along with the role that she'd implicitly been assigned in accordance with the projection of dissociated aspects of the patient's self (refusal to "wear the attribution," Lichtenberg, Lachmann, & Fosshage, 1992, 1996). The analyst finds herself objecting to the role she's been assigned by the patient to play, the way in which she is being seen by the patient, or covertly how she is being asked to act. The analyst may find these requirements personally repugnant, out of line with how she likes to see herself and/or not in keeping with how she typically behaves. As a result, the analyst may react vehemently by "saying it isn't so" – which I (R.T.) equate (in volleyball terms) as a "block at the net" that prevents the blocking players from having to contend with the ball making its way into their territory. The analyst's refusal to play along thwarts the patient's wish, expectation, or need and runs counter to the patient's sense of reality – defying his belief of who the analyst is and/or who he needs the analyst to be.

What sorts of attributions might an analyst find personally unacceptable? By and large, most analysts pride themselves on their capacity to understand their patients on a profound level – believing that accurate and empathic understanding is *an* essential, if not *the* essential, mutative psychotherapeutic agent. As a result, many analysts are intolerant of the insinuation that they either do not understand a patient or, alternately, are failing to provide the requisite healing experience. The patient may complain that he feels misunderstood or otherwise feels the analyst's offerings of concern, attention, and so on are insufficient, bogus, "hard to buy," and the like. In this regard, sometimes an enactment is the result of the analyst's failing to wear the attribution – the analyst's refusal to "play along."

Let's consider an example that illustrates this point. A patient who had been in analysis (with a supervisor) for several years announces he wants to end treatment so that he can "get on with his life." In response, the analyst earnestly outlines the value of the patient's continuing in analysis. The following day, the analysand describes the analyst's efforts as "desperate," leading the analyst to admit that while she'd put considerable energy into getting the analysand to recognize there was more that could be accomplished by continuing the analysis, she herself would not characterize her efforts as "desperate." So here we have a compound clinical situation involving, first, the analyst's becoming drawn into an enactment that has her strongly advocating for the continuation of the analysis, and second, the analysand's claim that her efforts smelled of desperation and the analyst's defensive response to that claim.

Taking issue with the analysand's characterization of her as desperate falls into the category of the analyst's "failing to wear the attribution." The analyst's "no" could alternately mean "I've been caught in the act of being desperate and can't face the fact" (negation) or "I can't stand being seen in that light" ("I hate being portrayed as desperate"). In this instance, the analysand appeared to need to view his analyst as desperately wanting him to remain in treatment against his own self-portrayal as un-ambivalently wishing to terminate. The analyst "took the bait," resulting in her prematurely outlining the indications for continued treatment. In this fashion, the patient succeeded at externalizing an internal conflict by making it appear as if it were a conflict between him and his analyst. At the same time, he succeeded at wresting from the analyst a covert admission of her investment in him and the treatment.

In the clinical moment that follows, the analyst recognizes – in retrospect – how she'd become drawn into a defensive posture, insisting that her intentions toward the patient were noble and not – as he imagined – off-the-mark as he experienced them being. The analyst's protestation that she'd been falsely accused constituted an enactment not unlike what many analysts have experienced at one time or another as the two got into what Benjamin (2004) refers to as a "doer/done to" situation in which the two parties each insist that they'd been the one who'd been "done to" (e.g. misunderstood). This brief essay highlights the interpersonal approach to the handling of enactments, which is not the approach Dr. Orbach applied at the time but one she recognizes in retrospect may well have been a more ideal approach.

The clinical moment

A social science professor, in his late 40s and divorced, Dr. N often spoke bitterly of his ten-year marriage. He felt thrust into the roles of primary caregiver of his two children and household domestic. Returning home from work, his wife would be quite fatigued and remain unavailable to him and the children. He felt taken for granted, without any appreciation or recognition for his hard work. Even post-divorce Dr. N declared that his ex-wife continued to presume – with minimal notification – that he would take care of the children when it was not part of the regular visitation schedule. In addition, she would frequently make important decisions about the children without consulting him – despite their having joint custody. Ironically, it was because of one such unilateral decision by his ex-wife that I had the good fortune to meet Dr. N.

His ex-wife had contacted me regarding the possibility of their then preteen son beginning psychotherapy. It was clear during our first meeting that she had initiated this consult without informing the father, Dr. N, of her intent or action. After completing my assessment, which involved meetings with the son and both parents, I recommended a brief psychotherapy. The son's increase in anxiety appeared to be related to difficulty in adjusting to a new school. Following a two-month period of psychotherapy and parent work, in which I saw mother and father separately, their son seemed to be back on track. He no longer appeared stricken by an inhibition that had been accompanied by self-deprecating remarks.

Throughout my parent work with Dr. N, I found myself impressed by his intellect, concern for his son, and what appeared to me to be a "stuck-ness." He conveyed a feeling of hopelessness around his adult relationships, particularly regarding his ex-wife and his mother. When he was with them, he often felt misunderstood and unimportant. I grew to see him as feeling generally depressed and defeated.

Based on my impressions I queried Dr. N about whether he had ever considered engaging in his own treatment. Initially, he shared with me that where he came from, a working-class neighborhood, this was not something people usually considered; however, he was familiar with people in the academic world who were in psychotherapy. He seemed interested; I pressed on and recommended psychoanalysis.

I found it important to keep in mind that I initiated the idea of his treatment. Historically he was often the helper, the side dish, but never the main attraction. Could he allow himself to feel like the desired one? He also knew that I was training to be a psychoanalyst at the Michigan Psychoanalytic Institute and was receiving supervision. Therefore, he was chosen by someone in need, and that was the most familiar role to him. It also was the place he found himself drawn to repeat with the most resentment.

The ways in which Dr. N framed his difficulties were not quite the same as mine. I perceived him as a man who felt hurt, diminished, and emasculated.

This primary burden of self-experience led him unknowingly to seek out and repeat behaviors and negative emotions with others. I saw his feelings of hopelessness and depression as a shadow that hung over all his relationships. Dr. N, however, saw himself as being emotionally assaulted and undercut by others. He would wonder why he kept getting the short end of the stick and often adamantly declare that others constantly undermined him. For most of his life, he could not entertain the idea that there was anything he could do to contribute to a different outcome. He saw his despair as justified based on his past family experiences and current encounters. The world was predictably disappointing for Dr. N.

Dr. N agreed to the recommendation of psychoanalysis. His primary concerns focused around his mother and severely cognitively and physically disabled brother, barely a year older than himself. He experienced dread around his mother's expectation that he would have to assume full physical custody and care of his brother following her death. Though he was unable to imagine any other possible outcome, Dr. N was willing to explore this dread in his treatment with me.

Always feeling the outsider, Dr. N grew up in a working-class neighborhood with his disabled brother and parents. The guilt he experienced around being the healthy sibling was expressed through the many ways he spoke of himself as the designated "responsible one," his brother's keeper. He looked after his brother at home and at school and would intervene physically, if necessary, whenever his brother was bullied. Quickly surpassing his brother in all developmental abilities, he nonetheless grew up feeling incidental, second to his impaired brother and often invisible. His disabled brother was the focus of his mother's life. Dr. N felt that his independent abilities and talents were often ignored, if not downright discouraged.

He grew up in a home in which there were few if any books. He remembers his parents as leading a dull and unhappy life. It seemed to Dr. N that his mother took little pleasure in her role as wife or mother. She allegedly cooked the same meal every night of mashed potatoes, creamed corn, and meat loaf. His father, an unskilled laborer, died one month prior to the birth of Dr. N's first child and three months before Dr. N officially launched his academic career. He described his father as distant and self-absorbed and recalled that when he did have contact with his father, this would often result in an argument, like around eating dinner. He would have to sit there at the table until he ate the whole meal. Dr. N decided that this unappealing, unvarying meal was worse cold than it was warm.

When I met Dr. N, I could see that he was highly intelligent and driven to succeed; however, he often seemed puzzled and frustrated in his communication with others. Interactions with co-workers and family members often left him feeling misaligned because he would end up feeling misunderstood and confused. Growing up, Dr. N lived in a world within which he felt taken for granted, invisible, and unprotected. He in turn developed a self-protective shield that had a thin membrane. He experienced much frustration and pain in his attempts to consociate with others, hence his profession: "I do not need anyone."

Even though he agreed to the analysis, Dr. N often acted as if he was an unwilling participant and had a difficult time initiating the sessions. His associations could be difficult to follow, or he would push away my interventions when I thought I was connecting to what he was trying to say. Early on, I wondered with him if he saw my recommendation for analysis as something more for my own needs than for his. He denied this, but was able to verbalize his fear that in lying down he would not be able to defend himself. "I guess I think I would lose some edge. Like what if I really get into things and then the time's up?" I then wondered to myself about the fear he felt in finding access to his feelings about our relationship. What about his deep, seemingly untapped well of longing for love and connection, his fear of being overwhelmed by his own needs, and his wish that something could really be just for him? These wishes seemed to be walled off by the anger that arose around the possibility that his desires would be cut off and he once again would be left alone to suffer the humiliation.

In hindsight, if I had not been in training at the time, I might have reconsidered introducing the couch so early in our work. I think it is clear how difficult relationships were for Dr. N, due to his narcissistic wounds and feelings of inadequacy. Lying down may have increased his counter-phobic state, punctuated by his need to alienate and disunite the two of us. If he had sat up, I wonder if he would have had to fight me off quite as vigorously as he did. Sitting up, he may have felt like he could better preserve his sense of independence and equality and ease more gently into some of these distressing experiences of himself with me.

After about six months in our work together, I began to see glimpses of his ability to work more deeply. For example, Dr. N introduced his thoughts about the film *The Piano*. He described the confusion he felt around the female protagonist choosing the "aboriginal guy" over her husband. Furthermore, he could not identify with either of these men, and he thought it was so sad that the woman had to give up her finger. Exploring this further, Dr. N spoke directly to the fact that the husband had cut off her finger to silence her and constrain her. "But he was lost at that point. He could not possess her."

I listened to this material much like a dream. I silently speculated that he seemed most identified with the woman and wondered if he feared becoming too dependent on me and losing an intact experience of himself. My shared thoughts were: "It could be that your thoughts may relate to the hesitation you have around lying down on the couch and talking. This is a rather unique situation and I can see how you may have some worries about what could come up and the depth and breadth of the feelings that could emerge." Dr. N responded: "It's risky, maybe. Like with this film. Why wouldn't I see it again? Because I would risk feeling something and disrupt my pattern and that shakes everything up."

Dr. N often would invite me in only to then push me further away. I would think about who was the disabled: His brother, himself, or me? He presented small, painful pieces of his past and then would make sure that I knew I was unable to help him. For example, he once explained: "A couple of sessions ago you said something about how my being so accident prone may have been a way to get my mother's attention. Maybe, but I didn't tell you that she did not always take me to the ER. Like one time I got a chunk of wood halfway into one of my nails. No one could take it out. At the ER, a doctor decided to cut my nail open without anesthetic. Nurses held my hand down and he was whistling. I could tell that my mother took a certain degree of satisfaction from this. Other times she said my accidents served me right." He seemed to fear that I was setting him up like a lamb to slaughter.

In contrast to his distrust and resentment of others, Dr. N often found himself taking care of them. It seemed to be that this was the role he knew best and was drawn to repeat. Most notably, he had a difficult time creating boundaries for himself around the demands of his mother and brother. This contributed to the cycle in which he felt guilt, sacrifice, and then resentment. He could dutifully give, and yet was highly uncomfortable being given to. I think in our work he felt like he was again giving to someone: the in-training psychoanalyst. Though this was in part true because I did need him as a patient to complete my requirements for graduation, I also hoped to provide him with professional help through our work together.

Gradually, more moments occurred in which he could begin to consider that he had a role in how he experienced and reacted to events in the treatment and in his day-to-day life. For example, he could say: "I think I was defensive because you were seeing things only your way. That wasn't the way I was saying it. I caught myself doing this at a meeting. I was in academic mode and halfway through my lengthy explanation there were many questions. I said let me finish talking. I felt irritated, like I was not getting heard out. I recognize that I get defensive about not being understood."

Dr. N struggled with his attempts to understand the feelings or motivations of the actions of others. In our work, at times he seemed oblivious to my possible reactions to him and his actions. One time, he failed to arrive to a session that occurred early in a week prior to my vacation. I called him and left a message letting him know that I was wondering where he was. I called because I thought it was important for him to know that he was not invisible to me and that I did think about him when he was not there. We had another couple of remaining sessions prior to my actual departure. He did not return the call but did arrive on time for his next appointment. It turns out that Dr. N had arrived at the wrong time, earlier on the morning of the missed session; however, he had the thought that maybe I was on vacation already. Though he had realized he had arrived at the wrong time once he got in his car, he did not return at the expected time or return my call. He said that he did not know what to do.

At this point, he could begin to see some connection between his missing the appointment and my upcoming absence. I encouraged further exploration, and he could tell me he did not imagine that people cared about him or thought about him when he was not around. I asked him what it would be like to know that I or others in his life did care and missed his presence. In his somewhat enigmatic way, he said: "If I experience openness that would mean that I would be honest and aware of all the things that are inside and letting the skeletons out of the closet." I listened and wondered with him: "To think that I care about you would mean we had a relationship. Possibly you fear that you could feel pain and disappointment around my going away. This allows for the possibility of your feeling at risk for repeating what you have had with your mother and ex-wife."

Around the middle of the second year, Dr. N more frequently appeared to soften, and our work together, at times, felt more like a collaborative enterprise. He was able to identify feelings and could share some of the more vulnerable sides of himself. I understood some of this change as having been facilitated by the many enactments that had transpired. The enactments resulted in what felt like a more authentically mutual emotional connection.

Toward the end of his second year of treatment, the clinical moment ignited around his reluctantly telling me that he had been awarded a prestigious grant accompanied by a monetary sum. In response to my curiosity, accompanied by my undeniable display of interest and pleasure, the patient became guarded and curt. He said: "Others are excited but for me it is just okay." He then explained that some of this money would compensate for his lower salary, since he had resigned from an administrative position the previous year. I had not known that his salary had been decreased, and I said as much. He then became even more guarded and visibly annoyed and said tersely, in an accusatory manner, that the "award is not about the money."

It felt like old times, and I asked with exasperation: "What's going on here, what just happened?" He then said: "I don't know, it is different. I suppose I'd tell my mother and it wouldn't mean anything to her. I don't think she would understand what I'd be happy for." Then I stated that he did not seem to think I was getting it either. To that he threw out: "Well it is not only about the money!" Awash with feeling misunderstood, guilty, and the bad one, I found myself caught up in my own need for him to see me as having only good intentions toward him. Feeling accused of something that did not belong to me, I was trying to convince him that my interest was not in the money. He was determined to convince me that my interest in him was motivated by something superficial and how I could not really know him or what is important to him. My part of this enactment involved trying to convince him, with some fervor, that I was being falsely accused of having less than noble intentions. After three or four volleys, I was better able to access what this accusation had triggered in me and then regain my ability to think more cogently. I could see that I had been identifying more viscerally with the patient's longings and fears of rejection.

Invited commentator responses: Andrea Celenza and Donnel Stern

Andrea Celenza

Enactments used to be viewed as bad things, unfortunate moments in a treatment where the analyst went off-game. Now we know they cannot be avoided and may even be useful if handled with care and humanity. I intend to elaborate this understanding further, not only by normalizing enactments as part of the ongoing psychoanalytic process, but as representative of a good fight, one long suppressed or in some inchoate, unpotentiated state that if actualized and metabolized can have strengthening effects.

What are actualized in enactments are those selves or potential selves that are forbidden to be realized, "bad" aspects of a self not yet represented or formed for fear of its potential strength, aggression (or other passions) that are the basis of its expression. This sense of oneself (and it's only a sense) is dangerous, prohibited, or desires something threatening. Yet these parts of the self relentlessly push to be realized because they are also (unconsciously) precious, held in tight embrace and guarded with possessive jealousy, despite being walled off or left unpotentiated in some unformulated haze. As patients, this is the dreaded fight we itch to provoke, yet we feel overwhelmed in its midst. This will be an intense fight, *excessive*, spilling over in ways that prompt the analyst to react with equal intensity and lack of poise. Yet if we dare to risk it, we have the possibility of gaining access to sources of inner strength, deep passions, and, not least of all, a pathway to becoming whole.

From the analyst's perspective, there is no perfect way of handling an enactment. We are taught that there will come a time when we will be the recipient of projected affects that feel dangerous, intolerable, and forbidden to the patient, maybe even to ourselves. We will fight back in a kind of "No, you! No, *you!*" kind of interchange. The analyst's first task is to sort out what belongs to whom and to own what is ours. Inherent in this sorting out is a deft redistribution of introjections and projections (from both the analyst's and patient's perspectives). This part, the art of analytic work, identifies these affects in ways that are not humiliating to us or to the patient but are humanizing. Phrases such as, "Of course you want to kill your brother," or "Of course you want to actualize your dreams," come to mind for Dr. N in the present vignette.

Yet, as analysts, we always look back upon an enactment with regret, wishing we hadn't exposed our vulnerability with such reactivity. Maybe there is a useful distinction here between the analyst's *reactivity* versus *responsivity*, the latter characterized by reflective, equanimous poise. The analyst in this clinical moment wishes she had not reacted so adamantly, revealing to Dr. N her dread of him seeing her in a bad light. It is so very human to react with a bit of defensiveness, especially given that vexing grain of truth in Dr. N's accusations. And we all want to be the good object, appreciated for our kindness and empathy, now, always, *forever!*

John Gunderson (1995) studied effective outcomes in long-term psychodynamic treatment of borderline patients. (This is not to suggest that Dr. N is borderline, but to generalize from Gunderson's results in a way that I believe is universal.) He utilized a wide range of therapists in his study, from trainees to highly seasoned psychoanalysts. Surprisingly, he found the best outcomes came from treatments where the therapists were trainees! There was a biphasic trajectory in these treatments where the first phase, spanning two to three years, can only be described as chaos. Lots of acting out, symptoms worsened, patients needed to be hospitalized – enactments galore. Then things calmed down, and gradually, the patients began to accept the limitations of their therapists and the limitations of reality. And they got better.

When these trainees/therapists were interviewed, they all looked back on the first phase of chaos with much regret, saying they wished they had set limits sooner, had taken better control of the treatment, and had made more pointed interpretations. In short, they wished their treatments looked more like those of the seasoned analysts – prettier, more reasonable, fewer enactments. But Gunderson was not convinced that a more ordered treatment would have led to better outcomes; indeed, his study reflects that it probably would not have. The implication is that there is something important in the tumult.

I've written extensively about Michael (Celenza, 2014), a patient whose analysis took a decidedly salutary turn after a vicious and painful episode in the fourth year of treatment. The enactment revolved around Michael's revelation of a secret fantasy to stab me repeatedly with a knife so that I would plead with him to stop and, most importantly, express my need of him in an intense state of bloody helplessness. I became alarmingly afraid of him for several weeks (an eternity) and felt acutely threatened, imagining him stalking me (he wasn't). Looking back, I could think of many things I might have said when he initially revealed this frightening fantasy to me, words that completely eluded me at the time. Something like, "Yes, we want to kill the one we love who will not return that love." Or, "Yes, we want to inflict the pain we feel onto the one who causes it in us." Would this have helped at the time? I have come to believe it would not have. I think Michael needed to see me overwhelmed. He needed to see *me* need *him*. If I had not been overwhelmed, I believe he would have had to up the ante. Another patient accuses me of not caring, being oblivious, then tells me not to take it personally! But these are personal moments; we are in these dyads mutually, authentically. It is a personal relationship at the same time that it is professional and asymmetric.

So the question is not how to handle an enactment *expertly*, as one would in retrospect, but how to have your authentic, experiencing affective self converge with your asymmetric analytic stance. How can I use my full self, my attuned affective engagement to inform my understanding of the patient so that together, he can more fully experience himself? Perhaps responsivity will combine with reactivity in these moments.

Dr. N is in the process of disabling himself. It is as if he is a character in Kurt Vonnegut's (1965) novel, *God Bless You Mr. Rosewater*, where a community lives under the belief that everyone should be equal. Those who were born with advantages wear weights commensurate with their talents. Ballet dancers are hamstrung by heavy blocks of lead that impede their arabesques. In Vonnegut's alternate universe, this is as it should be.

But Dr. N cannot help but feel gypped. He projects his anger onto the outside world and experiences it (and those who populate it) as stealing his talents from him, disabling him. In this way, he externalizes his agency, his authorship of this particular scene. Even though he agreed to psychoanalysis, for example, he acts as if he is an unwilling participant. He complains of others' imposition on him, yet this way of feeling put upon is a necessity – it holds him in. He fears his agency because if he were to embody his talents, he fears he might surpass his brother or provoke his envious mother. He colludes with his unconscious commitment – enjoying his ambition is strictly prohibited.

Any well-meaning analyst is bound to encourage Dr. N's growth, the expression of his dreams and the actualization of his desires. But how is he to allow this? He cannot have his analyst reflect enjoyment in his ambition or compliment him on receiving an award, for example. Ambition is dangerous. Perhaps there lurks a fear in his unconscious: If I exist, I could murder. Or, the other way around: I strive, (therefore) I am... bad.

As I mentioned, the bad self is not only private, a secret, it is also precious. Dr. N's world is populated with thieves, and so he is forced (in his idiom) into a self-sufficient defensive organization where he must protect and hide his bad, striving self from the light of day, lest the fruits be stolen from him.

Such is the nature of transference, that great big telescoper of time. The retranscription of memories is constituted by wishes and dreads – not veridical in the sense of a replica of the past, but rather made up of scenes within a much longer play. There and then is now and here. Dr. N might say, "I protected my brother from bullies. Now, I protect [my disabled self] from the bullying outside world. [That's why] I feel emotionally assaulted and undercut by others, constantly undermined."

"A man...is born and it is as though he has fallen into a sea, a dream," Stein advises Lord Jim (Conrad, 1900, p. 301). We enact scenes as acts from within a lifelong play. Dr. N is trying to communicate something about what happened, what *is* happening, how he feels immersed in a repetitious scene based on a script he is unconsciously writing but does not yet know.

Enactments help us see what the scene is about. At the same time, we need not get sidetracked, tempted by the siren song of some reality level, of the need to avoid being the bad object. The bad object, indeed, is part of the scene and has a crucial role within the play. This is what psychoanalysis has to offer: Actualizing the bad object as a character in the scene, externalized, the bad object within, the bad self within, momentarily ascribed to the other.

In retrospect, the author questions the use of the couch so early on in the treatment because, she wonders, perhaps Dr. N would not have had to "fight her off so vigorously." But was the fight a bad thing? Is it not a scene, a fight within himself that he needed to actualize? What if the money *is* part of his striving, despite his negations? What if he wants to make money from this prestigious grant in addition to the recognition and elevation of his career? Is this part of the bad self he might need to project onto his analyst?

Maternal envy is tough to metabolize – to recognize the envious, potentially destructive mother makes the world pervasively unsafe, the ground beneath one's feet unsteady, about to split apart. Worse, no one will come and rescue him, as Dr. N's father stood by or was absent, then died. Dr. N tells how he experienced accidents construed as his fault; he sensed his mother's satisfaction in his physical pain. Did she want him disabled? Did she disable his older brother? After all, it was her body that produced the disability; it was his brother's life that disabled his mother and caused her to want to diminish Dr. N as well. It is no wonder he felt the need to hide, to wear an invisibility cloak. We cannot know what really happened, but this is the internal world in which he lives.

The analyst in this clinical moment interprets Dr. N's experience of her as a repetition of his relationship with his mother, directly identifying the analyst's seeming lack of appreciation in just the ways he described his mother. No doubt these interventions helped him gain perspective on the there and then. What gets lost, however, is the theatrical/dreamlike way in which he constructs his narrative of his mother – was she like that or did he construct her that way so as to justify his remaining invisible? This is a fight he never had with his mother… Now he is having it with his analyst and there is more to learn.

Dr. N is dancing the dance he prompted with his mother just as she led him in mutual rhythm. The analyst responds by differentiating herself from Dr. N's mother, as if to say, "I won't dance that dance with you." This is the co-construction in the present when he says, "It could be something about wanting to keep it to myself." In other words, this is a dance I can't risk to dance. This is a solo, not a duet.

To me, this is a tango that is as yet unfinished; there are steps still to be learned, discovered, and co-created. I believe there are enactments yet to come and if all goes well, the two will fight the good fight.

Donnel Stern

Enactment concerns the part of subjectivity that has been dissociated, and that is therefore not organized as part of the self, but as unformulated experience. Unformulated experience is a vague "something," a global, affect-saturated, non-ideational state. It is potential experience – the source of what will become consciousness; its form is not entirely predetermined, but shaped partly by the interpersonal field within which it is formulated. Because dissociated experience has no symbolic representation in the mind, it can come to clinical attention only through enactment – which makes enactment a crucial part of treatment.

Subjectivity is dissociated when its acknowledgment – its symbolization – would require the acceptance that one is not, in some vitally important respect, the person one feels oneself to be. Enactment, in other words, occurs to protect one's ongoing sense of identity, of being recognizable to oneself (Philip Bromberg has made this point well).

When the interpersonal field threatens to compose itself in a way that would bring not-me into awareness, forcing acknowledgment that I can be something that I must not be, what do I do? I enact. I treat the other person as if *they* are whatever it is that I must not be. And often enough the other person – generally the analyst – takes on this reciprocal role for unconscious reasons that it is then the analyst's responsibility to sort out.

Shame is the affect that generally accompanies being unexpectedly forced to acknowledge that you are something you can't tolerate being. When an enactment is breached, it is because the patient can see and feel that the other person – the analyst – is not reacting in the way that originally made it impossible for the patient to acknowledge not-me in the first place. That is, the patient is not humiliated when he expects to be (without even knowing that he expects it); he does not face the criticism he thinks is about to come (without realizing he thinks it); and so on. But the analyst cannot do this in a planful way. Interpretation just doesn't work when you're dealing with psychic states that haven't been symbolized, because while there's "something" there, the something is not recognizable. The new perception of the other that breaches an enactment must be authentic and personal.

With these thoughts in mind, I turn to the material.

Let me say at the outset that understanding situations like this requires a close acquaintance with the affective atmosphere of the session, the kind it is not always easy to create even in doing supervisory work with the treating analyst. And so what I say will have to be guesswork. I will give myself a freedom I don't take as a supervisor to imagine both the clinical situation and the patient's history. I don't claim that what I am about to say is accurate in factual terms, but I do hope it serves to illustrate my point of view.

There is certainly a convincing source of shame here, a not-me. It is the patient's narcissistic pleasure and excitement about the award of his grant, and especially what we might imagine as his wish to display his accomplishment for his analyst, and his hope for her appreciation and admiration. To be excited about his accomplishments is, to him, selfish and despicable, because such a feeling implies to him a disregard of the privations of his mother and brother. Wanting the analyst's appreciation and admiration would be even worse, threatening catastrophic shame. I imagine the part of the patient that harbors these wishes to be dissociated: He simply cannot tolerate being such a person.

But of course the patient is far away from "knowing" this, partly because he obscures it by enactments such as the one described in the text. By accusing the analyst of being too excited about the grant, and then too excited about what he claims are the wrong things (the money), the patient avoids the whole scenario, especially his wish for the analyst's admiration: It's as if he were saying, "*I'm* not shallow; *I* don't lose perspective and get caught up in these superficial considerations. *You* do."

Now let's consider the other side of the interaction: the analyst's part. In what way did this analyst play a reciprocal, dissociated, interconnected role? How might we conceptualize her contribution to the maintenance of the underlying dissociation? How is this a *mutual* enactment?

As I began to think about these questions, my first inclination was to ask myself whether there might be some aspect of the analyst's positive response to the patient's accomplishment that was problematic. But what could the analyst have done about that? Nothing. Receiving the grant *was* a significant accomplishment, after all, and so it would have been disingenuous for the analyst to pretend otherwise. In the same way, while of course the analyst didn't need to make a point of being impressed, it would also have been disingenuous for her to actively pretend that the patient's accomplishment meant nothing to her.

No, in order to understand the enactment I think we need to look at responses that the analyst didn't have but could have had. And to do that, as is so often the case, we need to reimagine the nature of the patient's emotional impact. How might the patient have affected what the analyst could see and think? What, exactly, *couldn't* she think? What might the way he treated her have encouraged her to dissociate?

The important thing seems to me to be this: During the time of the enactment, the patient talks and behaves as if the analyst's involvement and excitement about the grant cannot be a genuinely affirmative thing, as if this part of the analyst's reaction can only be superficial and somehow selfish. The patient treats the analyst, in other words, as if her view of narcissism is as limited as his own. (*I'm* not shallow; *you* are.)

Why do I describe this view of narcissism as limited? Because the assumption seems to be that narcissism is, and can be, nothing but an indulgence. This is the patient's assumption, and he has influenced the analyst to think in the same direction, but she doesn't realize it. He has treated her in such a way that she has lost track of the possibility of a different view. He has made her defensive: She needs to deny that she is superficial. She seems to take it for granted that the only alternatives available to her are to agree with the patient or to disagree with him, and of course, given those alternatives, she disagrees.

That, from my perspective, is her unconscious participation in the enactment: She does not say, and apparently does not even think, about a different and more commodious view of narcissism, one in which it would be perfectly acceptable for the patient to take pleasure in status and money, and for the analyst to share this pleasure. From my perspective, the analyst is vulnerable to this effect on her, to this kind of unconscious participation and the defensiveness she feels, for reasons having to do with a vulnerability about the role of narcissism in her own life – a vulnerability that is very common in our culture. Many of us – maybe most of us – would be vulnerable in exactly this way, especially in the face of an attitude like the patient's.

Now, I have also been invited by the authors of this chapter to comment on what might be done about the situation we are discussing. How might I respond to this enactment? Well, that would entirely depend on my experience of the affective part of the relatedness between the patient and me, and on the thoughts that were available to me on the basis of that involvement. Let's say I began, as this analyst did, by responding defensively to the patient's subtle accusations of my shallowness. Let's say our interaction went along whatever lines developed from that kind of relatedness, as did this analyst's. But let's imagine that I am also able to think to myself, "What's going on with this guy? How come he's being so tough on me? Wait a minute! He's being tough on himself, too, isn't he? And what about my reaction to my own self? How come I'm being so critical of myself?"

Which is to say, let me imagine that I begin to feel an empathic appreciation of the patient's rejection of the narcissistic pleasure he might have taken for granted. If I felt that way, I might find my way to a perception of the patient as not so much a harsh and tough-minded accuser but as someone who unnecessarily deprives himself. If I did find myself with this new perception of him (and I could not control having it – it would "appear" in response to my questioning of myself), my imagination is that it would come to me, as these things usually do, as a new sense about him, a psychic picture of him – what I am calling a new perception. Also, I would have a new perception of myself, because my capacity to question my defensiveness would lead to the disappearance of that feeling, and its replacement by a greater acceptance of admiration for my patient. My sense of myself, of the patient, and of our relatedness would be changed forever – by which I don't mean that I would always respond consciously to these particular self-states in either him or me. No, I mean that I would forever be living with the sense of a man who I knew *could be that way*. In the same way, I would know, better than I did before, that I *can be that way*, and that we can be that way together. In the breach of an enactment, it is not only the patient who changes.

What would I actually do or say? Well, it seems to me that, once the relatedness shifts in the way I have just described, the most significant aspect of the therapeutic action has already happened. Without conscious intention, just because I see him differently, I will now treat the patient differently than before, and in response he will feel differently than before. But memorializing the change, and giving voice to it, are important, too. They reflect the new capacity to think about something that has been outside the range of thought up to now. And so I might say something like the following:

> You know, the way you're talking to me makes it sound as if taking pleasure in your accomplishment – either of us taking pleasure in it – would be a bad thing: shallow, superficial. As if to feel that way would somehow compromise you, or me, or both of us. Better we should keep a distance from it.

Note that I'm not suggesting that the analyst has to get deeply involved in what, from another point of view, would be called defense analysis. I'm content to make an observation about the nature of what's transpiring between us. I don't want this to become intellectualized.

In this particular case, I'd probably add something at this point about my speculations about the patient's history – because sometimes enactments reveal history, just as history can contribute to a grasp of enactments. In this instance, I'd use the history to make reference to my part (the analyst's part) of the enactment. I might say something like this:

> I noticed that for a few minutes there, I seemed to be prone to your view of being proud of accomplishment. I think that, without realizing it, I was buying into that feeling that it's shallow to feel that way. It made me defensive when you characterized me that way. I think that the way you spoke to me influenced me in that direction – you suggested it, and I responded to the suggestion – no doubt for reasons of my own.

Perhaps I would continue with something like this:

> Here's what I'm thinking: Just as I didn't question (to begin with) why you seem to assume that enjoying your accomplishment is a bad thing, your mother may not have questioned it, either. I don't necessarily know what she thought about you being proud of yourself, but I do have a pretty good idea that, whatever else could be said about her involvement in that part of your life, there's one thing she didn't do: she didn't take you aside and explain to you that you should feel free to enjoy your accomplishments without having to feel that they took something away from her or your brother. She could have tried to make sure that you felt good about your achievements, just as I could have. If you agree with me, maybe we can ask what that was like for you with your mother, and what it was about.

What I'd be hinting at here is the possibility of the mother's envy and/or the effects of what might have been an understandable, but overly protective, involvement with her disabled son. And I'd want the patient to understand my part of the enactment – which I would understand to be the absence of my awareness of the ways in which narcissism can be joyful and affirmative for all concerned.

As work on the enactment unfolded over time, I think I would begin to imagine a future in which the patient could feel more freely, and with less of a sense of selfishness and superficiality, his wish/need for approbation, pleasure, and pride from me, his analyst/mother. Over time, he might become angry with his mother for stifling him (if that seemed to be the case), and with me (the analyst) for whatever discouragement about narcissistic pleasure I contributed via my defensive enactments in the analytic relationship. I would hope for a freeing up of all his relationships as he became less worried about spontaneity. I am imagining, given the patient's apparent success in his work life, a future in which he could allow all kinds of events to evolve more freely between himself and others, because he would be less worried about being surprised by reactions from others that would threaten him with a flood of narcissistic feeling.

The heart of the therapeutic action would have taken place, though, not in all these interpretive imaginings, but in the moments when the patient had even a faint wish for the analyst's excitement for him without sensing an accompanying reluctance on the part of the analyst to offer it, or even a whiff of disapproval from the analyst of the pleasure the patient might take in it. The analyst would be able to participate in these healing moments only when her part of the enactment – her unconscious, defensive complicity in the judgment that narcissistic pleasure is selfish and superficial – became visible and thinkable in her own mind. And this enactment would need to take place repeatedly, over a long period of time, each repetition requiring a new breach of the dissociation, accomplished by a fresh approach to the same dilemma, but never with the same difficulty as the first time.

My intervention

I responded by stating that he was "not allowing me to understand what this award really means to you. I believe you are placing me in the role of your mother. You see her as unappreciative of who you are and what you have accomplished. I am actually the opposite of the way you describe your mother. I am very focused on your life and what goes on, and this seems to make you uncomfortable. This is why you may have to protect yourself by pushing me away." Thus, I interpreted his part of the enactment as one in which he was rejecting me as a person who cared, similar to the way he saw his mother.

Following this intervention, there were some less vehemently stated concerns about the award and the money. He then added how it really was not a big deal; he has gotten many other awards. Furthermore, he did not think I understood the value of it. I inquired as to what he thought I misunderstood, and he said: "There's a prestige to it. It is an award of recognition from the state! It felt like I was thinking one thing and it was not coming through. It could be something about wanting to keep it to myself."

We both could see the beginning of a self-reflective shift. The following hour took him further along this path. He brought up thoughts about his mother and disabled brother, from whom he said he takes very little pleasure. He acknowledged that he felt guilty about not wanting to meet his mother's expectations regarding the care required for both her and his brother. He added: "It's also the guilt of why is my brother disabled and I'm not? Doesn't seem very equitable. I did not ask for it. To have my own ambition was wrong. I felt my ambitions took a back seat to mother's and brother's needs."

I simply responded by restating that he seems to feel guilty about his good fortune, because of his brother's misfortune. He agreed and elaborated: "This award is hard for me to talk about with most people because I don't want positive attention. It draws my attention to the disparity between myself and my brother." He could see that this guilt played a part in how he had responded to me in the previous session. I added that I had felt "dis-abled by him" and how it resulted in neither one of us understanding what was happening. Because his brother can't have things, he feels he should not have them either. He then shared: "If the other is disabled, it would presume that I would have to relate to them and what if I don't want to relate. Or what if it is not about the other person being disabled. It's me wanting to feel able somehow. I don't know why it would work that way. If I want to feel able is it to feel in control or in charge?"

I felt that Dr. N could accept my participation in part because we shared in an authentic emotional exchange. I provided unexpected responses to what he was attempting to instill and provoke. Furthermore, I was willing to remain affectively engaged with him while he tried to push me away. I think he expected to be able to push me away in his anger, like he has with others. Following a sequence of his pushing and my pulling, along with my subsequent efforts to synthesize the enactment, he was able to see "the wall" as his need to push me away. He could then share and reflect on his internal state.

We shared in learning that he felt some safety in trying to see me as his mother and that this was a way to defend against his feeling greater intimacy with me. To feel closeness with me was another experience in which he would have more than his brother and mother. Furthermore, if I could be like his mother, he could maintain the wall and would not have to unearth his longings for love and appreciation.

Part of my ongoing countertransference was the submerged anger that I experienced because I felt shut out and defeated. I can remember at one point, prior to this clinical moment, fantasizing how I could replace Dr. N with another patient. When I became aware of these thoughts, I also became aware of my guilt. Certainly, there are reasons within my own history that would in part trigger the fantasy and subsequent guilt; however, I could also identify that this had to do with the way he felt in his family. He could not be appreciated for being a non-defective child; rather, he felt unplanned and unwanted. He felt guilty for being fully able and wanting to be the special child (maybe the only child) and experienced further guilt for his anger at having been marginalized. The evoked fantasy of his being disposable was a primary state that Dr. N carried within himself.

I find myself reflecting on how I might handle this enactment now, given that I am working as a graduate analyst reaping the benefits of having had more clinical and didactic experiences. In this vignette, I now see my interpretations immediately following, what I had thought to be a more centered approach, as still part of the enactment. The ways in which I declared how he felt and who he thought I represented were offered with some continued vehemence of conviction. He was right: I was acting like a mother!

Presented with the likes of this enactment again, I would more humbly present my response and thoughts as just that: my thoughts and reactions based on the way in which I experienced our interaction. I would hope to sound less accusatory and not as dedicated to the depiction of the transference. It is likely that I would ponder with him what it meant for us both to experience feelings of having been misunderstood. Furthermore, I may add how this led to my feeling shut out and deprived as the result of my not being able to share in the mutuality of pleasure over his accomplishment. This might have provided greater clarification for Dr. N, in addition to possibly heightening his awareness of the way he can affect others.

My work with Dr. N has contributed significantly to my interest and curiosity around the transformative nature of enactments. Throughout our time together, I could see more and more how our affective engagements appeared most helpful to him. I often visualized the emotional desert from which he journeyed and how isolated he felt from others and himself. The overt level of affective engagement with Dr. N eventually led to a shared gratification in that our work together became more enlivening, stimulating, and, dare I say, transformative.

Notes

1 As we shall see, this is not at all how interpersonalists think.
2 In distinction to earlier views of projective identification that posited the transfer of a wholesale piece of the patient.

References

Benjamin, J. (2004). Beyond doer and done to: An intersubjective view of thirdness. *Psychoanalytic Quarterly*, 73(1), 5–46.
Bromberg, P. (1998). *Standing in the spaces: Essays on clinical process, trauma, and dissociation*. Hillsdale, NJ: The Analytic Press.
Celenza, A. (2014). *Erotic revelations: Clinical applications and perverse scenarios*. London: Routledge.
Chused, J. (1991). The evocative power of enactments. *Journal of the American Psychoanalytic Association*, 39(3), 615–639.

Chused, J. (1996). The therapeutic action of psychoanalysis: Abstinence and informative experiences. *Journal of the American Psychoanalytic Association*, 44(4), 1047–1071.
Conrad, J. (1900). *Lord Jim*. London: Blackwood's Magazine.
Gabbard, G., & Westin, D. (2003). Rethinking therapeutic action. *International Journal of Psychoanalysis*, 84(4), 823–841.
Gunderson, J. (1995). *Effective treatment of borderline personality disorder: A longitudinal study*. Cambridge, MA: Grand Rounds, Cambridge Health Alliance.
Lichtenberg, J., Lachmann, F., & Fosshage, J. (1992). *Self and motivational systems: Toward a theory of psychoanalytic technique*. Hillsdale, NJ: The Analytic Press.
Lichtenberg, J., Lachmann, F., & Fosshage, J. (1996). *The clinical exchange: Techniques derived from self and motivational systems*. Hillsdale, NJ: The Analytic Press.
Stern, D. B. (1997). *Unformulated experience: From dissociation to imagination in psychoanalysis*. Hillsdale, NJ: The Analytic Press.
Stern, D. B. (2003). The fusion of horizons: Dissociation, enactment, and understanding. *Psychoanalytic Dialogues*, 13(6), 843–873.
Stern, D. B. (2004). The eye sees itself: Dissociation, enactment, and the achievement of conflict. *Contemporary Psychoanalysis*, 40(2), 197–237.
Stern, D. B. (2017). Personal communication.
Vonnegut, K. (1965). *God bless you Mr. Rosewater*. New York: Delacorte Press.

> # Part III
>
> # What Patients Want; What Therapists Can Provide

Chapter 6

Patient as Bean Counter

Rina Freedman

Editors' introduction

Many transferences involve the patients' paying meticulous attention ("counting beans") to what they are or are not receiving from the analyst in the way of praise, attention, love, adoration, and so on. This clinical moment involves a 40-year-old lesbian woman who'd been attending psychoanalytic psychotherapy sessions 3 days weekly for 15 months. Roberta is an academic who prides herself on being brilliant, powerful, and better able than anyone else to interpret her own process. Raised by an exacting and stingy mother, it wasn't surprising that the patient would eventually find occasion to question whether she was getting her fair share of what was due her in the way of the analyst's time and attention. This clinical moment began at the end of the patient's 50-minute hour marked by the analyst's noticing something was amiss given that the patient had a smirk on her face and a swagger in her walk as she left the room. The next session, the patient was unusually irritable, complaining of a long list of things about which she felt dissatisfied, ending with a furious outburst about her controlling and stingy mother. In response to the analyst's inquiry about her angry feelings, the patient exploded over the fact the analyst had cut short the previous session by three minutes. The analyst was willing to concede that she may well have shorted the patient's time, which allowed her to shift the focus of exploration onto how much the event had meant to the patient. What made this moment particularly challenging for the analyst was the question of how to explore the patient's transference without disrupting the mirroring function that the patient looked to the analyst to serve, which she urgently needed.

The moment in context (Richard Tuch)

There are a few noteworthy aspects to the clinical moment that follows: one having to do with the patient's vigilant, background search for subtle signs indicating how the analyst feels about her, the other involving the matter of how the patient reacts when she comes to believe she'd been short-changed by the analyst – setting off a powerful reaction that catches the analyst off-guard, throwing her off-kilter as she scrambles to gather her wits about her in the hopes of averting a more substantial and sustained enactment. Under such circumstances, the precipitous nature of the patient's reaction may momentarily impair the analyst's ability to think on her feet and to fashion a thoughtful response, which, in turn may lead the analyst to react in knee-jerk fashion, which she may come to subsequently regret. Quickly and gracefully rebounding from such a powerful countertransference reaction is the most ideal outcome of the potential outcomes given the circumstances.

The speed with which an analyst comes to her senses in the wake of feeling attacked varies from analyst to analyst – and there is an ever-present danger that the situation may further deteriorate if the analyst remains stunned, defensive, or engages in a retaliatory maneuver. Believing that analysts ought to never act in such manners is an unattainable ideal out of line with the realities of clinical practice. If there is anything analysts have learned about countertransference reactions over the last half-century, it would be this.

Such reactivity on the analyst's part represents an enactment of sorts, which may persist until the analyst comes to terms with how she had been reacting and shifts to a more self-reflective mode of thinking. Lichtenberg et al. (1996) refer to this process as "self-righting"[1] (p. 196) – "an intrinsic tendency during psychoanalysis to rebound from an altered (lower level) state of functioning to a more adaptive state" (p. 196).

In the clinical moment that follows, the intensity of the patient's transference reaction proved off-putting for the analyst. The patient charged the analyst with short-changing her by ending the previous session prematurely, and the intensity of her confrontation made it momentarily hard for the analyst to think. After initially reacting defensively, the analyst was able to quickly "self-right," enabling her to explore with the patient a particular aspect of what had amounted to a very brief enactment.

It is not unusual for patients to pay rapt attention to the matter of how the analyst manages the time aspect of the analytic "frame." Whether the analyst starts late, starts late but then ends the session on time, ends the session prematurely, or allows the session to "run over" – are matters that may become highly significant to the extent the patient interprets them as a sign of how the analyst feels about them. Taking the patient in late may indicate that the analyst was less than enthused about seeing her, and ending the session early might mean to the patient that the analyst has had as much as she can take of the patient. Letting the session run over might mean any number of different things, but it can be interpreted by the patient as "a precious gift" or a sign of how fascinating the analyst had found the patient to be, and so on and so forth. It could be interpreted as a sign of the analyst's lack of discipline, possibly reflecting her inability to end the session on time because she feared that doing so might fuel a developing negative transference or, alternately, because she felt she needed more time to drive home a point that she'd been trying desperately to make.[2]

Time is a precious commodity in psychoanalytic treatment. Patients are often remarkably attentive to the precise length of the session, making it necessary for the analyst to not only be remarkably punctual but to be vigilant about times she had in fact started a session late, ended it early, or allowed it to run over. Perfection is not the point; after all, sometimes circumstances may make it less than clinically optimal to end a session precisely on them. How the patient handles the situation can be quite telling. Some patients may even excuse the analyst's lateness to show themselves generous to show how "hang loose" they can be, or to find ways to defend against feeling hurt or angry about the lateness – for example, by imaging that the analyst had had an emergency that she could not control so, under the circumstances, "Who am I to get upset?"

If we narrow the discussion to instances when the analyst ends the session early, it is easy to imagine how such an event could leave the patient feeling rejected. If a patient reacts angrily, framing his protest in moral terms (about right and wrong, about what's due her, about being cheated, and the like), the feeling of being hurt will likely be pushed to the side, which may be the defensive purpose of talking about the event in this fashion. To whatever extent patients can or cannot admit to having such feelings and concerns, the psychoanalytic situation promotes the development of an intense attachment and a concomitant reactivity to the analyst in her role as transference figure. Accordingly, patients will forever take measure of the analyst's interest, investment in, and regard for them to determine whether they are favored, liked, or merely tolerated.

Beside the issue of the ways in which patients interpret instances when the analyst fails to maintain the "frame" relative to time, is the matter of *the intensity* of a patient's reaction when the analyst seems to have cut the session short. If the patient's reaction is sudden and intense, the analyst may find herself in the uncomfortable and emotionally challenging position of being on the receiving end of an attack that the patient claims had been triggered by the analyst's actual behavior. It's been said that one's empathy for another is the first casualty of war, and the same can be said when the analyst finds herself under attack – ambushed, if you will – caught off-guard, aghast at the charges being leveled and the unfairness of it all. It is not hard to imagine an analyst silently, or not so silently, protesting given how caring and patient she felt she'd been all these months and years. When under attack, the analyst is at risk for feeling stunned, leading her to become defensive or engage in counterattack. Given the circumstances, one can't fault the analyst for feeling like recounting "after all the things I've done for you, and now *this*?" I am not suggesting that these are the average, expectable reactions every analyst would feel under the circumstances; I am only illustrating how some analysts may feel and react – or, more to the point, be *willing to admit* to feeling and reacting. How and whether such feelings can be utilized productively in therapy is a matter of debate. Certain interpersonalists, for example, argue in favor of letting the patient know in no uncertain terms the effect the patient is having on the analyst (Ehrenberg, 1992, 2003). Other analysts see clinical value in the development of a full-fledged countertransference enactment. Here, I am limiting myself to the analyst's self-acknowledged, *but "checked,"* countertransference impulses, *not* enacted impulses, and I am suggesting how routine such reactions can be given the circumstances.

In the clinical moment that follows, the presenting analyst is candid enough with the reader to admit that she was personally prone to become stunned when conditions became unexpectedly heated. It is brave for an analyst to admit as much – not just because it enlivens the presentation, adding a dimension by introducing the element of subjectivity, but because such admissions go a way toward helping us all accept and admit the strength of our own countertransference reactions. It takes courage to make oneself vulnerable by sharing the truth of one's subjective responses because it exposes one to the potential judgment of a holier-than-thou, above-it-all type analyst who looks down her nose (tsk! tsk!) at an analyst who admits to having such reactions. If the countertransference reaction that the presenting analyst experienced is the "average-expectable reaction" that most other analysts would also have experienced given the circumstances, and not merely an idiosyncratic reaction on the analyst's part, this particular countertransference reaction would be considered bona fide "clinical data" or "evidence" that is highly relevant to the case. This, in a nutshell, is why an appreciation of countertransference reactions has become so central to psychoanalysis as illustrated in the clinical moment that follows. In this case, it seems reasonable to assume that the *nature* of this analyst's countertransference reactions is much like what other analysts would feel had they been in the room, though the *intensity* of her reaction seems to be the result of her own personal proclivities about which she is candidly aware.

The clinical moment

Roberta is a 40-year-old lesbian woman who is an academic scholar at a major university. Her field is International Affairs. She is a very attractive, tall, and athletic Nordic woman, well-dressed in a uniquely masculine/feminine way. The clinical moment I will be describing occurred in the third year of three-times-a-week treatment with me.

In the very first session, Roberta introduced herself saying: "I am a heat-seeking missile. I want to put myself in someone's hands whom I can trust. I have a lot of anxiety. Despite great academic success and professional accolades, I constantly worry that one day everything will fall apart and I will be found out to be just average, ordinary." As she admitted to having such fears, the patient smiled brightly, as was her typical way, in contrast to the inner horror she felt over the prospect of being found ordinary. She went on to report how she never feels content with her relationships or with herself, unless she receives constant attention and praise. Roberta's father is a brilliant man from a very wealthy family but was considered irresponsible and a bit of a "con man" by most who knew him. Her mother is a hard-driving, highly ambitious woman, who is financially independent. By the time Roberta was one year old, her mother divorced the father. Roberta has one brother, the "golden boy," who is four years older than Roberta. The brother is handsome, bright, and unconditionally adored by both parents. While the father tried to gain custody of his son, he did not wish to have custody of Roberta, claiming that she was a baby and did not know him at the time the divorce took place. The patient reported feeling very wounded and neglected by her father's rejection, though she declined exploring these feelings as the treatment progressed. Though the father had sought custody of his son, it turned out that both children went on to live with their mother. The father remarried and unofficially adopted the three children of his new wife with whom he lived a quasi-bohemian life style. When Roberta was 12 years old, Roberta's mother remarried a man who is a powerful politician and was a "nice guy" who cared about Roberta and was attentive.

Roberta's relationship to her father was marked by disappointments and a lack of the attention that she so dearly craved. Her mother was very present but in an intensely demanding way, expecting Roberta to shine in every respect, while the brother was just adored with nothing demanded of him. Roberta describes herself as "a star" in all areas – a super athlete, fabulous skier, mountain climber, and scholastically always at the top of the class. But while she is proud of her achievements, underneath she worries that she is a "fraud" (like her father?). Her mother, she said, expects top results and complains that Roberta demands too much attention and praise from her. Roberta always felt invisible unless she could produce some great feat at school or in sports, and now feels the same at work and in life in general. She expresses kind sympathy for me, guessing, correctly, that I am not a serious athlete, which she forgives me for. As the treatment progressed, Roberta reported that her mother felt jealous about the quality of her relationship with me.

Roberta drives herself onward relentlessly, both professionally and personally. In session, she takes over and explains to me how things *ought* to be and *are* to be. She alternates between viewing our relationship strictly in business terms ("I pay you just like others do") or in more personal terms ("I know I am your favorite patient and I am doing my best to keep it this way"). My interpretations regarding her quest to be my most special patient are met with a knowing grin and reassurances that I am "right on," noting: "I was trained by the toughest and best trainer, my mother! And I deliver!" Exploring how she feels about paying me "like the others do" gave Roberta an opportunity to tell me that I am "naïve" to the extent I don't see matters in the keen and businesslike manner that she sees matters. Furthermore, she believes I see myself as a "healer" when, in fact, I am just in it for the money. "Anyway, I don't want to waste my time here talking about *you*!"

At the time the clinical moment to be described took place, Roberta had been in treatment for three years, two and three times a week, depending on her travel schedule. From the start, she rejected the couch. "I feel good with you, but I need to monitor your face to see that you care for *me* in the way I need to be cared for, not per some psych manual." The transference was mostly very positive, and I felt rewarded by her trust and seduced by her idealization of me. Roberta has this way of knowing how to elicit from me signs that I like her and think highly of her and will do something special for her.

As an analyst, I am not very rigid about stopping at the 50-minute mark. I sometimes go over if a patient needs a couple of minutes to finish. So, I was stunned when Roberta came into her session furious with me because, per her watch, I had stopped the previous session three minutes short. Historically, I tend to shut down emotionally when confronted unexpectedly with another's heated reaction or explosive rage. So, somewhat numb and flustered, I told her that, as usual, I relied on my office clock. Roberta exploded: "Your clock? *I* have the best watch one can have – the very best! It is *always* right! Your clock is of no use to me, it is just an ordinary, tick-tock clock."

I thought to myself that she must be feeling crushingly unimportant at this point, just as she would with her father and often too with her mother. She experienced me as having short-changed her, resulting in her need to turn the tables by casting me in the role of the ordinary one with her expressing contempt from her position on high as the authority who knew right from wrong:

A: I can see this is very upsetting to you—you feel short-changed by me.
R: Damn right! How can I trust you to be a reliable professional?
A: You are worried that I may not be as reliable, as responsible, as perfect as your mother is [and as you were expected to be by her]. Perhaps you worry that I am more like your father? Loosie goosie! He short-changed you repeatedly.
R: Oh, give me a break with all this psychobabble.
A: Yes, and sometimes when we go over for a few minutes, how do you feel then?
R: I *know* when we go over and I *love* it! But that is *your* choice! I want my 50 beans in my pot every single time. I got 47 beans last time! You have no right to decide when I get less than my 50 beans. I should leave; I am so angry; but then, I'd lose my time here again.

Invited commentator responses 1: Robert Alan Glick and Judy Kantrowitz

Robert Alan Glick

I want to thank Drs. Tuch and Kuttnauer for this invitation to imagine myself in the therapist's "shoes" with her "Patient as Bean Counter." As a shared learning moment, I am drawn into the intense challenges of thinking, feeling, and acting as an analytic clinician. We all know that this rests on our clinical knowledge and experience, what we know about ourselves, our patient, and the treatment process.

In this intimate clinical moment, I try to place myself both inside the therapist's experience of the patient, and standing outside, next to her, to assess and infer what may be going on in her, what she is reacting to, and what she brings to the interaction. The same holds true for me. I will try to recognize those aspects of the clinical picture, of the interaction between patient and therapist, which pull me in one direction or the other, as I experience the inevitable temptation to respond from my own recognized and unrecognized transferences, my own clinical and personal life. In this regard, the teaching encounter can get very crowded.

I will structure these two inserted responses much as I would in a conference or supervision, beginning with the therapist's introduction of the treatment, followed by the first and second process moments, and finally, with a broader discussion of clinical and theoretical questions.

So we begin.

The therapist sets the stage, suggesting qualities that impress her about the patient. I feel that I am about to meet a powerful masculine woman, who stands strong and alone in her world, and carries the burden of continued disappointment in the women in her life. I feel a shiver of apprehension for the therapist.

The patient announces a paradox: "I am a heat seeking missile," very dangerous and destructive; and "I want to put myself in someone's hands whom I can trust." The therapist is telling me that she has a dangerous and challenging mission, a provocation about whether she is up to the task. The task has a further quality: the danger is paradoxical – "falling apart" and being discovered as "just average, ordinary." I feel that the immanent narcissistic crisis will be a loss of very precious and very fragile specialness. The therapist is on notice: Protect me from the risk of plummeting into the world of "the rest of us" ordinary people. The therapist's challenge involves facing the inevitable rage and grief that come with offering the patient an opportunity to give up deeply held aspects of herself for a different, more realistic, and more resilient sense of herself.

As I imagine sitting with her, I find myself "taking stock" of my own self-image, my professional and personal history that I carry with me into my work. We always bring all of ourselves into the consulting room, especially when the patient announces that narcissistic injury and rage, grandiosity and devaluation, loss and mourning, are all on the table. It gets very personal.

The patient alerts the therapist that she is an "attention and praise" addict. Without it, she is crushed, anxious, and enraged. She comes from wealthy, special people. Parents divorced when she was one, her father seeking custody of the golden-child son, who lives in an endless flow of the precious adoration. Her life is a series of family disappointments, and while she is indeed "a star" in virtually every aspect of her life, she is tethered to her critical mother, from whom she can never get sufficient nurturing attention.

After a brief passing comment about the patient's sympathy for the therapist's athletic inferiority, and the mother's jealousy, a sort of early missile warning, we are shown the patient's demeaning view of the therapist regarding money. Money lives in the patient with complex and conflicted meanings, woven into issues of identity, gender, power, and attachment. The therapist, in the patient's eyes, is quite naïve. I feel like I am hearing some very familiar family ideology that serves to define the superior and the inferior, the stars and the ordinary.

The clinical moment is announced with the patient's refusal to use the couch because she needs to monitor the therapist's flow of "caring" from the therapist whom she has come to trust. I sense the therapist's discomfort with having been trained to give the patient a form of "specialness" nurturance. The therapist has set the stage for the dramatic moment when the attack from the "heat-seeking missile" will come. As they say in the theater, when there is a gun on the set, it will eventually be used!

"Action"!

The missile is launched, and the therapist is shocked and disoriented in the explosion.

The therapist deploys some emergency tools to manage the crisis, seeming to scramble to point her analytic finger at the appropriate historical targets but the patient correctly and usefully bats it away, demanding that she stay in the room with her, stay in the moment, implying that the therapist should not leave, not die, not punish. The rage feels shocking and out of proportion. How is the therapist to find an effective "righting response," a way of staying in her seat – as Winnicott said, "staying alive" – and not be crushed or exploding with rage herself?

"Let's talk bean counting, money, and responsibility."

"You failed me! I should leave you but I won't."

First, I would want to ensure that the therapist has caught her breath, and feels "okay" with her shock and distress, that she is not embarrassed or ashamed. Then we could look at what and why this is happening, and what she can do to regain composure, optimism, and courage to continue. Then we could discuss some aspects of clinical theory to apply to technique at a moment like this.

Given that we are in the world of intense narcissistic dynamics, I would want to explore a combination of ideas: self-psychological constructs: the use of preparatory mirroring and mutual idealization phase, the necessary empathic failure, the rageful devaluation and transmuting internalization phase; the Bionian construct of containment/metabolism of intolerable affect/self states (alpha and beta functions that demand a willingness to receive these experiences in order for the patient to re-internalize them in a more organized and tolerable, thinkable form). Additionally, we might consider ideas from the Boston Change Process Study Group in Boston (BCPSG) (Stern et al., 1998). They offer an intriguing sequential view of clinical process from "present moments" – the familiar patterns in the flow of intersubjective unconscious ways of relating – to "now moments," when something new and unexpected happens between them that creates an opportunity for a "moment of meeting," their signature notion of the authentic mutative interaction, the essential opportunity for growth in "implicit relational knowing," those patterned ways one relates to oneself and others.

Our first process moment could be described as an example of a "now moment" and the second as a "moment of meeting." As the BCPSG describes a "now moment": "The most intriguing now moments arise when the patient does something that is difficult to categorize, something that demands a different and new kind of response with the personal signature that shares the analyst's subjective state" (Stern et al., 1998, p. 912). In this instance, the patient has had immediate affective impact on the therapist, in the form of shock and distress. When seized therapeutically (i.e., when the therapist "rights herself" and remains engaged and attuned), as in the second clinical moment, she allows for the creation of a "moment of meeting," an interactive intersubjective experience that deepens and enriches the shared implicit relationship and, as this Study Group suggests, changes the patient's implicit relational knowing as a feature of beneficial therapeutic change.

The therapist has given the patient needed empathic mirroring, in the form of loving attention and mutual admiration. But I sense that she also knew that it would have to be challenged, and the "honeymoon period" would end. The weapon had been labeled and would have to be used. I would reinforce her sense that, while it is shocking and painful, she managed the attack well. The patient's underlying rage and vulnerability demanded that she test the therapist's resilience and reliability in order to free herself from her narcissistic emotional bunker. The patient needed to feel she had *real* impact on the therapist "where she lived." She had to knock the wind out of her, to attack her moral core as a therapist. She had to find out that the therapist, unlike the internal representations of her primary objects, was truly strong enough, real enough, concerned and caring enough, to survive the test, and that they would both continue together. This has the quality of a morality play, but not a tragedy. It is about good and bad, pain, loss, disillusionment, repair, and, ultimately, a shared optimism about future emotional growth.

Interestingly, I share it too, and do not feel that supervisor's need to describe what I might have done in this moment. Rather, I might share similar painful and disorienting moments in my own experience to underscore the distress and disequilibrium I have felt in comparable situations. I would hope to convey a sense that this is very intimate, intense, and human work we do.

Judy Kantrowitz

Dr. Freedman's openness about her thoughts, feelings, and responses to Roberta provides information that inevitably influences my understanding of what is transpiring. I hear the material based on the dyad, not just as if I were Roberta's therapist. Dr. Freedman is "stunned" by the intensity of the patient's anger and arrogance. She recognizes the defensive aspect of her initial focus on reality – the time on her clock. Yet, I think what she refers to as a justification for her response, her intention to calm Roberta, is warranted. No one can take in information when so distressed. She is narcissistically wounded.

It seems that Roberta's idealization of her analyst has been paralleled by the fantasy that she is her analyst's favorite patient. Her fantasy of specialness is reparative of both her mother's hostility toward her and her father's neglect. I wonder if Dr. Freedman's focus on the "reality" of time – her clock – was also unconsciously a defensive reaction to Roberta's having said that she pretends to not care about realities like money, pretends to just want to be a healer. Pointing to the time on the clock, Dr. Freedman is saying in essence: I *do* tend to my realities and needs, not just yours! Previously, the patient may have been mocking her analyst for what she assumes was her self-abnegating stance, while enjoying the idea that she is "superior," wiser in her "knowing" of the world and complexity of people relative to the analyst. Dr. Freedman may have unconsciously been trying to correct this perception. While we understand such perceptions are transference, there can be an understandable pull to want to be correctly perceived, and Dr. Freedman has no quibble when Roberta perceives her as not athletic.

Roberta's perspective, even prior to this present incident, is one of superiority in this respect, looking down on Dr. Freedman as self-deluding, which the analyst sees as an identification with her critical mother who puts people down – especially Roberta. It is, as Dr. Freedman says, "a turning of the tables" for the patient to now attack the analyst. She attacks because her fantasy of being the analyst's special, probably favorite patient, has been shattered. She is humiliated. Yes, it seems her mother demands perfection and her father has neglected her – "short-changed" her – and both parents seem to favor her brother, but these genetic interpretations, at least initially, seem like "psychobabble" to her. At this moment, it is Dr. Freedman, not her parents, who has injured her and the patient seeks reparation from her analyst.

But then the analyst reminds the patient of another reality – sometimes she extends the sessions for a few minutes. And while the patient has registered this other reality of sessions with extended time, and acknowledges her loving it when it occurs – loving it because it supports her fantasy that she is the special, favored patient, which is why she had gotten extra time – this information does not quell her fury. She, of course, has no way of knowing that Dr. Freedman runs over with other patients as well, that her doing so is not an indication of Roberta's specialness. If she did know this fact, the meaning would have been different to her.

Dr. Freedman thinks that Roberta believes that she herself now has the power because she has caught the analyst in making a mistake. At first Dr. Freedman thinks of this "error" as breaking "the contract" that spells out her obligation, first and foremost, to take care of the patient and not herself. Later, both to herself and in the work with the patient, Dr. Freedman focuses on not being "perfect." And while I think both of her ideas are right and relevant, I think the humiliation of the loss of the patient's fantasy of finally being the favorite, finally having an idealized parent, is the more central issue here.

I do not identify myself with subscribing to any one psychoanalytic theory. If forced to choose, I'd think of myself as Loewaldian, but what is occurring here makes me think of Kohut – Roberta's shattered narcissistic fantasy of being mirrored by an idealized object, her analyst, who will restore a belief in her specialness by the analyst's admiration, and particularly by keeping that gleam in the analyst's eye for her, on her. How could anything be worse than her turning away, focusing on her clock, on herself, and not on the patient, and then trying to justify this by referring to other times when she gave Roberta more? How could the analyst imagine this would make up for it? Her fury seems the result of this shattered fantasy; arrogance is the patient's way of restoring her self-esteem, giving herself what she imagined her analyst was offering her – a way to feel specially favored.

Up to this point in the hour, I would be imagining that her narcissistic fragility was too great to take in her analyst as separate and that her rage was too intense for her to be able to be self-reflective. Whatever I might say to her would need to be empathic with her sense of injury. I imagine that she would need to be calmed in order to be able to listen and think. My first response would likely have been something similar to Dr. Freedman's, addressing her feeling short-changed and finding that upsetting. Although I'm sure I would have thought about her transference, I doubt that I would have brought up any reference to her parents right then. Rather, I probably would have tried to get her to elaborate her thoughts about me. I think it is not just that I (were I to have been her analyst) had been unreliable, but maybe she imagined that I had deceived her by giving her extra minutes previously, leading her to believe she was special – and so be seduced and abandoned by me.

Dr. Freedman noted how she has felt seduced by the patient's idealization of her – again, the patient conveys something of what is likely to have been her experience through her actions toward the analyst, enabling the analyst to feel what the patient has experienced. I'd be wondering about the history of this kind of seduction. We know much more clearly how she is left. I'd wait for her response to this kind of intervention. I would be wondering if she could acknowledge feeling tricked, seduced into believing she was special and then humiliated. If she could elaborate on it, I then would wonder what kind of person she imagines would do such a thing? Here, my inquiry would be informed by thinking in terms of Steiner's (1994) analyst-centered interpretations. Could she now allow her negative transference to come into the room, to perceive me not just as someone she could occasionally feel superior to – as when she had perceived me (Dr. Freedman) as not athletic and as naïve – but also as untrustworthy, manipulative, maybe even sadistic, wanting to laud my power over her. I doubt I would introduce any of these speculations at this point unless she herself went this far. But at some point in this hour, I would also indicate that I thought she was trying to communicate what it had been like for her when she made a mistake or disappointed her mother by giving me "a taste" of this experience – so I would really get it, feeling something more than just words could convey.

The session continues

(After the patient said, "You have no right to decide when I get less than my 50 beans. I should leave; I am so angry; but then, I'd lose my time here again"):

A: Oh Roberta, you are really showing me what it was like for you with your mother. The slightest flaw cancelled out what was good. You really had to be vigilant and perfect for her. It must have made you so anxious and alone feeling.

At this point, Roberta burst into tears:

R: That is how she is! That is how she was with my father, with me, and everyone, except my brother. I dreaded coming home from school if I did not have everything under control.
A: A full pot of beans every time.
R: (Smiling) Yes, a full pot of beans. [Then, noticing the time:] Oh, the hour is almost over; I wasted it and short-changed myself this time. Before I go, tell me something that is not about beans.

Invited commentator responses 2: Robert Alan Glick and Judy Kantrowitz

Robert Alan Glick

The therapist calls the patient by her name: "Oh Roberta." I find this a very powerful and crucial personalizing action. It says: "This is us, affectively stepping outside the constraining roles as therapist and patient (and into an authentic, affectively real interaction). We are talking to each other; I take you into account. I am not speaking as a disembodied, objective, judgmental voice. You are making me feel what you felt with your mother, that crushing, isolating cancellation. I am living in your shoes. I get it; I feel it; I am truly here for you."

The patient, bursting into tears, has a painful cathartic recall of her hurtful and dreadful past. What I can't know at this moment is whether she has ever cried, ever been so enraged, or felt so much distress in the immediacy of the treatment before this moment.

The therapist's response is ironic, stating that they have been here before. She underlines the meanings of bean counting, responsible caring, money, and control. She mitigates the intensity of the patient's tearful outburst. The therapist is saying, wisely and generously, we have lived through versions of this before, we are in this together, nothing truly bad has happened, we both survived the upset and we are continuing on together.

This is an excellent example of how a therapist "self-rights" and effectively rebounds from an intense attack on her as an uncaring, failing person. This goes to the heart of the clinical reality in our work. We are unleashing powerful, primitive forces that are real for the patient and become real for us. There is no escape from enactments of the intersubjective process. Over time, we learn to expect the "unexpected," to ride through the storm, to "self-right" without disaster if possible. Ultimately, and most often in retrospect, we cherish the surprises as the moments when things happen that move the treatment forward.

The patient's last comments support her need for reassurance and her wish to stay in the immediate moment, a self-directed but shared criticism of her intense emotions that she must experience as evidence of weakness and vulnerability. Clearly, she needs to recompose herself, to feel back in control of her emotions. A mutative experience is happening. As confirmation of the therapist's intervention, the patient expresses her relief and reminds them both of lessons learned. The clinical moment ends.

At this point, I would invite the therapist's questions: What does she make of these clinical moments? How does she feel about what happened? And what would she like to explore about the patient, the therapeutic process, technique, theory, or anything else?

Following where the therapist's question might lead us, I might be on the "look-out" for further recognized and unrecognized countertransference reactions, those enactments that shape their participation and engagement in the process. This is a patient whom I assume elicits strong feelings and all sorts of oscillating identifications, competitions, sexual and gender feelings, and the like that could be swirling about the room. At these moments, I am thrown back into my past with similar experiences that evoke and provoke familiar feelings of anger, shame, discouragement, especially in supervision where the process can be awash with transferences in all directions. This is difficult work and we are all vulnerable. Our self-analysis never ends. What I might aim to tactfully explore are possible countertransference responses and possible enactments. I hope I might stimulate the therapist's curiosity about what else might be going on "in the room." Depending on where our discussion goes and what the therapist allows, I might again use examples from my own experience, from those moments when I felt overwhelmed, needed to "right myself," and to find my way back into the process. I hope to normalize these challenges and demonstrate their therapeutic value.

If our discussion allows, there are two important topics in this treatment that I am particularly curious about: *money and sex* and how they have appeared in the treatment. This could tell us a great deal about the patient, but crucially about the transference/countertransference interaction and therapeutic change in the treatment.

We have heard something about money in the brief discussion of the family history and its connection to her parents and their self-images. Bean counting has a history, a learned art. We have not heard anything about the patient's views on money, her actual financial circumstances, and what she feels about and does with money. But we know that it is important in her story and in her treatment.

About sex, we know that, as is true for all of us, her sexual desires and fears have a history and are involved in her unconscious conflicts. They have shaped and are in turn shaped by her personality. We have only heard that the patient is a lesbian, and we have not yet heard what this means to her and about her; what her actual sexual life and relationship history are; what her desires, fantasies, anxieties, and inhibitions are; and most importantly, what has or has not been explored in the treatment. Has any suggestion or explicit expression of an erotic transference emerged in their interaction? Has the therapist sensed erotic transference or countertransference feelings? Has the therapist sensed that certain things remain "off-limits," or "too (potentially) hot to handle"?

Finally, we might discuss psychoanalytic theory and its uses. I have a particular interest in how we use our theories to guide and comfort us in our work. In addition, I think it useful to explore our ideas about therapeutic action. Patients and therapists all have conscious and unconscious theories of therapeutic action which can come into play in the treatment process with the patient's, and the therapist's, recognized and unrecognized wishes, fears, self-images, and so on. Amongst the questions I find useful to explore are theoretical preferences and the technical applications of favorite theories, and how these preferences may reflect transferences to theory serving other unconscious wishes. Theory can become part of our "spirit of the analyst I wish to be" that can accompany us throughout our professional lives. "Know thyself" is the burden and the gift of the work we do.

Judy Kantrowitz

Roberta is full of rage, tempted to leave, but is able to control her behavior with a recognition that this would be further depriving herself. I would feel encouraged that she could both express her fury in words and contain her actions, recognizing what is in her own best interest; despite her fury, she values her time with Dr. Freedman. And here Dr. Freedman interprets, as I would have, that the patient is showing her what it had been like for her to be with her mother. I am in total agreement with Dr. Freedman that Roberta "had acted out with (her) what she could not express in words" – so the analyst can feel it "in (her) flesh so she would really understand deeply." We would be in agreement that this communication was the central issue at this time.

Based on the material provided, all the other issues Dr. Freedman cites are pertinent, which I believe are clustered around her narcissistic vulnerability. Maybe Dr. Freedman's emphasis on perfection is the same as the patient's need to be seen as the special one by someone she idealizes, and maybe "perfect is the enemy of good" is the analyst's way of addressing what I suspect is the patient's sense that either she is special or she is devalued as unimportant, an example of her either-or way of thinking/feeling about both herself and others. My focus would be her self-esteem.

Roberta's relationship with her mother is so fraught. She conveys that she disappoints her mother unless she is a star. She is no more seen by her mother than she is by her father, who seems so absent and, therefore, disappointing. But there is an active, tortuous relationship going on with her mother. Even sado-masochistic relationships are better than nothing. This way of relating will need to be analyzed and understood, but I agree that this is not the central concern of the moment.

I was surprised that Roberta responded so readily and with so much affect to Dr. Freedman's interpretation that she was showing the analyst "what it was like for you with your mother. The slightest flaw cancelled out what was good. You really had to be vigilant and perfect for her. It must have made you so anxious and alone feeling."

Surprised not because I thought it was incorrect – though my emphasis would have been a bit different – but because I thought Roberta would have responded as she had when she declared genetic interpretations were "psychobabble." I suspect Roberta really felt Dr. Freedman's empathy for how she felt – that she was on her side, did not blame her for her attacks on the analyst, and did not retaliate; rather, she understood her distress. She "gets" the patient's need for vigilance and control – she understands and does not condemn. The music of her response soothes the patient, all to the good. But I would be less inclined to specify what it is the patient is feeling (e.g., "It must have made you so anxious and alone feeling") because I would want to help her find her own words for her states. To my ear, terror is more likely than anxiety – and feeling unseen, I believe, makes one feel even more awful than feeling alone. The analyst's affect words understate what I hear as the patient's state of pain. But I don't know at this moment whether these details matter to her. The analyst reaches her affect, and unlike her mother the analyst not only doesn't demand and retaliate, she conveys her empathy and wish to understand the patient.

Like Dr. Freedman, I think I would be listening for Roberta's affect, what she can and can't tolerate, and how this is related to her self-esteem, which to my ear is fragile. I would want to leave room for her negative feelings toward me – and hope that I could keep in mind that her grandiosity and arrogance are defensively employed to bolster her self-esteem, which I believe would help me not become too irritated by her boasting. I would need to remain alert to this unhelpful countertransference response that likely would be stirred in me. Simultaneously, I would want to be sure that in trying to help repair her narcissistic vulnerabilities I did not bypass the sado-masochistic engagements that permeate her relationship with her mother – and surely others. But I don't believe these struggles can really be addressed without being enacted and/or leading to her feeling ashamed and humiliated until her narcissistic fragility lessens and her affect tolerance improves.

My therapeutic stance would be to stay as close as I could to what was affectively available to her, to speak as much as I could about what she was conveying, to be empathetic with her experience, while slowly trying to find a way that she could explore what she disowns, projects, and/or mirrors in her relationships with others. I would be looking for her progressive edge. Ultimately, I would hope that both the positive and negative affects and relationship experiences could become alive in our interactions as a place where they could be contained and understood with empathy for both participants.

The session continues

(After the patient says, "Oh, the hour is almost over; I wasted it and short-changed myself this time. Before I go, tell me something that is not about beans"):

A: Maybe you want me to remind you that perfect is the enemy of good. [This was a phrase and concept that she and I traditionally would go back to because it captured the essence of her dilemma.]

R: (Looking relieved) So you aren't mad at me?! See you tomorrow.

Final thoughts (Rina Freedman)

There are many layers to this hour, but I would like to focus first on my countertransference. I had not before detected a hint of such anger and "arrogance" in her, nor had I noted such feelings either in her dreams or fantasies. I felt stunned. I wanted to calm her so I could think. So, I got defensive, though I justified what I then did by telling myself I was doing it for her good – to calm her down by introducing the reality that I rely on my clock, as usual. Big mistake! I broke the contract between us that stipulated that I would listen to *her* and take care of her rather than taking care of myself. She let me have it. "Your ordinary tick-tock?" She had the power, she had the real big gun.

After my initial reaction, I felt in more control of my countertransference reaction. I still wanted to defend myself, but I also wanted to understand more. When I asked how it felt when she got more minutes from me, her response poignantly expressed the pain and helplessness she felt at the dreaded possibility that she was not wanted by me, that – maybe – she was just an ordinary patient. She retaliated in her mother's manner. (I remembered my own analyst saying to me, years ago, that daughters and mothers are but a step away from each other.)

The "50 beans" told me so much. I now had to decide what among the various possible issues would be best to address. Should I address her rage at needing me, or her wish to be my only patient, for me to be totally devoted to her? Should I allude to her being deprived of her father by a powerful mother who had the authority, as I do in my profession? Was she getting less than another patient – one she imagined might be more admired by me – thus experiencing a repetition or reactivation of her sibling rivalry?

No, all that would be addressed later. In her horror, she had acted out with me what she could not express in words: how truly tyrannical her mother's demand for perfection was, and how she suffered from it. She let *me* feel it in my flesh so I would really understand deeply. Again, she had turned the tables and had given me a task of what it was like to be her vis-à-vis her mother.

These silent reflections informed my empathic interpretation: my wish to hold and contain her in this terribly difficult moment and my quest to help her see that our journey together is on track.

Notes

1 Borrowing from Waddington (1966) and Fajardo (1987).
2 Naturally, there are other ways that patients may interpret each of these situations.

References

Ehrenberg, D. (1992). *The intimate edge: Extending the reach of psychoanalytic interaction.* New York: Norton.

Ehrenberg, D. (2003). A radical shift in thinking about the change-process: Commentary. *Psychoanalytic Dialogues,* 13(4), 579–603.

Fajardo, B. (1987). Neonatal trauma and early development. *Annual of Psychoanalysis,* 15, 233–244.

Lichtenberg, J., Lachmann, F., & Fosshage, J. (1996). *The clinical exchange. Techniques derived from self and motivational systems.* Hillsdale, NJ: The Analytic Press.

Steiner, J. (1994). Patient-centered and analyst-centered interpretations: Some implications of containment and countertransference. *Psychoanalytic Inquiry,* 14(3), 406–422.

Stern, D. N., Sander, L. W., Nahum, J. P., Harrison, A. M., Lyons-Ruth, K., Morgan, A. C., Bruschweilerstern, N., & Tronick, E. Z. (1998). Non-interpretive mechanisms in psychoanalytic therapy: The "something more" than interpretation. *International Journal of Psychoanalysis,* 79(5), 903–921.

Waddington, C. H. (1966). *Principles of development and differentiation.* New York: Basic Books.

Chapter 7

Withstanding the Patient's Demand for Answers

Janet K. Smith

Editors' introduction

This clinical moment involves a circumstance that analysts occasionally encounter when patients become seized with the intractable belief that the analyst knows more than she is letting on, and could assuredly tell the patient how best to proceed given a particular dilemma. This clinical moment involves a patient in her late 40s who'd been in analysis for several years and had, at this juncture, become intensely anxious that she say the right things to her son, who was attending law school. The son had not been communicating with the patient directly, which she believed to be the result of his feeling too "embarrassed and stressed out" to face her given his shame over having delayed his advancement tests out of fear he'd flunk out. The patient felt quite sure there was one right thing she could do or say that would solve the problem, and she pressured the analyst to tell her what that was – revealing her fantasy that the analyst was omniscient but withholding. The patient insisted that analysis can and should be providing her with cogent answers to her real-life problems, and she talked as if she believed that nothing less than a concrete response from the analyst would suffice to solve the problem at hand. As the patient's frustration and worry mounted, she became less able to think clearly and more inclined to criticize the analyst and regress in session. The analyst confronted the dilemma of how to respond to the patient's demand for advice while maintaining an empathic analytic stance designed to help the patient accept the fact that there is no perfect "knowing" and no all-knowing other.

The moment in context (Janet Smith)

Two valuable lessons are illustrated in the following clinical moment. The first involves what might be called "the provision model of therapeutic action," which stipulates that therapeutically facilitated change comes about when the analyst provides the patient with the essential, development-promoting "ingredient" (an experience, tools, information, etc.), which the patient's parents had failed to provide during the patient's formative years. The other issue illustrated in this moment touches on the analyst's "adaptability" – her ability to recognize mid-session that the approach she is taking is escalating the patient's anxiety. The adaptable analyst realizes the need to shift gears expeditiously to stabilize the situation.

Therapists occasionally encounter patients who are convinced that they lack the psychic wherewithal needed to determine for themselves what course of action to take when confronted with choices. These patients frequently attribute this deficit to a lack of early environmental provision – the failure of caregivers to prepare them properly for life by instructing them about what to think, how to think, or how to behave, leaving them to flounder in social situations or when confronted with the need to make an important life decision. Such patients feel they've been left to figure things out on their own in contrast with peers whose parents either modeled effective problem-solving behaviors or guided them toward the same as a matter of course. Patients who see themselves as deficient commonly enter treatment believing that this "lack" can be rectified by the analysts providing them with the requisite answers, tools, and skills – *concrete* knowledge needed to make it in the world.

As certain as these patients are that provision is the solution, they are equally certain that their analyst has just such a solution and should expeditiously impart it to them. Failing to do so, the analyst is then experienced, in the transference, as a withholding and/or ineffectual parent, leaving the patient alternating between feeling angry and despairing that she is not getting what she needs and "deserves," all the while convinced that the analyst will eventually come through with the essential answers and tools.

Most psychoanalysts do not subscribe to the provision model of therapeutic action. They do not believe that the patient's difficulties are caused by a failure to have received the requisite supplies (knowledge, guidance, etc.), nor do they believe that the patient can be "cured" if provided such supplies.[1] While the patient sees himself as suffering from a *lack* of something within ("something is missing"), analysts who think in terms of repression and intrapsychic conflict that is contained within the individual see it differently. They see the patient's difficulties issuing not from a lack but, rather, from the presence of an *internal process* that interferes with the patient's ability to use his mind effectively.[2] Though the nature of this interfering process varies from patient to patient, it often involves persecutory anxiety that – in part – may result in, and/or be the result of, defenses that develop in response to unrealistic superego expectations that demand the patient be perfect. Expecting oneself to be perfect can make one's arriving at a self-determined plan of action an agonizing, risk-taking exercise that makes it difficult – if not impossible – for such an individual to reach a conclusion, form an opinion, choose between alternate options, or decide upon a course of action given that doing so becomes fraught with danger and accordingly triggers intense anxiety. One patient described this feeling as "being in a room with no exits." Her solution to this anxiety-driven dilemma was to imagine herself merged with the omnipotent analyst, projecting her own capabilities into the analyst who was then seen as knowing just what to do. This patient's connection with the analyst was intensified by her need to remain connected to the split-off, projected part of herself – her "capable self," which she remained identified with *as it existed in the analyst*. The alternative – the prospect of accepting herself as a *separate and responsible* agent capable of deciding for herself – terrified the patient to the extent she found separateness intolerable (Rosenfeld, 1964, 1971). She feared that vicious criticism (persecutory anxiety) was imminent if she dared decide on her own and that decision either turned out badly or turned out differently than she had hoped or imagined.

A patient who believes that she is deficient and in need of supplies is often at odds with an analyst who believes the solution lies in discovering and understanding the unconscious forces that inhibit action and prevent growth – thus placing the analytic couple on a collision course given their differing beliefs about what constitutes therapeutic action. From the analyst's point of view, treatment is designed to help the patient come to know herself better with the goal of becoming better integrated. If one thinks – for example – in terms of repressed psychic content, integration comes about by lifting repression, allowing buried psychic content to become conscious. Alternately, if one thinks in terms of the projection of aspects of the self, integration results from reintegrating split-off parts of the self – for example, by re-owning a "knowing" part of oneself that had been disowned and projected/attributed to the analyst. By so doing, the patient ultimately comes to know and accept what he presently projects.

The idea of projecting split-off aspects of oneself was advanced by Klein (1946), who called the process "projective identification" (p. 104). In the case of a patient who desperately seeks the analyst's knowledge, the "knowing" part of the patient is *projected* or *attributed* to the analyst, who then ends up being seen as an idealized, all-knowing figure. According to Steiner (1996), the theory of projective identification represents a radical and revolutionary extension of classical Freudian theory, one that enlarges upon, rather than replaces, Freud's original intrapsychic conflict model. Projection externalizes internal conflict, turning intrapsychic conflict into interpersonal conflict, with the aim of analysis being to help the patient to achieve an integration and to regain parts of himself that have become unavailable because they have been split off and projected.

Earlier, we spoke of the patient's *sense of lack* in terms of the *presence* of interfering internal forces. To this we now offer an additional perspective – that the patient's sense of lack (self-defined as a needed but missing skill or ability) can be understood as the result of an aspect of herself having been split off and projected into others – leaving the patient devoid of aspects of the self that are needed to function properly. The patient regains ego strength by re-introjecting parts of the self that had been projected, resulting in a new-found ability to resolve conflicts on his own, in his own way (Steiner, 1996).

The patient who clings to the belief that *it's the analyst who knows* has a different model of therapeutic action. The patient's demand for "guidance" or advice comes in many forms – as a simply stated request: "Tell me what to do, tell me how to think about the situation"; as a taunt: "You're the expert, doc, that's why I pay you"; or, as a plea: "Can't you just leave your role as analyst for once and give me your opinion?" Whichever form it takes, what becomes patently apparent is the patient's wish and sensed need for the analyst to fill the void by supplying the missing piece. If the patient regards her wish for provision as completely reasonable and therapeutically required, she will likely experience the analyst's frustration of that wish as an act of cruelty. While the analyst ideally empathizes with the patient's anxiety – the pain and narcissistic injury triggered when such provisions aren't forthcoming – she nevertheless understands that it cannot be otherwise. To pretend to be omnipotent would be a lie.

The patient's wishful thinking that the analyst is omniscient (*"le sujet suppose savoir"* – the one who is supposed to know – Lacan, 1949) constitutes an illusion that robs the patient of her own capacity to know as she projects imagined, idealized abilities into the analyst, thus weakening the patient's ego. Unanalyzed idealization typically is a harbinger of disaster to the extent it typically collapses into a devaluation of the analyst that can prove difficult to successfully interpret (Slochower, 2011). Before devaluation sets in, the patient basks in the glow of the analyst's supposed "superior knowledge" – a misunderstanding of the analyst's capacity, the analytic process, and her defining task – to help create a clinical environment that facilitates the patient's self-discovery that ideally eventuates in a working through of conflicts that interfere with her ability to recognize that she has a mind of her own and abilities she'd never dared imagine. Not until the patient comes to realize what the analyst can and cannot provide will she experience the analytic encounter as two partners participating in a collaborative effort that helps promote the development of independent thought.

The second point illustrated in this clinical moment has to do with the analyst's "adaptability" – her capacity to take note in real time of how the patient is responding to her interventions and to make rapid adjustments if the patient's behavior suggests she is not responding well to the analyst's method or message. Clinical adaptability involves a trial-and-error process that manifests in the analyst's readiness to change her approach if it appears to be making matters worse – that the analyst's present line of thinking or interventional efforts are proving intolerable. Clinical acumen is sometimes more apparent in the therapist's ability to adapt as the process unfolds – shifting track when clinically indicated – rather than in knowing from the get-go how best to initially intervene in the treatment.

There are a few published examples that demonstrate such adaptability. The first appears in an often-referenced article by Killingmo (1989) that offers a verbatim account of the interactions between analyst and patient illustrating how the analyst's interventions, based on the assumption that the patient was suffering from conflict-related repression, proved confusing and frightening for the patient, whom the analyst subsequently realized to be suffering more from deficit-based pathology. In this case, the patient's responses to the analyst's interventions were not initially recognized by the analyst as a sort of S.O.S. on the patient's part – signaling her indirect plea for the analyst to recognize that she was operating on a more primitive level – one that required the analyst adopt a somewhat different approach. The patient's responses to the analyst's interventions demonstrated that she did not "get" what he was driving at, nor did she understand why he continued to harp on a subject that was clearly leaving her feeling more and more frightened, desperate to get the analyst to notice her distress so that he might change his tack. Eventually the analyst caught on and shifted gears – which helped reestablish the working alliance.

A second published example of an analyst who found himself intervening in ways that made matters worse appears in Gill and Hoffman's (1982) volume of verbatim, audio-recorded psychoanalytic sessions with nine different patients. The one that illustrates adaptability is Patient E: Session 93 (pp. 91–115) – a young man, likely a college student, who appears to have developed a solid therapeutic alliance with his analyst until something happens midway through the reported session. The analyst pushes into territory that makes the patient increasingly uncomfortable when he suggests that they explore the patient's latent homosexual feelings toward a fellow classmate and in the transference as well, ignoring signs of the patient's mounting panic at the way in which the analyst was framing the matter. The analyst's continuing advance increasingly unnerved the patient, making it incumbent that he recognize what was happening and change course, which he ultimately does. Though this example illustrates "adaptability," it is not the sort of preferable or graceful adaptability demonstrated in Killingmo's paper in which the analyst proved able to make a much subtler shift – one that seamlessly continued his efforts to work analytically.

We now turn to the clinical moment itself, which illustrates both the issues discussed in this brief essay.

The clinical moment

What follows are a series of clinical moments that occur in rapid succession. These moments reflect a pattern in my work with the patient, Mrs. B, a woman in her late 40s who had been in four times weekly psychoanalysis for five years when this series of moments occurred. It is characteristic of the patient to feel that she is incapable of making life decisions. She is often filled with doubt about how to handle a matter at hand and at such times seeks my guidance by insisting that I tell her what she should do next. Mrs. B acts as if she cannot tolerate any ongoing doubt, and she becomes frustrated with herself and with me when her lack of confidence in her own decision-making abilities leads her to turn to me for answers, believing that I know best what she should do given the circumstances. When I sidestep the assigned task of sage, the patient typically gets annoyed and can become quite critical of me. The clinical management of such moments is illustrated in the following clinical process.

Mrs. B is 20 years into her second marriage and has two grown children: a daughter, 27 years old; and a son, Sam, 24. Mrs. B has a good life from all external appearances: Her children are well launched, her husband supports her and is more or less devoted, though she feels he neither listens to nor validates her ideas and opinions. Mrs. B wants more from him, and she feels frustrated to the point of sometimes feeling enraged that she's not been able to get him to change his ways.

Mrs. B has struggled in her efforts to maintain close friendships. She experiences herself as on the periphery of her circle of friends and distant from both her family of origin and her husband's family. Her disappointment and sense of isolation are agonizing, and her failed attempts to forge closer relationships leave her feeling miserable and unimportant. She is persistent in her efforts to build the kinds of relationships she so desires, but in the end never seems to win others over – which leaves her feeling that she doesn't matter to anyone but her immediate family. She exhibits intense narcissistic sensitivity around others and easily feels slighted. She responds by becoming tongue-tied, freezing "like a deer in headlights" for fear of outright rejection. By contrast, with her husband and children (and analyst), she is not afraid to speak up, which allows her to unleash her feelings unbridled without respect to their effect on the other.

In the transference, Mrs. B feels that she doesn't matter to me. She rationalizes her disappointment – telling herself "that's how analysis works." Signs of unconscious jealousy can be seen in her feelings about my other patients (her "analytic siblings"). Once, when I needed to shift one of her times to accommodate another patient, Mrs. B was able to recognize her competitiveness with the patient who became linked unconsciously with her next youngest sibling – a sister – who arrived when the patient was only 13 months old, leaving Mrs. B feeling displaced. Even when the link became conscious, Mrs. B could not forgive me (mother) for accommodating the new patient (baby), and she still felt "kicked out."

Mrs. B generally blames the "other" for her difficulty forging close bonds with others, exhibiting significant narcissistic pathology. Mrs. B sees herself through the eyes of others – those whose opinions are important to the extent they govern her self-esteem – and she depends on others for validation, which she measures by the compliments she receives. She hungers for recognition and cannot believe that she is significant or even *exists* unless such recognition is forthcoming. She is acutely critical of her appearance – her shape ("too fat"), her height ("too short"), her skin tone ("too pale"), and her hair ("too unruly"). She dresses to hide herself during the day, although she scrupulously attends to her appearance when she will be seen at a function by people she knows. Her tendency to project makes it difficult for Mrs. B to sort out whose judgment is whose, reflected in her tendency to become confused about what she thinks and feels and how to respond to others. The mechanism of projecting her own feelings into others and then believing those feelings are coming from them is called "projective identification." Given the strength of her need for and dependency upon the good opinions of others, Mrs. B rarely feels gratified by the compliments she does receive; she receives them as unspecific, tepid, and insincere. She envies others who seem more able to garner the admiration of others.

Mrs. B's self-esteem is further weakened by an intransigent belief that others are much more knowledgeable than she, manifesting as a transference conviction that I *must* know precisely why her friends are indifferent or hostile and why her mother is the way she is. Her conviction that I *do* in fact know why she has such difficulty forming relationships but withhold this critically needed information from her for whatever reason forms the basis of the clinical moments we are about to hear.

Mrs. B's low self-esteem is further compounded by her inability to take sufficient advantage of her genuine talents. She also routinely fails to take advantage of varied opportunities that might help improve her sense of self. When attempting the task of learning a new skill, she quickly becomes overwhelmed with the inevitable frustrations of new learning, believing that she can't succeed for lack of ability. Low frustration tolerance and a lack of faith in herself lead to the tendency to quit the task, rather than stick it out and see if the learning curve is in fact beyond her ability. Accordingly, Mrs. B misses out on opportunities to feel both accomplished and, as a result, more independent. For example, she was excelling in a graduate class but dropped the course when she grew frustrated by the challenges – even though she realized how much better she would have felt about herself had she completed the course and come away with documentation of the success and a new set of skills.

Mrs. B is the second of five children. Her older sister is four years her senior, and she has a younger sister and two younger brothers. Because the third child is only 13 months younger than she is, we came to believe that she'd been traumatized by the loss of her mother's full attention – an experience that must have been driven home with the subsequent arrival of the last two siblings. Such a loss at this preverbal stage must have had a substantial effect. Mrs. B's narrative is that she responded to feelings of competition and jealousy by becoming loud and demanding, overshadowing the baby, which she believes contributed to her being labeled "the bad one" with her sister being seen as "the good one." This persistent self-perception presently leaves the patient feeling that she is "too much" and "too demanding," fueling her belief that people find her unlikable.

Mrs. B's parents are married, and while they presently live in the same city as the patient, they rarely see one another. Both parents experienced much deprivation as children. Her father was orphaned at age 12, while the mother was orphaned during her teen years. Their marriage was tumultuous, and Mrs. B couldn't wait to get married and leave home.

Mrs. B describes her mother as nervous, socially awkward, and avoidant of social contact. Her parents did not celebrate holidays or birthdays; they hid when the doorbell rang and let the message machine answer the phone. They never had people over or entertained. Mrs. B reports that her mother was vague and prone to spouting platitudes. Mrs. B feels similarly about the compliments she receives today. She recalls that her mother treated her like a friend she'd confide in, leaving the patient hungering for mothering – which she presently seeks from her woman friends (and in the transference). Such tendencies likely contribute to her difficulties forming satisfactory peer relations.

In the transference, Mrs. B swings from feeling that I am a good analyst who is meeting her needs to feeling that I am a bad analyst who frustrates her expectation that I perform in particular ways. When frustrated, the patient can become highly critical of me – contemptuous and sharp-tongued. In particular, when she becomes overwhelmingly frustrated, she tends to unravel psychically, which manifests in her engaging in shaming and retaliating attacks on me. She'll lash out saying, for example: "You're not helping me – I don't know why I come here," or, mockingly, "just spit it out" or "that's a bunch of psychobabble."

Sometimes, the way she treats me frankly rattles me, making it hard for me to think. Her critical view of me triggers my own self-critical thoughts, which can disable my capacity to create useful interpretations or helpful interventions. At such times, I struggle to regain an empathic analytic stance, reminding myself that Mrs. B's attacks are manifestations of her anxiety – which helps me tolerate what feels to me like mistreatment. Sometimes, I remind her that we think differently and that my pace is different from hers, and that I can't produce "on demand" even though she is desperate to get relief. I think these moments mirror her own tendency to feel tongue-tied when she feels attacked or slighted by friends – that my countertransference feelings are concordant in nature – with me being assigned the task of containing the sorts of deer-in-the-headlight-type feelings she oftentimes experiences with friends. At such times, I feel caught by the need to say something to alleviate her (and my own) frustration. This is difficult when I am at the same time hindered by the feeling that I lack the tools needed to accomplish this goal, succumbing momentarily to the submerging effect of the countertransference – which recedes when I am finally able to come up for air. I eventually am able to regain my bearings, and with it my empathy, by reminding myself of the underpinnings of Mrs. B's feelings of persecution. When I remember that her reactions date back to infancy and her experiences of feeling bereft and untethered, I imagine Mrs. B as a small child, which engenders in me feelings of wanting to comfort her.

The following clinical moments occurred immediately following a gap in treatment due to a three-day Memorial Day weekend. The patient is tremendously upset that her son, Sam, has called her husband – not her – and confided that he is "freaking out" because he didn't feel prepared to take his law exams that would be held three weeks hence. He told her husband that he'd not been doing well on the practice exams and that he must pass the exam to graduate to the next level. The patient is reacting to a confluence of issues: the hurtful fact that her son had not turned to her, her uncertainty of how to respond to the information that Sam had confided in his father – meaning that she might feel as if she were betraying a confidence if she spoke up – and her own feeling of panic in response to Sam's panic:

MRS B: I told Sam about sleeping, studying without music, and running to relax. I knew something was wrong. I told my husband that one cannot study with music – that it divides the brain – but my stupid husband always undermines me. So he's the good guy and I'm the bad one. He says, "*I* always studied listening to music." When the children were small he undermined me by saying, "Mom has her time of the month and is in a bad mood. Let's get out and go to the park." So they learned to listen to him and ignore me. This is a crisis now and Sam is freaking out. If he fails this test he's out of law school. They don't offer a re-take. That was another one of my husband's gems. Sam never should have started law school when he did. He wasn't prepared, but no one listened to me. Once again my husband discounted me. For a change, what I predicted happened (said sarcastically). I'm worried that this will lead to something really bad for him. If he flunks out I hope there are no bridges in the area. He is so depressed. I don't know what to do. *Dr. Smith, do you see why I hate my husband?*

The patient is posing a direct question. Should I respond, let her continue to associate, or interpret her need for validation? What intervention makes sense? She is so distraught that an interpretation might prove ill-timed and un-empathic. And yet, perhaps the best support is a good interpretation. What to do?

Invited commentator responses 1: Jay Greenberg, Albert Mason, and Dominique Scarfone[3]

Jay Greenberg

What impressed me most in Dr. Smith's introduction of her patient is her own countertransference. Rightly or wrongly, and for better or for worse, I was unable to read the process without having thoughts about this foremost in my mind. And unlike in live supervision, I am able to refer back to the text as needed, so my thoughts about the countertransference are far more fully conscious than they usually are when I respond to clinical material.

Consider: "Mrs. B has a good life from all external appearances: her children are well launched, *her husband supports her and is more or less devoted, though she feels he neither listens to nor validates her ideas and opinions*" (my emphasis). Note the contrast: "her husband supports her," presented as an objective fact; "though she feels he neither listens to nor validates her ideas and opinions," presented as the patient's presumably distorted subjective experience. This colors everything that follows: Despite all that is available to her, Mrs. B is presented to us as unwilling or unable to make use of it and "blames the 'other' for her difficulty forging close bonds with others."

I assume that this dynamic formulation grows out of Dr. Smith's experience of the analysis; that is, I assume that it is an account of five years of the analyst feeling that her best efforts have been rejected. This is virtually certain to evoke what Heinrich Racker (1957) called a "complementary identification," that is, an identification with the patient's objects. Put in other terms, I imagine that it has led to something of a transference/countertransference impasse, what the Brazilian analyst Roosevelt Cassorla (2012) terms a "chronic enactment," and that the particular moments at which Dr. Smith wonders what could be said are what we might call "tipping points," in the sense that they are mini-crises that will shape the future course of the treatment.

Like all enactments, the one I sense in Dr. Smith's account is a two-way street. I was especially struck by this: "Once, when I needed to shift one of her times to accommodate another patient, Mrs. B was able to recognize her competitiveness…" The silences in this sentence speak far louder than the rather ordinary "insight" that Mrs. B was able to achieve. Why, faced with *another* patient's demand for a different hour, did Dr. Smith decide to change Mrs. B's session? Every analyst knows, although we rarely say it out loud, that there are some patients whose sessions we find it easy to change, while there are others with whom we would never dare even to raise the possibility. What is it about Mrs. B, and about the relationship between her and Dr. Smith, that makes her sessions easy to change? Dr. Smith has told us that Mrs. B's husband is "more or less" devoted to her; has the same "more or less" found its way into the analysis?

Perhaps even more striking, how does Mrs. B know that her session was changed so that Dr. Smith could "accommodate" another patient? We need to be clear that in changing the session and in disclosing her reason for the change Dr. Smith is introducing the "other" into the analytic relationship. One way of putting this is to say that she is introducing triangulation, and thereby introducing reality into a dyad that may have begun to feel suffocating. This is, of course, another manifestation of countertransference; it may be part of what Cassorla would call an "acute enactment." In light of this, I cannot follow the account of the session without being nagged by and skeptical of Dr. Smith's comment that "*In the transference* [as opposed to "as a result of our co-created enactment"], Mrs. B feels that she doesn't matter to me."

Because of this, as a consultant, I would be interested in why Dr. Smith was bringing the case to me just now, not when she was faced with the need to change Mrs. B's session. And I can't hold this moment without thinking of that one. And, of course, of all the other moments that lead us to this one.

All of this should make it clear that it is impossible for me to approach the exchanges I have been asked to comment on in anything like the frame of mind that the analyst was in; whatever I have to say should be read in that light.

It seems to me that the moment is saturated with Mrs. B's affect; it seems pointless to try to address anything else and pointless to try to find particular meaning in either the question itself or the associations leading up to it.

I would probably say something like, "I see that you are terribly angry [even to speculate about toward whom she was feeling the anger would feel like too much of a stretch] and that you feel helplessly trapped in your anger." *Contra* Dr. Smith, I wouldn't say that I see that Mrs. B feels scared for her son, because it's not yet clear to me that she is actually scared rather than contemptuous and angry. And I am sure that I would not say "I see *why* you feel scared for your son, and angry at being dismissed..." – first of all, because I wouldn't know why she feels that way, and second, because saying that I did would position myself as a "good object" who is more empathic and/or compassionate than her family members. Because of the considerations I noted in my general comments, I don't believe that Dr. Smith necessarily *is* so different from the others, and accordingly, I would find suggesting that she is to be misleading. It will be helpful to keep this in mind as the session unfolds, the analyst coming to believe that she must shift to a more "supportive" stance.

Albert Mason

The problem that is being addressed in this clinical moment is that of a patient who has transformed the understanding of her own unconscious anxieties (her analysis) into some other process wherein concrete help is felt to be the solution to her problems. The patient is demanding action from her analyst in place of understanding her own inability to act appropriately. In the case we are considering, the patient Mrs. B wants instruction from her analyst about handling a situation and saying the "right" thing to her distressed son. This situation is complicated by the fact that the patient feels that her son might actually kill himself ("I hope there are no bridges in the area").

We know that her son Sam is conveying and projecting extreme anxiety – even panic – into his mother. Is this a countertransference communication of suicidality from the son to the patient? Can we ignore that possibility? I, for one, could not and, moreover, I do not believe that Mrs. B or her analyst should make that decision. I would tell the patient that she and I are in no position to know how serious Sam's anxiety is and that he would best be served by seeing a psychiatrist for evaluation. It seems that Sam would be helped with his performance anxiety by consulting a mental health professional, and that his mother's own anxiety prevents her from being of assistance here. In fact, any attempt on her part to intervene might well make Sam worse by her collusion with a very distraught young man. The father's concern adds to the seriousness of the situation.

I think that underlying Mrs. B's more sophisticated anxieties is a very primitive anxiety concerning the baby and the breast originally, and the baby part of the personality and the life-giving aspect of the analysis or analyst in the present. This patient's infantile misconception is that if she doesn't get what she thinks she needs now (the answer, formula, interpretation, or omnipotent solution) she will die. Since the phantasy of what is needed is so vital and life-sustaining, the infant constructs an ideal image of the breast or mother – the supplier of this elixir of life. Not only must the feed be perfectly timed and exactly what is required, it must quench the inexhaustible thirst now and forever. This is clearly a delusional, unrealistic demand.

Since the infant relates to her object from birth onward by projection and introjection and builds her mind by these introjects, she introjects an object that is the product of reality plus her projections. These introjects form the primitive superego which is a distorted view of reality containing the infant's projected magical and perfectionistic phantasies. This introject (now a superego) demands of the child and later the adult exactly that which the child demanded of the breast or mother originally as a life-sustaining object. Mrs. B feels that she has to give her child today exactly what she demanded of the idealized breast-analyst originally to keep her son-baby alive. She must become the omnipotent all-providing breast that she requires the analyst to be.

I am suggesting that if this dynamic had been clarified earlier, the present situation or impasse may not have developed.

It is not easy to undo the patient's belief in the idealized analyst and her idealized powers and functions. The patient must be confronted with her refusal to accept the limitations of reality for fear of a deadly outcome if total satisfaction is not achieved. Klein's formulation that the breast is sought by the baby not only as a source of nourishment but as a relief of persecutory anxiety seems to be illustrated in this case in which the patient's urgent demand for answers is to obtain relief from persecution (her son will die) rather than insight or understanding. In addition, the patient's desire for a concrete response such as advice from the analyst is often from a baby part of the personality that wants physical evidence of being cared for – like holding. Words are too grown up.

Despite the fact that Mrs. B's anxiety may be exaggerated due to guilt – realistic or delusional – I believe that the real possibility of the son's suicide must be addressed. It needs to be made clear to this patient that neither she nor her husband has any way of objectively assessing the risk of suicide, and that professional help must be enlisted, one way or another.

However, addressing the central question of the patient breaking the analytic process is quite another problem. Since analysis frequently mobilizes anxieties which were heretofore unconscious due to suppression or splitting and projecting, it is common that defenses against these anxieties are immediately sought. Defenses can be obvious such as lateness, cancelling sessions, failing to pay bills, frank hostility, or seeking other treatments or analysts. They can also take the form of manic episodes to evade depressive anxieties, various enactments, and more subtle forms such as reversal of roles in which the analyst is seen as needing the patient rather than vice versa. These manic maneuvers could be described as negative therapeutic reactions, mild or severe.

Understanding and interpreting the anxiety defended against by these reactions is sometimes easy; they might be linked to the analyst's vacations, illness, or even normal gaps like weekends and the phantasies these gaps produce. Feelings of rejection are common, as are anxieties about the analyst's illness or death, and jealousy concerning others in the analyst's inner circle. Envy of the phantasies about the analyst and his or her life are also frequent sources of negative responses.

The associations, history, and repetitions of the patient will usually give clues as to which anxiety is presently mobilizing the defense. The analyst may be frustrated at these interruptions of treatment and feel he or she has addressed the unconscious anxiety many times, but will often be surprised at the various subtle misconceptions the patient has that have yet to be uncovered and worked through. The same symptoms may have many causations and different levels of origin – from the patient's infancy, to latency period, to adolescence, right up to the present day. Repetitive resistances that appear similar may spring from different sources due to internal phantasies, current or genetic, or external events, traumatic or happy.

In the patient in question, the search for an omnipotent analyst, answer, or magic formula for her problem is obvious and her wish to impart this incantation to her son equally clear. I suspect, however, that the idealization of the analyst and her supposed universal expertise has not yet been fully teased out. The secondary effects of the idealization are clear enough. As discussed above, the introjection of this ideal figure (the analyst) forming a superego demanding that the patient become ideal or perfect produces all the feelings of doubt and inadequacy from which this patient suffers. Furthermore, the attacks on and devaluation of the ideal object because of envy do not appear to have been made clear. The creativity of the ideal object and her fantasized magic as a defense against the patient's persecutory anxiety also need to be clarified.

Mrs. B's mother appears to have been significantly paranoid and would therefore be persecuted by her daughter's projections of anxiety and hostility. The inability of Mrs. B's mother to be helpful and understanding to her daughter would certainly contribute to the development of narcissistic defenses in the patient. This dynamic is repeated transferentially when the patient attacks her analyst, rattling her and preventing her from thinking. The early birth of Mrs. B's sister must have played a crucial part in the patient's attacks on her parents' intercourse, and the subsequent introjection and identification with the split couple then interferes with the patient's own creative endeavors. The transferential situation in which the patient splits the analyst's mind would be another version of the clinical moment, which can be seen as an attack on the analyst's attempt to think and work. At these moments, the analyst has lost the capacity to understand and respond appropriately.

Dominique Scarfone

A preliminary warning. Since I am not the analyst in the room and am therefore not exposed to the affective load that the patient's words, both in content and tone, would have put on me, I can only try to imagine what I would do or say. Mrs. B is, I believe, a rather difficult patient, one who poses many challenges to the analyst wishing to maintain the analytic process on track. Therefore, in reading my comments, the reader should keep in mind that my personal take on the material both suffers and benefits from the fact that I was not caught in the *actual* climate of this analysis, nor did I personally face the difficult form of transference that is at work here. Also, there are many threads that could be followed in the material offered here for discussion. Obviously, I will need to ignore many of them and concentrate on what I consider the main aspect.

To answer the question, "What do I do?", I think I would probably not respond to the patient's question and let her go on associating. Yet, I am well aware that this could frustrate her and make her insist that I say something. In that case, I would probably base myself on her sense that "no one listens to [her]," so, in partial agreement with Dr. Smith's intervention below, I think I would say something like:

> On the one hand, you *seem to feel* all alone in the present situation and want to know if someone is listening to you, *here, now, in this room*. You also seem to want me to validate your feelings towards your husband, *as if you could not trust your own reasons for having those feelings.*

The session continues

(After the patient asks the analyst whether she can understand why she hates her husband who had turned a deaf ear to her concern that their son was not ready to attend law school):

A: I see why you feel scared for your son, and angry at being dismissed by your family. I see that you feel alone and unsupported.
MRS B: Sam says he studies constantly – he's under tremendous pressure. He lives like a hermit, doesn't go to class, and downloads the lectures. I've told him there's a reason they hold classes – you get the information

twice – by hearing it and by reading it. Why do we pay for an apartment so close to the campus when he doesn't even attend the classes?
A: Maybe the pressure is too great on him but he is afraid of disappointing you.
MRS B: I don't think so. I've always told him, from the beginning, that all we expect from him is to do his best. It's not about outcome. "Just do your best Sam, and let it go after that."
A: Just because you said that doesn't mean that that is what he took in. He may have internalized a message that makes him feel he must succeed or he will be a disappointment.[The analyst reports thinking to herself: I suspected that her narcissistic investment in her son's performance and accomplishments leads her to need him to succeed so that she can then feel that she's a good mother].

MRS B: I can see that. His father didn't give him the guidance he needed. He wasn't out playing ball with him or helping him become athletic. As a result, he was bullied. It started in junior high school after my brother-in-law (who is a doctor) gave him the meds for his gastric condition. Sam changed after that. I looked up the side effects, which included depression. I think my brother-in-law wanted him to fail. There is a competition there and I don't think he gave him the best options and I don't think he is the best doctor. They sure worked hard to see their kids succeed but I don't think he did the same for my child. Sam is still taking those meds today.

[The analyst reports thinking to herself: Mrs. B is unable to be thoughtful and continues to feel persecuted. She blames her husband and her brother-in-law. The patient's anxiety is escalating to the point of the development of paranoid thoughts].

MRS B: My husband ran into a high school friend of Sam's who said that another friend of theirs "corrupted Sam." What does that mean? Drugs? Alcohol? This kid never came to our house – Sam always went there. Was he taking drugs? Sam was furious one night when we didn't allow him to go to the kid's house. Sam's sister is a combination of street smart and really able to pick herself up after she falls. I'm not so sure about Sam. He is anxious and doesn't have much self-esteem. Maybe it was the rotten start he got at birth – in the hospital when the doctors gave me an opioid medicine and forgot to discontinue it on time! Who knows what that did to his brain that was just beginning to get wired. Sam seems to need direction: Tell him what to do and he'll do it. He is not a self-starter. He is much less able to act for himself.

[The analyst reports thinking to herself: It occurs to me at this juncture that the patient may well be describing herself. She too is anxious, lacking in self-esteem, and is often seeking just such direction from me. She has trouble initiating action given her lack of self-confidence and her doubt about whether she knows what needs to be done. Her tendency to project – to attribute her own feelings and traits to others – was well known to both of us at this point, and helping her sort out who's who so that she'd be less inclined to become psychically merged with others was one of my goals for her treatment].

So…*do I suggest that the patient could well be addressing a side of herself that she sees in Sam? What do I say?*

Invited commentator responses 2: Jay Greenberg, Albert Mason, and Dominique Scarfone

Jay Greenberg

This is a good example of a point at which I wonder why the analyst is asking for help just now. To my ear the exchanges leading up to this moment reflect Mrs. B's increasingly desperate attempts to be heard by the analyst, along with her rage that these attempts will fail. When Mrs. B says that she's told her son that "there's a reason they hold classes – you get the information twice," I'm certain that she is referring to the present moment, to her despair that the analyst will ever learn.

So at that point I would say, "I think that there's some information that you're trying to communicate to me, and that I'm not hearing it, even though you've been trying to let me know in every way you can." But instead, Dr. Smith says, "Maybe the pressure is too great on him but he is afraid of disappointing you." This must be exactly what Dr. Smith is feeling at the moment – the pressure is on her and she is afraid of disappointing Mrs. B, but she deflects her own anxiety, externalizing it onto the figure of the son and, in the process, blaming the patient and instigating the paranoid turn that characterizes the next several exchanges.

This suggests that from my point of view the analyst is a full participant in this spiral. Mrs. B says that she has told her son that all that matters is that he does his best, to which Dr. Smith replies that perhaps the son has taken in "a message that makes him feel he must succeed or he will be a disappointment." What I find crucial here is not the content of the comment, which may be accurate, but the analyst's need to externalize her own countertransference response, a need that will register, at least unconsciously, in the patient's experience. The reflection that "Mrs. B is unable to be thoughtful and continues to feel persecuted" follows from this rejection of her transference experience.

All of this shapes my response to the second moment. I think what is needed is what John Steiner (1994) calls an "analyst-centered interpretation," or some comment that grows out of the analyst's awareness of what has recently been termed a co-created "bastion" or an "occlusion" in the bipersonal field. I would not comment on the content but on what is happening in the room. Something like: "You must be afraid that I have gotten so caught up in wanting to be helpful that I am driven to force ideas into you that just don't make sense. It is hard for both of us, each caught up in our personal crises, to acknowledge how bad it feels to be in the room together."

Of course if I were able to say these things – and I would be able to say them only if I were really on my game that day which is unlikely in the context of Mrs. B's emotional state – the session would certainly not unfold as it did. Accordingly, my subsequent responses will be even more hypothetical than they would be in different circumstances.

Albert Mason

I think I would say something like: "I think you are frightened and feel helpless and hate yourself for not knowing what to do. You want me to instruct you because you feel I am supposed to have all the answers. But if you think that your son is suicidal, it is clear that he needs an independent professional assessment, since neither of us is in the position of knowing what to do."

Dominique Scarfone

I agree with Dr. Smith that the patient is describing herself (and it is very possible that her son is indeed like she describes him, but this we cannot know for sure). With the advantage of hindsight, having had the time to think back to the earlier part of the session and the background information provided above – something the analyst could not do as easily in the heat of the session – I believe I would have said to her something like:

> As I listen to you describing your son, *I feel* you are *also* describing part of yourself, as if a very intimate relationship connected you to him, making you forget that he is now a grown-up. This may get you much too closely entangled in your son's life and therefore *overly concerned* with his difficulties.

The session continues

(After the patient enumerates her son's many handicaps – he is anxiety-ridden, lacks self-confidence and self-esteem, and is incapable of self-direction – which, to the analyst's ears, sound like traits she shares with her son):

A: That sounds like you. It doesn't mean he's not smart, just as it doesn't mean you're not smart. It means Sam is different from his sister and he struggles differently. Things happened over which you had no control and you are anxious that there was early damage.

[The analyst reports thinking to herself: I think about Mrs. B's guilt over Sam's rough start in life].

Dominique Scarfone's comment

I agree. Mrs. B feels guilty over Sam's rough start and his present problem. But since she strongly projected her guilt onto others, I don't think she was, at that moment, ready to access her own guilt feelings. This is why, in my imagined intervention, I would have used the expression "overly concerned," with no mention of guilt. In this way, however, I would still have implicitly addressed her narcissistic investment in her son and situated myself as a gently critical "Greek chorus" inviting her to reexamine the situation.

Editor's comment

After the analyst suggests that Sam may have internalized a message from his parents that made him feel that he must succeed lest he disappoint them, the patient launches into a campaign to lay blame for Sam's difficulties on others' shoulders: her husband, her brother-in-law, a high school friend who corrupted Sam, the hospital staff that overmedicated him shortly after birth. The possibility that the patient may have felt subtly blamed by the analyst for her son's problems is reinforced by the analyst thought that the patient was narcissistically invested in her son's accomplishment. While the analyst never verbalized such a belief, one can easily imagine the patient picking up on an undercurrent when the analyst wondered aloud whether Sam might be feeling pressured by the need to satisfy his parents' needs. Noting that the patient was feeling persecuted to the point of becoming paranoid, the analyst shifts tack by moving in the direction of providing more support. She tells the patient that she is smart, that she is not to blame – after all, in the final analysis, these are things over which she lacks control. This illustrates a process referred to in the preceding essay as "adaptability."

Dominique Scarfone's comment

I'd rather suggest that here the analyst's "change of gear" was needed to correct something that had been elicited by his/her earlier comments about Sam. The analyst now clearly wishes, with good reasons, to bring the patient back on a less paranoid track. As I said earlier, I also sometimes fall in the trap of commenting about something "out there," and what I usually get in return is indeed a paranoid stance. I find that, in spite – or because – of my efforts at being sympathetic and understanding, my patient and I get finally caught in becoming members of a "paranoid community." This is why I believe that we should avoid as much as possible comments on what may "really" have happened "out there." Sometimes, of course, this is impossible. But as I will indicate later, I believe another path was available in the present case.

The session continues

(After the analyst reminds the patient that things happened to her son "over which you had no control":)

A: Maybe Sam needs a less pressured career. What might happen if he succeeds at this point and discovers law isn't for him? Will he – and you – be OK with that?
MRS B: (There is a short silence) I asked him if he had second thoughts. He did research for a summer. He said he wanted to do litigation and was committed to law.

[The analyst reports noticing: As we talk, the patient appears to shift from being panicky about her son's panic as she turns more thoughtful and reflective].

A: I think when you put everything into one giant tumbleweed, you feel overwhelmed and one thing seems just like another: not being listened to, being overmedicated at birth, Sam's depression and panic, and your fear that he may jump off a bridge. You then can't separate out what is unlikely from what makes sense, and what you have no control over. It feels like everything is against you, and that makes you feel helpless and frustrated.
MRS B: I can see that but I don't know what to do. *I want to do something* but to say that he doesn't have to finish law school could be seen as the opposite of supportive. If I call he would know that I know he's freaking out. He didn't call me – he called my husband – and that could make him feel betrayed. I could send him a note, just "Hang in there – we're with you," but I would feel terrible if he took it the wrong way. I'm worried about him. What if this is the onset of schizophrenia? I want to know that I did everything possible to help in every possible way and then I can let go.
A: It sounds like you feel a note is the best way to go, as a note like that communicates support without being intrusive.
MRS B: Knowing all you know and given your expertise and training: Do you think that *is* the best way to go?

Editor's comment

This is the third in a series of clinical moments that require the therapist to think on her feet even though she doesn't feel certain how best to respond. As mentioned before, therapists don't always have the luxury of certainty – oftentimes, they rely upon their implicit clinical intuition, which is based on a combination of empathy, mentalization, past clinical experience, and knowledge of the patient's developmental background. This third clinical moment, like the first, is triggered by a direct question posed by the patient. In this case, the patient is directly seeking expert advice from the therapist. If you were her analyst, how do you imagine you might respond to such a request?

Invited commentator responses 3: Jay Greenberg, Albert Mason, and Dominique Scarfone

Jay Greenberg

This section starts with the Editor's comment that at this point "The therapist wisely moves in the direction of providing more support." I would note that the wisdom of doing so – we could skeptically characterize this as the wisdom of abandoning a more analytic approach – derives from the failure so far in the session to address what is actually happening in the room. "Support" under these circumstances seems to me to operate in the service of undoing an enactment. As a matter of principle, I don't think this is the best route to take. It may be accurate to say that the analyst is showing "adaptability," but it seems to me that there is something that is also and irreducibly self-protective about offering support at this point.

Interestingly, patient and analyst have arrived at the feelings of helplessness that I mentioned earlier. But what is addressed is only the *patient's* helplessness in the face of her son's struggle. In contrast, I am struck by the *shared* helplessness, analyst and patient joined inextricably in their despair about things ever getting better. Mrs. B wonders if writing a note to her son is the best way to go – is there some way that she can be of use while sparing her son from having to deal with her as a fully living and present person? And Dr. Smith wonders if giving advice is what she must do – sparing Mrs. B from having to deal with her as a fully empowered analyst. Because of the way things have evolved in the session Dr. Smith certainly can't say anything about this, but it is where I would hope to be. Dr. Smith's reflection that Mrs. B is "disappointed and frustrated with my response" suggests to me that she is hoping for a more genuine and personal exchange with her analyst.

Albert Mason

Again, the patient feels that either she or her analyst should know the best thing to do when neither of them is in the position of really assessing the situation. I would say, "Your love of your son makes it difficult for you to assess the situation objectively, even though you feel you should. Having him examined by a qualified mental health professional will place the responsibility for assessment where it belongs."

Dominique Scarfone

Thanks to Dr. Smith's intervention regarding other possible choices available to Sam, the patient is now more reflexive indeed. But, comforted as she was by the analyst's previous "reality comments," Mrs. B again resorts to a direct request for advice. Is the choice, however, simply between giving or not giving advice? I believe there is a third way – one that has to do with a significant aspect of the material that, in my view, was left unexamined.

Indeed, it is obvious to me that the patient induced the analyst into implicitly *sharing her belief* that Sam did not want his mother to know about his problems at law school. But not only is there no evidence of such a thing, this belief actually reflects the patient's own need to project in her son's psyche the idea of a total split between her husband and herself. How indeed could Sam possibly believe that his father would have kept his distress call a secret and not tell his wife? Her dilemma – to call or not to call her son – had therefore no basis in reality and resulted from an internal conflict.

Many factors certainly contributed to Mrs. B's projection and her ensuing pseudo-dilemma. As for me, I would have first addressed the patient's *resentment* towards her son for not having called her and having chosen instead to confide in his father. In my view, Mrs. B felt that in calling his father, her son contradicted her wish for a relationship like the one she herself had experienced with her own mother: being her confidante, forming a very intimate couple with the mother, thereby excluding the father. This sort of coupling creates a problematic, yet powerful kind of bond between parent and child, one that, I dare say, ultimately concerns the primal scene – or rather, in the present case, its very distorted, truncated form (father is the one being excluded).

Introducing the primal scene in the present context may seem far-fetched. After all, isn't the problem of who Sam called or not an issue that can be addressed directly, without recurring to such a "deep" kind of formulation? As a matter of fact, I imagine that when Mrs. B said that her son had called her husband but not her, and therefore that she feels uneasy at calling and giving him support, I would have simply asked: "What makes you think that your son didn't expect you to be informed of his worries?" And I would have added: "Could it be that your hesitation in calling him is in part due to your frustration and anger at not having been informed first-hand by your son?"

These are simple questions, but I believe they are directed at the core of the material in this session. And let me insist that in this material the primal scene is lurking. Not that I would have rushed toward interpreting this aspect of the question, but the primal scene – its truncated form, as noticeable in both the patient's childhood history (being her mother's confidante) and in her relationship to her son (wishing to make one with him) – appears to me as the background organizer of the clinical moments we are discussing. It is a matter of incest-like wishes on the part of Mrs. B's mother and Mrs. B herself, who both seem to wish to create a special bond with their child and to exclude the fathers.

Mrs. B's pseudo-dilemma ("Should I call my son or not?") therefore seems to stem from her unconscious urge to form a special couple with her son, and this is why she strongly resents the latter's communication with his father. She is angry at her son, hence she cannot bring herself to simply call and be supportive towards him. She is stuck in a conflict concerning aggression (she also does not want to compromise the chances of maintaining a special bond with Sam), so through a reactive formation against her anger she experiences an excessive concern about not breaking a confidentiality pact between father and son – a pact which, for all we know, exists only in the patient's imagination.

The reader will have noticed that I just used the term *conflict*. Indeed, I do not share the "provision" model described in the introductory notes. I hope I will have succeeded in showing that under the apparent space to be "filled in" by the analyst a desire is actually at work, a desire that must be analyzed so as to shed light on the actual motives of a given manifest situation.

The session continues

(After the analyst agrees that it might be best were the patient to write her son, to which the patient responds by seeking further reassurance that the analyst agrees this is so given her expertise):

A: There's no guarantee, is there? It would be nice if I just knew the right thing to say or do so that there would be a good outcome, but that's impossible. No one possesses the power to know with certainty someone else's mind. And there is no one perfect response that will cover all bases. All you can do is think about what you'd like to say, weigh the possible outcomes, and say it with love.

MRS B: I come here and tell you everything I can and it's like going to a doctor's office. I want a prescription. I'm not saying I'll follow it – I just want something more than, "you figure it out." I pay you for your supposed expert advice.

[The analyst reports thinking to herself: Mrs. B was disappointed and frustrated with my response, leading her to express herself aggressively. She acted as if nothing short of direct advice could provide the assurance she was seeking. She struck out at me and, by so doing, was provoking me to feel as small and impotent as she herself was feeling in the moment. The patient implied that she wasn't getting her money's worth and denigrated my clinical skills – my "supposed" expertise. In this moment, she sees me as "the ineffectual one" and strikes out accordingly. I believe this is a reversal of roles through projective identification, where she becomes the one who knows and I become the dumb charlatan.]

How would you respond to the patient's expression of criticism and disappointment?

Invited commentator responses 4: Jay Greenberg, Albert Mason, and Dominique Scarfone

Jay Greenberg

As I've said, I would hope not to be here at this point, and if I were, there might not be any way to salvage the situation. In such circumstances, it is reassuring to remind ourselves that the patient will be coming back tomorrow and that we'll both have another chance.

However, I might consider saying something like, "Perhaps you are afraid that through trying to be helpful, by trying to suggest what might work with your son, I have lost touch with your emotional state. Have we created a situation where we're both feeling inadequate, perhaps both flailing, not knowing how to work ourselves out of a situation that seems to be becoming increasingly out of control?" The Editor comments on something similar, noting that neither therapist nor patient "are truly in a position to know how best to handle the situation." But as things have unfolded this is talked about in displacement, rather than as something that is happening in the room, between the two of them, and to which each of them is contributing. That, to me, is where the real potential for therapeutic gain lies.

Albert Mason

I think at this moment I would say something like: "Your anxiety understandably makes you search for magical solutions and certainties from yourself and me. Your questioning me must also be related to your search for a mother who will listen and respond. I think you feel that you need more than understanding; you need the tone of the words to make you feel held, cared for, and safe. And I think your disappointment with me shows me that you feel unwanted and rejected if I can't offer a magic solution for your son's pain."

Dominique Scarfone

In my opinion, with the kind of interventions I suggested above, chances are this last expression of disappointment would not have come into being. I would expect indeed that my questions or comments to the patient about her false dilemma – which I deem based on a non-existent confidentiality issue between her husband and Sam – would have directed the session towards a different ending. I surmise that at some point we would have landed in the vicinity of her wishes for a special bond with her son, much in the manner of the one she was caught in with her mother. Repetition compulsion indeed often creates such similar patterns from one generation to the next.

By the way, Mrs. B's insistence on getting answers and advice from the analyst appears to me as invitations directed at the analyst to also enter into a special relationship with her – a relationship where the analyst would be willing, among other things, to let go of her analytic stance and give her "expert advice." But, in spite of appearances, this call to the "doctor" and to his/her prescriptions has nothing to do with "reality"; hence, I believe the analyst should resist the call for "adapting" her conduct, since the patient's request should be heard at the level of the transference. For one thing, the patient tries to secure with the analyst the kind of special bond that her son has apparently denied her in calling his father rather than her; moreover, she tries to solve her internal conflict by putting the onus of the decision on the "doctor's prescription," but she also immediately warns the analyst that she may not actually follow the doctor's advice – one more indication, I believe, that in "getting the analyst's advice," it's "getting the analyst" that matters to her, and not the "advice."

In my work as supervisor, I am often presented with similar situations where the analyst is put under pressure to give the patient a direct answer, be it advice, information, or the like. Obviously, this is never a comfortable position, and the analyst – I include myself, as I said earlier – may end up putting him/herself in what I would call the "problem-solving mode." This may at first appear as the reasonable thing to do. However, most often I find that trading analytic listening for the problem-solving attitude only produces more frustration and is sometimes conducive to a clinical impasse. Hence, while I believe that the analyst must indeed adjust his/her interventions to the patient's capacity to use them, I am not fond of "adaptability" if what is implied by this term is leaving the analytic stance for something else. Mind you, I, no less than others, am prone to going astray from the analytic stance, but I would certainly not elevate this sort of incident to the status of a special know-how.

The session continues

(After the patient demands she get her money's worth of expert advice from the analyst):

A: I suppose that if you want him to be safe and to do everything possible to keep him from hurting himself the only thing you can do is go there, take him out of school, take him to a psychiatrist, and have him put into a psych unit at a hospital. Even then, he could kill himself. People have been known to commit suicide in hospitals and jails.

[The analyst reports thinking to herself: I believe that Mrs. B saw the impossibility of what she was asking, fell silent, and become more reflective. She realized that she is ultimately not in control of her son's life and can only do so much, that the two of them are separate, and that the control of Sam's life rests with Sam.]

MRS B: I think I will write a note. I'll just say something short and encouraging. [The analyst reports thinking to herself: She said this in a relaxed tone of voice with no hint of aggression. It appears as if the patient has resolved about how best to handle the matter without being told what to do].

Dominique Scarfone's final comments

The patient has apparently resolved her pseudo-dilemma all by herself: She decided she will write her son a note. A "solution" was found without the analyst giving the requested advice. The analyst should be commended for not having given the direct response the patient wanted. The fact remains, however, that the issue was dealt with only at the manifest level, when, as I have explained, in my view the issue lay elsewhere. Conflictual desires were lurking and could have probably been brought to consciousness, concerning both the patient's desire for a special bond with her son and the transferential version of the same.

Notes

1 Self psychologists would disagree to the extent they believe that psychopathology emanates from the caregiver's failure to serve as a growth-promoting selfobject.
2 Further along, we will see how an analyst who thinks in terms of projective identification would see the matter differently.
3 This is the only clinical moment to contain comments from three commentators. This was the result of the Editors erroneously assigning three commentators to the same moment.

References

Cassorla, R. (2012). What happens before and after acute enactments? An exercise in clinical validation and the broadening of hypotheses. *International Journal of Psychoanalysis*, 93(1), 53–80.

Gill, M., & Hoffman, I. (1982). *Analysis of transference, vol. II: Studies of nine audio-recorded psychoanalytic sessions*. New York: International Universities Press.

Killingmo, B. (1989). Conflict and deficit: Implications for technique. *International Journal of Psychoanalysis*, 70(1), 65–79.

Klein, M. (1946). Notes on some schizoid mechanisms. *International Journal of Psychoanalysis*, 27(3–4), 99–110.

Lacan, J. (1949). The mirror stage as formative of the function of the I as revealed in psychoanalytic experience. In *Écrits: A selection* (A. Sheridan, Trans.) (pp. 1–7). New York: W. W. Norton & Co.

Racker, H. (1957). The meanings and uses of countertransference. *Psychoanalytic Quarterly*, 26(3), 303–357.
Rosenfeld, H. A. (1964). On the psychopathology of narcissism: A clinical approach. *International Journal of Psychoanalysis*, 45(2–3), 332–337.
Rosenfeld, H. A. (1971). A clinical approach to the psychoanalytic theory of the life and death instincts: An investigation into the aggressive aspects of narcissism. *International Journal of Psychoanalysis*, 52(2), 169–178.
Slochower, J. (2011). Analytic idealizations and the disavowed: Winnicott, his patients, and us. *Psychoanalytic Dialogues*, 21(1), 3–21.
Steiner, J. (1994). Patient-centered and analyst-centered interpretations: Some implications of containment and countertransference. *Psychoanalytic Inquiry*, 14(3), 406–422.
Steiner, J. (1996). The aim of psychoanalysis in theory and in practice. *International Journal of Psychoanalysis*, 77(6), 1073–1083.

Chapter 8

To Attend or Not to Attend the Exhibit?

Nancy Kulish

Editors' introduction

From time to time, therapists are invited by patients to attend a ceremony, performance, or the like: for example, patients who've struggled finding a mate might find it highly meaningful to have their analyst present at their wedding ceremony. This particular clinical moment involves a bisexual artist in her 40s whose capacity to express herself artistically improved dramatically as a result of her analysis. At the outset of treatment, the patient had considerable difficulty expressing herself verbally. In place of words, the patient brought her art into session as a way of communicating with the analyst. As therapy progressed, a pattern of emotional neglect at home during childhood, boundary violations by teachers, as well as outright sexual abuse by both her father and her brothers was revealed. An intense transference developed that was erotic in nature. Gradually, over the course of the analysis, the patient's art changed in tone, and she was ultimately able to sufficiently overcome her inhibition to finally permit her work to be exhibited at a local gallery. The patient asked the analyst to come to the exhibit, leaving the analyst to grapple with the question of whether to go. The reasons for going, given the analyst's understanding of the patient's dynamics and the state of the transference/countertransference at the time, are considered. The ramifications of the analyst's decision for the subsequent course of the analysis are discussed.

The moment in context (Richard Tuch)

In clinical moment 4, we began a discussion of extra-analytic (out-of-the-office) encounters between analyst and analysand, which we now continue given the fact that the following clinical moment involves the possibility of just such an encounter. Extra-analytic encounters may come about in a variety of different ways. Some occur inadvertently – analyst and analysand "bump" into each other outside the office, mutually unaware that such a thing was going to happen. Other inadvertent extra-analytic encounters can involve an analysand learning something personal about the analyst in passing –

having been directly informed by another or having "stumbled upon" the data (e.g., by overhearing something being said about the analyst). Intentional instances of extra-analytic encounters include instances when a patient shows up at an event knowing beforehand that the analyst would be in attendance, catching the analyst off-guard, likely wishing to position the analyst accordingly. In the clinical moment that follows, the analyst is considering the possibility of intentionally stepping outside the analytic "frame" by accepting the analysand's invitation to attend an important life event. When analysts decide to accept such an invitation, they likely do so believing that the dangers of purposively compromising the therapeutic frame are outweighed by the therapeutic benefits of doing so (e.g., when attending the event effectively counters the patient's deeply ingrained pathogenic beliefs about how those in their lives will predictably react; Weiss et al., 1986).

Most analysts subscribe to the importance of maintaining the analytic frame because doing so helps contain the anxiety associated with the emergence of regressive wishes, which – in turn – helps facilitate treatment by providing the patient with a safe environment that encourages the patient's trust. Accordingly, extra-analytic contact is never initiated without the analyst giving it due consideration. Psychoanalysis begets regression, and regression, in turn, begets powerful infantile impulses and wishes that, in turn, can press for satisfaction. Proper analytic technique helps provide a safe environment that permits the patient to re-experience and express these powerful longings, reassured that it is safe to do so given how the analyst has conducted herself by making clear that the analyst appreciates the "as if" quality of the transference, respecting the fact that the past is being relived somewhat independently of other realities that also characterize the analytic relationship.

Early in training, analysts are taught about the vital importance of tending to "the frame," which includes – but is not limited to – the matter of maintaining proper boundaries between analyst and analysand. Langs (1973, 1992, 1994, 1995, 1998; Langs & Stone, 1980) wrote extensively about the subject and was insistent about the absolute and essential importance of maintaining the analytic frame. Patients may experience a mixture of feelings when the analyst elects to do something that strikes the patient as lying outside the bounds of what the patient sees as strictly professional behavior, stimulating a mixture of excitement and fear over feeling that one had received more than their fair share of attention/gratification. Such an experience can lead to a sense that one's importance and position have suddenly been elevated, which can leave one's head swimming with a wondrous, yet disorienting, floating feeling associated with a sense of lacking limits, potentially leaving one feeling as if one might be capable of nearly anything. Accordingly, gratifying certain of the patient's wishes historically has been considered to be the undoing of a proper analysis, seeing that analysis is designed to help patients come to terms with, and work through, the inevitable frustrations of life played out in the analysand's relationship with the analyst.

One of the chief concerns about agreeing to engage in extra-analytic contact has to do with the issue of "transference gratifications." Freud (1914) was clear about the dangers of gratifying certain of the patient's libidinal wishes – though he did not, would not, and could not deny that some of the patient's needs were in fact being gratified in the act of being given the analyst's undivided attention. Though some analysts speak as if they think it is indisputably so, it is hard to place stock in the idea that granting a patient's wish to – for example – attend an important life event would necessarily prove to be the undoing of the analysis, though the inverse might prove true in certain instances with certain patients – when refusing a request has a detrimental effect on the analysis.

Freud's original suggestions about technique included recommendations that analysts conduct themselves in particular ways: abstaining from gratifying the patient's infantile wishes (maintaining "neutrality") and remaining more or less anonymous to provide the patient a "blank screen" upon which to construct the analyst as she sees fit in accordance with transference expectations. Recently, some analysts have challenged the value of adhering to what they regard as outdated techniques, arguing as Henry Friedman has (quoted in Tuch, 2001) that one is better off satisfying a patient's needs rather than adopting techniques that generate regression and, with it, intense infantile desires that the analyst cannot hope to satisfy (see also Renik, 1995, 1998). One wonders how far these analysts may be willing to go in the name of providing for what they believe to be the essential developmental needs of patients – needs that had gone unsatisfied during the patient's childhood. Might the satisfaction of these needs constitute growth-promoting, self-object functioning sufficient to facilitate the treatment, which these analysts may believe is better than leaving a patient aching with a repetition of dissatisfaction?

Several writers have addressed the matter of extra-analytic contact (Ganzarain, 1991; Strean 1981; Tarnower, 1966; Weiss, 1975). Writing during an earlier era of psychoanalysis, both Greenacre (1959) and Langs (1976) were adamant about the need for analysts to maintain proper boundaries at all cost. Of particular concern – expressed by many – is the belief that stepping outside the frame by having any extra-analytic contact constitutes a boundary violation – a crossing of the line that will irreparably damage the analytic relationship forever, introducing reality that will inevitably disrupt that patient's continuing ability to describe and explore his transference beliefs and longings.

Many would consider such situations in clinical practice as potential and risky boundary crossings, which could lead to serious boundary violations. Gutheil and Gabbard (1993) assert that the therapist's office is, and should be, the locale for almost all therapies, and that exceptions can constitute boundary crossings with varying effects, some harmful and some constructive. These authors stress the complexity of such invitations and the importance of careful consideration and discussion on a case-by-case basis between therapist and patient before acting upon them. Such variations in the therapeutic frame, if not boundary crossings or violations, are at the very least clinically complex and frequently can become prime material for enactments and important transferences and countertransferences.

The two chief concerns raised about engaging in extra-analytic encounters are concerns about stimulating the patient's infantile wishes, and fear of contaminating the transference by exposing the patient to aspects of the analyst's outside life. Tarnower (1966) notes, "The psychoanalyst has good technical reasons for avoiding his patient outside of the hour. He does not want to burden his patient with impressions gained from reality contacts, thereby distorting or confusing transference reactions" (p. 412). Strean (1981) warns about how extra-analytic encounters "[c]an heighten latent transference and countertransference themes... [and] can also interfere with an analysis by raising false hopes for the patient and can dilute the analyst's position as a fantasied object" (p. 238). Sandwiched between these concerns, Strean inserts the potentially positive effects of such encounters: their ability to clarify resistances and "serve an index of therapeutic progress" (p. 238). Ganzarain (1991) takes the position that introducing reality in the form of extra-analytic contact is not likely to have as much of a disruptive effect on the patient's transference as is commonly thought, because "[t]he analyst actually 'exposes' only a small fraction of the analyst's reality... [hence] the patient's transference will prevail and deform the 'real' meaning of such extra-analytic encounters" (p. 138).

Tarnower (1966) approaches the topic of extra-analytic contract from a two-person psychological perspective[1] by describing tension between wish and prohibition stimulated by the prospect of extra-analytic contact, which hangs over *both* analyst and analysand – each harboring wishes to gratify certain of their own personal needs through such contact (e.g., mutual wishes to satisfy curiosity about the other, which some may equate as a repetition of the primal scene when the patient is the one doing the looking). Tarnower alerts us that "countertransference may seriously interfere with analytic work if the analyst needs to deny awareness of wishes to have social contacts with his patients" (pp. 410–411). Strean (1981) elaborates on this theme when he notes that:

> While the analyst may justify his wish to avoid this type of contact as an effort not to contaminate the transference, this avoidance may serve defensive purposes for him ... Whether an extra-analytic contact is viewed as valuable or hazardous depends to a large extent on how the analyst feels about meeting his patient outside of the consultation room. If he is anxious that treasured transference and countertransference positions will be altered, if he is worried that he cannot contain regressive wishes in the patient or in himself, if he is uncomfortable in departing from his anonymous, unseen role behind the couch, then he will in all probability find reasons to explain why the meeting should be avoided.
> (p. 256)

With certain sorts of patients, therapists have good reason to be wary of any extra-analytic contact. Tarnower (1966) catalogues the sorts of patients for whom extra-analytic contact might prove troublesome – in particular, impulsive patients who "might well get out of control when temptation is increased and the controlling structure of the analytic situation is not available" (p. 410) (e.g., women who've formed strong erotic attachments to the analyst and who are intolerant of frustration). Ganzarain (1991) outlines how extra-analytic contact may:

> Forcefully occupy the centre of analytic attention, bringing up temptations by exciting the participants' curiosity and exhibitionism, by often replicating the "primal scene," reactivating oedipal wishes and jealousy, and also oral cravings and envy.
>
> (p. 134)

Such may be the dangers with certain patients, but certainly not with all patients, leaving one to wonder whether it is a mistake to extend the practice of avoiding all extra-analytic contact to all patients – particularly when a well-considered weighing of the clinical pros and cons might lead a therapist to see clinical value in – for example – accepting a patient's invitation to attend a meaningful life event, as is well illustrated in Dr. Kulish's following clinical moment. Rather than inevitably proving problematic, Tarnower (1966) advances the idea that extra-analytic contact can provide important material for the analysis, and Ganzarain (1991) observes that "every analyst has observed how ruptures of the setting may bring up new, positive clinical developments" (p. 136).

The clinical moment

Ms. B, a 45-year-old artist, became depressed when her female partner betrayed her with another woman. This situation brought a whole upheaval into her life: She had moved out of the state to be with this woman and now had to return to the area where she got a job teaching art. She considered herself as bisexual and was involved with a man at the time she sought treatment with me some months after this move. We began a twice-a-week psychotherapy.

During the first months of the psychotherapy, she brought in her artwork and laid the pieces down on the couch for me to view and comment upon. At the same time, she said that she knew there were deeper things bothering her – she suffered frequent nightmares, had sexual difficulties, and could not stand to sleep next to anyone. She said she had no words for what was bothering her: "I do not do narrative." Indeed, it was evident that she was trying to communicate with me by literally showing me her inner life via her artwork. Her images were dark, full of sharp and disparate elements. All I could say was that I understood she was trying to help me to understand her. I did not comment on the artistic aspects of her work, although I thought they were beautiful, but jarring. It was evident that Ms. B needed and wanted an analysis, which we began after six months.

It was painful and difficult for Ms. B to relate her history. She was in the middle of eight siblings in an Italian Catholic family. Her father was harsh and sadistic and probably an alcoholic. He was demeaning, humiliating, and exploded arbitrarily. When he was drunk, he became meaner and more violent. While he was verbally and physically abusive to all the children, per the patient and her siblings, he was especially hard on her. He did favor the four boys and especially the oldest son, the "golden boy," who excelled in sports. Her mother appeared softer, but never stood up for the patient or any of the children and always was subservient to and defensive of the father. She also tried to mold the girls to be super-feminine, by dressing them up in identical frilly dresses and bonnets for church. The patient resisted these attempts and always played with the boys, whom she envied for their freedom and status. Ms. B herself was very athletic and excelled in sports throughout school and college. Her parents never came to any of her events to see her play but always attended those of the brothers, especially of the "golden boy." Her family tolerated her "tomboyishness" until middle school, when they cracked down on her hard, especially her father. The patient also showed early talents in the arts and in music. She felt that these too were not appreciated by the parents.

In her high school and college years, there had been several instances of female coaches whom she had observed taking sexual advantage of some of the players. She expressed her anger at, and disapproval of, such situations. She contrasted these memories in terms of her growing trust of me.

Ms. B took very well to psychoanalysis, which I suggested after several months of the psychotherapy. Being creative, she had easy access to her fantasy life. She dreamed profusely and vividly and was able to associate well. I felt we had a very good working alliance. She was able to work with the transference – that is, to express her feelings and fantasies about me openly, but also take some distance to observe herself.

During the analysis, we reconstructed early sexual trauma. When she was about three, her father held her over his knee while seated in a rocking chair in the basement. She was naked, and he probably became sexually excited, so that she felt the erection beneath her. There were also scattered memories of sexual touching by her older brothers during bath time. In the early transference, the rocking chair played a repeated theme; it was also the chair in which her mother sat to teach her sewing. A rocking chair sometimes appeared in her art.

Rapidly shifting maternal and paternal transferences were interwoven in the first years. Sitting behind her I became her stern, harsh, and sadistic father judging her; walking away at the end of a session I was her rejecting and disappointing mother; neither accepted her as she was. For example, in the first year of analysis, she brought in another picture. She said, "Another mother moment last night – I was reprinting my resume and I thought that I should bring it in and show it to you. It's [the resume] the same thing as art. I want approval, help, guidance. I've never been able to get anything like that from my parents. That's another sad one. I had talked about that strong image of you walking away from me. It reminded me of the image of that rocking chair in one of my works, *with its back to me*. Something is going on behind my back."

I asked, "Me walking away from you and something going on behind your back?"

She replied, "It's like the uneasy feelings I have with M [her boyfriend at the time] – like he'd grab me from behind. A certain paranoia. Never knowing what my father's mood was." She continued haltingly to talk about her father's verbal abuse and blowing up for no reason. "He would look around at dinner to see who he could find fault with."

As one can see in the above example, Ms. B became more and more able to tell her story – to "do narrative" and not to rely on the visual. Nevertheless, she often brought in a piece of art on which she was currently working to show me.

Much later in the analysis, intensely erotic material emerged in dreams and more and more directly in the transference. She yearned for sexual closeness with me, both imagined as a male and as a female, or sometimes both, as in reoccurring bisexual imagery. I would be the perfect bisexual lover who has it all – both father and mother in one object. For example, she dreamed a beautiful male lover, with soft skin like a woman's, a figure she associated with me.

Meanwhile, in her life, she was more able to spend time with her family and became closer to some of her siblings. She began to produce more art. Its content had changed – less violent and disturbing imagery, and also from dark to brighter colors. She became recognized as a fine teacher, winning awards and getting a lot of satisfaction from her work with her students.

In the third year of analysis, Ms. B was gaining some recognition in the area as an artist. She had a show with other artists in a small gallery. This was a fruitful period in the analysis as we explored her interrelated feelings toward males and females and her conflicts about her own gender and sexuality. The erotic feelings toward me were at this point submerged and disguised, but I was aware of her sexualized yearnings for closeness with me. For example, in the context of feeling anxious about having to miss a few sessions because of work, she reported a dream with the image of herself as an infant: "I was looking at myself, the sensation was sexual... My legs, labia were open." She associated to "making love to another woman and kissing her down there. It's a combination of an adult thing and also being a kid who wants to feel good, masturbating but it involves somebody else."

"Masturbation implies an idea of a relationship?" I asked.

"But no one was there."

"It doesn't mean that you don't want someone," I answered.

"You got me there."

Around this time, Ms. B was invited to give a solo show by a local university's art department. She was very pleased about this and worked hard to produce many new pieces. She brought in many if not most of these pieces and talked about the problems she had with the framing, matting, and arrangements in the gallery. Then, a few weeks before the show, she handed me the invitation to the opening, leaving me to wonder whether to accept the invitation or gracefully decline. It seemed that each of the two options offered rich opportunities as well as distinct problems.

Invited commentator responses: Morris Eagle and Joe Lichtenberg

Morris Eagle

Contributors to this volume have been asked to address two questions related to the "clinical moment" presented to them, namely: What do you think about the situation, and how do you imagine that you yourself would choose to respond given the circumstances? In the "clinical moment" that I was asked to address, the patient, Ms. B, invites her analyst to attend the opening of her solo show at a local university art department. The analyst "wonder[s] whether to accept the invitation or gracefully decline." The analyst, Dr. Kulish, notes "that each of the two options offered rich opportunities as well as distinct problems."

Given the explicit and implicit assumptions we have internalized from our training and from presumed clinical wisdom, the clinical moment presented is seen as a difficult situation, a dilemma in which it appears as if one is damned – or blessed – if one does, that is, accept the invitation, and equally damned – or blessed – if one declines. The extent to which the situation is experienced as fraught appears to be due to the following factors. First, the fact that it is experienced as a superego dilemma – that is, if one accepts the patient's invitation, one is engaging in gratification, which violates a taboo internalized during our training; if one declines the invitation, one runs the risk of hurting the patient, a feared consequence that also elicits guilt. Second, the assumption that it is the analyst's action of acceptance or refusal of the invitation that is the critical factor. Third, the explicit and implicit assumption that relative to other patient–therapist interactions, the analyst's decision as to whether to accept or decline the patient's invitation is especially consequential for the treatment.

Regarding the first assumption, it seems likely to me that it is not primarily the analyst's decision itself that may be important, but how the patient's request is dealt with. I can envision an option something like: "I appreciate your invitation and would like to share the event with you. But let's talk about both of our feelings, your feelings about extending the invitation to me, about my being at the show, and what effect, if any, it might have on our work here; and my feelings of both having an immediate Yes reaction to your invitation as well as some lingering questions as to whether I'm violating some norm or taboo and wondering whether I'm interfering with the treatment in some way." (Let me add here that the above scenario is a reasonable one if, and only if, the analyst herself mainly *does* want to attend the show and would feel reasonably comfortable doing so.) I can also imagine a scenario in which after an open and honest examination of the patient's and analyst's feelings and thoughts, the analyst – and perhaps even with the agreement of the patient – might decide to decline the invitation.

Whatever the analyst's decision, an essential consideration is allowing space in some way for the patient to be able to reflect on her own feelings and thoughts that are linked to her invitation, as well as the fantasies, feelings, and thoughts she may have regarding the analyst's reasons for either accepting or declining her invitation.

The Control-Mastery theory of Weiss and Sampson and their colleagues (e.g., Silberschatz, 2005; Weiss et al., 1986) seems especially pertinent to the clinical moment vignette presented here. A core idea of the theory is that both unconsciously and consciously, patients often present tests to the analyst that can be either passed or failed. There is systematic evidence that test-failure is reliably followed by increased defensiveness and other indices of lack of clinical progress, and that test-passing is reliably followed by the relaxation of defense, the emergence of warded-off material, and other indices of clinical progress.

In general, the essence of test-failing lies in the patient's subjective experience that the analyst is behaving in a manner similar to problematic parental behavior, thus constituting a mini-retraumatization in the treatment; the essence of test-passing is the patient's experience that the analyst is behaving in a manner different from the problematic behavior of the patient's parents, a manner that facilitates the patient's feelings of *conditions of safety*.

The idea of test-failing versus test-passing is quite simple to grasp. However, like other important and seemingly simple ideas, it can be a generative and nuanced one. The clinical usefulness of the idea is largely a matter of being able to assess what constitutes test-passing versus test-failure for a given patient, a given patient–analyst pair, and a particular patient–analyst interaction and context. Bringing to bear the concept of test-passing versus test-failure to the clinical moment material presented by Kulish, I have suggested that the important clinical issue is not primarily a question of whether the analyst accepts or declines the patient's invitation, but rather of how he or she deals with the invitation. And how the analyst deals with the invitation needs to be guided by his or her clinical judgment of what will further the treatment in a particular case rather than by general "rules" about abstinence, neutrality (often misunderstood), and the dangers of gratification, or on the other side of the theoretical divide, general "rules" about the patient's presumed need for re-parenting, "analytic love," and overly facile and not sufficiently clinically informed notions of empathic understanding, corrective emotional experiences, and so on. The clinical question, of course, is what specific therapeutic interventions and behaviors are experienced by the patient as constituting empathic understanding, a corrective emotional experience, and so on.

Based on the particular clinical material presented, my clinical judgment would be that, putting aside for the moment other considerations and factors, accepting the patient's invitation would be more likely to constitute test-passing and rejecting the patient's invitation would be more likely to constitute test-failure. I will say more about this a bit later.

Regarding the second factor, as noted, the assumption is made that certain "clinical moments," which Tuch describes as presenting "a clinical quandary that leaves the therapist unsure about how to proceed," are especially consequential for the treatment. As Tuch writes, the analyst "mulls over his choices believing that his response could either create an unbridgeable rupture or forge a... deeper bond." In regard to the specific clinical moment I am addressing, there appears to be the implicit assumption that either choice of accepting or declining the patient's invitation will be especially consequential, far more than other ongoing interactions and interventions in the treatment. It is this assumption that I believe needs to be examined. One consideration, already noted, is that the analyst's experience of a dichotomous and fraught choice, with either choice leading to unpredictable and momentous consequences, may in fact, be illusory and may obscure recognition that *how* the patient's invitation is dealt with and responded to may be more consequential than the analyst's decision – accept or decline – itself.

To make this point particularly clear, imagine for a moment that the analyst's acceptance of the patient's invitation is made in an offhand manner – "sure, why not" – or in a manner that reflects a sense of carrying out an irksome duty – "I guess I should go";[2] contrastingly, imagine for a moment that the analyst's declining the patient's invitation is given in a thoughtful and empathic manner, reflecting the analyst's serious aim of understanding the patient's feelings. I think we would all agree that in the above imaginary scenarios, the acceptance of the invitation in the manner described would be likely to constitute far more of a threat to the treatment than a decline of the invitation presented in the manner described.

What this imaginary exercise reveals is that because all actions, therapeutic decisions, and interventions are carried out in a particular personal manner, we cannot escape revealing who we are to the patient, including the degree and nature of our "affective presence" at any given moment (Stechler, 2000, p. 75). And further, it is likely that *how* interventions are carried out – in this case, *how* one accepts or declines the patient's invitation – will reveal who we are in relation to this patient, and will be at least as consequential as (perhaps more consequential than) the decision itself.

Who we are in relation to our patients is continually revealed in every session throughout the treatments and is likely to be, if I may coin a term that parallels the concept of cumulative trauma, "cumulatively consequential." It is likely, I believe, that the degree of consequentiality of the "clinical moment" will reflect, at least to an important extent, the cumulative history of the patient–therapist relationship. And, I would suggest, the cumulative history of the patient–therapist relationship will have a powerful influence on the treatment consequences of either decision, accept or decline.

Let me turn now to how I think I would respond. My inclination would be to accept the invitation. In the present case, as the analyst observes, there is a history of the patient, at least to an important extent, bringing in her art work as a means of "trying to help me to understand her." As Kulish notes, during the first six months, the art work was the main means of communication for the patient – "I do not do narrative," she states. After a period and after entering analysis, the patient *is* increasingly able to communicate verbally; she reports her dreams, expresses her feelings and fantasies, and so on.

This sequence suggests to me that bringing in the art work to the sessions is not simply or primarily a defensive means for avoiding narrative, but rather the means of communication that was most available to the patient at the earlier period of treatment and both complementary and preparatory to a fuller engagement and relationship with the analyst. Of course, as the patient openly acknowledges, she also wants approval from the analyst, an experience sorely missing in the patient's life.

From a Control-Mastery theory perspective, one can speculate – and this is only speculation and requires more clinical evidence to evaluate – that the patient's communication mainly through her art during the first six months of psychotherapy may, in part at least, constitute an unconscious test as to whether "conditions of safety" obtain. Through her response to the patient's art work, the analyst passes the test, which enables the patient to begin a fuller and more intense relationship with the analyst. One can also speculate that in inviting the analyst to attend her art show, the patient may be attempting to show the analyst her progress in integrating the "private" showing of her art work to the analyst during the first six months of therapy with the now more open public showing. If my speculation has any plausibility, it would be an additional reason for me to accept the patient's invitation.

Joseph Lichtenberg

Based on what I have been told in the clinical vignette, I would lean toward accepting the invitation to attend the opening. I would tell Ms. B of my intention and take it up with her in the analysis. I would try to help *us* learn about and understand the *meaning to* her of my decision. Might Ms. B hear my decision as a counter to her parents not attending her athletic events? Is it for her an indication of my caring about her progress and success? Is it an opportunity to sense, along with her, her aesthetic struggles with the setting and placements in the show? Does she picture it as an opportunity for me to be empathic with her responses to praise and to criticism? I would look for whatever other meanings emerged, especially those that would be unpredictable and open new pathways for the analysis. Given any or all of that, I would attend.

But what if when we talked about my attending the opening, her associations, fantasies, and dreams revealed it would make her intensely uncomfortable? What if she would be so self-conscious of me – my reaction – or of other people knowing of or not knowing of our relationship – that her distraction would detract from her full appreciation of the opening? What if her erotic arousal stirred by my presence would cause her shame and embarrassment? I would suggest to her that the invitation has served us well in that it has opened the analytic inquiry to new issues for us to understand. Let's continue to work with it and hold open my attendance for a future opening at a time when we could both relax and enjoy. The above are my reflections as of today. These reflections are clearly not "the preservation of the frame" designed to lead to an uncontaminated transference projection on a pristine blank screen that in my training I had been told I must follow. I tried but I could never resolve the paradox that speaking to an analysand in an elevator or answering a question would adversely influence the analysand's responses while not greeting or refusing to answer would not! I do believe deeply in preserving the explicit and implicit elements of a frame that my analysand and I have agreed on – setting, frequency, timing, payment, reliability, honesty, and consistency of interest, inquiry, and caring.

Two clinical moments during my training affect my belief in and adherence to the avoidance of what I regard as mutually dehumanizing experiences. My analysand – my first control case midway during the session while on the couch – said, "God it's hot in here. I am so sweaty and uncomfortable I can't think." I said, "I'll see if I can turn off the radiator and open a window." Returning to my chair, I had the immediate thought – Boy, am I going to get into trouble. I said to her I know you were referring to the temperature in the room but could there be another meaning? – feeling very foolish. When I recounted this to my supervisor, she became so exasperated she stammered – if you ever interrupt an analytic session in this way again, you might as well discontinue your training. The paradox: opening a window is interrupting (like Freud reaching for a cigar), but ignoring my patient's complaint that I shared and doing or saying nothing would not be interrupting our relatedness, our working alliance, and her free spontaneous associations.

The second clinical moment occurred with a patient who was doing very well in her analysis. In a session at Christmas, she brought me a small present. I worked with her associations during the session and at the end, against my personal inclination, returned her present explaining I couldn't accept it. Not surprisingly, she was furious. Further analytic work revealed her mother had regularly rejected her attempts to be altruistic. Now we understood the transference meaning of her gift and my rejection but nonetheless something changed. A sourness, a distrust, a bitterness emerged that took a long time to be worked through and resolved. Some five years after the successful completion of her analysis, I met my former analysand at a social gathering. We greeted each other with pleasant eagerness until she said – I know how much you helped me but I still can't forget your returning my present! Was I protecting the frame – or putting it in great danger?

Returning to Dr. Kulish and Ms. B in the clinical moment of decision about accepting the invitation, hadn't the analyst already accepted an invitation to alter the frame? Ms. B brings into the consulting room not only her associations and dreams but her artwork. I regard Ms. B as saying, "If you want to know me, to really get who I am, you have to see what is central to my sense of self, my identity. Much of my heart and soul is in my creativity – and here it is. Look, share, react, respond. My narrative comes in two forms – verbal and visual." Then what about the analyst's anonymity? How can she preserve it? She can't. Either she knows something about art or she doesn't. Either she has a degree of aesthetic sensibility or she doesn't. Her office – that part of the frame will already tell Ms. B a lot in answer to those questions about her analyst, just as Freud's interest in antiquities was to be seen all over his consulting room. How did Dr. Kulish look at the art? They must have talked about it. She tells us Ms. B brought her paintings in for her to view and comment on. Also, Ms. B claimed she didn't do (verbal) narrative, so the artwork was to be a substitute.[3]

Additionally, the artwork served as an indicator of progress – increasing in volume with "less violent and disturbing imagery, and also [changing] from dark to brighter colors." The paintings provided a parallel interactive metaphoric narrative for the changes taking place in Ms. B's psyche and the dyadic relationship. The sensual erotic emergence in the transference and the shift from dark to bright color in the paintings provided a vivid correlation and opportunity for exploration.

Could they talk about the artwork and be within the frame? I believe so. Could they not talk about it and still have a meaningful frame? I doubt it. An analysand asks his analyst, did you see a movie, or a TV show, read a book, attend a meeting, participate in a march. Repeated analytic experience indicates that themes and interactions in movies, TV shows, books, and events can provide model scenes that crystallize and reveal critical formative dynamics of an analysand's lived experience. These model scenes then become available for joint analytic explorations that open to shifting enlightening perspectives.

An analyst has three possible responses to the analysand's question: don't answer directly and/or play the game of "I'm curious why you ask," answer yes, or answer no. Refusing to answer directly, ostensibly to preserve anonymity, will shift the focus off the theme in the event that has caught the analysand's imagination. Instead, the focus will go to the analysand's emotional response triggered by not being able to get a straight answer to a simple question. The aversive response may be explicit. Alternatively, often in the more traditional analytic mode, analysands become indoctrinated into the regimen of the analyst being unresponsive to direct inquiry and behaving as though nothing of his or her personal thought, feelings, preferences, and predilections were being or should be being revealed. Once an analysand accepted this convention, he would stop asking, or if his inquiry slipped out, he might try to repress his frustration. In any case, the analysis would be able to proceed carried forward by the analyst's genuine interest in the analysand's experience with the movie, book, or event and the analysand's reservoir of need, trust, and goodwill.

What if the analyst's answer was "Yes"? The analysand would naturally assume they had some commonality of experiences. The analyst might then ask the analysand to describe her experience gaining as full as possible a sense of the analysand's perspective. Inevitably, the analysand will wonder about the analyst's take on the same scene. Did the analyst see it the same way, did it have a similar meaning? The analysand may wonder if the analyst is judging her as an observer or as one who makes "incorrect" inferences from the shared scene. And the analyst will have his own read on the scene – affected by what memories and judgments were evoked. No empty clean slate, no absence of memory, bias, and desire is possible or would be desirable if it were. When analyst and analysand are free to share similarities and differences in their reactions, understanding, and meaning of the scene – things about it that caught each other's attention – the metaphoric range of joint understanding expands. How the experience relates to significant narratives of the analysand's life as the analyst knows them will help the exploration go forward. How the experience relates to significant narratives of the analyst's own life often can enrich the empathic perception or may need to be set aside as irrelevant to the inquiry.

What if the analyst's answer is "No"? The analysand will recognize the necessity to fill the narrative envelope so the analyst can absorb the information he wishes to convey. Similar to relating a dream or a description of an encounter or a memory, analysands vary in their skills as narrator. Many need to be helped, or, as Ms. B, will use auxiliary information – a painting, a poem, a photograph, a song, or mimicking in gesture or tone the behavior of a person being described. If the analyst in the clinical example does not attend the exhibit, Ms. B will wonder if Dr. Kulish really gets from her description a true picture of what happened and what it meant to her. The analyst will wonder how much of what Ms. B is relating is actual, how much fantasy, how much distortion or dissociation, and how much designed to impress, provoke, seduce, or avoid her.

To summarize, my reflection on the clinical moment of to attend or not is that each decision will have consequences that can be successfully worked with in an analytic frame that privileges relatedness, openness, empathic inquiry, and exploration of meaning. As it was construed during my training, the analytic frame severely constrained an analysand's freedom to interact and participate emotionally. These constraints of the frame paradoxically introduced other interferences that often worked to rigidify and dehumanize the experience. So go or not go is less the issue than if the meaning of either choice can be explored to gain understanding for the analysand, the analyst, and especially for the dyad. I have tried to illustrate how discussion with the analysand of the impact of either choice, attend or not attend, both before and after the exhibit, can enhance reflection on the meaning of the event and of the analyst's participation for the analysand and the analysis. Reflecting on whatever form the narrative takes carries an analysis forward. Flexibility in the frame facilitates enriched narrative experience and exploratory reflection.

My intervention

I questioned myself about whether to go or not to go. I felt, given the patient's worries about boundaries being broken, that this was a tricky situation. At the same time, I knew she was sensitive to rejection, and I did not want to hurt her. We talked about the invitation across several sessions. I brought up the issue of boundaries. I wondered with her how she would feel about my presence there with friends, colleagues, and any family that showed up. For instance, how would she explain my presence? She had kept her being in analysis from her family. She said that there would probably be a lot of people there so that perhaps that might not pose a problem. Another consideration was that she had already showed me most if not all of the pieces that were to appear in the show. Finally, feeling more comfortable with being more conservative, I decided not to go. Ms. B seemed to understand and be okay with this decision.

After the show, Ms. B appeared satisfied. Apparently, it had been a big success, and she had even sold several pieces. The opening had been well-attended. Then I did not hear much more about it. In the months that followed, she got recognition and pleasure in the prize-winning work of her students. She described new projects – photography and even some writing. She thought perhaps she might do an experimental film. She talked a lot about the meanings of her art to her; she brought in slides of older, bigger pieces and analyzed their meanings. In her sessions, the focus moved onto other matters: She continued to work on her feelings about being female and returned to feelings of betrayal by her former partner and her mother. At this point, the transference appeared to be primarily centered on her mother. In one session, she murmured, "Feeling needy… getting attention." I asked about how that related to me. She answered, "It reminds me how I got my mother's attention [i.e., by being sick]." I said, "So inside you there is no conviction that my attention, or anybody's attention, is steady or is to be counted on." "That's true," she said, her voice breaking. "Her attention was like for a little doll. Any real attention is from art… I've been so sad. You are leaving in two days…"

After many months passed, it became increasingly apparent that she was not producing any new art. Instead of bringing in current works, she brought in a little viewer and some slides to show me all the art she had done over the years – a kind of retrospective. Her attitude seemed nonchalant. I remarked that I knew she thought her art was good and it came from something very important to her, but at the same time the way she was talking about it was like, "Oh well."

"That's exactly how it was. That was the attitude in my family – like oh well I wasn't important." Then she spoke of the power of a teacher who looked at her first artwork when she had had no training and had said, "You are an artist. All you need is a studio."

She began to speak of being stuck and fantasies of quitting her analysis. She blamed the analytic process for stopping her work. That is what she had feared before she started analysis – that it would cause her to not be able to produce art. She spoke of the "terror" to go inside herself to find out "where all this comes from" – that is, she was terrified of finding out where the images and feelings that she had poured into her art came from and what they meant.

We realized that the problem of not being able to produce art had begun after the show. At first, I wondered if it had to do with her fear of success and recalled to myself a dream she had had a few months before. In the dream, she had a crush on an unknown woman. Her associations had somewhat unexpectedly led to feelings that it was dangerous to be noticed, with memories of her father's arbitrary brutality if one happened to come into his sight.

More than a year and a half after the show, she was feeling despair: "I don't have my art any more, but it was dumb art. But the process has taken away my art. At least I can see that now and what's the point."

Finally, I began to put the pieces together. I told her, "You are more self-conscious now about your work, but I realize that your art stopped since the show, and we did not really realize it – I did not realize it at the time. We had talked about issues around success. But more than that, I think, this is about a feeling that you want something, many things that you cannot have."

"Yes, I can't have what or who I want, so I don't want anything. Exactly right."

Then we went back to the art show. After some discussion, I said, "I wonder now, after looking back at it with some distance and considering what you have been talking about lately, that my not going – although you seemed to understand why I did not go at the time – was like your father not going to your games, your parents not appreciating you."

With sadness, she said, "Yes, my art is like my newborn child. Other people bring you their newborn children to see. I need for you to *see*. I didn't have the newborn child and you didn't see my art." (In the very beginning of treatment, she was approaching menopause, and she had had to mourn the fact that she would never have the children she had wanted.)

In retrospect, I believe I would have done it differently. I think I would have gone to the show, not to the opening but quietly at some other time. I think that my not going had a devastating effect on the patient and her work, which we did not even realize for over a year. I did not consider the facts of her history – her parents, and especially her father's disregard for her accomplishments – when I was thinking through what to do about the show. Certainly, if I had had in my mind these meanings of my not going and had been able to *talk* with Ms. B about these issues beforehand, the painful repercussions might have been forestalled. With this understanding, my choice to not go might not have turned into a repetition of the painful past. What occurred was an enactment or a reenactment of the disregard and rejection that had been so traumatic for this woman. Thankfully, she and I could work this through eventually.

Now I think that an unconscious countertransference on my part obscured thinking about these particular transferential meanings. Early on, in the first months of analysis, I had a consultation with a renowned analyst about this case. We had discussed the danger of a certain countertransference in this case – my desire for the patient to be a successful artist. During the time of the show, I was not aware consciously of such desires on my part, but I think they were there. I backed away from these desires – my *wanting* to go to the show and *wanting* to share in her success. Following the rules and staying more "neutral" was my unconscious compromise. In a sense, both to go and not to go to the art show were transference/countertransference "enactments."

Notes

1 Not that it was called that back when he wrote.
2 I am not suggesting that any responsible therapist would actually respond in this way.
3 This brings to mind an adolescent I analyzed. Whenever we were stuck – she in the telling, me in the understanding – she would bring in a poem she had written. I would go over it line by line, and we would parse it together and new meaning always emerged.

References

Freud, S. (1914). Remembering, repeating and working through. In J. Strachey (Ed. & Trans.), *The standard edition of the complete psychological works of Sigmund Freud* (Vol. 12, pp. 145–156). London: Hogarth Press.

Ganzarain, R. (1991). Extra-analytic contacts: Fantasy and reality. *International Journal of Psychoanalysis*, 72(1), 131–140.

Greenacre, P. (1959). Certain technical problems in the transference relationship. *Journal of the American Psychoanalytic Association*, 7(3), 484–502.

Gutheil, T., & Gabbard, G. (1993). The concept of boundaries in clinical practice: Theoretical and risk-management dimensions. *American Journal of Psychiatry*, 150 (2), 188–196.

Langs, R. (1973). *The technique of psychoanalytic psychotherapy* (Vol. 1). New York: Jason Aronson.
Langs, R. (1976). *The therapeutic interaction.* New York: Jason Aronson.
Langs, R. (1992). *A clinical workbook for psychotherapists.* London: Karnac Books.
Langs, R. (1994). *Doing supervision and being supervised.* London: Karnac Books.
Langs, R. (1995). *Clinical practice and the architecture of the mind.* London: Karnac Books.
Langs, R. (1998). *Ground rules in psychotherapy and counseling.* London: Karnac Books.
Langs, R., & Stone, L. (1980). *The therapeutic experience and its setting.* New York: Jason Aronson.
Renik, O. (1995). The ideal of the anonymous analyst and the problem of self-disclosure. *Psychoanalytic Quarterly,* 64(3), 466–495.
Renik, O. (1998). Getting real in analysis. *Psychoanalytic Quarterly,* 67(4), 566–593.
Silberschatz, G. (2005). The control-mastery theory. In G. Silberschatz (Ed.), *The control-mastery theory of psychoanalysis* (pp. 3–30). New York: Routledge.
Stechler, G. (2000). Louis W. Sander and the question of affective presence. *Infant Mental Health Journal,* 21(1–2), 75–84.
Strean, H. (1981). Extra-analytic contacts: Theoretical and clinical considerations. *Psychoanalytic Quarterly,* 50(2), 238–259.
Tarnower, W. (1966). Extra-analytic contacts between the psychoanalyst and the patient. *Psychoanalytic Quarterly,* 35(3), 399–413.
Tuch, R. (2001). Questioning the psychoanalyst's authority. *Journal of the American Psychoanalytic Association,* 49(2), 491–513.
Weiss, J., Sampson, H., & the Mount Zion Psychotherapy Research Group. (1986). *The psychoanalytic process: Theory, clinical observation and empirical research.* New York: Guilford Press.
Weiss, S. (1975). The effect on the transference of "special events" occurring during psychoanalysis. *International Journal of Psychoanalysis,* 56(1), 69–75.

Part IV

Having Impact: The Balancing of Power

Chapter 9

How Far Do We Enter into a Child's Fantasy When We Play?

Bernadette Kovach

Editors' introduction

While play therapy can provide a seemingly safe transitional space within which analyst and child can work together, the analyst must never lose track of the fact that play can be deadly serious, and accepting the child's direction to assume a certain role can render both partners vulnerable, potentially disrupting a tenuous balance between the two. When five-year-old Adam started his analysis, he did not want to speak or be spoken to, though his fear and rage were palpable. When he did speak, it was to bark out short two-word commands. Sessions typically began with rejecting silence. Attempts by the analyst to speak were met with enraged screams: "Stop talking! Don't look at me!" Adam had suffered through a series of challenging medical procedures early in life that left him frightened and enraged – manifesting in angry outbursts characterized by incessant screaming, a tendency to strike out, and an incapacity to soothe himself. After working with his parents and with Adam for several months, Adam seemed ready to try to speak about these unspeakable feelings and memories, ushered in with his announcement "let's play a game," indicating the "real games were about to begin" – games that would require the analyst to wear a paper bag over her head and be wrapped tightly in a blanket, making her vulnerable to Adam's every emotional urge. Could it be helpful for her to allow him that much power? Was there another way to help this child put into words his feelings and memories? The analyst's decision helped this child move forward developmentally. He began to speak, form friendship and experienced a lessening of the rage.

The moment in context (Bernadette Kovach)

Our understanding of the motivations behind behavior is an important component of how we respond to each other in general and when working with patients. As psychoanalysts, we know that our own histories and unconscious bear upon every interaction we have with patients young or old, and we strive to remain neutral in our interactions, aware of our varying states of mind.

However, a child's behavior is often more evocative than most adult behavior, easily eliciting an intense emotional and sometimes immediate response. Therefore, how we understand and have understood a child's behavior may greatly influence how we engage with that child both in and out of a treatment setting. Do we consider the behavior a means of expressing emotion, a demonstration of their experiences, a symbolic representation of universal struggles, or as anomalies that cannot truly be understood? Trying to help children and their parents understand behavior, and what is being expressed by that behavior, is important for the growth of the parent–child relationship as well as that of the individual child. With understanding comes emotional strength and a heightened ability to think about thoughts and feelings. Alternatively, when we attempt to stop a behavior, or offer coping strategies in place of understanding about what the behavior is about or what the child was or is experiencing, everyone involved may become frustrated and sadomasochistic battles may ensue.

Children have historically been considered miniature adults, blank slates, and apprentices (Locke, 1894; Vygotsky, 1986). In Freud's (1893) analysis of Little Hans (Herbert Graf), he considered Hans' behavior to be indicative of castration anxiety arising from competition with his father. On examination of the relationship with his mother, Frau Graf, it is also possible to understand Hans' behavior as an outgrowth of trauma and an identification with a silent, submissive father (Blum, 2007; Chused, 2007). As was often the stance at the time, the "material reality" of the situation was not taken into consideration in deference to "psychic reality" and, as such, the environmental trauma that influenced Hans' symptoms was not fully considered (Kovach, 2012; Ross, 2007). The difficulties posed by new accounts of Herbert Graf's life, based on letters and interviews with his father Max Graf, are characteristic of the struggle we encounter with any recounting of an event: "Which reality is it?" Just as dreams are subject to reworking, so too is episodic memory. The reworking of memory causes numerous difficulties for those suffering from traumatic experiences as well as those attempting to help them (Breuer & Freud, 1895; Schimek, 1987). Symbolic linking of screen memories to material realities may cause us to make one-to-one correlations that are not verifiable (Arlow, 1991; Ofshe, 1994; Terr, 1994). However, understanding memories as a "construction" that mixes several realities and fantasies can help us remain outside of the true/false dichotomy (Alpert, 2001; Freud, 1896, 1926). While some might argue that infants have little or no memory of early events, I think it prudent to consider the ingredients of a memory that can include wishes, fears, and perceptions based on the cognitive and emotional age of the individual and their environmental influences.

Barish (2006) suggests that a child's behavior represents, in part, a search for security through affective discharge of conflicting internal motivations such as pleasure and envy. Compromise formations, evident in the child's behaviors, are used until conflicting motives are smoothed out – affording relief. In his article on reparative processes in childhood, Barish asks an important question: "If conflict is universal why is this child symptomatic?" (p. 93). A more encompassing question that has impact on technical considerations is: If conflict and trauma are universal, then are we pressed to ask not only why is this child symptomatic, but why have the symptoms manifested in this particular way? Considering the environmental impact on a child is one area of general agreement across many disciplines, from educators to environmentalists to psychoanalysts. Albert Bandura (1977) developed the theory of *reciprocal determinism* underscoring the relationship between cognition, environment, and behavior: Each area influences the other. By combining reciprocal determinism with analytic understanding of the unconscious, we can include the unconscious mind as part of everyone's cognition: each person with their own defenses, conflicts, and affective expression. The mosaic of influences on any individual's development is, at first blush, incomprehensible. Yet, over time, we begin to see a pattern that allows us to piece together some understanding of what happened. Looking closely at the miscellany allows us to consider why this person in this circumstance reacted in this way. An important piece of the mosaic is the medical community and the family's involvement with many doctors during the first three years of this child's life.

As Coates (2016) addresses in her article, the medical community has often denied the impact of physical pain, citing the assertion that children have a natural amnesia about the implementation of medical procedures early in life. Despite the medical community's reluctance to consider the physical and emotional pain a child experiences, psychoanalysts have long considered early medical procedures to be traumatic for the parent and child alike. Though each child and each child-parent pair differ with regards to the sorts of difficulties that child has putting his trauma into words, including that associated with witnessing parents' illness, the trauma is present and real nevertheless. The mixture of the real, the perceived, and the felt experience of a child needs to be recognized and acknowledged, not treated as something the child will forget or get past without recognition. Some children are fortunate enough to have parents who recognize their child's needs and help put those needs and struggles into words, thus facilitating the child's capacity to understand and work through what it is he has been experiencing.

At times, children and adults alike look to others to help them put feelings into words. When working with children, this can be a difficult task, because children often find that talking makes their feelings more intense and moves them to action. It is difficult to talk about something if you cannot yet differentiate between what is inside and what is outside (Furman, 1992; Kernberg, 1980). Some children find expressing their feelings to be disorienting, particularly if they have insufficient ego strength to help modulate the feeling. These children become anxious and "act out" by becoming aggressive or "hyper" in an effort to "get the feelings out" so that they can recover a modicum of control.

How do we put words to something we do not understand? What if the experience is preverbal? Witnessing the child's behavior and putting words to it for them is one way of helping children understand what is happening to them, letting them know that their behavior is telling us that something is wrong or is troubling them. Witnessing by engaging in the child's play as an assigned character is another way to help a child re-experience his past without becoming overwhelmed by it. Engaging as one of the play's characters allows the analyst to help the child develop the capacity to use imaginary play as a bridge between inner and outer reality. The analyst becomes a "player, to regress in the service of the ego with the child" (Chethik, 2000, p. 51). By becoming a character within the child's play, we engage in a safe enactment with the child, thus allowing the child to make new connections within the relationship and within himself. Play in the therapeutic setting may be one of the purest forms of finding a neutral space between various influences and between id, ego, and superego (A. Freud, 1966).

The clinical moment

In our first meeting, five-year-old Adam's parents, Karen and Dan, described their son as a very bright and challenging child. Smiling, they indicated that he loved to read and had been reading on his own since age four. With a more worried look, Karen added, "He reads silently, and his speech is not very advanced. He only says a few words and at times doesn't speak at all. His pediatrician isn't concerned but we are." Adam's father quickly added, "He may not speak but he is certainly capable of screaming. Sometimes he screams so loud that my ears ring for hours afterward. It's really difficult not to become irritated and snap at him." In what appeared to be an effort to change the subject and calm her husband, Karen said she had wondered if the speech delay could be connected to the birth of Adam's little sister, Kay. They agreed that Adam became less inclined to speak to anyone after Kay was born. Dan added, "I wish he could tell us what he is so upset about, but it doesn't seem like he can. It just comes out in fits and screams. Karen can take it better than I can." In a supportive tone, Karen replied, "We are both kind of laidback people, but you have tinnitus, I don't. It's easier for me because it's not painful when he screams. Sometimes I wonder if he does it because he wants to hurt Dan." I inquired what might cause Adam to want to hurt his father. Haltingly, Karen replied, "I don't know really, but I think Adam wants him to know what it was like when Dan did not respond to him." Dan explained that he has a hearing problem including tinnitus. He also began to become excessively tired and developed migraines after Adam's birth. At times, he needed to turn the lights off and lie down to control the pain. He had little energy to play with Adam. He couldn't understand what was wrong because he had wanted a child and was happy to have a boy. Initially, he thought it was just something guys go through after having a baby because of the changes in demands on him and getting up for late-night feedings. After just a few weeks, Dan found himself yelling at Adam to "just go to sleep!" Both parents anxiously chuckled as Dan added, "Like that would make any child go to sleep!" Karen became worried about Dan's impatience, "not that he would hurt Adam or anything, but he was usually more patient with endless energy." In addition to the challenge of being new parents of a child with medical issues, they found out that Dan had cancer.

I met with the parents for several sessions, discussing their experiences. During these interviews, I was impressed by their openness and the way they comforted each other. They frequently looked at each other to confirm their views and to ask if they were "remembering it right," as if they both held part of the story and didn't trust their own memories. They detailed their understanding of being new parents with fears and insecurities. Those fears were complicated by Dan's cancer treatments, Adam's medical issues, and their own histories.

As Dan and Karen became less anxious, they were better able to recall some of the details of Adam's first two years of life. They waited to have children until Dan was in a stable position with his company and had received a promotion that would allow Karen to stay home if she chose. They began their family agreeing to two children and that Karen would stay home until the children were in school full-time. "Well that didn't happen because once Dan was diagnosed with cancer everything changed." Karen and Dan took turns speaking as they recounted the numerous office visits, and being told that it might be best for them to have another child before Dan began chemotherapy and radiation treatments. "It was all so much coming at us at one time that I don't think we could hardly even think. We just acted. So, it was probably too soon to have another baby but we did," Karen explained. Dan comforted his wife as she began to cry. "Then I realized how afraid I was that he would die. How was I going to manage to take care of two children by myself? It was just crazy." Dan inserted, "I was worried about the same thing. How would she manage? It wasn't about the money, it was about taking care of the kids. There were so many other struggles."

The other struggles Dan was referring to included his son's medical issues. Adam was born with muscular weakness, a skull malformation that required him to wear a helmet, and hip dysplasia requiring a harness. When Dan became too tearful to continue, Karen took over the story, "Adam needed a lot of attention and he seemed to be sensitive to everything." Based on their description, Adam was very sensitive to clothing, could not stand tags or seams, and would cry if the material was at all rough. What was worse was that Adam did not like to be touched and would "freeze" when they tried to pick him up to comfort him. Karen was the first to admit that she was concerned that I might judge her and find them lacking as parents. Tearfully, she added that she believed she was lacking as a parent for the first two years of Adam's life. Dan sighed, "It was hard on all of us but mostly it was tough for Karen. She felt so guilty."

Karen said she felt guilty because she was not able to care for Adam the way she would have liked to. She was aware that she had become more withdrawn, paying attention to herself when she wasn't caring for Dan or working. I wondered if we could consider that her becoming more inward-focused was, in part, because of her pregnancy, and because she was overwhelmed and frightened. This observation seemed to decrease her sense of guilt and allowed her to talk more openly about her own anger and disappointment. Karen was sad that something was "wrong" with her child. She was unhappy because as the cancer treatments increased Dan was unable to work, which required her to go back to work full-time. At the same time, she felt somewhat relieved because she was so unsure how to help Adam with his physical and emotional troubles.

Initially Dan tried to take care of Adam while he was home, and on his "good days" things were challenging but "bearable." As Dan became increasingly tired and irritable, he recognized it was impossible for him to be a good parent. His mother took over caring for Adam while Karen was at work. Dan and Karen were concerned about the arrangement because his mother was in her 60s, and they were worried that Adam would be too much for her. Karen said she consoled herself with the fantasy that Grandma Bev would be able to give Adam what he needed and what they could not. As we spoke, Karen became aware that it was both a wish and a fear. Similarly, she worried that Adam might find me to be a better "parent" than she or Dan could be. Over time, we established a working relationship by talking about both parents' fears and wishes about what my becoming a part of their family might mean to them. We also decided that it would be best for me to meet Grandma Bev.

Grandma Bev was supportive of Adam being in treatment. She was concerned about his developmental delays and understood that his early years had been traumatic for him. During our meetings, Grandma Bev described Adam as a very angry child who bit his cousins, screamed inconsolably at times, and would fly into fits of rage. After several sessions, Grandma Bev recalled having left Adam in his crib to "cry it out" on several occasions. She would go into his room to check on him but did not pick him up. She added that he was difficult to look at with his helmet and his red angry face. Tearfully, she explained that she didn't know what to do for him as he wouldn't allow her to comfort him like other children. "There was no holding him or petting his hair, oh no, none of that!" she lamented. Grandma Bev hoped that being in treatment might help Adam feel differently: "It seems all he feels is anger. He is never happy and seems to not want others to be happy. He becomes so jealous, worse than I have seen with my own children, or with the other grandchildren. I don't think he is a bad child, I think he is in a lot of emotional pain."

I continued to work with the parents and grandparents to help them to understand Adam's feelings and to translate his behaviors into emotional expressions. With some effort, they were also able to remember and discuss their own emotional outbursts, jealousies, and wish to have it all when they were children. When they were able to consider that Adam was behaving in ways that could be understood and helped, we agreed it was time for me to meet him.

Although Dan and Karen still struggled with feelings of inadequacy, they also thought having Adam in analysis was less of an indictment of their inability to parent and more a way to further care for their child. We agreed that he would call me Ms. Bernadette so that he did not relate me to the numerous doctors he had seen early in his life. In addition to his own doctor visits, Adam had accompanied Karen when she picked Dan up from radiation and chemotherapy. Karen recalled Adam screaming he would not go to the pediatrician because "they will make me sick like Daddy." We agreed they would explain that he was going to see someone that would help him with his big feelings.

When I met Adam, he appeared unable to form complete sentences, speaking in telegraphic speech with a very infantile tone. Although able to make eye contact, he refused to acknowledge my presence and would only allow me to quietly sit and watch him play games with his parents. After several sessions of gentle encouragement from his parents, Adam gave me the opportunity to play a game of "chutes and ladders." I made sure I lost. Eventually, he agreed that he could come in and play alone with me under one condition: *"No talking!"*

Over the course of six months, Adam's imaginative play increased. He used paints and drawings to illustrate his feelings. I would attempt to put words to his feelings, each time being met with a firm and insistent *"no talking!"* I decided it might be helpful to use a picture book with printed words as I knew Adam could read, so I cut out many animal photos that expressed different feeling states. Adam was very intrigued by the facial expressions or behaviors of the animals that represent joy, sadness, anger, loneliness, fear, contentment, and love. He decided he was a wild dog who could yelp, bark, and most importantly growl. When I commented that a dog doesn't talk, Adam smiled.

Anger, jealously, and hatred dominated the sessions along with silence. Hitting me was transferred to hitting, kicking, and stomping on stuffed animals. I was ordered about by pointing and using simple sentences. Adam would command, "Draw a dog." As I drew, Adam scribbled on the paper, adding many colors to his creation. I commented that I thought his artwork was wonderfully colorful. He scoffed at me, grabbed my drawing, and tore it to pieces. "That was so ugly." These reproachful remarks extended to how I was dressed and how I looked. I was ugly, wore ugly clothes, and looked stupid. During this time, I commented that I was fearful that there was nothing right with me and that I couldn't do anything right. Adam told me he hated me and that everything I did was ugly and awful. Each session began with "I hate you so much." After weeks of my tolerating his hatred and anger, an important session took place. Adam came in and announced, "Let's play a game." He found a paper bag in the art supplies and cut tiny holes out for my eyes. "Put this on." Given his propensity for physical rage, I hesitated. I was worried about my own safety given the limited sight I would have with a paper bag over my head. Adam screamed, "*Put it on!*" I held the bag in my hands while he put a small rug on the floor and walked over to the light. He commanded, "Sit there and put it on and shut up."

Invited commentator responses: Susan Donner and Alan Sugarman

Susan Donner

In times of analytic uncertainty, often the best practice is for the analyst to keep an open mind and follow the patient's lead. In psychoanalytic treatment with children, the analyst literally plays along and uses whatever material emerges from the play sequences – including verbal utterances, nonverbal communications, and the transference-countertransference constellations and enactments – to understand the child's internal world. As a child analyst comfortable with play and action as well as the ubiquitous experiences of confusion and uncertainty, Dr. Kovach intellectually "knew" when Adam engaged her in this "paper bag play" that her participation was absolutely necessary for the meanings of the actions, symbols, roles, and affects to come alive and to help give meaning to previously unrepresented or sequestered overstimulating or traumatic memories, fantasies, and internal states. So when Dr. Kovach stopped her narration at this particular moment, *her pause should give us pause*. Dr. Kovach signaled that she was feeling something markedly "different" from her usual interactions with Adam.

Part of our valuable training as psychoanalysts is to recognize important moments of change, omission, or affective vulnerability in our patients as well as in ourselves. In her introduction, Dr. Kovach quite casually mentioned that Adam's physical aggression had shifted from "hitting her to hitting the stuffed animals," thus revealing that she had been a target of his sadistic and violent actions. At the paused moment, however, her tone shifted, and she specifically noted her worrying about Adam's "propensity for physical rage."

In this suspended moment, Dr. Kovach communicated to us, and likely also to Adam, her ambivalence; that is, her simultaneous willingness and hesitation to enter into an enormously complex and demanding enactment that is at the heart of Adam's difficulties. The courageous and hopeful part of her (and of Adam, too) wished to understand these tangled strands of what she was anticipating as painful and frightening sadomasochistic dynamics, for which there apparently were no effective solutions till perhaps this moment. Could this play sequence allow Adam's terrors and traumas to be elaborated and re-experienced in a separate and different form, potentially less terrifying and toxic to Adam's experience of himself and his object?

And yet there was an element of terror and unpredictability that was conveyed in Dr. Kovach's hesitancy to embark on this adventure. Her experience of how threatening, frighteningly aggressive, and even deadly serious this play could become signaled her sensitive grasp of his internal reality and her acceptance of Adam's exploratory projections of his most prominent primitive anxieties, such as likely annihilation, castration, and claustrophobia. The first step of effective therapeutic action was Dr. Kovach's availability to receive Adam's communications and contain them until she could metabolize the intense and complex affects and meanings.

Perhaps a combination of her constitutional sensitivity, autobiographical history, and clinical training rendered her open for this kind of specific bonding. More important, however, was Adam's contribution in expertly training Dr. Kovach early in the course of treatment, by helping her develop the verbal and nonverbal vocabulary needed for his analyst to be able to grasp what Adam was conveying without saying it explicitly. The playroom became a relatively neutral zone in which forms of aggression could be uniquely tolerated and where Adam might be the focus of one-on-one attention without the distraction of an ill and exquisitely noise-sensitive father, an overwhelmed mother, or a needy baby sister. Dr. Kovach had learned well enough, both consciously and unconsciously, how to receive and interpret enough of Adam's style and messaging, and how to respond in a safe and containing way so that his attacks did not ricochet back in retaliation and sadistic revenge. And so, this "moment" should be considered within the frame of the previous weeks and months of careful testing and preparation.

Heinrich Racker's (1957) concepts of concordant and complementary identifications, the former being internal states of the patient and the latter being ways he experienced his objects, might be helpful terms to organize Dr. Kovach's possible feelings of bombardment and attack by Adam. In my clinical experience with traumatized children, the more overwhelmed and isolated a child felt during the original states of terror and aggression with internal representations of both victim and aggressor, the more forceful and rapidly fluctuating the projected and enacted states with the child analyst.

As an infant and again, like an infant, Adam knew intuitively that there was no better way to have another person feel what you feel than having them feel it first-hand. This way words – with their expressive delay, complex meanings, and potential distortions – do not get in the way. Dr. Kovach could get the full impact of the experience, as in immersive virtual reality. Thus, Adam put Dr. Kovach in a passive role with a bag over her head and small holes that made it difficult to see. Most ingeniously, Adam recreated in her his experience with a helmet on his head with limited visibility that made it difficult to move safely and predict what was looming around the corner. With her sight limited and her other senses on alert, he put her perfectly on the defensive.

Given the surprising and painful events, both enormous and imperceptibly small to outside observers, such as his father's illnesses and treatments, his baby sister's appearance and enviable normal growth and development, unpredictable caregiving, sensory pain, discomfort, overstimulation, and physical weakness, Adam had so very much to communicate to his willing and able partner. Her therapeutic burden was to endure the feelings of vulnerability and unpredictability. Would she be able to prepare for a possible surprise? Would she feel underprepared and overwhelmed or, on the other hand, over-prepared and silly for her exaggerated reactions to a five-year-old? Adam created a scenario where the correct state of readiness was elusive; thus Dr. Kovach, like Adam, would likely be wrong and out of sync. She might then become fearful of an aggressive attack or anxious with her own fantasy and response. As a result, Adam has impinged upon her sense of her own realistic power and strength in several sensory modalities, so now, with this next step, she might feel further encroachment and even greater claustrophobia than just the confining feeling of the bag.

Thus, another layer of Adam's experience was conveyed – that is, he could not do anything right. As a baby, he tried to communicate but his cries were too loud and strident. Adam's projections were essentially too toxic to his parents to be absorbed; there was clearly a mismatch in his transmission of his distress and the parental containment. Neither parent could transform them to a less toxic state, and/or Adam could not introject these alpha elements without his own attack on them (Bion, 1962). As an older toddler and preschooler, he tried to explain his feelings of overstimulation, neglect, frustration, competition, and rage but could not make himself clear and/or overwhelmed his parents with his inconsolability and aggression. In the clinical setting, he was effective in conveying his experience to Dr. Kovach, who heard his orders to obey and heeded them to stay still and quiet.

Perhaps there was also the sensation of exclusion that Adam needed Dr. Kovach to feel. Always too slow, too weak, and too miserable, Adam had never been able to catch his objects unless he was aggressive with them. They were too big, too sick, too busy, or too impatient for him. Might Dr. Kovach let herself be caught by this little boy with all the complex intense longings, for instance, sensual, sexual, envious, jealous, competitive, that are communicated and need to be endured in this particular compressed time and space? Equipped with few mechanisms but projection, Adam has turned his environment into a claustrophobic and terrifying nightmare, and Dr. Kovach must allow herself to experience the terror and experience of being caught, squeezed, trapped, and tortured.

This paper bag robbed Dr. Kovach of her identity as well. Adam could look at her as faceless and replace her with any of a number of individual or amalgamated objects, including his own self-image. On the other hand, in that anonymity, there could be dehumanization leading to an intensified sadistic impulse. In this way, he could convey his concordant experience of not being seen and understood and the complementary one of his extraordinary and seemingly limitless rage.

At a more abstract level, we might consider Adam's sense of himself as being a leaky, unmanageable, flimsy bag with two holes for excrement – the weak, klutzy, ineffective, nonverbal baby self magically transformed before him into the therapist with the bag on her head whom he can direct and appear to "control." In terms of complementary identification, the bag might also be a metaphor for his experience of his environment, easily torn and fragile, obscured and obscuring, stifling but nevertheless ineffectively containing. Adam had not been able to have his parents reliably soothe his distress with his sensory hypersensitivity and motor hypotonicity, let alone their own limitations. As Klein described, his rageful, envious and jealous attacks on his sick and distracted internal objects were then introjected (Klein, 1948). One can imagine that his worlds, outer and inner, were constructed of flimsy containers that perpetuated Adam's fantasy that he is a terrifying and omnipotently destructive monster. The environmental confirmation of these fantasies may have perpetuated this delusion as a *folie à deux* between the child and parents (Mason, personal communication).

Might Dr. Kovach prevent a recapitulation of Adam's traumatic history by assisting him to shift his concordant and complementary representations as they reemerge in this play scenario? In an effort to master trauma, play scenarios and enactments can operate as an opportunity to have a "do-over," as children call it on the playground. Like other overwhelmed and overwhelming children, Adam used the analytic space to rule and direct the play and action and force Dr. Kovach to adopt the role of the passive and submissive victim bearing the affects of weakness, vulnerability, helplessness, and powerlessness. What was undoubtedly therapeutic was that Adam, in spite of what had been limiting developmental delays, could now communicate and give verbal orders in a more age-appropriate way and active form (e.g., "Don't talk").

Now, six months into the psychoanalytic treatment, begins the real work of playing and reworking the pains of his past. Adam found a partner who might help him locate his realistic locus of control and power, authentic sense of agency, and perhaps even responsibility for his actions. She must first be willing to play in his scenario, and, most importantly, she must simultaneously guarantee that no irreparable harm will come to either of them. This implicit reassurance cannot be simple since his infantile omnipotent aggression had the power of weakening his father, stripping him of his hair and masculinity, and sending him away to the hospital. Dr. Kovach will need to frustrate his grandiosity, hopefully gently, as she must ultimately demonstrate competent containment, that is, that he is a little boy and she is the grown-up who can keep him safe, in a way that does not destroy his creativity, realistic power, and true self.

Again, Adam has intuitively created a situation where Dr. Kovach is held hostage to a mental state where she must be submissive to his controlling rules or break the frame of the pretend mode, which supports his fragile self-esteem and limited self-regulation. Adam already had ordered her to stay quiet multiple times, thus allowing her to experience his own experience of his father's rage and pain and critical attacks. This prelude signaled Dr. Kovach to prepare herself to endure preverbal experiences and tolerate the intolerable – which, up until now – had been unspeakable. She would be tested, time and again, about whether she could bear the affects and tolerate his aggressive and erotic attempts to engage her, without rejecting him or withdrawing from him. Could she not only survive his real and fantasied attacks in a way that his parents couldn't, but also turn the unspeakable into words.

Back in the real-time playroom, there is no time for analytic dissection of meaning. Before a child analyst can think about what dynamics might be unfolding, the first order of business must be safety. Could this five-year-old with low muscle tone really be dangerous to himself or the analyst? Only Dr. Kovach would be able to assess his potential given his previous attacks. Did the analyst feel that intensity of the excitement and sadism escalating so quickly that she needed to intervene in some way to protect herself physically? Would she be able to protect Adam from the overwhelming affects of persecutory and annihilation anxiety – let alone retaliatory action – should he do actual harm? Or could she find a way to bear and, especially, to verbalize the feelings of being vulnerable, passive, and helpless in this scenario?

In the moment, Dr. Kovach was on a tightrope – too much submission and she could overstimulate Adam's sadistic fantasies of revenge and retaliation. Too much resistance to her passive position and she could destroy the field of pretend play that Adam might experience in his limited paradigm not only as too real, but also – in sadomasochistic terms – as her domination with constraint and control. How and when to join with a patient and follow his lead and how and when to introduce separateness and differentiation in a tolerable form is truly the art of psychoanalytic treatment. Although Adam was only five and had no weapon other than his limbs, his mouth, and a paper bag, I would suggest that his feelings of terror should not be minimized. However, at the same time, Dr. Kovach needed to assess how much of the terror she must emotionally and physically contain. Adam needed to have her feel that the tables could be turned safely, but, if she began to feel too threatened and too uncomfortable so that she could not think clearly, then she would need to address the danger of the situation to herself and to Adam. Ultimately, the child analyst has the responsibility to be the guardian of safety, both physical and emotional, of the analytic space.

Responding to the sense that something new might emerge, the analyst might see the potential for "playing with reality," to use Fonagy and Target's (1996) term. Here, Dr. Kovach could have the opportunity to mark the sequence in a way that affectively matched the intended communication but exaggerated it so it is differentiated from reality (what Fonagy et al. 2002 refer to as "marked mirroring," p. 156). The emotional communication back to

Adam could reflect "I understand what you need me to understand" but "we know I am pretending and will therefore survive." For example, wordless dramatic expressions of affect like pretend screams, or short bursts of "I'm scared," might be very helpful in communicating that the analyst understands the intent of the play but can mark it as separate from reality and decompress tensions, a crucial function of play.

This transformation of the once intolerably toxic elements through play sequences and co-created meanings is another crucial component of therapeutic action, although it may need to be repeated and worked through in many variations as remodeling of earlier procedural organizations of affect and experience and new constructions emerge. The use of narrative, character, and role elaborations as well as variations of play scenario outcomes can become internalized and thus modify Adam's previously limited ego and superego components. The hope is for Adam's eventual restoration to what Anna Freud called "a path of progressive development" with greater creativity, flexibility, and resilience.

Alan Sugarman

Let me begin by thanking Dr. Kovach for providing such a vivid and emotionally moving description of Adam, his parents, and his difficulties leading up to the clinical moment in question. Her material is so rich and empathic toward Adam and his family that putting oneself in her shoes when confronted by his demand to put a bag over her head is immeasurably easier. The rich descriptions of Adam, Dan, Karen, and Grandma Bev also suggest Dr. Kovach's implicit formulations about the underlying causes/meanings of Adam's speech delay and rage attacks. These formulations are important because they will be the basis for the technical decision about how to handle the clinical moment in question. My assumption, based on the literature that she reviews and her sympathetic descriptions of the cast of characters, is that trauma is viewed as the primary cause of Adam's difficulties. To be sure, Dr. Kovach demonstrates a realization that the experience of trauma is only a construction that mixes realities and fantasies. But her statement that the child's experience needs to be recognized and acknowledged suggests to me that she still prioritizes the environmental situation(s) that the child has experienced as traumatic.

I (Sugarman, 2008, 2017) have expressed concern that such formulations can lead to subtle shifts in technique that fail to enhance the child's experience of himself-as-agent and realization that he is responsible for managing his reactions to his feelings and the meanings he has given to whatever he has experienced in the external world. In order to avoid this danger, I do my best to maintain my clinical focus on the immediate present, particularly in terms of what is happening or has been happening recently between the child analysand and myself. This way of working is consistent with my understanding of the dynamic, nonlinear systems theory that so many of us currently find useful for thinking about development. That model implies that any symptom or problematic behavior or personality trait is best understood in terms of its current context and the patient's current level of mental organization regardless of its chronological origins. Development is characterized by regular nonlinear transformations that change the meaning and function of any pathological phenomena. Hence, patients of all ages, even children as young as Adam, are best helped by facilitating their abilities to look at and understand their mind's workings in the immediate present. This emphasis may be even truer for pre-latency children such as Adam because of their cognitive concreteness and developmentally less mature senses of time.

Another element of the theoretical biases that inform my clinical listening and technical interventions is the ubiquity of intrapsychic conflict (Nagera, 1966). Although I work in a very relational fashion and use a theory of mutative action that emphasizes both Bionian and Contemporary Freudian ideas, I find the concept of internal conflict very helpful in organizing the material in the room, particularly inter- and intra-structural conflict. From my perspective, everything experienced by patients, both young and old, is experienced through the prism of internal conflict and gives rise to subsequent conflicts. Implicit in this model of the mind and mental functioning is the notion that the major function of the mind is maintaining a harmonious equilibrium between all the psychological functions that comprise it and interact with each other. Such a homeostatic equilibrium is challenging because these functions interact with each other; they are not developing in linear and parallel fashion. Furthermore, they also develop according to different timetables. Adding to the mind's task is the need to ensure that this internal equilibrium helps the patient to adapt to the internal world.

Thus, I try to help my patients, even the very young ones, to observe their mental functions interacting in our interactions. This task is particularly difficult with Adam's age group because they are so afraid of their affects (Bornstein, 1949; Hoffman, 2007). Hence, direct reference to them in the session is likely to only cause intense anxiety and intensify defense or resistance. It is this reason that necessitates working within the play, including sometimes taking the role of a character in it. I do not always wait to be assigned such a role as Dr. Kovach advocates. Instead, I may find a way to insert myself into the play either by taking on the role of a character or by using a toy to begin talking about what is transpiring. I see my role as more than just "witnessing" the child's behavior and putting words to it or helping them to "re-experience [their] past without becoming overwhelmed by it." From my perspective, I am working and interpreting in the displacement offered by play. This displacement is necessary because of their developmentally limited affect tolerance and their not yet integrated psychic equivalence and pretend modes of functioning (Fonagy et al., 2002). Until these modes are integrated, direct interpretation of internal states can feel terrifying because the child's ability to realize that ideas and feelings are not the same as reality is limited. That is why staying in the pretend mode of playing feels safer and allows them to discuss internal states.

Because of my emphasis on internal conflict, I emphasize interventions that will help a child like Adam see and realize his internal conflicts as they are externalized in the play and interactions between us. For this reason, I would look for ways to address the internal conflicts necessitating his control of me by forcing me to silently watch him and his parents play games or in his commands of no talking when I tried to put words to his feelings. Certainly, Dr. Kovach was quite sensitive to his anxiety in her careful silences or creative introduction of animal photos with emotional expressions on them. But, from my internal conflict perspective, such interventions skipped over the possibility of helping him to see the anxiety and/or narcissistic vulnerability presumably stimulating such extreme defensive control of the environment.

For example, while making sure that I lost when playing Chutes and Ladders, I might take on the masochistic, loser role and lament feeling so bad about myself because I was never smart enough to win. Or I might talk about how unsafe I feel if my mommy and daddy aren't with me and how lucky Adam is that he has his mommy or daddy there to make him feel safe. My experience is that such interventions can be done playfully so that the child is clear that I am talking from the role of an imaginary character, not expressing my own feelings. Obviously, none of these interventions might have worked and I might have been forced to take the passive role taken by Dr. Kovach. My point remains the same, however. Such an outcome would still be understood as reflecting internal conflict between Adam's unexpressed emotion and some sort of intense signal anxiety triggering defensive externalization. I would not see it as simply an ego regression caused by the various traumas he had experienced.

This perspective holds true, also, for the attempts to put words to his feelings. My approach would be to find ways within the play to talk about fears of knowing feelings, either as a character in the play, or by using a puppet or other toy to express the conflict. For example, I might pick up one of the stuffed animals and have it say it wants to paint, also, because that helps it not talk about its feelings that feel "so big." Again the point of this approach would be to draw his attention to the defensive way that his mind functions, but in the displacement so that he can observe it without feeling overwhelmed. There is research data showing that young children can talk about complicated internal phenomena within the play that they cannot discuss when it applies directly to them (Mayes & Cohen, 1996).

The point of this preamble is not to second-guess Dr. Kovach. She obviously has a much deeper understanding of her patient than I possibly could from only an abbreviated summary about him. Instead, I am trying to lay the groundwork for how I would experience and react to the clinical moment when he demands that I put a bag over my head. I certainly would have felt great pressure given the intensity of Adam's demands and his fury when frustrated. But my reaction would also be informed, probably preconsciously in the heat of the moment, by my thoughts of what had been transpiring between us. The sessions leading up to this demand were characterized by his devaluation of the analyst and her work. Her drawings were ugly; so was her appearance. And she was stupid to boot. Hence, he hated her and she was awful. What are the conflicts driving this devaluation and hatred would be the questions going through my mind at the time. I would have been testing out various hypotheses and verbalizing various elements of the possible conflicts in the displacement of the play.

For example, I would wonder if he was externalizing onto me his own feelings of being ugly and repulsive. There is certainly evidence that his family saw him in that manner at certain points. From this perspective he is not simply communicating his own feelings caused by the trauma of being seen by one's family as so physically hideous. Instead there is an internal conflict between such a self-representation, formed in part from actual experience, and a defense that tries to maintain narcissistic equilibrium by defensive externalization and devaluation. To test out such a hypothesis, I would start by being a character who voices how ugly and hideous he feels. After playing out that theme for some sessions, I would voice its defensive value by saying that I wish I could feel as good as he does. Such work would lead into my talking about how he must be glad that I'm the ugly one. It is important that he ultimately see that his mind is actively conflicted and that he treats others quite poorly, at times, to protect himself from feeling ugly and unlovable.

Another possibility that I would consider would be that his anger and devaluation indicated an attempt to rid him of angry feelings that his superego found objectionable. Coen (1992) has talked about patients who externalize to avoid the self-recriminations of a sadistic superego. I find that many children behave the way Adam did to avoid superego criticism. In such an instance I would take the role of feeling ugly and bad because I was so angry. I might alternate such laments with wishes that I could be nice. Eventually, I would work my way around to realizing that I could feel good by making others feel that they are bad. Still another possibility I would be thinking about would be an unconscious masochistic attempt to provoke others into rejecting him as a way to atone for his own sadistic rage about which he felt guilty, or as a reflection of the omnipotence that characterizes masochists (Novick & Novick, 1996). Masochistic behavior might also be the only way he can conceive of attaching. Such play and interactions could also involve an unconscious attempt to enlist the other as an auxiliary ego to help him with his problems with regulating his intense affects, particularly his rage. Finally, he might even be defending sadness and loneliness with sadism.

I am sure that there are other possible dynamic conflicts that might also be driving such behavior in the sessions. My interventions would involve taking on the role of a character or using a toy in the room to voice possibilities while using his reactions to modify, emphasize, or reject the particular conflict I was hypothesizing to be the driver of the negative transference in the room. In this context, I would see his demand that I put a bag over my head as a continuation of such a conflict. This way of looking at material would determine my response. For example, I might exclaim, "Oh goody! Nobody will see how ugly I am if my face is covered by the bag." In this way, I would be interpreting the narcissistic defense being externalized. Or, if I was feeling the worry for my physical safety reported by Dr. Kovach, I might say from the role of a character (not my real self), "I'm so afraid. If I can't see what's happening around me very well, something bad could happen to me!" In this way I would be interpreting the existential vulnerability that I thought was being defended. I might even go on to say, "I want my mommy or my daddy. I'm really scared to be alone." Or if I was using the hypothesis that trauma was being reduced via an enactment, I might respond, "Wow. This reminds me of how my head felt when I used to have to wear a helmet that made it hard to see."

These interventions might not seem very different from Dr. Kovach's emphasis on putting words to feelings. In my mind, the significant difference is my assumption that whatever feeling is being voiced is not a solitary internal experience. Instead it is part of a complex compromise formation that includes all elements of a conflict-impulse, defense, signal affect, and superego. Hence, I start out voicing one part of the conflict and work my way around to covering the multiple facets of the conflict. Eventually, I look for signs that the child is ready for me to move out of the displacement and to talk about the fact that they might feel similar to the play character. But it is important to begin with, and spend much of the working through process in, the play itself (Sugarman, 2003, 2008).

The clinical moment with Adam demands that Dr. Kovach find a way to try to work with its meaning in the play. If interventions like the ones being suggested fail, I would simply insist that one of the animals in the office wear the bag. At one point, she insisted he physically mistreat stuffed animals instead of her. I would make a similar demand. Were that to inflame him, I would simply look for another role from which to talk about my disappointment when others won't do what I want and then about the conflicts I thought were making such control feel so important to him in the moment. But throughout the work stemming from this clinical moment, my interventions, both verbal and behavioral, would be guided by my theories of pathogenesis and mutative action. That is, his behaviors all reflect internal conflicts and he needs to learn to see inside and observe his mind's conflictual functioning in order to master it using verbal, symbolic insightfulness.

My intervention

Although anxious, I sat down on the floor and put the bag on my head. Adam began to speak in full sentences. He turned the lights on and off while he spoke. "I am going to place you in a small cage and you will have nothing to look at because you have to wear this thing on your head. I will peel your skin off your body and I will poke your eyes and they will pop and all the eye juice will come out of them. You will not be able to stop me, *ever*. You can't see me coming because when you try to turn your head and look the bag thing is in the way. You will hear sounds, me laughing and talking, other voices. You are going to be so afraid and if you cry I will tell you to shut up! Stop crying. Then I will scratch your arms and your face until you bleed and I will yell at you for making a mess with your blood. You will watch all your blood come out and you won't be able to stop me." Adam handed me a blanket and told me to wrap it around myself so I could not move my arms. He began again, "I am taking all your blood and you can only lay there and watch me do it. The thing is tight around you and you cannot stop me from taking all your blood." He walked over to me and poked my arm, then walked away. "The hole I made will let all the blood out and you will die." I would occasionally say how frightened I was and that if a child had to live through all this, it would make them feel so scared and so angry. I wondered how else a child might feel if they had to live like this. I wondered if it would ever end. Adam replied loudly, "*It will never end!*" I thought to myself I would rather die.

The tormenting sessions continued for two weeks, during which time we made a cage out of construction paper and paper towels. Adam began each session saying, "I hate you, I hate you, I hate you. You are ugly and you're going to be ugly forever and you will always be scared. Now put this on your head." I said I felt trapped and afraid. I worried that I might not ever be able to get out of this stupid bag. I didn't want to remain in a bag forever. He assured me I would die after all the blood was drained from me. My hair was to be cut off and my eyes would be pinched. I felt frightened and tormented and told him how I felt. "That is right, that is how you will always feel." I disagreed and said I did not always have to feel tortured and in pain. "Yes you do, shut up, you are and will feel hurt all the time." I said it would be horrible if a child felt like this, and I wondered if he knew someone who felt as if they were ugly and they couldn't understand why their mother would leave them to be hurt and frightened. I said I bet a child who was so scared would have so much to be angry about that they wouldn't know where to put it all and they wouldn't want to speak about any of it.

After some reconstruction, Adam was able to begin to put words to his feelings. He remembered the helmet he had worn, the numerous blood draws, the eye patches he had to wear, and the brace on his legs. I worried that he would stop coming, also realizing I wished for him to stop coming to stop the torture. After three weeks of torture, Adam came to session asking if I had somewhere for him to put his anger. I sincerely wanted to cry from all the sadness I felt and out of a sense of relief. I asked where he wanted to leave his anger. He replied, "On your desk." Adam took out a marker and headed for my desk. I quickly placed a sticky note down, and he drew out his anger, one sticky note after another. Once my desk was completely covered in layers of sticky notes, Adam began to smile. He said, "I pooped all over your desk. You have to keep it here until I say so." Adam added, "Now we can play another game."

While Adam continued to express anger, a wish to be beaten, and a wish to beat, his screaming and rages subsided at home. In session, his beating fantasy began to be acted out using stuffed animals, and his fantasy play began to contain more Oedipal elements. As his anger diminished in session, he asked if we could pretend he was being born. We built a tent out of blankets, and he curled up in the tent waiting for his mother to give birth to him. He directed my narrative by first telling me that the mother and father would go to the hospital. The mother would "push the baby out," and when they saw the baby, it would be perfect. He wanted to be perfect and to undo all the struggles he had as an infant. My taking on the role of the tortured child and putting words to his feelings helped Adam speak and put his anger out there for both of us to see. I have wondered if it might have sufficed had I suggested early on that we use stuffed animals or baby dolls. I remember at the time thinking that he needed to trust me, to see what I could tolerate. It was not just a need for me to feel what he felt but a quid pro quo. If I honestly spoke my feelings, he would be able to speak about his.

References

Alpert, J. (2001). No escape when the past is endless. *Psychoanalytic Psychology*, 18(4), 729–736.
Arlow, J. (1991). Methodology and reconstruction. *Psychoanalytic Quarterly*, 60(4), 539–563.
Bandura, A. (1977). *Social learning theory.* Oxford: Prentice-Hall.
Barish, K. (2006). On the role of reparative processes in childhood: Pathological development and therapeutic change. *Journal of Infant, Child and Adolescent Psychotherapy*, 5(1), 92–110.
Bion, W. R. (1962). *Learning from experience.* London: Tavistock, pp. 2–10.
Blum, H. (2007). Little Hans: A centennial review and reconsideration. *Journal of the American Psychoanalytic Association*, 55(3), 749–765.
Bornstein, B. (1949). The analysis of a phobic child: Some problems of theory and technique in child analysis. *Psychoanalytic Study of the Child*, 68(1), 98–143.
Breuer, J., & Freud, S. (1895). Studies on hysteria. In J. Strachey (Ed. & Trans.), *The standard edition of the complete psychological works of Sigmund Freud* (Vol. 2, pp. 1–321). London: Hogarth Press.
Chethik, M. (2000). *Techniques of child therapy: Psychodynamic strategies.* New York: Guilford Press.
Chused, J. (2007). Little Hans "analyzed" in the twenty-first century. *Journal of the American Psychoanalytic Association*, 55(3), 767–778.
Coates, S. (2016). Can babies remember trauma? Symbolic forms of representation in traumatized infants. *Journal of the American Psychoanalytic Association*, 64(4), 751–776.

Coen, S. (1992). *The misuse of persons and analyzing pathological dependency*. Hillsdale, NJ: The Analytic Press.

Fonagy, P., Gergely, G., Jurist, E. L., & Target, M. (2002). *Affect regulation, mentalization, and the development of the self*. New York: Other Press.

Fonagy, P., & Target, M. (1996). Playing with reality: I. Theory of mind and the normal development of psychic reality. *International Journal of Psychoanalysis, 77* (2), 217–233.

Freud, A. (1966). *The ego and the mechanisms of defense* (rev. ed.). Madison, CT: International Universities Press.

Freud, S. (1893). The psychotherapy of hysteria. In J. Strachey (Ed. & Trans.), *The standard edition of the complete psychological works of Sigmund Freud* (Vol. 2, pp. 253–305). London: Hogarth Press.

Freud, S. (1896). Heredity and the aetiology of the neuroses. In J. Strachey (Ed. & Trans.), *The standard edition of the complete psychological works of Sigmund Freud* (Vol. 3, pp. 151–156). London: Hogarth Press.

Freud, S. (1926). Inhibitions, symptoms and anxiety. In J. Strachey (Ed. & Trans.), *The standard edition of the complete psychological works of Sigmund Freud* (Vol. 20, pp. 75–176). London: Hogarth Press.

Furman, E. (1992). On feeling and being felt with. *Psychoanalytic Study of the Child, 47*(1), 67–84.

Hoffman, L. (2007). Do children get better when we interpret their defenses against painful feelings? *Psychoanalytic Study of the Child, 62*, 291–313.

Kernberg, O. (1980). *Internal world and external reality: Object relations theory applied*. New York: Jason Aronson.

Klein, M. (1948). *Contributions to psychoanalysis (1921–1945)*. London: Hogarth Press.

Kovach, B. (2012). The scent of the other. *Psychoanalytic Study of the Child, 66*, 60–80.

Locke, J. (1894). *An essay concerning human understanding* (A. C. Fraser, Ed.). Oxford: Clarendon Press.

Mason, A. A. Personal communication (unpublished paper, Fast Leopold and Slow Otto).

Mayes, L., & Cohen, D. (1996). Children's developing theory of mind. *Journal of the American Psychoanalytic Association, 44*(1), 117–142.

Nagera, H. (1966). *Early childhood disturbances, the infantile neurosis, and the adulthood disturbances: Problems of a developmental psychoanalytic psychology*. New York: International Universities Press.

Novick, J., & Novick, K. K. (1996). *Fearful symmetry: The development and treatment of sadomasochism*. New York: Jason Aronson.

Ofshe, R. (1994). *Making monsters: False memories, psychotherapy and sexual hysteria*. New York: Scribners.

Racker, H. (1957). The meanings and uses of countertransference. *Psychoanalytic Quarterly, 26*(3), 303–357.

Ross, J. (2007). Trauma and abuse in the case of Little Hans. *Journal of the American Psychoanalytic Association, 55*(3), 779–797.

Schimek, J. (1987). Fact and fantasy in the seduction theory: A historical review. *Journal of the American Psychoanalytic Association, 35*(4), 937–965.

Sugarman, A. (2003). A new model for conceptualizing insightfulness in the psychoanalysis of young children. *Psychoanalytic Quarterly, 72*(2), 325–355.

Sugarman, A. (2008). The use of play to promote insightfulness in the analysis of children suffering from cumulative trauma. *Psychoanalytic Quarterly*, 77(3), 799–833.
Sugarman, A. (2017). The importance of promoting a sense of self-agency in child psychoanalysis. Marianne Kris Memorial Lecture.
Terr, L. (1994). *Unchained memories: True stories of traumatic memories, lost and found*. New York: Basic Books.
Vygotsky, L. (1986). *Thought and language* (rev. ed.). Cambridge, MA: MIT Press.

Chapter 10

A Shocking Revelation

Deborah Harms

Editors' introduction

This clinical moment involves a 31-year-old struggling writer who seemed full of promise when he was young, though his life did not pan out as many had expected. He sought help for his sadness, depression, and low self-esteem related to his inability to sustain a romantic relationship. Jake's childhood history centered on secrecy and the shock he'd experienced upon learning of his father's infidelity – a life-changing event that demarcated his life into two phases: "before" and "after." Subsequent to its coming to light, the event was never spoken of again in the family; furthermore, the patient himself had never shared the experience with anyone else until he entered treatment. After a period of twice-weekly psychotherapy, the patient was seen in four-times-weekly, on-the-couch analysis. The patient was remarkably passive, withdrawn, and isolative. He seldom dated, and when he did, it never seemed to work out well. He preferred to watch TV, smoke pot, and lounge about rather than work to overcome his social anxiety in order to realize his deepest desire: to find a woman and settle down. While the patient seemed unconcerned about his heavy reliance on drugs, the analyst sensed he was, in fact, conflicted about this habit, though she was loath to confront him about the matter lest she be experienced as judgmental. While he attended sessions religiously, the patient would rarely continue the work between sessions, to the extent he would often act as if an important piece of work from the previous session had never happened. He adopted an "ignorance is bliss" policy and seemed dead set against exploring his internal life. Efforts to get him to recognize how unhappy his childhood had been led the patient to violently disagree. At times, his analyst would despair about the patient's prospects and struggled against tendencies to succumb to his pervasive negativity. Then, several years into the analysis, the patient suddenly divulged a secret he had kept from the analyst, the exploration of which forms the basis of this clinical moment.

The moment in context (Richard Tuch)

Instances when a patient consciously chooses to knowingly withhold information from the analyst violate the only instruction that Freud deemed worthy of calling a rule – the "fundamental rule." Freud (1913) would educate patients about their responsibility to the treatment by reminding them: "Finally, never forget that *you have promised* to be absolutely honest, and never leave anything out because, for some reason or other, it is unpleasant to tell it" (p. 134, italics added). In his classic volume on technique, Greenson (1967) argued that:

> The secret, by its very nature of being a secret, is a significant psychic event and has to be analyzed. There can be no compromise on this point... The slightest concession to secrecy, for whatever reason, is incompatible with the analytic situation. *One permissible secret means the end of effective analysis.*
>
> (pp. 128–129, italics added)

Such thinking is in keeping with Freud, who – in a footnote – underscores the need for patients to be completely forthcoming:

> It is very remarkable how the whole task [of analysis] becomes impossible if a reservation is allowed at any single place. But we have only to reflect what would happen if the right of asylum existed at any one point in a town; how long would it be before all the riff-raff of the town had collected there?
>
> (Freud, 1913, p. 135, footnote 1)

Against the backdrop of what's just been said – the seemingly absolute demand that the patient hold nothing back from the analyst – is the realization that patients can and do keep secrets from their analysts. In his paper "The Secret," Gross (1951) writes about how "this delight in harboring a secret, as an end in itself, is a phenomenon which obtrudes itself rather frequently in psychoanalytic work" (p. 534). In mid-century, psychoanalysts (Dickes, 1968; Gross, 1951) tended to think of secrets in bodily terms – in particular, as withheld feces (secret = secretions) that could be bestowed as gifts (anal-phase thinking), or as a child contained within (Fraiberg, 1954) protected just so long as it's kept secret.

While some analysts are adamant about the corrosive effects of secrets on analysis, some authors acknowledge the fact that some patients may feel a need to keep certain matters secret – if only for a time – and, accordingly, such secrets are best regarded as "something to be respected and not crushed, coerced or begged out of the patient" (Greenson, 1967, p. 202). Ekstein and Caruth (1972) – building on the work of Tausk (1933) – asserted that the growing child's ability to keep secrets from his parents helps further his sense of having a mind of his own, which means that sharing one's innermost secrets can involve "a risk of losing that which is 'mine'" (Meares, 1976, p. 260).

Writing about the clinical management of secrets in psychotherapy in a well-reasoned manner, Hoyt (1978) takes the position that:

> Clinical judgment is primary here, but as a general guideline I would suggest that the desideratum be *what function the secret seems to serve*. Is it salutary to the patient's present development, or would growth be better facilitated by its exposure? The handling of the secret requires patience and sensitivity if we are to have impact without trauma in our therapeutic endeavors. Patients must feel secure enough to give up their secrets, must feel that the therapist is trustworthy and that the advantages to be gained will outweigh the expected pains.
> (p. 239, italics added)

At first blush, we might regard the act of consciously keeping a secret from the analyst to represent acting out insofar as the patient is willfully refusing to comply with the demands of treatment. While secret-keeping may be considered a form of acting out, Roughton (1993) is quick to add:

> We would now say that they contain meaningful analytic material, not just opposition. The focus here is on the analytically useful aspects of acting out, a point of view based on Freud's concept of acting out as repetition in the transference and, therefore, as a way of remembering. In order to focus on this, we must move away from the narrow way of thinking about resistance, in general, and acting out, in particular, as representing only opposition to the analytic process.
> (p. 446)

Countertransference reactions to patient-held secrets can vary. Annie Reich (1951) wrote about the voyeuristic tendencies of some analysts who "are still fascinated by their being entitled to pry into other people's secrets... they live out their infantile sexual curiosity" (p. 29). If the patient intimates that he is harboring a secret, the analyst is wise to consider the possibility that the patient is attempting to tease the analyst into a desperate wish to know – quite possibly re-enacting something from his childhood whereby the patient himself was dying to know something that he experienced was being kept from him – possibly experienced as a sadistic tease. Hence, understanding what motivates the patient to want to keep something secret often represents the most the analyst can hope to accomplish at the moment. The function of the kept secret may represent power and control (Margolis, 1974), and an exploration of the hopes and fears associated with disclosing the secret becomes a paramount feature of the clinical approach to the situation. Hoyt (1978) notes how "secrecy and secreting continue to function as a means of asserting autonomy and hiding shame in later relationships, including psychotherapy" (p. 234).

Therapists often pride themselves on proving they are trustworthy enough to encourage patients to divulge a closely held secret that they'd never told to another soul. The promise of strict confidentiality can help patients open up about matters they imagined they would take to their graves. Naturally, sharing such matters with the analyst can be a tremendous relief for patients, particularly if their worst fears about doing so – the exploration of which often prefaces the disclosure – fail to materialize. Margolis (1974) writes about how:

> In the formation of neurosis the child feels there are certain aspects of his life that he must hide from his parents and he then hides some of these from himself (renders them unconscious). In an analytic situation properly set up, the ego reverses this whole process. The analysand pours out all his thoughts, revealing secrets he has never dared to speak of before. This leads to more personal associations involving secrets he has hidden from himself. Instead of hiding things from his parents because of the danger of disapproval, punishment or rejection, he reveals everything to his analyst ... The analyst consistently helps the patient to see that his motives for hiding things from his analyst and himself are unrealistic and that there is great advantage in knowing himself better.
>
> (p. 295)

As we will see in the clinical moment that follows, the patient was able – early in the course of treatment – to bring himself to share an extremely painful, life-altering experience that had taken place around the onset of adolescence. Paradoxically, as we are about to see, the patient ended up keeping from his analyst an important detail about his adult life that went unmentioned for several years – constituting the particular clinical moment about which this presentation is based. This type of secret-keeping differs markedly from the type that has thus far been written about in this essay. Furthermore, once this secret was ultimately divulged, it constituted a relatively shocking disclosure – shocking because it had gone unmentioned throughout the course of the patient's treatment. Quite naturally, for an analyst to suddenly learn about an important detail of the patient's life about which she had been completely clueless is shocking; it fills the analyst with so many emotions that it can figuratively make her head swim as she tries to come to terms with this new knowledge. Feelings run the gamut: How dare he keep this from me? Why would he do such a thing? Who does he think he is? Who does he think I am? Did he not feel me trustworthy enough to share this information? Was there something I did or did not do to contribute to that feeling? What else might I still not know? Has this all been a sham? Was analysis even occurring? And... what the hell is this all about? – with this latter question being the most important and salient of the questions asked. One cannot assume much about the meaning of the secret-keeping unless one keeps an open mind, considers the patient's history, then works to make sense of the situation – which is precisely what Dr. Harms is able to do in the end.

The clinical moment

Jake, a 31-year-old aspiring writer, first appeared in my office because of his sadness and loneliness. He had worked in Hollywood as a writer and producer and had hoped to achieve fame and fortune just as his friends and family had predicted, but after some initial success, he was having difficulty selling his scripts. He returned home and began to work in the family business as an office manager, earning a modest income. He was socially withdrawn, lacked motivation, and was passive in his orientation to life, which left him feeling hopeless and defeated. He was particularly distressed that he could not sustain a romantic relationship with a woman; his longest and only relationship had lasted eight months.

Jake appeared unkempt, unshaven, and carelessly dressed in tattered jeans, giving him an adolescent appearance. I found him bright, likeable, warm, and sincere. I expected him to be an interesting and enjoyable patient. As a writer who appreciated symbolism and metaphor, Jake found it interesting that treatment involved exploration of symbolic, metaphoric meaning of his thoughts and feelings, but he preferred to believe that these ideas did not apply to him.

Jake was the elder of two children in a stable, child-centered family with loving, caring parents. Though he insisted his childhood had been blissfully happy, this claim seemed unsupported by any specific memories from his younger years. Jake was particularly close to his mother's father – a pillar of the community, a successful and wealthy man who lived in grand style. The patient idealized his grandfather who, in turn, treated him as the "favored grandson." Jake's assertion of his "idyllic" childhood stood in stark contrast to the one memory that he did recall from age 13. This experience shook him so deeply that his life was never the same, and, as I later observed, he tended to speak of his life as divided into a "before" and an "after." Upon returning from school one day, Jake found his mother sobbing uncontrollably. That – in and of itself – must have punctuated his life in a way nothing had before. His mother turned to Jake for comfort as she blurted out that she had just learned that his father was having an affair with an employee. On top of that, the employee's husband had delivered the news with threats of violence directed toward the father, which added fear to his panoply of emotions. The event was never spoken of again by the family, and though never explicitly stated, Jake understood that he had been charged with the responsibility of keeping the family secret. I found it highly significant that Jake emphasized repeatedly that this event had "absolutely nothing" to do with his current state of affairs, which led me to believe that it had everything to do with his current distress.

Jake was particularly perplexed about how to reconcile his previous view of his father – who had always emphasized doing the "right thing" – with the newly emerging view of his father as a cheater. This was compounded by his awareness that his father took an inordinate interest in a 12-year-old female actress who played the starring role in a community stage production. His family frequently entertained this girl, and the father even flew to New York for visits once she left the area. Jake wondered whether his father was "weird."

Jake emphasized that he was nothing like his father – a "metrosexual" who was inordinately interested in clothing and in his outward appearance. By contrast, Jake could best be described as "rumpled" – and it was a source of constant contention with his mother because she was forever after him to get a haircut and wear different clothes. He experienced his mother as brutally judgmental as evidenced by her comment about one of the young ladies he had brought home, whom she had described as being rather "rodent-like."

During the early phase of treatment – and sporadically throughout our work – Jake emphasized his wish "not to know," which I connected to the discovery of the father's affair. Jake denied any such connection, insisting that "ignorance is bliss," which we discovered was related to his anxieties about what he might find out about himself in the course of treatment. His greatest fear was that he might discover that there was something terribly wrong with him.

During the first several months of treatment, Jake's depression abated, though he continued to experience episodic despondent feelings that he attributed to rejections from various women. He described numerous instances when friends took him aside to explain that he had been offensive to their girlfriends. His father had done likewise, telling him he needed to apologize to his mother even though Jake never quite knew just what it was he had done. He recalled that he and his father shared a secret communication in which they would roll their eyes behind his mother's back to express disdain for her hypersensitivity and emotionality. This revelation led me to wonder aloud whether he might be anticipating the same thing happening in session – that either he or I might be hiding from the other our angry or disdainful feelings. As I addressed the possible transference manifestations of these feelings toward women, I learned that Jake was particularly concerned that I would be offended if he spoke of his ambivalent feelings about women, which he feared might cause me to terminate his treatment. In response to this exploration, Jake expressed the opinion that a man can never really know when he has offended a woman because women are so devious about what they feel.

I found Jake to be exquisitely sensitive to slights. My attempts at transference interpretations were, for a long time, met with protestations, denial, and a sense of humiliation, which led me to offer my ideas gingerly and to focus on his intolerance of affects and vulnerability. Jake came to acknowledge that it bothered him to think he might enjoy feeling close and connected to me.

I felt frustrated by Jake's insistence that there was nothing to be learned about his sensitivity to slights, seeing as "the fates" were just against him. At times, I privately reacted to his recitations about the inevitable doom of all of his aspirations with momentary resignation that, perhaps, he was right – that he and the treatment were doomed. At these times, I would step back and wonder what I was missing, why it was that I was now feeling hopeless and despairing. Did he have a need to defeat himself in this endeavor as well? Did he need to defeat me? Or might his mother have felt defeated and depressed, leading him to unconsciously engender such emotions in me? Was this his way of identifying with her – connecting with her through her depression? Was I expecting too much of him? Was I imposing my goals on him by hoping he could find satisfaction and happiness in life? After such moments of despair, I would gather my enthusiasm and try harder to find a way to help Jake and to engage him more deeply in the work.

As treatment progressed, Jake appeared to be taking better care of himself – he was feeling less depressed, sleeping better, feeling more confident, functioning better in his job, and making more attempts to socialize despite his considerable social anxiety.

Jake brought in one of his scripts and asked me to read it, which I did. I found it interesting that the main character was a domineering mother and the "surprise ending" involved the revelation of a major family secret. Jake was amazed when I pointed out this connection to his own family history, adding that he had not done it consciously. Following this revelation, Jake became more curious about his own unconscious and seemed to participate with me more in the treatment process.

Jake reported a dream in which he noticed with horror that his beard had been half shaved off. Associating to the dream, he said that a beard is a symbol of manhood, bringing to mind Samson and Delilah. I told him that I thought he saw me, and women in general, as dangerous Delilahs seeking to emasculate him. Furthermore, I pointed out, his passivity protected against the expression of his aggressive and sexual urges, which he feared might get him in trouble. I further suggested that his heavy reliance on marijuana (which he had gradually revealed) was not only a way of anesthetizing himself but, furthermore, a way to render himself passive. He thought this was right on.

Jake's thoughts moved on to his fascination with hair. He talked about people who hide things, and when I asked him to elaborate, he confessed that he had discovered that he and I go to the same hairdresser. In spite of the hairdresser's mention of "hairdresser–client confidentiality," the hairdresser further revealed to him that he also cut my daughter's hair. I was surprised how this conversation had come about, and I wondered what other secrets he knew and what else he was not telling me.

Simultaneous with this work were recurrent themes about a secret desire to "get away with something." Jake gleefully recalled how, during his school years, he had maneuvered to be assigned to lunch and study hall back to back so that he could sneak away to the local arcade and play video games for hours while simultaneously maintaining a reputation as a stellar student. I wondered how his wish to get away with something might be manifesting in our work.

I realized that Jake was superficially compliant, attending his sessions faithfully – never cancelling or coming late. Nevertheless, once he left the session, he did not give another thought to what we had worked on, so each day seemed as if we were beginning anew. Days when I thought we had made an important breakthrough were followed by Jake's ridiculing me the next session for having thought something meaningful had occurred. While this abrupt dismissal of me and our work sometimes stung, I found it mostly perplexing. How could he not recall what we had discussed the day before and how could something that seemed to surprise and interest him one day be so meaningless the next? It made me wonder about the effect of the marijuana use.

Jake was adamant that he had no interest in exploring his marijuana use, though he often complained that using pot left him feeling like a "criminal." Such feelings alternated with glee about getting away with purchasing the drug. He brought in numerous dreams in which he was falsely accused of raping women, or was caught stealing, or was being pursued by police. These various themes led us to some meaningful work around his issues of "conscience" about his sexual, aggressive, and competitive feelings.

An interpretation that arose in response to an episode when he had acted out a rivalry with his "analytic siblings" produced one of the first textured memories of his childhood. Jake enacted his rivalry by refusing to go to the waiting room to wait his turn. Instead, he stood outside my door, sometimes blocking another patient's exit, demanding that I see him right away. I told Jake that I thought he felt rivalrous with my other patients and furthermore felt overlooked and neglected by me, just as he had by his parents, who tended to favor his sister. I further mentioned that I thought he was angry with his parents and with me – whom he accused of being neglectful – though he seemed bothered about having such feelings. A bit surprisingly – since it was out of character for him – Jake seriously considered my idea, which generated a memory. He recalled how his sister had pestered him to play Monopoly with her, which he agreed to do on the condition that she let him punch her in the stomach ten times. She agreed, he punched her accordingly, but then refused to play. I said I thought this recollection said a lot about how angry he now felt toward me and his other "analytic siblings." Also noteworthy was the fact that he had not played fair insofar as he had failed to keep his end of the bargain.

Since Jake had begun to reluctantly acknowledge these more personal feelings, I took it a step further. Jake complained that he was lonely and that all his friends had disappeared. I thought about how few childhood memories he had reported, his insistence that his childhood had been perfect, and how much this contrasted with his current life situation, and decided to venture out. I said that perhaps he had felt lonely as a child (knowing that he had spent hours in front of the television alone). Jake protested vigorously, "I can't agree with that. I had a best friend all the way throughout school." In response, I said perhaps his deep sense of aloneness had occurred earlier, maybe when he was two or three. "I was *never* lonely," he insisted. "I had an intact family, a stay-at-home mom, four grandparents, and a dog. I was watching a lot of television by then. Everyone agrees, it was a good thing. I surprised my parents by reciting the pledge of allegiance when I was three.

People are always putting down kids watching television, but it was a very good thing for me. When I came home from school, my mom had a snack for me on the counter every day. What more could I want?"

Noting the intensity of his protestation, I commented that it seemed very upsetting to him to consider the possibility that he might have suffered any disappointment during his childhood, and I further suggested that he felt it was disloyal of him (a violation of his pledge of allegiance) to express anything but the most positive feelings about his earliest years – that he seemed to work very hard to maintain his belief that his childhood had been picture perfect.

It was rare for Jake to speak up and participate more actively in treatment by offering his own insights. I addressed his reluctance to participate more actively in session and, in response, Jake volunteered that he thought his lack of participation came from a fear that making progress would lead to the termination of his treatment. He warned me that he had an addictive personality and worried about becoming too dependent on me and the analysis. I too had concerns along these lines – wondering whether he might be relying on the analysis and on me as a substitute for a real-life relationship given his social anxiety, his degree of withdrawal and isolation, and his fear of rejection, which together kept him from venturing out. I addressed his fear that he would lose me if he made any progress, and I related this to his difficulty with outside relationships, which he likewise feared would always result in loss. In response, Jake became more curious, more accepting of transference interpretations, and more willing to acknowledge feeling conflicted about his dependent tendencies, which allowed me to address his use of marijuana as a substitute (oral) dependency that was displaced from the transference.

In one particular session, Jake announced suddenly that he was thinking about taking a couple of weeks off from his analysis. This stunned me seeing as Jake had never taken any vacations or even one day off from analysis. It stunned Jake as well. He complained that I had all the control and that he had none because he had made a commitment to the analysis. Jake then realized that he felt trapped by his own dependency on me. His dawning awareness of the degree of his dependency on the analysis and on me frightened him. He then reported a dream in which he was dancing with a young, underage girl. Her mother gave him a disapproving look, and so he stepped back. After associating to his father's inordinate interest in the young actress, he backed away abruptly from any further discussion of this material, insisting that he did not want to discuss his father anymore. In the next moment, he revealed something he had essentially kept from me for over six years – confessing that he had been struggling with a very serious gambling addiction. It had now been over a year since he'd been in a casino, but during his 14-year-long gambling addiction he had come to owe huge sums of money that necessitated he turn to his parents for loans. He had not wanted to share these details with me out of fear that I would be at risk knowing about such matters – though he didn't elaborate. He said he didn't know whether the treatment had helped him conquer this addiction since he had never addressed it directly in treatment. However, he believed our work together may have somehow helped seeing as it was during this period that he had finally overcome this lengthy habit. Finally, he divulged that all those times when he told me that he was sad because a woman had rejected him had never really happened. At the time, he had been too preoccupied with his gambling worries to have actually pursued women. The only woman who had disappointed him was "lady luck." Those complaints about being rejected by women had been his way of talking about the fact that he had lost at the casino the night before. And then he stated, adamantly and defiantly, that he did not want to talk about this any further.

Jake's abrupt confession felt like a punch in the stomach. All these years and all these sessions during which I had worked hard trying to connect the dots to move the analysis along, and yet I had been operating in the dark. The shock of it produced in me anger and a sense of betrayal when I thought about how hard I had struggled to help him with his painful feelings of rejection when he had led me to believe that women were mysteriously and uniformly rejecting him. I struggled with the question of what to do with these emotions, and how to respond in a helpful way while feeling so blindsided and off-kilter. This was the dilemma I faced the day that Jake decided to pull back the curtain.

Editors' note

This clinical moment differs from most of the others in this volume in one important respect. Most of the clinical moments contained in this book arrive at a point when the analyst feels uncertain about how to proceed. This is not nearly the case in this instance, unless one focuses on the patient's adamant insistence that the topic was closed for discussion and the analyst was expected to say no more. Naturally, such a revelation is shocking to the extent such things aren't supposed to happen in analysis. The patient is directed to say whatever comes to mind – to obey the basic rule – which this patient had clearly violated by keeping an important piece of information secret for the longest time. Thus, if this moment doesn't confront the analyst with the question of how to proceed, it nevertheless leaves the analyst with the task of grappling with a host of different feelings stirred up by this dramatic and shocking revelation, which the patient essentially forbade the analyst from addressing.

Invited commentator responses: Stefano Bolognini and Mitchell Wilson

Stefano Bolognini

I want first to express my appreciation to the presenting colleague for her generous, clear, and thoughtful report, and for her admirable capacity to bear and to analyze difficult passages during this treatment.

One can understand how possible expectations of an ideal continuity of the process and of a methodical approach to the truth have been periodically "discombobulated" (a term she utilizes in her script, which gives perfectly the idea of the ups and downs of the transference/countertransference experience she had to pass through) because of unforeseen disclosures by the patient which changed the whole picture and dismantled his previous statements, completely displacing the analyst.

I think Dr. Harms described very well the real work in progress that led to these "shocking revelations," and, having shared the "punch in the stomach" experience, like her and like Jake's sister in the past, I share her technical reflections afterwards too.

In contrast with other previous commentaries on clinical materials, where I mainly explored the process in itself more than the content of the exchanges between analyst and patient, here I want to deliberately focus more on the specific underlying fantasies, which, in my opinion, seem to characterize this patient and consequently his clinical story. Then I will reflect on the countertransferential position that, in my opinion, the analyst could be engaged in.

My first association, while reading about the initial presentation of Jake's family by the patient as reported by Dr. Harms, was about a movie: *Far from Heaven*, by Robert Zemeckis (2003), where the protagonists were also involved, like in Jake's case, in an apparently "perfect family life" external representation, because of their need to protect and to confirm an ideal model of emotional harmony both within and outside the home and within and outside themselves, until the underlying secrets were dramatically discovered with cataclysmic effects.

This sort of original exterior scenario – depicted on the basis of the glossy family self-representing style – seems to have been heavily internalized by Jake, whose defensive ego works following the implicit and sometimes explicit injunction which had come from his parents: to look the other way, to brush the dust under the carpet, to keep secret, to forget, and finally to deny something experienced as awful and unbearable, in order to preserve a respectable perfect façade; otherwise, Jake would betray his family secret.

We could say, psychoanalytically, that this looks like a classic case in which the shadow of the object falls onto the subject's ego and conditions its further defensive functioning: Jake's defensive ego has to intrapsychically function as Jake's parents directly and interpersonally did with him, by censuring, repressing, and denying.

So, the patient starts an analysis asking consciously for help and officially accepts the fundamental rule; but we will discover he is seriously split. "One" Jake wants to work analytically, the "other one" silently and unconsciously opposes.

The analyst inherits this complex dysfunctional situation, and she starts the analysis exactly (and coherently) asking the patient to comply with and respect the rule: not to hide associations, to be as frank, honest, and sincere as possible, and not to be reticent with her when lying on the couch.

Which is actually impossible, as we know: Were the patient able to do that from the beginning, he/she wouldn't need any analysis. However, as analysts, we all know that paradox, and we are aware of the partial "impossibility" of that expectation when we present our request: Basically, we indicate to our patients at least an orientation, when presenting the task.

Dr. Harms allows us to participate, through a wonderful, countertransferentially honest, and very touching clinical report, in the development of this really interesting treatment.

I will go directly to some crucial points which attracted my attention, starting from some considerations on the deep maternal environment and its implications in little Jake's fantasies.

I had in treatment some patients who had a specific biographical element in common with Jake: an extremely successful, rich, respected, and prestigious maternal grandfather, who openly loved his male grandchild and who projected onto (projection) and into (projective identification) him very high expectations, both as a follower and as a potential successor, also via the mother's unconscious messages.

When this unconscious constellation of fantasies is effectively "installed" inside the child, the narcissistic benefit is initially huge and valorizes his "golden boy" status; however, it implies such high expectations that the child (and then the boy, and then the young adult) feels forced to perform beyond his real limits and capacities, falling down like Icarus for an excess of self-confidence and illusion (as seems to have happened to Jake, with his unfortunate Hollywood experience).

At an Oedipal level, in many of these cases the real father is devalued and bypassed, since a secret underground line connecting the mother's father to the mother's child is unconsciously created. In an implicit and condensed way, it offers the child an apparently advantageous escape from the Oedipal confrontation, conflict, and mourning, thanks to a possible unconscious grandiose identification to the maternal grandfather.

The original collective unconscious incestual myth which reproduces this fantasy is the Immaculate Conception (*Immacolata Concezione*) of Mary by God through the Holy Spirit, while St. Joseph is given the collateral role of Putative Father (*Padre Putativo*), a role which sounds insubstantial for the deep identity formation of the individual.

The mentioned "Lady Luck" (that I would define as "The Big Deceiving Mother"[1]) of the gambler Jake is an Oedipal unconscious representation of the idealized, unconditionally adoring mother, who secretly proposes and confirms the absolute exceptionalism of her "God/Son of God" child: a special, privileged, and omnipotent magical human being who will naturally share the capacities of his admired, reassuring, "immensely powerful" maternal grandfather.

In many cases, this grandiose fantasy is hosted from the beginning in the depth of a secretly incestual mother, who is fixed to her idealized father and inclined to recreate this fantasy in the child, by deluding him about his future glorious destiny full of fame.

To some extent and with some limits, this maternal fantasy can be intrinsically physiological and universal, working as a helpful and necessary primal narcissistic gift which constitutes a basic capital for the baby's early sense of self; however, in some cases, it goes beyond its sane limits, and it colonizes the child's mind in an unconscious and split delusional area shared by the two.

The megalomaniac secret expectation to be such a super-gifted and exclusively beloved individual looks for intrinsic/implicit confirmation via the fast-track of the gambling solution – and *this is the real secret Jake has been protecting for years*, in order not to lose omnipotence and not to come back to (or more realistically, to reach) a disappointingly "normal," human, limited condition.

The price for this solution is dramatically high: We know Jake had to withdraw from real meaningful relations and isolate himself for years. Why?

My hypothesis is that a part of him – a split, hidden, but also dominant part of him – had to actively and carefully avoid achieving something normal and limited in order not to lose the illusion of achieving something exceptional and megalomaniac, and I think, after reading the impressive analytic report on the work done by this colleague, that the main defense at stake in this case was not repression: It was splitting.

Incidentally, I have to add that I found something similar in several children or grandchildren of famous entrepreneurs who, one or two generations previously, had unexpectedly "jumped" from an initially very low socio-economical condition to huge success and wealth. Their fast and glamorous upgrade had generated high idealization by their daughters towards them; correspondingly, years later, secret jealousy, envy, humiliation, and rage were generated in their daughters' husbands, who had to struggle to compete with those extra-powerful fathers-in-law, as well as an additional fear of insufficiency and incapacity in their grandchildren, who had been expected to repeat and to renovate the maternal grandfather's epic, hyper-idealized achievements.

So, the patient has remained unconsciously entrapped for many years in a split early fantasy which only now can be recognized, worked through, and integrated, with some reluctance, together with the analyst.

And finally, who or what could be the analyst now in Jake's mind?

It would almost certainly be an oversimplification to classify her transferential role and countertransferential condition in a univocal, simplistic way.

From my point of view, I would be inclined to underline an evident primal maternal role when she welcomes him regularly for years and gives him "special" care, continuing to pay attention to him and to tolerate his resistances and lies without rejecting him.

But at a deeper Oedipal level, the analyst also acts as a father who works for separating him from the "Lady Luck"/idealized, omnipotent adoring mother: so, a presence and a figure Jake needs, more or less like Telemachus needed Ulysses returning home for limiting his own internal Proci-like symbiotic parasitical part, but also one he wouldn't like to be faced with, in order not to lose omnipotence.

The "punch in the stomach" metaphor reminds me of the patient's sister, of course, but before her, the mother had been the first in the family story to have spoken about that traumatic experience.

As we know, when patients produce strong unexpected emotional impacts in the analyst's countertransference, they need to actively repeat and to share something, before they can receive any clarifying interpretation; because of their transgenerational chain of traumatizing discoveries, the analyst is implicitly requested first for sharing, which is one of the primal maternal tasks, and then for containing and working through, at an Ego level, the mutual experience of the Self.

Frankly, I think that Jake, in spite of his unfortunate story, has at least finally been quite a lucky patient: It occurred to him to bring his severe, secret pathology to treatment (which is not at all an obvious step) and to find such a thoughtful, generous, and authentic analyst, who is able to wait the long time required for analytical discovery, co-experience, understanding, and possible reintegration of deeply split parts, which probably come from a multiple transgenerational heritage.

I felt very touched by this clinical presentation, and I experience a sincere desire to know more about further passages of Jake's and his analyst's analytic story.

Mitchell Wilson

Perhaps it goes without saying – though I feel it is very necessary to say – that serious psychoanalytic work, while never immune from thoughtful critique, always deserves respect. This seriousness comes through in the ways in which the analyst lays it on the line, the ways in which, as Lacan once wrote, the analyst "pays with [her] being." Dr. Harms' dedication to the analytic task is palpable. And there is no doubt that her work with Jake has produced felicitous results for the patient. I believe that the clinical moment I have been asked to comment on is evidence of this progress in Jake's analysis.

There is no way for me to know how I would actually feel, as Jake's analyst, in this particular moment in which he tells his analyst about his gambling "addiction," which, we should immediately add, he has not indulged in for about one year.

While there is no way for me to know how I would actually feel, I can say what I think I would have felt and how I think I would have proceeded in the analysis at that moment. Before I cut to that chase, I need to set up this seemingly concluding moment with an orienting backstory. The backstory goes something like this: As psychoanalysts, we know that *all saying is partial*. There are different psychoanalytic traditions that describe this "partial saying" in different terms. Bion talked about "alphabetizing" "beta"-experience; but there is a lot more "beta" than "alpha," so there will always be a remainder, there will always be something left out of the thinking or telling. Lacan talked about the Real resisting symbolization; it is impossible to descriptively cover the waterfront of the Real. And recently, numerous analysts have been writing about the "sub-symbolic" realm of experience or about patients who struggle to "represent" their internal world. How many times have we sat in our chairs and waited to hear more of the patient's story and been rewarded in so waiting? We hear new information that changes, sometimes completely, what we had just thought to be the case. We would be wrong to believe that the patient had been "hiding" something. What emerges in the here and now is emerging for the first time, less being "uncovered" than newly expressed.

This partial saying is structural. In Lacanian language, there is a *lack* that is constitutive of any symbolic system (the "glitch" in the *Matrix*, and Russell's paradox, are two famous examples). Given this structural fact about descriptive representation, the moment of Jake's big reveal is, to put it plainly, *just further description*. But it is not just any old description; clearly, it is new and important and meaningful description. Because it is important and meaningful I would view its emergence as positive, undeniably advancing the analysis. It may appear that Jake *is* pulling back, but in fact, he has revealed that he *had been* pulling back. He is coming closer now. It is testimony to the good analytic work that led up to this moment.

I believe that it is both epistemologically true and clinically advantageous to view Jake's statements about the gambling as freshly expressed rather than finally revealed. This view should give one pause about the soundness of the question of whether Jake was lying. Be that as it may, I will take up this question, because it points to an inherent conflict in the patient's ethical obligations to himself and to the analyst. Did Jake lie? Any more than any patient who chooses to withhold? I don't know. But I do know that all patients, no matter how faithful they are to the fundamental rule, are never totally faithful to it. Not only is it impossible to be totally faithful to it, as Donnet (2001) made clear in his masterful paper, "From the Fundamental Rule to the Analyzing Situation." The particularity of the patient's relationship to such a rule (which is an important feature of the transference) is what is of analytic interest. The analyst's desire for full disclosure is bound to cause significant difficulty if the question of the transference does not include the subtleties of the patient's orientation to what it means for this particular patient to speak to this particular analyst. In most circumstances (I'll discuss an exception in a moment), the question of lying signifies a problematic analytic stance on the analyst's part: It puts the analyst in a position of suspicion in relation to the patient. This is especially true if the analyst is dedicated to gradually building an explanatory narrative of the patient's troubles.

Another aspect of the question of disclosure and "honesty" is the nature of the patient's relationship to himself. I'll never forget Tom Ogden talking to our first-year candidate class about the fundamental rule:

"Who here," he asked, "believes in the fundamental rule?"

My hand shot up: "I do."

"Why?"

I gave some answer about the "psychoanalytic method" and the like.

"What about the patient's right to privacy? What about the patient's capacity to be alone? To have a space within that is his own?"

While I still think patients should attempt to say what comes to mind, I've never forgotten Tom's point, and it relates directly to this moment with Jake. Jake told his analyst about his gambling when he was ready to tell his analyst about his gambling. I do believe that psychoanalysis places an ethical burden on both parties to take responsibility for one's actions as best one can, and to give an account of those actions, again, as best one can. And yet, though it often feels to us like the patient owes us something besides showing up at agreed-upon times and paying us for our services, they actually owe us nothing else.

There is one exception to what I have just written in the previous paragraphs regarding the pace at which the patient speaks to us about important aspects of his or her life. This is the case of the patient who uses the analysis for *perverse* purposes. What I have in mind are those patients (and they are rare, because they rarely come into analysis) who use the analysis and the analyst so that they can *continue* to act in the world in ways that are "beyond the law." For example, consider the patient who exposes himself to children or adults, and is "waiting" to "understand" his behavior in the analysis before he stops his behavior in the world. In such a case, the analysis is being coopted into the perverse structure; it becomes part and parcel of its machinery. *If* Jake were continuing to gamble his and his family's money away *while talking* about it month after month to his analyst in analysis, I would say it is likely he is using the analysis perversely. But, as far as I can tell, this was not the case with Jake and Dr. Harms.

I have already mentioned that a key feature of this analysis that is important in understanding Dr. Harms' reaction to the news about Jake's gambling is her desire for narrative coherence, a desire for gradually building an explanatory narrative of Jake's difficulties and problems. There is, I believe, a clash of desires in this case: Jake wishes "not to know" and the analyst pushes to know and to build a story. We can see this conflict at various points in the case report: "I felt frustrated by Jake's insistence that there was nothing to be learned about his sensitivity to slights"; "Was I expecting too much of him?" And finally, after hearing about the "14-year-long gambling addiction": "Jake's abrupt confession felt like a punch in the stomach. All these years and all these sessions during which I had worked hard trying to connect the dots to move the analysis along, and yet I had been operating in the dark."

As I've been insisting upon, there is an important sense in which we are always operating in the dark. This is a fact that I try, as an analyst, never to lose sight of (to use a metaphor that captures the paradox of "seeing in the dark"). Here, I am following a basic Lacanian tenet: all of us, including us psychoanalysts, are desiring beings because we are lacking beings. This, again, is a structural fact that I find enormously helpful as a kind of analytic compass or, better, analytic gyroscope (Wilson, 2006). It is a way of keeping one's balance when confronted with sudden changes of direction. In this context, the effort of narrative coherence – an endeavor that all analysts pursue to some extent – is problematic as a central orientation for the analyst. It is problematic because narrative explanations tend to *create their own demands for coherence* as they get built. There is not much difference, arguably, between a psychoanalytic narrative that seemingly explains, if partially, the present state of the patient, and, on the other hand, a more rigidly held paranoid explanation. This is especially true if the storyteller, the constructor of the narrative, is narcissistically invested in the story he or she is putting together. Dr. Harms' case report, like any case report, is filled with clues that we only appreciate in retrospect, *after* the gambling tell: The father was a "cheater"; the "hiding" of feelings; "people who hide things"; "so that he could sneak away"; "using pot left him feeling like a 'criminal'"; the "addictive personality." The coherence is built retrospectively. This effort is not without value, but it should not be confused with a psychoanalysis as it is lived. The difference between a narrative and a psychoanalysis is one of kind; they are different species. If we are too interested in "connecting the dots," then moments of newness, surprise, oddity, confusion, contradiction, and repetition tend to get ignored. "[T]he unconscious is what closes up again as soon as it has opened, in accordance with a *temporal pulsation*," Lacan stressed repeatedly in Seminar 11 (Lacan, 1981, p. 143, my emphasis). These are moments of potential significance. While we all do this story-building to some extent, it is hazardous to make it the central focus of the analysis.

This is why I believe that the position of the psychoanalyst is best described as leaning in a *futural* direction, interested in and alert to what comes next. The "next" is a syncopation, a beat within the rhythm of the patient's discourse, or in the analyst's experience of the field as he or she listens to the patient. It may be, in other words, the "beat" of an image or metaphor that pops into the analyst's mind. Whatever it is, it is synchronic, momentary, and *potentially* significant. We may comment on it or keep it in abeyance as we listen further.

I want now to look more closely at the session in which Jake suddenly announces his "thinking about taking a couple of weeks off from his analysis" and reveals his gambling history. I wish we had more verbatim material from the session; so much is elided. And yet, we all know that in sessions such as these, note-taking tends to cease because we need both hands to hold tight to our chairs as we find ourselves, all of a sudden, on the ride of our lives. In fact, the sequence of events is not easy to bring together. Within the analysis, the uppermost question I would have is: How is it that Jake came to tell the analyst about his history of gambling then and there? It appears to be connected to the dream in which his identification with his father is made clear, about which, Dr. Harms says, "He did not want to discuss... anymore." It seems that the moment of identification with his father as a "cheater" who keeps secrets, and a philanderer, is simultaneously one of *dis*-identification with him, and one of subjective appropriation for Jake himself: "I am a gambler." In ways that we can speculate about but never really know for sure, Jake had reached a moment of truth. He decided to come clean, but on his own terms, as Dr. Harms tells us (again): "He did not want to talk about this any further." The feel of the session is clipped, staccato-like, as Jake leapfrogs from one meaningful topic to the next, and then the next.

Among things missing from the vignette is anything about how Jake was speaking to his analyst in these crucial moments. A speech-act is, after all, an action. A speech-act has pace, force, tone, and is embodied. We have no sense of these important aspects of the interchange. Was Jake comfortable or tense in the session? The word *confession* is used several times. Is this Jake's word, or Dr. Harms'? Again, it's not clear. There is a big difference between the former and the latter possibility.

As analysts, we have no choice but to meet the patient where they are at the moment, as best we can. If Jake is done talking about something, then I assume he is done, for the moment. I would let him know that I was glad he told me about his gambling. I would underscore the moment as important for him and for our work together. I would have confidence (which I would keep to myself) that what got discussed in this session would be revisited. We'd get back to it, down the road. And in the getting back to it, I would hope to find out Jake's view of why he told me about the gambling when he did. What had changed in him or in his view of me that led him to tell me when he told me? Perhaps this would lead to a clearer view of how he saw me as his interlocutor within the transference? What kind of object had I been to him? Was he pushing back on my efforts to make sense, to connect the dots? What did he mean by worrying about me "being at risk"? There is more than a suggestion of another world that Jake is beginning to speak about: money, risk, debt, cheating, and perhaps darker things yet, such as bodily harm. Whatever questions and key signifiers are on my mind, it is much more important for me to listen to Jake with curiosity and interest as things move forward, and not impose too quickly my own ideas of what went on.

With all of this having been said about lack, and partial saying, and the analyst's futural position, it is quite possible that I too would have felt gut-punched by Jake's revelation. And even if I didn't in this particular instance, I have no doubt that at some point or points in the analysis, my desire and expectations and ways of working would come into direct conflict with my patient's interests, in a manner that caused me great internal distress and self-questioning. I am not aware of an ongoing intensive psychoanalysis that does not have these searing moments and periods of questioning, in which the analyst feels his or her very being is at stake. These are precious times in psychoanalytic work in which the most therapeutic benefit can be achieved, *if* the analyst comes to terms more directly with his or her desire as it has contributed to the impasse or struggle – to *think* about it, in the Bionian sense – and in so doing move into a more receptive, open, and interested place, so the patient is freer to speak to us, as the analysis moves into the future.

My intervention

I spent part of the abovementioned session debating whether to address Jake's confession or the dream material. In retrospect, I find it unfortunate that I was so flooded with emotion triggered by this shocking revelation that I felt stunned and unable to address Jake's confession in the moment. My first reaction was to feel shocked, betrayed, outraged, and then ultimately to feel relieved that at least some things that had perplexed me about Jake now seemed to make sense. I considered this a sign of progress, regardless of how it had come about; Jake had made good use of our work. As I thought about my feelings of shock and betrayal, I recalled his childhood experience with his father in which he too felt shocked and betrayed. I told Jake that I thought he had recreated his experience of his father's affair in the treatment with me by lying to me, much in the same way his father had lied to him and his mother. I said I thought he had felt deeply hurt and betrayed and had resolved the matter by acting like his father, maintaining a secret life he could not reveal – a secret life that kept him at a distance from others and kept others from knowing the whole truth about his life. He surprisingly agreed and further volunteered that he was relieved that he had finally been able to tell me about this part of his life, which he also felt represented progress. We eventually discussed how he had recreated the traumatic experience of his childhood with me by surprising me with his secret the way he had been surprised by his father's secret, and then trying to impose a code of silence. I had felt at times during the analysis as if I was forbidden to speak, and I now shared that feeling with Jake – telling him that it seemed that he was trying to "tie my hands" with regard to our work. Eventually, Jake acknowledged that, in retrospect, he believed that the secret he had known and been required to carry was the reason he struggled so in life and the reason his sister, who had no exposure to the secret, had been more successful in life (a marriage, successful career, two children, and a close and cozy relationship with his parents).

As I look retrospectively at this clinical moment, it seems that I had become so caught up in trying to make sense of the lie and struggling with so many competing emotions that I had neglected to attend to the dream – the material that preceded this confession. It seems to me now that this confession had also been his way of stepping back from the sexual material that was surfacing in the dream and his fear of my disapproval. Perhaps we had both wanted to distance ourselves from that material. Going forward, it now seemed as if the analysis had also been divided into a "before and after" the confession of this secret. Fortunately, Jake continued in treatment for several years after this clinical moment and was kind enough to provide me with many other opportunities for us to look at these issues together.

Note

1 I.e., when a mother wants to create for the child the illusion that his father is Oedipally losing and he (the son) is winning as her real husband.

References

Dickes, R. (1968). Some observations on lying: A derivative. *Journal of Hillside Hospital*, 17, 94–109.
Donnet, J.-L. (2001). From the fundamental rule to the analyzing situation. In D. Birksted-Breen, S. Flanders, & A. Gibeault (Eds.), *Reading French psychoanalysis* (pp. 155–172). London: Routledge.
Ekstein, R., & Caruth, E. (1972). Keeping secrets. In P. Giovacchini (Ed.), *Tactics and techniques in psychoanalytic therapy* (pp. 200–215). New York: Jason Aronson.
Fraiberg, S. (1954). Tales of the discovery of the secret treasure. *Psychoanalytic Study of the Child*, 9(1), 218–241.
Freud, S. (1913). On beginning the treatment (Further recommendations on the technique of psycho-analysis I). In J. Strachey (Ed. & Trans.), *The standard edition of the complete psychological works of Sigmund Freud* (Vol. 12, pp. 121–144). London: Hogarth Press.
Greenson, R. (1967). *The technique and practice of psychoanalysis* (Vol. 1). New York: International Universities Press.
Gross, A. (1951). The secret. *Bulletin of the Menninger Clinic*, 15, 37–44.
Hoyt, M. (1978). Secrets in psychotherapy: Theoretical and practical considerations. *International Review of Psychoanalysis*, 5(2), 231–241.
Lacan, J. (1981). *The four fundamental concepts of psycho-analysis*. New York: Norton.
Margolis, G. (1974). The psychology of keeping secrets. *International Review of Psychoanalysis*, 1(3), 291–296.
Meares, R. (1976). The secret. *Psychiatry*, 39(3), 258–265.
Reich, A. (1951). On counter-transference. *International Journal of Psychoanalysis*, 32, 25–31.
Roughton, R. E. (1993). Useful aspects of acting out: Repetition, enactment, and actualization. *Journal of the American Psychoanalytic Association*, 41(2), 443–472.
Tausk, V. (1933). On the origin of the "influencing machine" in schizophrenia. *Psychoanalytic Quarterly*, 2, 519–556.
Wilson, M. (2006). "Nothing could be further from the truth": The role of lack in the analytic process. *Journal of the American Psychoanalytic Association*, 54(2), 397–421.

Chapter 11

Considering Third Parties
The Question of Allegiance

Michele Gomes

Editors' introduction

Patients occasionally place the therapist in an awful bind, as was the case in this particular moment. Ben, a single man in his late 50s, had been in twice-weekly psychoanalytically oriented psychotherapy for eight years when the following instance occurred. When the therapist opened the waiting room door, Ben was not alone. He was carrying a newborn kitten he'd found in a nearby park. The tiny kitten, supported by just two fingers, meowed loudly. Without warning, Ben nonchalantly dropped the kitten, trusting that the therapist would scramble to catch her. Once they sat down, Ben pleaded with the therapist to take the kitten or, more precisely, to protect the kitten from him. The therapist was aware of the potential harm that could befall the kitten given Ben's history of severe trauma, his tendency to identify with the aggressor, and – most importantly – his penchant for abusing animals early in life. These stories of torture, which the therapist had had to stomach on several past occasions, seemed particularly difficult to bear in the kitten's presence. As he retold these tales, Ben would pause to delight in the kitten's antics, occasionally responding to her meows as though he understood her. He demonstrated concern for her safety when she began to lick and then chew the leaf of one of the therapist's plants, and he patiently redirected the kitten's attention with the use of an enticing toy he cleverly fashioned by braiding tissues together. A decision loomed that would need to be resolved by the end of the session: Would the therapist keep the kitten to ensure its safety or entrust the kitten to Ben's care?

The moment in context (Richard Tuch)

It may seem rather peculiar to be writing about the analyst's concern for a third party – for someone who has been introduced by the patient into the analytic situation for whatever reason. The most obvious situation is one in which the patient is treating a child in a cruel or inhumane fashion, which will likely mobilize the analyst to feel an urge to speak up on the defenseless other's behalf. Sitting by and silently witnessing another being's abuse is something many analysts cannot abide. In such a triangular situation, "siding" with the individual who is not one's patient is bound to test the analyst's relationship with her analysand.

Exclusivity – manifesting in the analyst's undivided attention and unassailable allegiance – helps fuel the treatment by gratifying some of the analysand's most essential, narcissistic needs to be the center of the analyst's attention and devotion. The analyst's interventions make abundantly clear to the patient the degree to which the patient's inner world is being attended to on a moment-to-moment basis; even unconscious content fails to escape the analyst's notice. The analytic experience is unique to the extent the patient feels himself to be tended to in ways and to a degree that happens in no other arena of the patient's present life.

The Oedipal configuration (desire for an exclusive, dyadic relationship with one parent; fear of being attacked by the excluded parent) leaves the child in conflict to the extent he grapples with the growing realization that his relationship with his two parents is inherently, and undeniably, triadic. Eventually, the child must come to terms with the indisputable fact that the parental bond relegates him to the position of the excluded third – which Britton (1989) identifies as the origin of an individual's capacity for reflective thought – the ability to stand apart from a situation, to see things from the vantage point of the uninvolved party. When it comes to intimate love relations, Kernberg (2011) identifies unconscious fantasies about an "excluded third":

> An idealized member of the subject's sex – the dreaded rival replicating the oedipal rival... somebody who would be more satisfactory to their sexual partner, and this dreaded third party is the origin of emotional insecurity in sexual intimacy.
>
> (p. 235)

While the analytic situation is not wholly analogous to an intimate love relationship, it mimics, borrows, or echoes certain aspects from exclusive love relationships and, by so doing, nurtures a unique type of professional relationship unlike any other. Larry Friedman (1997) spelled this out when he described how Freud recognized he was:

> Doing something forbidden to physicians; he was deliberately courting a personal, affective intimacy... [and] was honest enough to recognize that the intimacy he wanted from his patient might be the sort of personal surrender that counts on a love relationship.
>
> (p. 25)

Friedman argues that Freud undoubtedly knew that his method, which involved the analyst's "constant, exclusive, selfless attentiveness" (p. 26), created an impression ("illusion"?) of the analyst's "deep and lasting attachment to the patient" (p. 26), which Friedman argued would prove so personally appealing that it would be hard for the patient to resist. Friedman dares to call this "seductive," though he rushes to assure his readers that "this seduction is unique, careful, modulated, responsible, therapeutically intended, unselfish, and nonabusive" (p. 25).

Such conditions not only mimic aspects of intimate love relations, they also stimulate the twin illusions of the analyst's *selfless attentiveness* (i.e., that the patient's needs always come before the analyst's needs) and her *singular dedication and devotion* (i.e., the belief that the analyst has promised that the patient's needs come before those of all others) – reminiscent of primary maternal preoccupation (Winnicott, 1956), the selfless and devoted stance that parents ideally sustain for several weeks (if not for months) during the infant's earliest days. Regression contributes to the fantasy that pictures the analyst's existence as amounting to her sitting in the office, there for the patient and the patient alone, without an outside life of her own.

Patients who succumb to these twin illusions[1] are in for a rude awakening; they soon learn that the analyst isn't nearly as selfless as they'd imagined, nor is she as singularly focused on them alone. Against the fantasy of the analyst's selfless attentiveness are instances when the analyst either appears to place her own needs ahead of the patient or appears to favor other patients – whether evidence supports the belief or it's purely transference-based conjecture on the patient's part. The patient may imagine that the analyst is saving better appointment times for her favored patients – patients she prefers, patients she will go out of her way for, patients she is more generous with, and so on and so forth. Such patients are seen as preferred because they make the analyst feel good, make her laugh, are fascinating creatures, are – all in all – better patients, more appealing patients. Naturally, there is no denying the fact that analysts respond differently to each one of their patients, and patients who surmise this to be so may be greatly pained by what they see as the analyst's betrayal in a triangular situation that imagines other patients as preferred, relegating them to the position of the envious outsider – the excluded third, whose nose is pressed up against the window as he watches others eating heartily by the hearth.

In the context of psychoanalysis, there are instances when another person, who was expected to remain in the position of the excluded third (relative to the analytic couple), suddenly appears to have gained the analyst's concern and attention – leaving the patient crestfallen. Concern for others may be stimulated by the strength of the patient's suicidal or homicidal impulses, leaving the analyst conflicted about the limits of confidentiality, as will be discussed in greater length in clinical moment 12.

There are other, more subtle instances when the analyst's consideration of someone other than the patient is deemed by the patient to be a betrayal of the analyst's singular allegiance. Take the example of a male patient I was treating who had a strong and aversive reaction to someone we both knew in the professional community. Hours were spent processing and analyzing how strongly the patient felt about this individual, leading up to a point when this particular individual made it known that he was entertaining the idea of seeing me for supervision. Word of this made it back to the patient who could not believe I would even entertain the possibility of supervising this man, and he went so far as to forbid me to do so – arguing that I needed to remain allegiant to him and him alone – that supervising this other therapist meant, essentially, that I was choosing him over my patient. No amount of analyzing succeeded at helping the patient understand the absoluteness of the position he was taking. In his mind, it was a simple matter – I was not to consider the needs of this other who, forever more, needed to remain in the position of the excluded third – to say nothing of my own wishes to supervise.

In the clinical moment that follows, the consideration of the well-being of another occupies the analyst's mind. As we shall see, the situation was unique, and her concern for this other being was powerful. She grapples with the matter and isn't sure which way to turn.

The matter of third parties and the question of exclusive allegiance is but one of two issues that arise in the clinical moment that follows. The other matter – one that is not a specific feature of the clinical moment as it is presented – has to do with the reporting of cruelty on the patient's part. Psychoanalysis is all about sharing one's innermost thoughts – one's wishes, impulses, desires, beliefs, and so on – which can often reveal a raw aggression that exists below the surface in the form of fantasies contained in every one of us. While analysts are comfortably acquainted with, and duly equipped to hear reports of such fantasies, the same cannot be said for reports of outright, enacted cruelty, which analysts are likely to find off-putting, if not personally offensive. It is one thing to think about aggressing on others; it is another matter to have actually engaged in such behavior. Learning how to endure reports of outright cruelty is a challenge for every analyst; thankfully, such instances are rare – though when they occur, they may cause the analyst to feel an urge to be rid of the patient – to not have to associate with someone who would do such things. Empathy often fails us when we hear about such matters, since empathy is typically predicated on the assumption "there but for the grace of God go I" – and imagining oneself capable of such acts is beyond many analysts' imaginations. I believe the reader will struggle, as did I, having to hear the outrageous report of a patient who pays insufficient respect for the existence of another.

Beyond the odious nature of such reports, a patient's disclosure about acts of cruelty can leave the analyst wondering: If the patient is capable of such cruelty, how might I fare when things heat up and the patient is in touch with such powerful impulses *toward me* – impulses he had previously lacked the capacity to contain? If the patient doesn't end up physically attacking the analyst, might he act out his sadistic pleasure by treating the analyst in ways that leave her squirming? And, might the situation be experienced differently by female analysts seeing male patients? In the clinical moment that follows, we cannot rule out the distinct possibility that the patient was expressing cruelty in the fashion in which he conveyed his story to the analyst – knowing enough about her personal life to know just how painful his story would be for her to hear.

Guntrip (1967) didn't mince words when he noted: "There is a healthy hate which a mature person will feel as a response to, say, intentional evil such as deliberate cruelty" (p. 41). In a paper describing his supervision of a therapist whose patient had acted cruelly toward a pet, Chrzanowski (1980) writes:

> The cruel incidents reported by the patient, indicative of his impulses and actions, should be upsetting to any listener. There need not be an excessive fear of being judgmental when reacting honestly to acts of cruelty and inhumanity. I do not consider it respectful to a patient to look politely the other way when a humanly reprehensible form of behavior or attitude is expressed.
>
> (p. 361)

Misguided idealism leads an analyst to believe that her capacity to hear, tolerate, and contain the rawer edge of human experience should be limitless – which sets the analyst up to feel ashamed and insufficient when she finds herself incapable of living up to such an impossible ideal. In the following clinical moment, the analyst is able to avoid falling into such a pit, as we are about to hear.

The clinical moment

Ben, a single man in his late 50s, has been in twice-weekly psychoanalytically oriented psychotherapy for eight years. I was beginning my postdoctoral training at a clinic where he was a patient. The Postdoctoral Fellow whom he had been seeing was graduating and opening her own private practice. She approached me saying that she had hand-picked me to take over his treatment because – in her words – we were a "perfect match." I felt flattered, which kept me from wondering why she had decided to not continue seeing him in her private practice or why she had selected me in particular to assume his treatment. It would take some time before I would come to realize how challenging a patient Ben would prove to be.

Our transition was quite bumpy. Ben was more sensitive than most other clinic patients to the experience of being left behind – a situation that pained and angered him, and reignited early experiences of having been abandoned as a child. He spent the first few months of treatment angrily "retelling" the story of his life, upset with me for not already knowing all he'd shared with his former therapist and complaining about having to pay for me to "catch up." It seemed natural to interpret his wish for competent and reliable caregivers, and the expression of my empathic understanding of these wishes often moved him to tears.

As the treatment progressed, Ben began to bond to me, which stirred up many conflicted and complicated feelings. He knew that it was just a matter of time before our relationship would be tested. The therapy progressed; we met two to three times weekly for nearly two years. Then, as the time approached for me to leave the clinic, I consulted with my supervisor about whether it was wise to take him with me into private practice – weighing the likely possibility that not doing so would be experienced by him as yet another instance of abandonment that would leave him feeling like a discarded child.

Ultimately, I elected to take Ben with me, and a bit naively expected that he would feel pleased and even a bit grateful. Instead, he found multiple ways to poke holes in our connection and to question my intentions. After I had made the offer to see him privately, Ben kept me hanging, refusing to say whether he would accept my offer. This dance proved maddening and deflating, though he did finally agree to continue seeing me, waiting until the last possible moment to give me his answer.

Moving to my private office not only afforded Ben a greater glimpse into my personality, it also stirred up envy over my development. Ben was particularly angry and hostile during the months following this transition. It was during this period that he began to disclose more details about the extent of his early trauma – the history of physical, sexual, verbal, and emotional abuse that began with his biological parents and extended through his time in the foster care system from ages 6–18. I had known much of this, having read his chart, but living through the first-hand experience of its retelling made it far more alive and painful for me to hear. He has told me horrendous stories and equally horrifying fantasies, and I have vacillated between periods of deep empathy and fondness and utter repulsion.

Time passed, and Ben loyally attended sessions week after week. He never cancelled and always expected to be able to reschedule if, for whatever reason, I needed to miss a scheduled appointment. Despite his consistency, I went through a period of wishing that any phone call I received was Ben cancelling his session. By this point, Ben had been in treatment with me for four years. Ben met a woman and quickly began a romantic and sexual relationship with her. This was the first time in his life – in his 50s – that he had had a girlfriend. Previously, Ben's sexual experiences had been limited to a handful of clumsy one-time encounters with prostitutes. He would often say, "I have no idea how to fuck a woman!" He spoke about women in a deeply misogynistic and disdainful manner. He shared fantasies of sadistically violating women and would pepper me with questions such as, "Do you *really* believe there's a single man out there who wouldn't rape a woman if he knew he'd never get caught?" He could fixate on just such a question for an entire session, mocking my attempts to make links or find meaning in the process unfolding between us.

Ben's relationship with his girlfriend became a central focus of the treatment. Their relationship had an adolescent quality, bringing forward both of their trauma histories and attachment difficulties. They lacked boundaries and fought constantly. After three months, Ben's girlfriend moved in with him, and their fighting escalated to the point of becoming violent. These fights were all-consuming for Ben. He spoke at length about the ways his girlfriend treated him poorly. He showed little guilt or remorse as he spoke about how they would hit one another – leaving cuts, bruises, and open wounds. Instead, he railed at the injustice of being accused of being a "batterer" when his girlfriend was equally violent toward him. They embodied one another's early abusers with abandon. This went on for nearly two years.

In the transference, I often became the woman who victimized Ben as well. My questions felt like attacks; silence felt like disgusted abandonment. Treatment proved challenging for me, so I sought consultation from a senior analyst. I found myself attempting to convince the consultant that Ben needed a more seasoned clinician or perhaps someone with an expertise in trauma or domestic violence. Somewhat to my disappointment, this consultant steadfastly encouraged me to continue on with Ben, saying, "You two are deep in it." The consultant provided a lot of reassurance, which helped to normalize the intensity of my feelings. I found this comforting but continued to have fantasies of fleeing the treatment. I felt guilty about my countertransference wish to terminate Ben but held on by reminding myself of the changes I had observed in him over time.

When their relationship ended, the heat once again fully concentrated on me. Ben was open about his desire to "possess" me, though he denied having any romantic, erotic, or violent feelings toward me. He expressed endless frustration at my refusal to disclose whether I was married as he openly shared his fantasies about the type of man he imagined I would marry. It was notable that this imagined man was nothing like Ben – he was tall, socially capable, and potent – and he knew how to "fuck" a woman.

We spent the next few years talking about Ben's mother, who shared the same name as his girlfriend, and about his relationship to me. Over time, Ben was developing an increasing ability to wonder, reflect, and put his feelings into words. Our sessions never became "easy," but we found a mutual capacity to do the work. This cut the sharp edges off Ben's personality, which allowed us to get closer.

This brings us to our clinical moment. Before the session began, I heard unrecognizable noises coming from the waiting room as I approached. My stomach tightened. This was Ben, after all – so I never quite knew what to expect. I opened the door to find Ben standing far too close to the door. I was suddenly transported to a time earlier in the treatment when Ben would do this regularly. He positioned himself in a way that made it impossible to open the door fully without it hitting him. He would then tell me that he experienced this as yet another violation of his body and his personal space, something he was all too accustomed to experiencing.

I felt a bit flustered by the return of this confusing behavior that cast me in a particular and uncomfortable role, but quickly was brought back to reality by a loud, clear "meow." Ben smirked a sarcastic smile, then presented a tiny kitten, supported by just two fingers. As he walked past me to enter the consulting room, he nonchalantly dropped the kitten, trusting that I would scramble to catch her. It was clumsy, but I did catch her. Instinctively, I held her close and immediately felt her body stop shaking as I pressed her to my chest.

Ben waited on my couch as I fumbled with the kitten. When I joined him in the consulting room, he appeared visibly distressed. I held the kitten out to return her to him, but he waved me off and asked me to continue to hold her. His face was red, his breathing labored, and his legs were shaking restlessly. I asked him the obvious question, "Who is this?" Tears came to his eyes. Ignoring my question, he launched into a string of horrifying memories – flashbacks perhaps – of his having abused and killed animals in his youth.

One story stands out as particularly horrifying. Ben got a hamster when he was six years old and still living with his mother. He was thrilled to have a pet – something "to give him love." Ben explained that the hamster quickly became unhappy and aggressive. Ben's mother kept the hamster food locked away and would regulate how much food he was allowed to give her. On occasion, the hamster would go without food for a span of two to three days. She began to gnaw incessantly on the bars of her cage, particularly at night, keeping Ben awake, which led to his using a broken television antenna to poke her through the bars to quiet her. He described how he poked her harder and harder over time, sometimes pinning her to the corner of her cage with the sharp broken end of the antenna. After a few months of such treatment, Ben had a violent animal on his hands. In a fit of anger, he took the hamster outside and attempted to smash it with a shovel. He could not recall if he was unable to hit the hamster or if he "chickened out," but he decided instead to catapult the hamster over the back fence onto a slope densely covered in ivy. He then dug a fake grave and told his mother that he had found the hamster dead – from *her* malnourishment – and that he had buried her.

I believe it is worth pausing to comment a bit more on how I felt hearing such a story. I was flooded with disgust and disdain – an intensification of the sorts of feelings I had been accustomed to feeling with Ben. The abuse that befell these vulnerable beings brought hot tears to my eyes. I managed to fight them back, afraid that Ben would pounce and attack my vulnerability. I felt angry at my supervisor and the consultant who had both encouraged me to continue working with Ben and felt momentarily convinced that he was beyond help. My mind drifted out of the room to a memory from my days in middle school when we'd read *Lord of the Flies* and were asked to debate the question, "Is there such a thing as inherent evil?" As a young girl, I had passionately argued that evil was nothing more than a social construct.

Ben dramatically paused to tell me that I would never believe the next part of the story. He returned home to find the hamster back in her cage in his room, with a heaping pile of food. His mother beat Ben and said that she'd found the hamster walking along the gutter in the direction of their house.

Ben went to bed that night in pain from the beating. He decided to poke the hamster to be sure it was his. At this point in the story my heart began to race. The kitten who had been soothed and was sleeping peacefully on my chest started to squirm and struggle out of my hands. I put her down on the ground. Ben shouted at me to pick her back up, but I assured him that it was safe for her to explore, adding that she clearly did not want to be held.

Ben broke from his story to observe her. He was becoming calm for the first time in the hour, watching her sniff and run in the sort of adorably uncoordinated way that kittens do. We giggled and smiled together. He told me that he'd found her outside my office under a dumpster near the tiny park that belongs to the doggy daycare situated next door. He saw her eyes glowing in the headlights of cars and he struggled to reach her. He assured me that he looked around for "a mommy" but that there was "no mommy to be found." He inquired at the doggy daycare and they knew nothing of the kitten's presence or how she had gotten there. He said, "My thought was that I needed to either kill it or rescue it."

My heart continued to pound quickly as Ben fussed after the tiny kitten who was now attempting to chew the leaves of my plant. Ben asked me if the plant was poisonous. I didn't think so but told him I couldn't be sure. He asked permission to move the plant higher, out of the kitten's reach. I was delighted and relieved by this gesture and said he was welcome to move it. The kitten followed him. She could jump a lot higher than he'd estimated. I could see Ben becoming frustrated as he tried to reposition the plant, but I wanted to let the incident unfold. The kitten was singularly focused on reaching and chewing the plant. Ben exclaimed, "We need to give her an alternative!" and began to fashion a braided toy out of Kleenex. He jokingly asked if I had any tuna to make the toy more appealing. Between braiding the toy, Ben would gently pull the relentless kitten away from the plant. Once the treasure was fashioned, he began to call to her in an enticing manner. She immediately leapt for the toy. He said, "Quick, put the plant in the closet!" I dramatized my steps as I rushed across the room to hide the plant. We were playing! The three of us! Or... so it seemed to me.

Addressing me, Ben announced: "You love her. You already love her *more than you love me*. You've never gone on a top-secret, plant-hiding mission on *my* behalf!" He threw the toy he'd fashioned to the corner of the room, breaking their beautiful connection as well as ours. The hamster story continued, and as it did my stomach dropped. I had hoped I wasn't going to hear the end of this story, at least not tonight. "I buried her alive. I put her in a small shoe box, pummeled it with the shovel a few times just to get her to stop being a wild beast, and then I buried it in the fake grave." He locked his eyes with mine as he said this to take measure of my reaction. He looked angry and quite different from the man I'd seen just moments before. He needed me to hear and to know about this experience – this part of him. I could feel the importance. "You killed her," I repeated. He began to sob.

Ben continued to cry as he paced about the room. He gestured toward the kitten and then pointed to the top of my bookshelf. I suddenly remembered the night, many years prior, when Ben first learned about my love of cats. It had been a particularly frustrating session. Ben was angry and felt abandoned and left alone in the room. He begged me to "tell him something real, to be human, to have a self, dammit!" Caught off-guard, my response was not thought out – it wasn't the type of timed, therapeutically indicated self-disclosure about which I had read. Unthinkingly, I responded to address the challenge, to satisfy his curiosity but – most of all – to defensively prove I wasn't the monster he was accusing me of being. An enactment – no doubt. I said, "I love cats! I have a cat and I love her!" He laughed at me and retorted, "Whoop dee do, I love corn dogs. Fuck you!" and stormed out of the session. What a disaster. I strained to remember whether I'd had the courage to share that embarrassing moment in a process note with my supervisor. Probably not.

Back to the moment at hand. Ben was still tearful and pacing. He told me calmly that he needed me to take this kitten from him. He asked repeatedly, "Will you take her from me? You'll know what to do and you already love her more than you love me. Just take her. Maybe I could raise her? No, I'll kill her or I'll hurt her. Will you take her from me? Tonight?"

Ben looked intensely at me for a response. What was I to do? I was all too aware of the potential harm that could befall this kitten if left in Ben's hands. Ben's trauma history was severe, and it had been his tendency, since adolescence, to identify with the aggressor. A decision was looming and needed to be reached by the end of the hour. Who needed protection tonight? Could I trust the "protective Ben" to prevail – the Ben who'd saved the kitten in the first place and who had cleverly fashioned a distracting toy to protect her from eating a potentially poisonous plant? Or would sending the kitten home with him seal her fate to be abused? Was it my job to protect the kitten from Ben? Or Ben from himself? Or Ben from an internalized version of himself that no longer made all of the decisions? I truly am a cat lover. I cannot bear the idea of a kitten being abused. I look daily at my cat and feel fulfilled knowing that she has received 14 years of love. I wanted the same for this kitten. What would my fellow cat-loving therapist friends think if they knew? Surely they would side with my taking this kitten from Ben. Would anyone disagree? Why did I disagree? Is it foolhardy to want to believe in him?

Invited commentator responses: Edgar Levenson and Nancy McWilliams

Edgar Levenson

I am grateful to Drs. Tuch and Kuttnauer for their invitation to comment on this extremely interesting clinical vignette. I admire the professionalism and devotion of the therapist, confronted with this spectacular crisis. She is faced with a terrible dilemma: Take away the kitten and perhaps reject the patient's claim for trust in his essential goodness; or give him the kitten, seduced by the dreadful sentimentality common to abusers, and precipitate a therapeutic disaster with the kitten assaulted or killed, the malevolence of the patient confirmed, and the therapy essentially over.

I believe the dilemma to be the consequence of a categorical error; that is, both the therapist and patient see what is occurring as content *within* the therapy. I see it as a boundary violation, a break in the frame, the dreaded "acting-out." Acting-out traditionally has carried with it a psychoanalytic obiter dictum. One doesn't analyze acting-out – one stops it! To attempt to analyze acting-out behavior puts the therapist, as in this case, in an impossible situation: having to make a real-life choice in a situation that is beyond her immediate comprehension. Once the behavior is contained, only then may it be possible to examine it.

The categorical error is itself a consequence of viewing therapy as an extension of real life; one hopes it is better, more caring, less mystified than the patient's real life, but it is *not* real life. In actuality psychoanalysis is a game, play, circumscribed and defined by rules – the containment of the frame – and would be otherwise impossible to sustain. One would be asking the therapist to be the one thing therapists aren't – wonderfully superior people able to undo the vicissitudes of their patients' lives. Like any professional relationship, captain or dentist – we do our work defined and protected by our roles. I saw this first made explicit in Bateson (1972) and later elaborated it myself (Levenson, 1983).

Recognizing that the therapist's effectiveness depends on the protection of the rules of the game would save therapists much anguish whilst attempting to meet the needs of patients. Particularly in "empathically" oriented therapies, there is often confusion between the affective categories of sympathy, compassion, pity, and empathy: The first signify concern for the suffering of the patient; empathy, on the other hand, implies that the therapist can identify with the patient's distress. That is often not the case, certainly not in this vignette – unless the therapist has struggled with the same animal abuse problems as her patient. Valorizing empathy can end in boundary diffusion as the therapist tries to experience the patient's experience. At the extremes, every good clinical idea becomes a countertransference.

I believe that the patient should have been informed that he was putting the therapist in an impossible situation, that what he was doing was essentially breaking the rules that make the therapy possible. I would prefer to tell him that he must take the kitten to a rescue station. He cannot keep it; that would make the therapist responsible and him possibly irresponsible for any subsequent disaster. If he wants to keep a pet, they should discuss it at length and arrive at some safe plan.

Let us say that in the best of all possible outcomes the patient has taken the kitten to a rescue station and is now ready to settle down and look at what was played out between them. Here, we have another problem: If the therapist and patient sit together trying to figure out why the acting-out took place, they will most likely be stymied, particularly since the precipitating event – a mewing lost kitten – was fortuitous.

It is also quite possible that the acting-out might not have happened in the first place if the detailed inquiry into the historical event had been more extensive. So, rather than rehashing their encounter looking for dynamics, it would have been more fruitful to re-examine the original event with the mother and the storied hamster. What really happened? Why did he end in special services? Where is the father? Siblings? Is she a single mother? What are her financial and work conditions?

Is this the usual story? Child wants pet, usually dog but maybe cat. Parent can't deal with the additional problems. Says, let's get a hamster and see whether you can take care of it and then we'll see. Child asks for love, gets responsibility. Is supposed to clean cage and feed the pet. Usually fails to do so, parent and child fight. Child comes to hate the hamster, which by the way (like a rabbit) can be or become ill-tempered and bite. The stage is set for murderous behavior.

The part of the story about the mother finding the battered hamster walking "in the direction of" home alongside the road sounds very suspect to me. A frightened hamster would head for the first cover and stay there; certainly, it wouldn't know the way home, and the coincidence of the mother finding it hobbling home seems terribly unlikely. Then she doesn't say anything, and the child finds the resurrected hamster, as in a Stephen King story, back in its cage "with a heaping pile of food"! Why would she quietly put back a hamster he tried to kill? Why not protect him (and the poor hamster) from his destructiveness? Do we begin to hear resonances with the acted-out incident?

The patient, at this point, interrupts the story to enact elaborate concerned gestures towards the kitten and then tells the therapist that he buried the hamster alive. I'm not sure I believe that part of the story. What happened after he buried the hamster? What did he tell his mother? What did she ask? What happened then?

More likely, this is a prime example of a narrative distortion, particularly since the therapist – breaking frame – had previously blurted out her love of cats as a defense of her challenged humanity. Is he then not challenging her definition of humanity? These distortions in the narrative can open portals for the therapy, to deeper dynamic meaning: for example, the child's rage at the mother's lack of nurturing, his compassion for her depression, his sibling rivalry (with the pet), his identification with the hamster – ministered to but not really loved or nurtured.

Obviously, once the narrative is "unpacked," the extended story permits of a variety of interpretive sets. Of dynamic formulations, there is no end. There is never a clear priority amongst often mutually exclusive perspectives on events. The mutative impact may come more from the expansion of the narrative and the patient's subsequent tolerance of multiple viewpoints and ambiguity than from the achievement of some superordinate view that makes it all clear at last, or even some superordinate experience with the therapist that makes healing possible. Patients refuse new experience and insight; that is what resistance is about. Mutative change depends more on the patient's grasp of what is happening around and to him than any explanatory set.

One hopes that the patient can now engage his rage at the hapless hamster, not as the manifestation of his Evil Self, but as a multilayered effort to deal with his and his mother's anguish. Will this free him? Perhaps not at once, but this initial opening would usually be followed by small incremental enactments in the analytic process that allow for a growing sense of the analyst's reliability and his own capacity for humanity. These incremental episodes of mutual caring and loathing and fear will make for change.

But isn't this acting-out as I defined it? What is the difference between acting-out and therapeutic enactment? Acting-out, some wag said, is whatever makes the therapist nervous. It means the limit of the containment has been breached. Enactment, on the other hand, is part of the psychoanalytic cycle first described by Menninger in 1938 (Menninger & Holzman, 1958). Therapy proceeds through free association (or its modern equivalent, the detailed inquiry) into resistance and transference and then automatically into history and then back again. Transference (and countertransference) is the replay of the narrative content. Put in a more interpersonal perspective, the treatment praxis is first a detailed inquiry into the patient's narrative that unpacks the story, opens up elisions, and mystifications (as I suggested in the discussed case). This challenging of the patient's narrative provokes anxiety, and the anxiety provokes a simultaneous enactment in the therapy of what is being talked about. In other words, what is talked about is simultaneously replayed, but replayed in the analytic space and at a manageable level. To repeat, it is the frame, the containment that makes that feasible.

Clearly, my psychoanalytic perspective implies that change emerges from a process of demystification in the telling, the narrative, and the showing, the relationship of the two participants. I believe that caring, respect, and trust in the patient play a vital role in treatment. But I do not believe that therapy proceeds by the therapist providing some restorative love or empathy experience for the patient. I believe the cure comes via the working through, the traditional arduous replay of show and tell that epitomizes psychoanalytic psychotherapies.

To summarize, the issue here is not of understanding dynamics or even the nature of their interaction. It is recognition of boundaries, frame, and rules that define the limits of the relationship and protect *both* participants from becoming overwhelmed. This is why we do not treat our mates or children or even close friends. In the real world, alas, we have no claim to healing powers.

One last caveat: Why did the referring therapist refer to them as "a perfect match"? Why did the consultant suggest she carry on with this frightening and perhaps untreatable man, rather than rescue her? Did she have a reputation for unflappability or endless patience and caring? At the risk of being discursive, I would like to remind the reader that some patients having experienced what Sullivan (1953) called a malevolent transformation, are not really treatable, at least by psychoanalytic methods.

Happily, we work in a field of great diversity of opinion and process. The therapist might well disagree with my comments. I am most interested to learn how she found her way. And again, I commend her on her caring and devotion for this difficult man.

Nancy McWilliams

Having been trained in the tradition of Theodor Reik, who emphasized the analyst's intuitions as a royal road to the meaning of clinical material, I begin by observing my own affective, impressionistic responses and then move to relevant ideas that arose while I was "listening with the third ear" to this compelling vignette. Different patients stimulate associations to different writers, theorists, and models, which I find variably valuable in understanding each person's unique issues.

The metaphorical cat has now been dropped on me. I viscerally feel for the analyst. My main responses are sympathy and admiration: Michele Gomes describes an agonizing clinical moment with uncommon emotional honesty. I assume that, via Epstein and Wallerstein's "parallel process," this combination of sorrow on her behalf and admiration mirrors the predominant attitudes of her patient, who seems, despite his challenges to their relationship, to have the capacity to be sympathetic and to admire his therapist's integrity enough to trust her for help with his sadism. And so he brings it to her in multiple ways; here, via a Hobson's choice.

In this enactment, Ben appears to be treating the therapist sadistically – perhaps not fully consciously, but not entirely unconsciously. In the clinical moment, he seems in a slightly dissociated, agitated, sadistic self-state. He gives Michele a choice in which neither of her options – to protect the kitten or to convey her confidence that he can protect it – is hazard-free. Her discomfort probably brings him a pleasurable reversal of the dominance-submission pattern that individuals with sadistic preoccupations tend to focus on in any dyadic interaction. She may be the therapist, but right now, he's "on top."

We are all mammals, sensitive to dominance issues and capable of sadistic behavior with prey. Most of us discharge our sadism in activities such as teasing, parodying authorities, watching graphic movies and slapstick comedies, reading true-crime literature, and generating vengeful fantasies when our narcissism is wounded. Ben's sadism seems more dominant and far-reaching than is typical, making it hard to maintain empathy with his psychology. Ben's rather ego-syntonic sadism seems to derive from the interaction of his childhood victimization with whatever was his constitutional endowment of aggression. He feels pleasure in domination and subtle glee at the other's discomfort, as is evident in several of the behaviors mentioned here. For example, his reaction to his therapist's offer to see him privately appears to be a sadistic defense against gratitude and its implicit recognition of dependency. He can't let Michele know how much she matters to him. He teases her until the last possible minute, implying that maybe he will and maybe he won't be her patient ongoingly. He seems to want to make her "beg for it," a familiar gambit in the dominance-submission rituals favored by those who frame life in terms of dominators and dominated, whose only safety lies in being the former.

Ben seems excited by his therapist's being tortured. Recreating his own childhood torment, during which he was given a pet he was forced to starve, he aggressively recruits her into a drama choreographed by his psychopathology. He gives her an animal in jeopardy, a potential pet she may not be able to care for adequately. It is a good sign that he remembered his ill-fated hamster and told that story with affect; that is how enactments are supposed to work. He trusted the therapist to tolerate and contain the excruciating feelings that his memories would provoke, and she did. Although his abreacting some aspects of his boyhood did not resolve Michele's dilemma, it moved him along in grieving his childhood subjugation, a necessary precondition for his eventually finding adaptations other than sadistic dominance.

As Davies and Frawley observed, individuals with traumatic histories frequently put therapists into predicaments in which their choice is to be experienced as either persecutor or victim, seducer or seduced, omnipotent rescuer or negligent abandoner, and other starkly polarized roles characterized by Benjamin as either "doer" or "done to," from which dichotomy some potential third way must be extracted. The Editors of this volume highlight this element: the patient's difficulty expanding the dyadic struggle into a relationship that can include a third.

Reading the case, I found myself associating to the "control mastery" theory of Sampson and Weiss, who emphasized the "tests" that patients impose on therapists. In this empirically derived model, patients know at some level what they need in order to change, and they repeatedly test therapists to see if they can provide it. If they need a greater sense of safety than their childhood allowed, for example, they may urge us to make exceptions to the frame and then see if we can maintain it despite their pressure. If they need to feel they could matter to someone, they may not show up, to see whether we care. What feels like resistance to us often feels to patients like taking the risk of opening themselves to the lesson that life does not have to be defined as their prior experiences have defined it. A therapist's passing the tests is emotionally reparative.

In many enactments, however, it is hard to know what the test is, and thus what passing it would entail. Is the depressed woman who asks to borrow a book testing to see if the therapist is, like her father, too rigid to be generous? Or is she trying to reassure herself that the boundaries of *this* relationship are impenetrable, unlike her childhood boundaries, which her father violated? Is the anxious man who wants to reduce his session frequency testing to see if we, unlike his negligent mother, truly want to see him more? Or is he seeing whether, unlike the parents who failed to support his autonomy, we can view him as the best judge of his needs? In Michele's situation, would it be passing the test for her to take the kitten, or to entrust it to Ben?

Sampson and Weiss identified two kinds of tests: *transference tests* ("Are you going to behave like my early caregiver, or is there another possible version of caregiving?") and *passive-into-active* tests ("If I treat you as I was treated, can you respond in ways I couldn't as a child, exemplifying a different response to the challenges I faced?"). Michele's situation seems particularly dicey because it has elements of both kinds of tests. On one hand, Ben seems to be asking her to be a loving mother to the kitten, unlike his own sadistic mother: If she can do this, he will take another step in mastering his childhood legacy. Via lived experience, he will see that some mothers are not sadistic, that love is possible. On the other, he is casting himself as his mother and the therapist as himself, giving her a pet as his mother gave one to him, under conditions in which the only outcome that reliably protects it reinforces his conviction that he is too sadistic (as he was with the hamster) to be entrusted with a vulnerable other.

There is no "right" response to such clinical challenges. There are somewhat better versus somewhat worse options, but choices in quandaries like these are always trade-offs. Sometimes one passes one element of a complicated test and fails another. The fantasy that there exists a therapist so competent that she would know exactly what to do is a remnant of the infantile fantasy of perfect, rescuing parental goodness. It is partly because one can never do the fully "right thing," provide the completely corrective emotional experience, that exploration and interpretation are essential to engaging with most enactments. It matters what we say as well as what we do. This may be especially true for dilemmas that come up later in treatment and exemplify what Paul Russell called "the crunch."

In my experience, the crunch tends to come when a patient has made changes that are so visible and significant that they provoke a crisis. The person cannot deny the progress, realizes that it results from being profoundly influenced by the therapist, begins to trust and hope more deeply than ever before, and panics. It is at this point that people with borderline-level psychologies (a formulation that may apply to Ben) may make suicide gestures, engage in self-harm, or implicitly threaten the therapist's well-being. They are managing terror that allowing themselves to depend emotionally on the therapist, and believing that life can actually improve under her care, will expose them to an utterly unbearable disappointment. Ben may be frightened by his own progress and by the strength of his attachment to Michele.

Foremost, and probably most terrifying among the attitudes of which he has now become capable, is love.

I find it hard to comment on clinical material without thinking through what I would do in the situation. My behavior would be specific to my own treatment frame, my personality, and what feels authentic to me as an individual. My solution might or might not be of use to Michele, who has a different personality and perhaps a different frame, both of which need to be honored. She also knows Ben in much more depth than I can extract from one glimpse at her work. With that caveat, I find myself thinking that in her place I would probably accept the kitten. I would do it with trepidation, knowing that in the next sessions I might have to deal with Ben's devastation because my actions betrayed my doubt about his readiness to be trusted with it. I would expect those sessions to be difficult, but I would be operating out of a core psychoanalytic principle, seared into my psyche by my own experience as an analysand, that processing intense negative reactions is essential to healing. Here are my conscious reasons for accepting the cat.

First, I would do it for the sake of the animal. It seems the only choice that guarantees its welfare. If I did not want a pet, I might agree to take it temporarily but would also engage Ben in a conversation about what service agencies could accept it. This would call attention to the larger social context, modifying the "It's either you or me" binary that he has imposed. The mother–son exclusivity evoked in the dyad can thus be reminded that there is an authority, a third, outside their either/or world, that defines options larger than the sadism-versus-masochism polarity.

Second, by taking the kitten, I would protect myself from worry and guilt. For my own sake, I would want to preempt possibilities of future torture. If Ben were to take it, he could report in subsequent sessions on his lapses in care, or, worse, his forays into sadistic mistreatment, thus subjecting me to harrowing real-time stories of abuse and complicating even further the clinical dilemma.

I have come to view the success of any patient–therapist dyad as partly dependent on the therapist's sense of security and ease in the relationship. This includes physical safety, but may additionally involve explicit provisos to prevent one's traumatization. I often tell patients that I have to protect my sense of basic comfort in the work. I may say something like, "I won't be in a position to do you any good if I am feeling resentful or enraged or highly anxious." With potentially suicidal people, for example, I insist on a promise that they will stay alive throughout the treatment, and I establish consequences that I then implement if they make a suicide gesture. I thus monitor my "conditions of labor," which include everything from fees and cancellations to limits on how patients may behave in my office. They may be irritated by my foregrounding my own welfare, but they understand. I hope it gives patients an image of self-care that differs from that of their childhood caregivers and from what they could do for themselves growing up. Here, I would be trying to refuse the masochistic position without flipping into a sadistic one.

Third, if I were in Michele's position, I would take the kitten because the patient explicitly asked me to do so. It would show respect to take Ben at his word, even though he will likely be angry that I have honored his wishes. I have learned (the hard way) that treating patients as if they are further along than they are – especially when they are expressing their deepest self-doubts – erodes their confidence in my judgment. They worry that I am seeing only what I want to see. In fact, sometimes that worry is the *stimulus* to a patient's acting out: It may express a dynamic that translates as, "What do I have to do to get you to see how troubled I still am?!" I have come to believe that in work with individuals with characterological difficulties, respect is even more important than what is conventionally construed as empathy. What the therapist views as empathic attunement is felt by some patients as a regressive pull toward refusal to take realistic adult responsibility.

Fourth, rescuing the cat opens more possibilities for processing what has happened between patient and therapist. Anger expressed in words is not a problem in therapy, but wordless acting out is. Ben needs to experience his own ambivalence: He wants his therapist to take the cat. At the same time, he wants her to act as if his sadism is not as much of a problem as he knows it still is. He needs to hold his sadistic and loving self-states in co-conscious equilibrium. In Bromberg's evocative metaphor, he needs to "stand in the spaces" between his contrasting states of mind.

I might also verbalize my dilemma. When patients put me in binds, I frequently articulate my conflict in terms of my effort to do the right therapeutic thing. In effect, I ask patients for supervision. I try to exemplify the attitude of holding in mind two antithetical positions. In this instance I might say, "Let's take a minute. I'm noticing I have diametrically opposing feelings about what should be done here. Part of me is responding to your own fear that you will hurt the kitten, and I want to respect that by taking it home. But another part of me knows you have made a lot of progress toward being less sadistic, and wants to insist that you can do right by this animal. What do you find yourself hoping I will do? What would you say is the 'right' thing for me to do?" And so on. This conversation would not rescue me from having to make the choice, but it might be a valuable contextualization.

In this commentary, I feel as if I have survived a test involving the welfare of Michele, Ben, the cat, and myself. I hope Michele feels similarly about her own endurance as a force for good despite the tortures of this vexing clinical moment.

My intervention

I spent most of this session with Ben and the kitten reeling – afraid for all of us. I was afraid of Ben's aggression, mostly toward the kitten but also toward me. I was afraid of how I would feel about myself if I knowingly sent this vulnerable being home with someone who might harm her. I was afraid that my work with Ben would be undermined no matter what choice I made. Was this one of those moments that Ben would benefit most from by virtue of my having faith in him? Or, would it be therapeutic for me to see Ben clearly and to help him limit his dangerousness? These questions spiraled through me as the session went on.

Interspersed were more moments of play and genuine delight. I watched closely as Ben interacted with the kitten. In eight years, I had never seen him smile as much or as naturally. He couldn't quite cuddle her or allow her to get as close to him as she wished to be. He seemed especially sensitive to her attempts to lick his face and mouth. Nonetheless, his characteristic vigilance and the stiffness of his body – which reflects a lifetime of trauma – seemed slightly more relaxed. As a cat lover, I couldn't help but believe in the healing power of a connection with a loving animal.

Ben and I thought together about his options. Should he take the kitten home to raise her? Should he drive her straight to the shelter that we'd located in a quick Google search? Should he take her home as a trial run, making sure to keep the shelter's number close at hand "just in case"? Should he leave her with me, wherein I would inherit the problem of ensuring her safety? I was heartened by the clarity of his thought process. He was taking this seriously and reflecting honestly upon his limitations and his potential for danger. And, we were working together.

As the end of the hour approached, I was feeling more and more pressured to answer Ben's question. I looked at Ben and asked him, "Did you think about naming her?" Quietly, with a shy smile, he said yes, that he had already picked a name for her. He gave the kitten his great-grandmother's name – the name of a woman he never met but longed to know. I replied, "You made her part of your family." He rebuffed this and said he picked the name simply because it's pretty. After some silence he added, "Of course I named her. It's dehumanizing not to. Everyone deserves a name."

Hearing this was a pivotal moment in my decision-making process. Ben recognized the value of her life. Just minutes prior, he told me a horrific story where he admitted that he did not value the life of his childhood pet – or, more precisely – that his own traumas and sadistic impulses could overtake whatever value he placed on this being's life. His identification with the aggressor won out as he violently killed the hamster. I recalled that he never called the hamster by a name, nor did he say "my hamster," which might demonstrate a sense of relatedness. This difference felt important and, in the moment, I clung to it as a sign of hope.

I said to him, "Right now, in this moment, the part of you that wants to rescue her is bigger than the part of you that wants to kill her." He stayed silent, looking nervous. I continued, "You picked her up and brought her here, you protected her from the potentially poisonous plant, and you gave her a name that made her a part of your family. You even made her a gift."

In that moment, my decision felt clear. I realized that the triangle was not simply between me, Ben, and the kitten. There was another important triangle between me, the destructive part of Ben, and the protective part of Ben. He found this idea compelling and was able to talk about the conflict between these two parts that rage on inside of him. His eyes watered as he sat staring at the kitten who had fallen asleep on one of the pillows on my couch. He responded, "You know I could still hurt her, right?" I said, "I know."

As Ben left, kitten in hand, I gave him some tips about what he needed to buy to feed her tonight. He stopped in the doorway and asked, "If I brought a kitten in a few years ago, you would've taken her away from me, right?" I nodded affirmatively. It felt important to be honest so that he knew my risk was thought out and based on a changing potential in him.

Ben and the kitten have been together for nearly two years now. During her kittenhood, he would occasionally bring her to session strapped to his chest in a Baby Björn. It has not been perfect or without pain. Ben has admitted to hitting her on at least two occasions, both times prompted by her play escalating into aggressive biting. However, she has become a profound source of analytic material in all that she stirs up in Ben and we are able to make use of it together.

Note

1 Naturally, not all patients are so inclined. Many remain skeptical, disbelieving that the analyst is anything of the sort, tilting in the direction of cynicism rather than romanticism.

References

Bateson, G. (1972). *Steps to an ecology of mind*. New York: Ballantine Books.
Britton, R. (1989). The missing link: Parental sexuality in the Oedipus complex. In R. Britton, M. Feldman, E. O'Shaughnessy, & J. Steiner (Eds.), *The Oedipus complex today: Clinical implications* (pp. 83–102). London: Karnac Books.
Chrzanowski, G. (1980). Collaborative inquiry, affirmation and neutrality in the psychoanalytic situation. *Contemporary Psychoanalysis*, 16(3), 348–366.
Friedman, L. (1997). Ferrum, ignis, and medicina: Return to the crucible. *Journal of the American Psychoanalytic Association*, 45(1), 21–36.
Guntrip, H. (1967). The concept of psychodynamic science. *International Journal of Psychoanalysis*, 48(1), 32–43.
Kernberg, O. (2011). The sexual couple: A psychoanalytic exploration. *Psychoanalytic Review*, 98(2), 217–245.
Levenson, E. (1983). *The ambiguity of change: An inquiry into the nature of psychoanalytic reality*. New York: Basic Books.
Menninger, K., & Holzman, P. (1958). *Theory of psychoanalytic technique*. New York: Basic Books.
Sullivan, H. S. (1953). *The interpersonal theory of psychiatry*. New York: W. W. Norton.
Winnicott, D. W. (1956). Primary maternal preoccupation. In *Through paediatrics to psychoanalysis* (pp. 300–305). London: Hogarth Press.

Chapter 12

Worried Sick about a Patient

Richard Tuch

Editors' introduction

Sometimes analysts experience remarkably powerful countertransference reactions in response to how the patient is behaving. These reactions can be conceptualized as instances of projective identification, of role responsiveness, of countertransference enactments, and so on, and they can be clinically managed in a host of different ways, including making the patient aware of the effect his behavior or way of relating has had or is having on the analyst. When a patient's fear that nothing he does can, or ever will, affect the analyst intersects with a deep desire to profoundly affect the analyst, the stage is set for a clinical moment of a certain sort. In this particular case, the analyst's intense countertransference reaction to a patient's sudden disappearance may have gone so far as to contribute to his literally worrying himself sick. The patient's response to the analyst's suddenly being out of commission due to his need for emergency surgery fueled fantasies of why the analyst had fallen ill and what, if anything, the patient had to do with this development. The patient's wish to powerfully affect the analyst was driven by a fantasy that impacting the analyst could help reassure the patient of his existence. This case presents not a single clinical moment but a series of related moments, each of which left the analyst wondering about how best to proceed.

The moment in context (Richard Tuch)

In the earliest days of psychoanalysis, an analyst's reaction to a patient – his countertransference – was considered a troublesome matter – a sure sign that something hadn't been fully worked through in the analyst, requiring he undergo further analysis to mitigate such tendencies. In the middle of the last century, with the publication of a series of seminal papers (Heimann, 1950; Racker, 1957; Tower, 1956), the tide began to turn in how the field regarded countertransference phenomena. Psychoanalysts ceased to see countertransference strictly as an impediment to treatment, and – as the decades wore on – more and more analysts began to see countertransference reactions not only as a highly effective tool but even as the essential way par excellence by which analysts come to know their patients, with countertransference seen as commentary about the patient's deepest dynamics.

While some insist that countertransference can never be de-contextualized – considered apart from the analyst's interactions with a given patient (a two-person or intersubjective perspective) – others believe it's still possible to encounter countertransferences from time to time that are chiefly, if not wholly, the product of the analyst's transference-readiness – his own idiosyncratic tendency to react to a given patient because that patient reminds him of someone from the analyst's past – with the patient a *more or less* "innocent" bystander who'd unwittingly stimulated an intense reaction in the analyst (Gitelson, 1952) – meaning that the analyst's reaction is on balance much more about him and much less a commentary on the patient to the extent other analysts would not have reacted to the patient in this same way or, if they had, would not have reacted nearly to the same degree as this particular analyst had (see Kernberg, 1965).

There are a number of different ways in which countertransference reactions have been conceptualized. One of the original formulations is that of "projective identification" (Klein, 1946; Malin & Grotstein, 1966; Ogden, 1979), defined as:

> a group of fantasies and accompanying object relations having to do with the ridding of the self of unwanted aspects of the self; the depositing of those unwanted "parts" into another person; and finally, with the "recovery" of a modified version of what was extruded.
> (Ogden, 1979, p. 357)

The recipient of the disowned part of the projector's psyche is not experienced as a separate entity in his own right – rather, he is experienced as if he's part of the projector's own being (Klein, 1946), resulting in a depletion in the projector's ego to the extent contents of his ego had been evacuated, making them only available to him as something that now exists within the other – as something he must control in that other. The process of projective identification is thought to be set off by interpersonal interactions that pressure the "recipient" of the projection to think, feel, and behave "in a manner congruent with the projection" (Ogden, 1979, p. 358), which accounts for the oftentimes profound effect this process can have on the recipient of the projection.

While many analysts continue to find great value thinking in terms of projective identification, others challenge the viability of the concept, going so far as to literally declare that no such thing actually exists as described (Stolorow, 2017) and that the clinical application of such thinking can even prove counter-therapeutic (Stolorow et al., 1987). What some analysts find objectionable about how projective identification is conceptualized (Demos, 1999; Eagle, 1999; Meissner, 1980; Stolorow et al., 1998) issues in part from the thinking of analysts like Heimann, who wrote about the subject in the mid-twentieth century. While most analysts would agree with Heimann's (1950) assessment that "the emotions roused in [the analyst] are much nearer to the heart of the matter than his reasoning, or, to put it in other words, his unconscious perception of the analysand's unconscious is more acute and *in advance* of his conscious conception of the situation" (p. 82, italics added), many would take issue with her assertion that countertransference is essentially "*the patient's creation*, it is a part of the patient's personality" (p. 83, italics added). For decades, many analysts believed that projective identification involved the wholesale transfer of an aggregate and reified (thing-like) aspect of the patient's psyche into the analyst's mind lock-stock-and-barrel, where it thereafter existed as a foreign body within the analyst, experienced as such. This view of projective identification fails to take into consideration pre-existing aspects of the analyst's psyche upon which the projected contents play – what it is within him that is his – the "hook" within the analyst upon which the projection gets hung (Gabbard, 1995). Some analysts also fault the concept of projective identification for failing to take into consideration the reciprocal, back-and-forth, chicken-or-egg nature of influence (Stolorow et al., 1998).

Projective identification stimulates a stirring in the analyst that sets in motion a process that may culminate in a variety of different mental states: reverie, a reawakening of personal memories, the experiencing of particular feelings, an irresistible urge to enact that is only appreciated after the fact, and so on, all of which can serve *as commentary* about the analysand's psychic condition. These mental states are the analyst's own reactions – not foreign contents evacuated by the analysand into him. The analyst's job is to fathom how his own internal state, or enacted behavior – if it goes that far – is connected to the internal state of the analysand so that he might then have something meaningful to say to the analysand.

In the 1970s, Sandler (1976) refined the field's thinking about countertransference by proposing that patients implicitly assigned roles for the analyst to assume. Analysts who are available to be "used" by the patient in this fashion (who "wear the attribution" rather than fighting against it – Lichtenberg et al., 1992, 1996) were said to be "role responsive." Sandler noted that analysts sometimes *find themselves* unwittingly acting in ways that are uncharacteristic of them for reasons that escape them. In his paper, Sandler presents the case of a patient to whom he'd handed tissues each and every time she cried, which was out of character for him. Sandler never mentions whether he'd come to terms with what it was about him that the patient had acted upon to cause him to behave in this manner, and another ten years would pass before the practice of openly admitting the analyst's personal contribution to an enactment would come into vogue. What Sandler decided to do was to cease handing the patient tissues, which proved clinically productive to the extent that shift in behavior led to material that clarified what it was that was being enacted – a role the patient assigned the analyst to play that was tantamount to his functioning like a mother cleaning her baby's bottom after defecation – a realization that went on to become invaluable to the treatment. Sandler did not see role responsiveness as a function of the analysand's efforts to impose a role upon the analyst – instead, he saw it as "a function of the analyst's receptivity, not of the analysand's unconscious intention, and should not be regarded as projective identification, as something that the analysand wants to 'put into' the analyst" (Sandler, 1993, p. 1105).

In the 1980s, Jacobs (1986) introduced the concept of the "countertransference enactment" – defined as instances when the analyst acted out his countertransference rather than containing it and utilizing it for the good of the treatment. Jacobs went a step further than Sandler by exploring how particular factors in his own background led him to engage with the analysand in an enactment – illustrating what had specifically gotten stirred up in him *that is his*. Over the course of the last 30 years, many analysts have come to believe that enactments offer an unparalleled opportunity for analyst and analysand to further the treatment by analyzing the enactment, which oftentimes reveals critical material that had heretofore gone unmentioned. Some analysts have gone so far as to assert that a successful analysis necessarily and invariably hinges on the development and working through of enactments (Boesky, 1990; Chessick, 1999; Renik, 1993). This position is epitomized by Boesky's (1990) often-quoted remark referenced as a sort of rallying cry for those who see the analysis of enactments as an essential – quite possibly *the* essential – mutative agent: "If the analyst does not get emotionally involved sooner or later in a manner that he had not intended, the analysis will not proceed to a successful conclusion" (p. 753). This position is thought by some to represent an extreme pendulum swing in counter-reaction to prevailing beliefs about countertransference that had been in effect a half-century before (Tuch, 2015). The universality of countertransference enactments – the belief that they are an everyday occurrence in every analysis – was furthered by Renik's (1996) over-the-top claim that countertransference can *only* be known after the fact – meaning that analysts can't hope to know much about how they are responding to patients in the moment until those responses manifest behaviorally, after which time they can retrospectively analyze the meaning of what they'd unconsciously acted out.

How one chooses to clinically handle the emergence of a countertransference reaction has much to do with how one conceptualizes the origin and function of the reaction. For those inclined to think in terms of projective identification, the intermediary goal of adequate containment of the projected content sets the stage for the ultimate goal of returning to the patient his disowned psychic content, made possible by first transforming the contents into a more easily acceptable form (turning beta elements into alpha elements; Bion, 1962). Sandler's particular approach was to cease engaging in the chronic enactment once he'd come to realize that this is what he'd been doing all along. Jacobs went a step further by coming to terms with what it was about him that contributed to his engaging in the enactment as a precondition to reversing the process. Finally, interpersonally oriented analysts like Ehrenberg (1992, 1996) approach the patient's effect on the analyst in a direct fashion by making the patient aware of how interacting with the patient makes the analyst feel. Underlying such a confrontation is the belief that the analyst's countertransference is the average expectable reaction that most analysts would have were they in the analyst's shoes, rather than an idiosyncratic reaction that constitutes the analyst's transference to the patient. Ehrenberg believes that patients are helped by their becoming aware of how their behavior impacts others, which is very much an issue in the case of the next clinical moment to be presented. Whether one conceptualizes this moment alternately as an instance of projective identification, of role responsiveness, or of a countertransference enactment may make a difference in the precise way in which the moment ends up being addressed clinically by the analyst.

The clinical moment

Like certain other clinical moments contained in this volume, this isn't a single moment but a series of linked moments. These moments were set in motion when the patient uncharacteristically and unexpectedly dropped out of sight, unresponsive to his parents' and his analyst's attempts to reach him over the course of several days. At the time this occurred, Mark – a grad student in his mid-20s – had been in five-day-a-week, on-the-couch analysis for 15 months. He'd initially sought treatment because he was intensely anxious and often lost in a fantasy world, which made it hard for him to just get through each day. He couldn't relax or think in a clear-headed fashion. He had no sense that he had a mind of his own, which left him yearning to be directed from without – hoping that someone would tell him what to do, what to want, how to be and think. He hadn't a clue about how to "be himself"; he couldn't even say what he liked or disliked, and he was amazed that others actually knew such things about themselves. He was forever "acting the part," making sure to never expose his "true self" – unsure of what that might even be, terrified he'd be "found out" to be the "shitty little kid" he had been when young. He tried to act "cool" around women he was interested in, but he was so rehearsed that he often came across as stilted. His dating history was sparse, and he had never been with a woman romantically. It would take another couple of years of analysis before he'd finally be able to have intercourse with a woman.

Mark lived much of his day in fantasy. He'd spend inordinate amounts of time watching a particular type of porn, the theme of which involved a woman who turns away from him to be with a man who – in whatever way – puts him to shame by being so much better, larger, more sexually satisfying, and so on and so forth. His inability to extricate himself from this time-consuming habit filled him with shame and self-loathing. I came to believe his porn-related fantasies involved more than mere Oedipal dynamics, though his idealization of his dad – "the smartest man I ever met" – clearly played a role. His fantasies were essentially masochistic insofar as he reveled in the thought of being rejected in this fashion.

Mark was deeply pained by how much of a struggle his mother had found life to be. Her life seemed filled with failed hopes and dreams, and Mark felt deeply obliged to save and restore her. He worried that his own success – to develop a successful life of his own – would make matters worse for his mother by demonstrating that success was achievable for some, if not for her. He'd always felt as if he existed solely to satisfy his mother's needs, and while he knew she loved him dearly, he hadn't a sense that she really understood who he was as a person.

Though he was quite bright, Mark found it difficult preparing for his classes and studying for exams, though he was making his way through his graduate program without a hitch, which I suspect was due to the sheer strength of his intellect. Thinking about graduating filled him with angst; he couldn't imagine setting aside his porn addiction, settling down, and attending to the task at hand were he to be employed. Furthermore, the thought of competing and succeeding (e.g., as the cuckold victor) left Mark feeling guilty because he imagined his success would pour salt in the wounds of those less gifted than he was. Surely, he reasoned, they would envy his success, against which they'd measure their own failures and inadequacies. After all, he knew about such tendencies since he was prone to envy the success of others, which left him feeling meek and inadequate in comparison. Mark was particularly uncomfortable experiencing or expressing assertion and aggression. Never once had he openly expressed anger toward another, or even displayed anger in the presence of others, fearing that doing so would destroy them.

The patient was emphatic that he was *never to be caught trying* to accomplish any particular thing. Everything should just come to him naturally without his having to exert any effort since accomplishments that required effort could never prove his inherent worth; "anyone can 'make it' if they just tried hard enough." Furthermore, trying meant wanting, and wanting left him vulnerable to being discovered and being known (by virtue of wanting particular things).

For the first several months of his analysis, Mark spent the better part of each session presenting a series of dreams he'd had the night before. While analyzing these dreams proved clinically productive, filling sessions with dreams seemed to reflect an effort to keep things from becoming "more real" in the room – replicating tendencies to live life through fantasy, which kept him from having to deal with "the real world."

By the time this series of clinical moments occurred, our therapeutic relationship had strengthened considerably. I sensed he felt quite attached to me; he came every day on time without exception. He was dedicated to the task of doing the work, though he found the treatment challenging. There was, however, a subtle threat that hung over the treatment. Mark warned me that if I ever forgot to show up for a session – were he to come to the office and find I was not there – he would never return and would not respond to my calls. He seriously questioned my interest in him and my commitment to his treatment, imagining that I might be playing him for the fool given his fantasy that I wasn't actually an analyst but was merely playing the part. Mark would remind me on a regular basis that he could end the analysis at the drop of a hat – that I should be prepared for the distinct possibility that one day he'd not show up, and that would be that! Naturally, this left me feeling a bit on edge – vulnerable, though I suspected that this was Mark's way of making *me* be the one who'd have to worry about being abandoned, not him.

In the week preceding the one during which this series of clinical moments occurred, Mark mentioned a dream about a young boy who was screaming at the top of his lungs but no one comes to help: "I'm screaming and another part of me tells myself to 'shut the fuck up!'" The following session, Mark spoke openly about his transference feelings – that talking openly in session felt like he was "going out on a limb," that he needed my approval and felt very attached to the interpretations I'd offer him. He also expressed a fear of improving: "To succeed is to be separate and to separate is to be alone!" He likened our relationship to Geppetto and Pinocchio: turning the wooden puppet into a real boy and, in his mind, his progress would need to be of another's making and, in his mind, another's glory.

This series of clinical moments was set in motion at the beginning of the following week. It is now 6:30 p.m. on Monday evening, and Mark has yet to show for his 6 o'clock appointment. This is very unlike him. Should I call and inquire as to his whereabouts or should I just assume he'll show for our next appointed session?

Invited commentator responses 1: Darlene Ehrenberg and Ted Jacobs

Darlene Ehrenberg

Before responding to Dr. Tuch's questions, I would like to note that in my view his description of how he thinks I work misses the essence of and the complexity of my position. *I do not see my interventions as "confrontational," nor do I see my reactions as "average expectable" countertransference. I think they are unique to the specific interactive dynamic between myself and my patient at that moment.* My focus is on trying to clarify what might be in play unconsciously between us when this seems to be an issue. Sensitivity to my own feelings as I engage with a patient, especially when these make no sense to me, often is what provides the clue that something complex might be going on unconsciously between us. Even if I know that my reactions relate to my own issues, I have learned the importance of two questions: "Why am I having this reaction now and not at other moments with this patient?" and "Why do I not have such reactions with my other patients?" What I might simply ask about, however, is what the patient is feeling at that moment.

I find that patients often then realize that they are feeling something they may not have thought to acknowledge even to themselves. Recognizing this often surprises and intrigues them. If a patient then tells me something they observe about my own reaction that I was not aware of, this intrigues me. Realizing that we each can help the other see something we could not have seen on our own leads to further "scaffolding" on each other's input, which allows each to take our own thinking forward in ways we could not have done on our own. This makes the interaction feel "alive" precisely because neither of us can predict where this might lead. Often very emotional associations and memories, which had been inaccessible up to that point, begin to emerge, leading to new experiences of hope and desire in place of a sense of hopelessness and despair. It can also help set in motion an important process of mourning for what might have been possible earlier in one's life had things been other than how they were. I think of one patient's comment that he felt "the ceiling lifting on his imagination." In this way, attending in an ongoing way to subtle shifts in feeling in the moment can make a difference in terms of how things might develop. I have described this as working at the "intimate edge" of the relationship (Ehrenberg, 1974, 1992) in which transactions between patient and analyst are treated as primary data (Ehrenberg, 1982).

Consider the moment when Dr. Tuch's patient warned Dr. Tuch that if he were ever to forget a session the patient would never return and would not return Dr. Tuch's calls if he were to want to talk with the patient about his decision. Also consider the very important questions Dr. Tuch struggles with about how his own bodily symptoms might be a response to his patient and whether he should have acknowledged to the patient that he understood the degree of the patient's pain and increasing despair. In my view, each of these concerns highlights the *mutual vulnerability* of patient and analyst as they engage with one another. My experience has been that focusing on how patient and analyst are being affected by, and are affecting one another becomes a way to keep things from escalating in problematic ways.

Dr. Tuch also tells us:

> Naturally, [the patient's warning] left me feeling a bit on edge – vulnerable, though I suspected that this was [his] way of making *me* be the one who'd have to worry about being abandoned, not him.

We all have moments like this, and these moments reflect our own unique responses. The question is how we can use these reactions to help inform a response that might help unravel what is in play interactively at that moment. Sometimes we are only able to find ways to do this after the fact, which is fine as well. In such instances (whether during or after the actual moment), simply asking the patient what he thinks he wanted me to understand about him by telling me this – what he wanted me to know about his vulnerabilities and his issues with disappointment and anger – would let the patient know that his comments have registered with me. I might also ask if this reaction is unique to his interaction with me. If I did react with fear that "I would be dropped" I would also wonder to myself how this patient got "under my skin" this way and why I was vulnerable to this.

The patient touches on a series of issues that seem rich and important. He dreams about a young boy who was screaming at the top of his lungs but no one came to help, and the patient's comment is, "I'm screaming and another part of me tells myself to 'shut the fuck up!'" He reports "that he feels he needs my approval and is very attached to the interpretations I offer him." Then he shares his fear that "to succeed is to be separate and to separate is to be alone." He associates to Geppetto and Pinocchio: "turning the wooden puppet into a real boy," and expresses his opinion that his progress would be of another's making and, in his mind, another's "glory."

Dr. Tuch doesn't specify how and whether he addressed these specific issues with the patient. It would seem important to ask the patient how he understands the conflict about wanting to be heard vs. telling himself to "shut the fuck up" and how such concerns might be influencing what might be going on between patient and analyst. I would also encourage the patient to share his thoughts and associations to the powerful image of Geppetto and Pinocchio as well as his concern about whether his progress would be of another's making and lead to another's glory. Might the patient fear the degree to which he feels attached to the analyst's interpretations as well as his need for the analyst's approval? Do such feelings render him vulnerable to the analyst? I might also wonder if all of these concerns relate to issues with his mother based on fears that he had expressed about upsetting or hurting his mother in multiple ways *if he were to try to become his own person.* I would be especially curious about the patient's idea that you are either the other's puppet (as in the relation between Geppetto and Pinocchio) or you are all alone. But apart from these kinds of questions, I would be interested in the actual clinical data about how each of their responses influences the other's next response. This can begin to bring into focus what each might be afraid to acknowledge, not only to the other but also to themselves – the disavowals of agency that may be involved and the fears of, or prohibitions about, "thinking" or "seeing" that may be in play from either side.

Though I believe that listening silently and not intruding at all often would be important, I think there are times when not addressing what is in play becomes the medium for collusion and enactment. Might this have been the case when Dr. Tuch remained silent when the patient spoke about his pain and despair? Was this in collusion with the patient's own expressed fears of being known or heard?

Would working in a more active way have prevented the patient's escalating despair and suicidal thoughts from developing? Would doing so have prevented the analyst's physical symptoms from developing? I do not know. But I think that tracking the moment-by-moment process could help clarify boundary confusions and demystify the idea that either of them "made the other feel" what he was feeling. Together, the two could wonder about the idea that someone else can "make me do" something I would not choose on my own to do. What about the disavowal of agency this would imply? It may become clearer why closeness is experienced as problematic when patient and analyst clarify the belief that closeness requires "giving over one's will" to the other and letting oneself be dominated, compromised in the process. Discovering that it is their choice if they forfeit their own freedom to know their own feelings and to be "real" with others can be a very liberating but also a sobering and disturbing "revelation." This might be very important in this case to the extent that being able to risk experiencing and expressing one's anger is essential to being able to feel one can be "real," and Mark expressed very clearly his fear of his own anger and his fear that others could not survive it. What is fascinating here is Dr. Tuch's worry that he is vulnerable to being physically compromised in a way that is out of his control as he engages with Mark. This opens onto complex and fascinating issues about how things that bypass consciousness may be played out not only interactively but sometimes in our bodies.

What is fascinating to me is that I have found myself at times suddenly in the role of a patient's mother or other family member with no clue how I got there. This becomes complex on multiple levels because letting this play out can end up reaffirming a sense of hopelessness and could even be re-traumatizing for both patient and analyst. I think proceeding with great sensitivity and care in such instances, and viewing these moments as important "analytic data" that can be profitably explored, can become a medium of *therapeutic interaction*.

To finally answer Dr. Tuch's question about what to do when a patient does not show up, I would call without hesitation. I would want to know if there was a misunderstanding about the time and if all was okay. Regarding his question about whether to respond to the father's email, I would confirm immediately that the patient has not showed up and that I do not know where he is or how he is and that I am concerned as well. (If there was even a slight risk of suicide, though I probably would not say this, I would be hoping that the father could find him and I would think that time is of the essence.)

Ted Jacobs

I would feel very much as you did: puzzled, anxious, and concerned for my patient's welfare. I would also be aware that the patient has signaled that he might act out feelings of anger, revenge, spite, or anxiety by not showing up for sessions. This prior warning about acting out by missing sessions or disappearing suddenly would modify my anxiety to some extent about the patient's welfare, as would the fact that he had shown no indications of suicidal thoughts. However, I have seen patients who did commit suicide without giving any indication of their intent, so the fact that he had not spoken of suicide or given any indications of suicidal intent would not fully eliminate my anxiety on that score.

I would definitely respond to the father's message of concern. Not to do so when a parent is so anxious would be cruel. And I would explain to the patient just how I felt: that it would be heartless not to respond to the father. I would explore with him what he was thinking that led him to disappear in the fashion that he did.

When and if I felt calmer about the situation, I would undertake a detailed review of the patient's last three or four sessions in an effort to determine, if possible, what in the therapy might have precipitated the patient's behavior.

My intervention

I call but Mark doesn't pick up. I leave a voicemail message noting that he'd not shown up, and I express my hope that everything is "okay." Mark never shows and, surprisingly – because he is usually quite responsive – never responds. I find this a bit troubling – particularly in light of his repeated warning that one day he might stop coming to treatment altogether and I'd never see him or hear from him again.

I'm more than a bit worried – but I try to put it out of my mind. It's now 10 p.m. I am lying in bed checking my emails when I see that Mark's father has emailed me: "Did Mark make his session today? We've been trying to reach him all weekend and have gotten no response. Please let us know." This intensifies my concern. I'd been trying not to imagine the worst – that he'd dropped out of treatment – but now an even scarier possibility floods my mind, leaving me deeply concerned about my patient's well-being.

So, what do I do now? Should I respond to the dad's email? Not doing so would seem inhumane, though responding to the email would constitute a breach of the patient's confidentiality. I know Mark well enough to know that he would not be bothered if I responded to his father's concern. But what about my own anxiety about Mark's well-being? Do I have cause to be concerned? Maybe it's a false alarm. Or… maybe, just maybe, Mark has… done himself in? Could that be? Is that possible? So now I'm confronted with two dilemmas – whether to respond to Mark's dad and whether I have cause to be thinking what I am thinking. What do I do? How should I feel? Am I getting myself worked up for no reason?

I email the father to let him know that Mark hadn't shown up for his appointment. He emails me back asking me to let him know if Mark shows up for his next session. In the meantime, he's made plans to be on the first flight out tomorrow morning and expects to arrive in L.A. around 9 a.m. His decision to fly down fuels my own fear. I am not alone in worrying about the implications of Mark's disappearance. What in God's name has happened to Mark?

It's now 12:30 a.m. I'm still awake. I begin to entertain the possibility that Mark had, in fact, committed suicide. After all – his life has been very, very hard – in ways, impossible. Frankly, he was miserable – though he rarely put it in quite those terms. But I knew that to be the case, though I'd never told him that I knew he struggled mightily just trying to get by. I steel myself against my mounting fear by reminding myself that Mark had never so much as mentioned a suicidal thought but – who knows – maybe I'd fatally erred by not telling Mark that I was very much aware of how miserable he was and how desperately he struggled with life. Maybe it would have made a difference had I said such things to him – maybe then he'd have felt like someone really understood what life was like for him – and maybe, then, he wouldn't have taken his own life. Clearly, my fears were getting the better of me.

I find it nearly impossible to sleep and awaken with a terrible stomach ache. I've worried myself sick, and the pain serves as a moment-by-moment reminder of my worst fear as I prepare for what surely is going to be a catastrophic day – convinced by my imaginings that are fueled by the fact that I've yet to hear back from Mark.

I get to the office to see my 7:30 patient. I am in considerable pain, but I carry on. The pain accuses me of having been less than adequately vigilant, careful, and caring. After my first patient leaves, I check my messages but there is still no word from Mark. My second patient comes and goes. It's now 9 a.m. Wait! There's an email from Mark's father. He'd finally gotten through to Mark. Everything is okay! It's a false alarm. *Phew!* I feel relieved, though now I'm left curious about what this had been about. With my curiosity piqued, I look forward to seeing Mark a couple of hours hence. Strange, my stomach still hurts. I felt sure my having received word would have set it to rest.

It's now 11:15, time for Mark's appointment. I go out to the waiting room but… no Mark. I check my messages, and I see that Mark had emailed me 30 minutes earlier asking to be reminded of his appointment time – which isn't so peculiar seeing that we'd just changed his Tuesday appointment time to better suit his schedule. I respond to his email, reminding him that our session was just now beginning. Several minutes later, Mark emails me back saying he won't be in today. My curiosity will have to wait another day, but at least I am relieved that Mark hadn't dropped out of treatment or out of life. I had worried myself sick about Mark, and it had been for naught.

The day goes by, but the pain persists. In fact, it's gotten a bit worse. By the time I arrive home, I think I know what's wrong. I am a medical doctor and had noted that the pain had lodged in the right lower quadrant of my abdomen. So… it *must* be appendicitis. Off I go to the hospital, but the emergency room doctor is not impressed. She palpates my stomach and is unable to elicit pain where I'd felt it earlier in the day. Accordingly, she figures it can't be appendicitis. She rules out kidney stones and gall stones and sends me on my way. I guess I'd gotten myself worked up for no reason – which, frankly, is like me.

When I awake the following day, I am still in pain but relieved that nothing is terribly wrong with me. I go to work and look forward to finding out what's up with Mark, who shows up right on time for his 9 a.m. session. The session begins with a brief silence, followed by Mark's offering that he didn't have much to say. He complains a bit about how little he's gotten from treatment, acknowledges in passing that he knew that his father and I had been in contact over the weekend, then mentions that he'd reread *The Fountainhead* over the weekend and how doing so had given him a sense that life could be good if he loved what he was doing to the degree the character in the book did. "That book helped me realize what it's like *not* to be depressed." Mark then launches into a litany of complaints about his life, leading to his faulting people who don't try to help others by providing them easy-to-understand explanations as one would for a child. Instead, people just show off what they know by explaining things in overly complicated ways that are hard to follow and provide no help: "No one tries to help me understand. It's a worldwide con!" Insofar as the patient had intermittently accused me of conning him, I suggest that he might have me in mind. Mark responds by talking in more general terms about "people who pretend to know things they don't actually know about," and how no one calls out these people because pretending to know staves off despair. At the end of the session, the patient is talking about having realized that others cannot provide him with self-respect – that he has to earn it by trying – though, he laments, "trying sucks." The session ends without my knowing anything more about what had taken place the weekend before. I had not actively explored the question as I believe I should have, which I attribute to my still being in considerable pain. Call it an excuse – and maybe it is.

As it turns out, I cannot get through the rest of the day. I cancel my last three patients, go home, get into bed, and begin to shake. My gastroenterologist calls, hears me out, and asks me to come in post-haste. After examining me, he renders his opinion that I indeed have appendicitis, which is confirmed by CT scan a few hours later. It is now 10:30 p.m. I am in the emergency room awaiting admission, scheduled for an emergency appendectomy the next morning at 7 a.m. I begin calling my patients to let them know I won't be able to see them until next Monday.

So, how much should I tell my patients about what is happening?

Invited commentator responses 2: Darlene Ehrenberg and Ted Jacobs

Darlene Ehrenberg

I would tell Mark that I was not feeling well and that I would be in touch as soon as I knew when I could meet next, but I imagine that I would probably also want to let him know that I appreciate how much there is for us to talk about.

When they do meet, Dr. Tuch tells us that the patient complained about how little he felt he had gotten from treatment, that it's "a worldwide con!" and how "no one calls out the other because pretending to know helps stave off despair." But he also reports that at the end of the session, Mark talks about having realized that others cannot provide him with self-respect – that he has to earn it by trying. Though this seems to be an important insight that the patient comes to on his own, when Mark laments realizing that others cannot provide him with self-respect – and that he has to "earn it by trying" and that "trying sucks" – it suggests that there were times when he wanted to feel he could rely on another to be there for him, and that this did not happen, and he was devastated. What kind of disappointment and trauma might he have suffered, how early, and with whom? These are questions that I think might help to open the work at such a point. One thinks of children who were not taken care of early on and how traumatic that must have been. Spitz's famous studies show some of these children did not survive. What kind of trauma might account for what was in play here? Does this have bearing on Dr. Tuch's idea that working with Mark had affected him in his body? This could be a clue to possible issues the patient may have in terms of how he may respond in bodily ways that bypass conscious awareness. Dr. Tuch does not tell us any details about Mark's issues in relation to sex, but we might wonder about this as Dr. Tuch does tell us that it took years of work before Mark was able to have his first sexual experience.

Ted Jacobs

I would call my patients and tell them that I would be out for a few days and expect to resume the following week. I would say that I will let them know just when I would be resuming.

If one is going to be out for a considerable time due to an illness, I think it is best to inform the patient of this fact without going into unnecessary details or giving a false (often overly reassuring) picture of what is taking place. The same is true if one is faced with a chronic illness with an uncertain prognosis. I believe one should be honest and forthcoming without giving the patient more than basic information.

In the present circumstances, I would probably not say anything more than that I would be out of the office for a few days. Realistically, the recovery period from an appendectomy is usually pretty rapid and I would not expect to be out for more than three to four days. Under the circumstances, I see no reason to reveal information that would unnecessarily worry some patients. I do not feel strongly about this position, however, and I would be comfortable with the analyst explaining the actual situation or saying that he was having minor surgery and would be out for a few days. This is a reasonable alternative, if the information is given in a matter-of-fact way that does not arouse any unnecessary anxiety.

My intervention

I try to fashion my explanations about what is happening to me to suit each patient as best I can. I'm not able to reach Mark directly, so I leave him a voicemail message informing him that I had developed appendicitis, would undergo surgery in the morning, and expected to be at work on Monday. I fear that he might not get the message, show up, find the office door locked, and follow through on his threat to never see me again. Thankfully, Mark responds, leaving a voicemail message ("That sucks") and wishing me good luck.

The next time Mark and I meet is the following Monday. It is now one week to the day since Mark had failed to show. After positioning himself on the couch, Mark begins:

> I'm a little worried about myself. I realize now that the thought of dying kind of makes me happy. I used to think people kill themselves because they can't take it. But dying... the thought of it makes me happy! I smile when I think of dying, when I think of killing myself. Like how some people react to smelling fresh flowers. Not having to be here!

The patient had never before spoken, even obliquely, about feeling suicidal or about wishing to die, and his doing so now makes me think that my imagining that he'd committed suicide wasn't nearly as "off the wall" as I'd come to think it to be. I ask Mark whether he thought the possibility of suicide had crossed his parents' mind when they'd not been able to reach him the previous weekend. Mark dismisses the possibility as highly unlikely – if anything, he imagined they might have thought he'd been in a car accident (ignoring the fact that he doesn't even own a car). At any rate, the patient added, he could never commit suicide because his parents would blame themselves and he could never do that to them. I persist: "Still, what effect do you think it had on them to not be able to reach you? After all, that's not like you." Mark said he suspected his mom had worried, though his dad was "the voice of reason," and, accordingly, would have been disinclined to make much of the matter. I press on, inquiring about why he'd been unreachable, leading Mark to explain: "My phone died and I had left the charger at a friend's house. My parents called, I didn't respond. So they emailed me, but I didn't respond to that either, until Tuesday morning. I was sick all weekend, so I just shut myself in."

I ask whether Mark had any feelings about my having spoken to his father. He responded by noting: "They contacted *everybody*. My sister even ordered food to my house to see if I would answer the door. I didn't, I was sleeping." I point out just how anxious everyone was feeling about his being unreachable, leading the patient to admit, "Yeah, everyone was freaking out." Then, I ask how he imagined his disappearance had affected me, leading to his response:

Concern. Anger. I didn't want to come last Monday because I was sick and when I'm sick I feel more vulnerable. I thought, maybe I'd just stop coming, period. But I was glad that during the previous session we'd finally gotten around to addressing the self-esteem issue head-on... finally! But it left me wondering – why haven't you figured this out yet! Are you really trying?

I press on, asking the patient if it had occurred to him that I might have been worried about him. The patient responded: "Of course. It wasn't attention-seeking so much. But it was one way to prove that you have emotions beyond just our professional relationship. To see if I could affect you."

Mark then talked about how he'd felt increasingly hopeless as time went on and nothing seemed to be changing. I mentioned that I could well imagine that death might feel like a relief given how hopeless he sometimes feels, which evoked a strong affirmative reaction from Mark, who added: "I am super-anxious. I've gotten so good at hiding what is wrong with me. I pretend. I can never be myself. To be myself would be a shock to *anybody*."

This sets me to wondering whether Mark believes that he has succeeded at keeping me from realizing the depth of his angst and despair. I venture a guess that Mark might have felt the need to protect me from the shock of realizing the depth of his problems, to which Mark emphatically responds: "*Yes!* I am still not entirely comfortable being open here. I protect both of us from that shock. It's anger. *If I was myself I'd end up killing myself.*" As if to complete Mark's thought, I add: "...to be done once and for all with the pain and your terrible sense of helplessness and hopelessness." Mark answers back:

> But killing myself would not be good. I wouldn't be around. To get involved with the world, to see the world is real. Once I thought it was vital to be trustworthy, but I can't trust myself. I don't have a concept of reality.

This last comment gets me thinking, leading me to speculate aloud: "Maybe you felt that if you were to have had an effect on me when you disappeared that *that* would feel real," which evoked a swift and unequivocal response from Mark: "Yes, versus your merely saying 'I care...'" I pressed on: "What about the fact that last week those around you thought – for a time – that you might not exist anymore?" – which led Mark to finish my thought: "And now I think about it too. Maybe their thinking about it allows me to think about it as well."

I go even further out on a limb by surmising the patient's unconscious motive. It wasn't hard to imagine that the patient's action had intended – if only unconsciously – to affect those around him, but this is pure speculation. I ask if he'd gotten anything from the worry his actions had triggered, to which Mark responds, saying:

Maybe, a little. *But I didn't do it to create that.* And, besides, I wish I were emotionally connected so that everyone's worrying affected me more. It's the difference between a news story about someone else and it's happening to you yourself. It just doesn't feel like it's about me, per se.

I take yet another leap, asking Mark, "Maybe you sometimes see me as being as dead and disconnected as you feel?" Mark, who seems to still be thinking about how hopeless life seems, responds by saying:

I just wish this would end. Also, I had a thought that I feel bad about sharing. Not that you were seriously enough injured, but maybe if you died then I could leave the analysis, but I am not saying that *I actually caused you to fall ill* by supernatural forces.

I take this to be an instance of "negation" – stating a wish in the negative both to admit to such a wish and to simultaneously insist it isn't so. If this be the case, the patient's last comment would represent an unconscious wish to powerfully affect me in order to feel, for once, that he is an actual entity in the real world – and not a Pinocchio.

The following session the patient admits that the previous session:

… made me put more stock in the treatment. Just talking about dying made me less happy about dying. Talking about it made it real. That people were so concerned about me. And that I could be so out of it; that I could think of killing myself and that I could *do it*. What if I didn't have treatment to reality check? I could see it: Kill myself if I weren't in treatment. It worries me how disconnected I am. And – *wow* – people *are* worried about me, it makes me feel more real. Maybe if my parents were more worried I could open up to them and they could understand my suffering. I guess I did unconsciously want my parents to worry. It scares me to have unconscious thoughts and feelings. With an unconscious – what do I believe?

Invited commentator responses 3: Darlene Ehrenberg and Ted Jacobs

Darlene Ehrenberg

Dr. Tuch focuses on the question of whether the patient had thought about how his analyst and his parents might have been worried when he disappeared. Clearly, there is much emotion on both sides at this point and I imagine being in that situation would feel very complicated, so whatever I say here is offered to raise questions rather than to suggest that I can know how I might have actually responded myself at the time.

What strikes me most here is the patient's comment:

> I was glad the session before we'd finally gotten around to addressing the self-esteem issue head-on – finally! But it left me wondering – *why haven't you figured this out yet! Are you really trying*?

Dr. Tuch notes that he pressed on, "asking the patient if it had occurred to him that I might be worried about him," in effect ignoring the words, "why haven't you figured this out yet! Are you really trying?" Mark tells Dr. Tuch that he was trying to prove if Dr. Tuch had emotions beyond "just our professional relationship" – "to see if I could affect you." The patient is clear now that he wants to know that he can affect Dr. Tuch and that he felt increasingly hopeless as time went on because *things were getting worse*.

Dr. Tuch's response to how frustrated and hopeless the patient feels seems to touch the patient to the point that he lets go of his prior disappointment, and replies:

> I am super-anxious. I've gotten so good at hiding what is wrong with me. I pretend. I can never be myself. To be myself would be a shock to ANYBODY.

Dr. Tuch responds, acknowledging the patient's feeling that it is necessary to protect him from being shocked by the depth of Mark's problems. Mark notes:

> I protect both of us from that shock. It's *anger. If I was myself I'd end up killing myself.*

Dr. Tuch then asks if Mark had gotten any pleasure out of the worry he'd triggered. The patient replies to this question, "Maybe, a little. *But I didn't do it to create that."* Dr. Tuch then suggests to the patient: "Maybe you sometimes see me as being as dead and disconnected as you feel." Mark replies:

> I just wish this would end. Also, I had a thought that I feel bad about sharing. Not that you were seriously enough injured, but *maybe if you died then I could leave the analysis, but I am not saying that I actually caused you to fall ill by supernatural forces.*

This is striking because it is almost the opposite of what Mark announced in the beginning of their relationship when he told Dr. Tuch, "if you miss a session I will never come back." Now he is saying, "I cannot leave you unless you die!" An important question here is why the patient feels the only way to be free is for the other to have to die.

The following session, the patient reports that the previous session:

... made me put more stock in the treatment. Just talking about it made me less happy about dying. Talking about it made it real. That people were so concerned about me. And that I could be so out of it: that I could think of killing myself and that I could *do it*. What if I didn't have treatment to reality check? I could see it: Kill myself if I weren't in treatment. It worries me how disconnected I am. And – *wow* – people *are* worried about me. It makes me feel more real. Maybe if my parents were more worried I could open up to them and they could understand my suffering. I guess I did *unconsciously* want my parents to worry. It scares me to have unconscious thoughts and feelings. With an unconscious – what do I believe?

It is very moving to see that they reached this point and how the period of work that has been presented ends in such a moving place. I think trying to clarify together what led to the crisis and what made the difference now, and what could have made a difference earlier, and how they each understood all that happened between them unconsciously as well as consciously, would all be very important. Trying to address whether there might have been less pain and trauma for both analyst and patient if they had been able to deal with these issues earlier could be very meaningful and might help illuminate how to take our thinking forward, including how to minimize the risks of suicidal acting out when this may be an issue.

My experience has been that attending to times when things begin to become problematic, before they can escalate, is one way to maintain safety and make it possible to work with patients who may have been severely traumatized and who otherwise would have been deemed "unanalyzable." This is something that I have written about as being of special concern to me (Ehrenberg, 2004 and in press 2017).

I want to thank Dr. Tuch for inviting me to respond to such moving process and to join in this larger conversation, and for the ways it has not only allowed me to share my thinking but also stimulated my own thinking.

Ted Jacobs

It is easy, of course, and quite unfair for a commentator to look back over a colleague's work with a patient and, with the gift of hindsight, proclaim what he thinks would have been a better way to handle a particular situation or phase of treatment. One cannot really be in the shoes of the analyst who not only knows his patient in a way that an outsider cannot, but has to contend with transference-countertransference forces and unconscious transmissions between himself and the patient that no one outside the immediate situation can either experience or truly understand.

Having said that, I will proceed to make pronouncements as though I knew a way of working that would have been preferable. I don't. I will, however, for better or worse, offer my spontaneous reaction to the patient and the situation that developed.

My overall view is that the patient fell into a state of despair after the last few sessions that broke through his defensive armor. This, I think, was because he felt he was not making progress and he questioned whether Dr. Tuch truly cared about him. He wanted more evidence of that together with interventions that were more helpful and caused him to have hope and to find a pathway for himself in life.

With this feeling of despair came conscious suicidal ideation, which took the form of a thought that it would be desirable to die and thus find relief from the pain and turmoil that he felt.

In this state, the patient unconsciously acted out these feelings by disappearing and causing both his parents and his analyst to be alarmed and in fear for his safety. Both his analyst and his parents were understandably worried about the possibility of suicide.

The patient knew in some part of him that he was not at a point at which he would, in fact, attempt to take his own life, but he did sense that he was closer to being in that place. And he wanted others to know that he was in a state of despair and that his pain was leading him to think of his death in a way that he had not done before.

This message got through to his parents and analyst, and both responded with concern and anxiety, responses that demonstrated to the patient, as words had not, that they truly cared.

As to his approach, I think that Dr. Tuch got on the right track by recognizing and responding to the patient's genuine pain. This response made a huge difference to the patient who recognized and appreciated his analyst's true concern for him. This important response of Dr. Tuch's, however, came later in the session after he had questioned the patient about how he imagined his parents felt about his disappearance and whether he was aware of what he was doing to them.

In other words, Dr. Tuch's initial response was primarily focused on the patient's behavior, its consequences, and his motives for it.

What the patient was experiencing that led to his behavior was explored somewhat later in the session. I think it would have been better to focus first on what the patient was feeling as his pain at the time was severe and was the cause of his behavior. The patient needed to feel Dr. Tuch's empathy, and when he did feel this later in the session, this gave him not only a feeling of being understood, but some hope for the treatment.

My guess is that, in part, Dr. Tuch's initial focus on the patient's behavior toward his parents and his analyst was a countertransference response that grew out of the fright and anger that he felt when his patient suddenly disappeared. This is a fully understandable reaction that would have been felt by any analyst who cared deeply about his patient.

Dr. Tuch's movement toward exploring the patient's feelings of pain and hopelessness put the treatment on the right track and helped strengthen the therapeutic alliance. This, in turn, fostered the possibility of more fruitful analytic work and demonstrated to the patient that his analyst genuinely cared about him. This, in turn, sparked hope that the treatment could actually be helpful to him.

References

Bion, W. (1962). *Learning from experience.* London: Heinemann.

Boesky, D. (1990). The psychoanalytic process and its components. *Psychoanalytic Quarterly*, 59(4), 550–584.

Chessick, R. (1999). Contingency and the unformulated countertransference: A case presentation. *Journal of the American Academy of Psychoanalysis*, 27(1), 135–149.

Demos, E. (1999). The search for psychological models: Commentary on papers by Stephen Seligman and by Robin C. Silverman and Alicia F. Lieberman. *Psychoanalytic Dialogues*, 9(2), 219–227.

Eagle, M. (1999). A critical evaluation of current conceptions of transference and countertransference. *Psychoanalytic Psychology*, 17(1), 24–37.

Ehrenberg, D. B. (1974). The intimate edge in therapeutic relatedness. *Contemporary Psychoanalysis*, 10(4), 423–437.

Ehrenberg, D. B. (1982). Psychoanalytic engagement: The transaction as primary data. *Contemporary Psychoanalysis*, 18(4), 535–555.

Ehrenberg, D. B. (1992). *The intimate edge: Extending the reach of psychoanalytic interaction.* New York: Norton.

Ehrenberg, D. B. (1996). On the analyst's emotional availability and vulnerability. *Contemporary Psychoanalysis*, 32(2), 275–286.

Ehrenberg, D. B. (2004). How I became a psychoanalyst. *Psychoanalytic Inquiry*, 24(4), 490–516.

Ehrenberg, D. B. (in press 2017). The power of silence: Intergenerational considerations. *International Forum of Psychoanalysis*.

Gabbard, G. (1995). Countertransference: The emerging common ground. *International Journal of Psychoanalysis*, 76(3), 475–486.

Gitelson, M. (1952). The emotional position of the analyst in the psycho-analytic situation. *International Journal of Psychoanalysis*, 33(1), 1–10.

Heimann, P. (1950). On countertransference. *International Journal of Psychoanalysis*, 31, 81–84.

Jacobs, T. (1986). On countertransference enactments. *Journal of the American Psychoanalytic Association*, 34(2), 289–307.

Kernberg, O. (1965). Notes on countertransference. *Journal of the American Psychoanalytic Association*, 13(1), 38–56.

Klein, M. (1946). Notes on some schizoid mechanisms. In *Envy and gratitude and other works 1946–1963* (pp. 1–24). New York: Delacorte.

Lichtenberg, J., Lachmann, F., & Fosshage, J. (1992). *Self and motivational systems: Toward a theory of psychoanalytic technique.* Hillsdale, NJ: The Analytic Press.

Lichtenberg, J., Lachmann, F., & Fosshage, J. (1996). *The clinical exchange: Techniques derived from self and motivational systems.* Hillsdale, NJ: The Analytic Press.

Malin, A., & Grotstein, J. (1966). Projective identification in the therapeutic process. *International Journal of Psychoanalysis*, 47(1), 26–31.
Meissner, W. W. (1980). A note on projective identification. *Journal of the American Psychoanalytic Association*, 28(1), 43–67.
Ogden, T. (1979). On projective identification. *International Journal of Psychoanalysis*, 60(3), 357–373.
Racker, H. (1957). The meanings and uses of countertransference. *Psychoanalytic Quarterly*, 26(3), 303–357.
Renik, O. (1993). Analytic interaction: Conceptualizing technique in light of the analyst's irreducible subjectivity. *Psychoanalytic Quarterly*, 62(4), 553–571.
Renik, O. (1996). The analyst's self-discovery. *Psychoanalytic Inquiry*, 16(3), 390–400.
Sandler, J. (1976). Countertransference and role-responsiveness. *International Review of Psychoanalysis*, 3, 32–37.
Sandler, J. (1993). On communication from patient to analyst: Not everything is projective identification. *International Journal of Psychoanalysis*, 74(6), 1097–1107.
Stolorow, R. (2017). Personal communication.
Stolorow, R., Brandchaft, B., & Atwood, G. (1987). *Psychoanalytic treatment*. Hillsdale, NJ: The Analytic Press.
Stolorow, R., Orange, D., & Atwood, G. (1998). Projective identification begone! Commentary on paper by Susan H. Sands. *Psychoanalytic Dialogues*, 8(5), 719–725.
Tower, L. (1956). Countertransference. *Journal of the American Psychoanalytic Association*, 4(2), 224–255.
Tuch, R. (2015). The analyst's way of being: Recognizing separable subjectivities and the pendulum swing. *Psychoanalytic Quarterly*, 84(2), 363–388.

Index

The letter 'n' after a page number refers to the endnote number.

acting out 12, 19, 90, 95, 108, 123, 150, 241, 252–4, 259, 271; acting-out/enactment distinction 254; child 203, 219; containment 254; definition 254; secret-keeping 224; suicidal acting out 280, 281
adaptability: analyst's adaptability 155, 157–8, 171, 173, 177; therapeutic action and 75, 105, 110
addiction 106; 'addiction to near death' 106
adolescence 62, 69n1, 196n3, 226; *see also* child/childhood
adoption 89, 94; mother, issues related to 94, 95, 96, 98, 101, 102, 104, 105, 107, 109
affect: affect attunement 26, 123; affective engagement 132; affective intimacy 243; child 214; transference and 16
Akhtar, Salman 3, 98–100, 101–103, 105, 109–10
alpha elements 144, 210, 235, 265
Alvarez, Anne 3, 7–8, 103–104, 105–107
ambivalence 99, 208, 227, 259; ambivalent feelings toward the analyst 48, 56, 61
analyst 27; adaptability 155, 157–8, 171, 173, 177; anger/anger at the patient 97, 98, 99–100, 132, 144, 231, 240, 281; asymmetric analytic stance 10, 103, 123; being tested by the patient 8, 10, 59, 145, 188, 212, 243, 256–7; dependency on 230; empathy 8, 26, 28, 105, 152, 172, 246, 252, 281; guilt 100, 101, 121, 132; hostility towards 8, 10, 66, 74, 75, 78, 79, 99, 138, 139, 146, 161, 166–7, 175, 245–6, 247; idealization of 48, 56, 58–9, 61, 64, 66, 69n2, 142, 146, 147, 156, 166; intervening unthinkingly 13, 19, 251; listening, observing 11, 27, 67; neutrality 182, 188, 196, 201–202; patient's impact on 10, 13–14, 20, 139, 145, 262, 266, 277–8, 279; personal life 89, 96, 101, 102, 108, 143, 192–3, 228, 246, 247, 251, 264; sadism 94, 97, 108, 258; safety 258; 'seduction' by 26–7, 244; self-analysis 149, 150; task of 64, 68, 157; thoughtfulness 27; traumatization 258; *see also* countertransference enactment; provision; speaking up
analyst-centered interpretation 82, 147, 169; *see also* interpretation
analytic frame 5, 53, 92, 193; break in the frame 252, 253; compromise of 92, 181, 191–2; constraints of 193–4; containment 252, 254; flexibility in 194; importance of maintaining the analytic frame 181; preservation of 191–2; *see also* 'time' aspect of analytic frame
anger 48, 53, 54, 78, 80, 83, 101, 124, 130, 132, 133, 144, 146, 164, 246, 259, 277, 279; analyst's anger/anger at the patient 97, 98, 99–100, 132, 144, 231, 240, 281; anger at God 54, 57; child 79, 85, 201, 206, 207–208, 216, 218–19
anxiety 1, 15, 25, 30, 37, 39, 41, 44, 78, 140, 164–6, 266, 277; analyst's anxiety 100, 271–2; child 203, 214, 215; defense against 166; enactment and 91; perfectionism and 155; projection of 166; relational perspective 42; sense

of lack of provision and 155–6; social anxiety 222, 228, 230; suicidal patient 164–5; *see also* persecutory anxiety
Arlow, Jacob A. 50
attachment: patient/analyst attachment 28–9, 98, 257, 267
attunement 27, 53, 65, 145; affect attunement 26, 123; empathic attunement 259; misattunement 54; tuning out 54, 66

bad object 121, 124–5, 160; bad internal object 98; bad self 124, 125; *see also* good object
Balsam, Rosemary 3, 59–63
Bandura, Albert 203
Barish, Kenneth 202–203
Barth, Jill Model 90–8, 100–101, 104, 107–109
Bateson, Gregory 252
Benjamin, Jessica 116, 256
beta elements 144, 235, 265
Bion Wilfred 2, 81–2, 144, 214, 235, 239; analyzing without memory or desire 37, 49
bipersonal field 169
Blass, Rachel 3, 4–5, 6, 51, 64–8
Blum, Harold P. 49, 50
Boesky, Dale 265
Bohleber, Werner 90
Bolognini, Stefano 3, 231–5
Boston Change Process Study Group (BCPSG) 144–5
boundary violation 12–13, 104, 180, 182, 252, 257; boundary crossing 182–3, 194; boundary diffusion 252, 271; recognition of boundaries 254
Britton, Rondal 243
Bromberg, Phillip 114–15, 126, 259
Busch, Fred 3, 5, 6–7, 9, 17–18, 34–8

Caruth, Elaine 223
Casement, Patrick 75–6
Cassorla, Roosevelt 163
castration anxiety 202
Celenza, Andrea 3, 5, 8, 9, 122–5
child/childhood 5, 8–9, 48; abandonment 246, 247, 248, 251; acting out 203, 219; affect 214; anger 79, 85, 201, 206, 207–208, 216, 218–19; anxiety 203, 214, 215; behavior 202, 204; capacity for illusion 50; child analysis 60, 209, 213–14; childhood needs 26, 203; conflict 203; containment 209, 210, 211; depression 78; enactment 209; environment 203, 210–11, 213, 215; excluded third 243; hostility towards the analyst 207–208, 212, 216; intrapsychic conflict 214, 215, 216–17; jealousy 206, 207, 211; masochism 216; memory 202; neglected child 180, 275; physical/emotional pain 203, 206; projection 165, 209, 210, 233; sadism 208, 211, 216; sado-masochism 202, 208; secret 223, 225; sexual abuse 180; trauma 202, 203, 206, 213, 240; troubled childhood 53, 57, 72, 77–8, 79, 118, 247; whining child 106; *see also* adolescence; infantile wish/need; play therapy
Chrzanowski, G. 246
Chused, Judith Fingert 91, 113
clinical moment 1, 14–16, 19–21, 189; clinical moments appearing in the literature 12–14; common denominator of 15; 'now moment' 15–16
Clinical Moments Program 1–2, 4, 20
Clinical Moments Project 2–4; clinical moments 19–21; commentators 2–4, 17–19, 21; Editors 3, 4, 19, 38; experimental design 16–19, 21; goal of 20; lessons from 12, 19
co-construction: patient/analyst co-construction of relational field 38
Coates, Susan W. 203
Coen, Stanley 216
compromise formation 217
confidentiality 175, 176, 225, 228, 244, 272
conflict: child 203; conflict resolution and integration 156; interpersonal conflict 156; loyalty conflict 57, 59; unconscious conflict 38, 40, 41; *see also* intrapsychic conflict
constructivism 38, 39; 'constructivist' position 39
containment 8, 36, 144, 252; acting out and 254; analytic frame 252, 254; child 209, 210, 211; countertransference reaction 265
Control Mastery theory 8, 21n5, 188, 190; passive-into-active test 257; test-failing/test-passing 188, 256; transference test 257
corrective emotional experience 189, 257

Couch, Arthur S. 50
countertransference enactment 15, 20, 37–8, 52, 60, 81–2, 89, 94–110, 162–3, 262–3; analyst, regaining sense of psychic equilibrium 114–15; analyst's defensiveness 108, 110, 122, 127–8, 130, 138, 146, 152; anxiety and 91; de-contextualization 263; definition 90, 113, 254, 263, 265; dissociation 113, 114, 125–7, 130; enactment/ projective identification distinction 91; extra-analytic encounter 90, 91–2, 183, 196; impact of unanalyzed countertransference 91; inevitability of 91; interpersonal school 113, 115, 139, 266; intersubjective perspective 263; intrapsychic conflict and 114, 116; maternal countertransference 104, 108, 161, 271; as the patient's creation 264; pervasiveness of 91, 265; as product of the analyst's transference-readiness 263; as projective identification 263–4, 265; regression and 91; relational school 114; religious belief and 52; resolution of 115, 122, 128–30; value of 112, 113, 122, 123, 124, 126, 130, 132, 139–40, 239–40, 263, 265; *see also* analyst; countertransference reaction; role responsiveness; wearing the attribution
countertransference reaction 13–14, 76, 91, 95, 138, 149, 152–3, 262, 268–70; bodily symptoms 269, 271, 273, 275; complementary countertransference reaction 89, 108–109, 110n1, 163, 209; concordant countertransference reaction 89, 97, 109, 110n1, 209; containment and 265; cruelty report and 248, 249–50; externalizing the countertransference response 169; secret-keeping, reaction to 224, 225, 231, 234, 237, 239–40; subjective response 140; suicidal patient 271–3, 277–8, 280, 281; *see also* countertransference enactment

Davies, Jody 13, 14, 19
defense analysis 9, 35–6, 45n3, 45n4, 45n5, 129; *undoing* 35, 43
deficit-based pathology 158
depression 76, 80, 106, 117, 118, 184, 222, 227, 274; childhood and 78

devaluation 74, 143, 144, 157, 166, 216
Dewald, Paul A. 50
disjunction 15
displacement 109, 159, 176, 230, 232; play therapy 214–15, 216, 217
dissociation 9–10, 69n1; countertransference enactment 113, 114, 125–7, 130; interpersonalization of dissociation 114; subjectivity, dissociation of 126; *see also* 'not me' aspect
doer/done to 116, 256
dominance-submission pattern 255–6
Donner, Susan 3, 5, 8–9, 208–13
Donnet, Jean-Luc 236

Eagle, Morris 3, 21n5, 187–90
Eckstein, Rudolf 223
ego psychology 2, 6, 9, 59, 60, 61, 235; body-ego trauma 96–7, 106; ego regression 215; id, ego, superego 204; superego 67, 155, 165, 166, 187, 204, 213, 216, 217
ego strength 156, 203
ego weakness 35, 37, 157, 203
Ehrenberg, Darlene 3, 6, 21n7, 266, 268–71, 274–5, 278–80
empathic failure 6, 48, 53, 54, 56, 57, 58–9, 60–1, 144; idealizing the analyst 48, 56, 58–9, 64, 69n2; self psychology 60; 'transmuting internalization' 69n2; tuning out 66
empathy 74, 121; analyst 8, 26, 28, 105, 152, 172, 246, 252, 281; empathic analytic stance 154, 161; empathic attunement 259; empathic listening perspective 7, 40; empathic mirroring 54, 137, 144, 145; empathic understanding 189, 246; 'empathically' oriented therapy 252
enactment 5, 54, 83, 85; acting-out/ enactment distinction 254; acute enactment 15, 163; benefits of 5, 90, 124; child 209; chronic enactment 163, 265; content of 9; definition 90, 113–14; play therapy 211, 217; projection and 113–14, 122; repression and 113–14; split off aspects 113–14; *see also* countertransference enactment
envy 26, 103, 108, 109, 160, 166, 184, 247, 267; maternal envy 125, 129; *see also* jealousy

excluded third 243, 244, 245
externalization 215, 216
extra-analytic encounter 89, 90, 91–3, 108, 183; analyst, impact on 93; analyst's home office 102; analytic frame, compromise of 92, 181, 191–2; boundary crossing 182–3, 194; boundary violation 182; chance encounter 92, 108, 180; countertransference enactment 90, 91–2, 183, 196; gratification 182, 187, 188; impact of 92–4; infantile wishes 182, 183, 184; patient's invitation, dealing with 92, 181, 187–94, 195; planned/intended encounter 92, 94, 181; potential positive effects 183, 184; regressive feelings/wishes 92, 93, 181, 183; test-failing/test-passing 188, 189, 190; warning against 183, 184
extra-transference interpretation 49–50, 58, 59, 60, 64, 68; transferential/extra-transferential distinction 59–60; see also interpretation; transference interpretation

father 93, 109, 118, 185, 226–7, 238–9; abusive father 13, 186, 195; analytic father 96; idealization of 267; infidelity 222, 226, 238–9; mother's father 233, 234; neglected by 140–1, 146; see also parents
Ferro, Antonio 2, 45n4, 60
Fonagy, Peter 2, 73, 121
Fosshage, James 3, 7, 9, 38–43, 115
free association 28, 33, 73, 167, 191, 254
Freidman, Lawrence
Freud, Anna 35, 213
Freud, Sigmund 16, 26, 59, 156, 192, 214; affective intimacy 243; analyst/analysand rapport 28–9; Anna O. 12, 21n6; defense analysis 45n5; 'evenly suspended attention' 49; females, vision of 62; fundamental rule 223; gratification of patient's wishes 182; hypnosis 73; Little Hans 202; religious beliefs/God 50, 51; 'timing and tact' 61
Friedman, Larry 26–7, 182, 243–4
frustrating object 65, 67
fundamental rule 11, 28, 73; secret-keeping and 223, 231, 232, 236–7

Gabbard, Glen 113, 182–3, 264
Ganzarain, Ramon 92, 183, 184

gender identity 61–3; female identity 61
genetic interpretation 49–50, 146, 151; see also interpretation
Gill, Merton 38, 49, 50, 60, 158
Glick, Robert 3, 8, 10–11, 142–5, 148–50
God 50–2, 63, 233; anger at 54, 57; a composite figure 54, 58; as delusion 50, 51; as illusion 50, 51; as metaphor within a psychoanalytic frame of reference 53–4, 67; Mother/God 51; a 'phantasy self-object' 52; relationship with 64–5, 67, 68; transitional space and 51; 'unique primary object' 51; see also illusion; religious belief
good object 8, 67, 123, 164; see also bad object
Gray, Paul 2
Green, Andre 2, 36
Greenacre, Phyllis 182
Greenberg, Jay 3, 8, 16–17, 18, 162–4, 169–70, 173
Greenson, Ralph 60, 223
Gross, A. 223
guilt 6, 26, 37, 118, 120, 132–3, 206; analyst's guilt 100, 101, 121, 132; projection of guilt into the analyst 66; projection of guilt into others 171
Gunderson, John 123
Guntrip, Harry 246
Gutheil, Thomas 182–3

Heimann, Paula 264
Hoffman, Irwin Z. 158
Hoyt, M. 224

idealization 52, 233–4; analyst, idealization of 48, 56, 58–9, 61, 64, 66, 69n2, 142, 146, 147, 156, 166; father, idealization of 267; mourning the loss of idealizations 61; self psychology, idealization of 74–5; unanalyzed idealization 157
identity 11, 95; enactment and 126; identity crisis 63; see also gender identity
illusion: child's capacity for 50; God as 50, 51; religious belief as an 'illusion' 50, 51; transitional space and 50, 51; twin illusions 244
infantile wish/need 26, 27, 28; extra-analytic encounter 182, 183, 184
intellectualization 5, 91, 112, 129; extra-transference interpretation and 50

interpersonal perspective/school 2, 6, 9, 254; advantages of 7; countertransference enactment 113, 115, 139, 266; interpersonal conflict 156; interpersonal field 7

interpretation 7; intolerance to 49; leading edge interpretation 41, 45n6; offering of interpretations 4, 28, 49; saturated interpretation 6–7; tentative interpretation 6; therapeutic alliance as prerequisite for interpretation 28–9, 44; trailing edge interpretation 45n6; unsaturated interpretation 36, 45n4; *see also* analyst-centered interpretation; extra-transference interpretation; genetic interpretation; transference interpretation

intersubjective perspective 9; countertransference enactment 263; intersubjective field 38–9, 40; intersubjective process 149; two-person perspective 9, 263

intrapsychic conflict 39, 40, 41–2, 155, 174, 177; child 214, 215, 216–17; countertransference enactment and 114, 116; projection 156; religious belief and 52, 54; ubiquity of 214

intrapsychic perspective 5–6, 35, 38, 39, 40, 41; disadvantages 42, 43

Jacobs, Theodore 3, 90–1, 265–6, 271–2, 275, 280–2

jealousy 108, 122, 141, 144, 159, 160, 166, 184, 234; child 206, 207, 211; *see also* envy

Joseph, Betty 60, 106

Judaism/Jewish 108, 109; davening 56, 57, 58; disdain for 89, 96, 97, 98, 99; Nazism and 96, 97, 99, 106; Orthodox Judaism 52–3, 62; Passover 54, 62, 66, 69n3; prayer 55, 56, 57, 68; rebbe/rabbi 55, 56–7, 59, 61, 62, 63, 68, 69; Talmud 54, 62; *see also* God; religious belief

Kantrowitz, Judy 3, 145–8, 150–2
Kernberg, Otto 2, 243
Killingmo, Bjorn 157–8
Klein, Melanie 60, 81, 156, 165, 211
Kohut, Heinz 40–1, 69n2, 73, 86n1, 147
Kovach, Bernadette 201–208, 218–19
Kris, Ernst 35
Kuttnauer, Lynn 1, 4, 48–59, 68–9

Lacan, Jacques 2, 157, 235, 236, 237; temporal pulsation 10, 238
Lachmann, Frank 7, 40, 45n6, 115
Langs, Robert 181, 182
Levenson, Edgar 3, 8, 11, 251–5
Lichtenberg, Joseph 7, 11, 40, 115, 138, 190–4
Loewald, Hans 59, 60, 147

Margolis, Marvin 1, 224, 225
masochism 106, 216, 258, 267
Mason, Albert 3, 164–7, 170, 173, 176, 211
McWilliams, Nancy 21n5, 93, 255–9
medication 84
Meissner, William 50, 51
Meltzer, Donald 104
Menninger, Karl A. 254
mental functions 214
mentalization 73, 172
Michels, Robert 83–4
Michigan Psychoanalytic Institute 1, 3, 117
'moment of meeting' 10, 145
mother 11, 56, 57, 69, 76–7, 118, 152–3, 267; breast 165; demanding mother 141, 143, 146, 148, 151, 153; guilt 206; incestual mother 233–4; internal mother 62; maternal countertransference 104, 108, 161, 271; maternal envy 125, 129; mother/child bond 174, 175, 176, 177, 178; mother figure 63; Mother/God 51; neglected by/hungering for mothering 160, 161, 176, 194; sado-masochism 151, 152; traumatic experience with 75–6, 76–8, 105, 120, 125, 131, 132, 166; *see also* parents
mourning 55, 61, 64, 67, 269

narcissism 10, 25, 73, 82, 144, 145, 147, 171, 233; affirmative, joyful nature of 129; limited view of 127–8; narcissistic crisis 143; narcissistic defense 217; narcissistic desire 26, 27; narcissistic injury 35, 39, 113, 143, 146, 157; narcissistic needs 243; narcissistic pathology 159; narcissistic pleasure 126, 128, 130; narcissistic sensitivity 159; narcissistic vulnerability 35, 95, 119, 128, 147, 151, 152, 215
narrative coherence 237–8

neurosis/neurotic 32, 225; transference neurosis 49, 96
New Center for Psychoanalysis (NCP) 1, 3
nonlinear systems theory 214
'not me' aspect 9–10, 113, 114, 115, 126; *see also* dissociation
'now moment' 10, 15–16, 145; as an instance 15; transference 15

object relations 59, 263
objectivism 38, 39; 'objectivist' position 39
Oedipal dynamics/configuration 184, 219, 233, 234, 243, 267
Ogden, Thomas 2, 16, 236–7, 263
Orbach, Susan 112–21, 130–2
organizing pattern 39, 40, 42, 43

paranoia/paranoid 75, 80, 83, 84, 166, 168, 169, 171, 186, 238; paranoid community 171; *see also* persecutory anxiety
parents 118, 160–1, 174–5, 185–6, 204–206, 244; analyst, test-failing/test-passing 188; analyst as withholding provision/ineffectual parent 155, 160, 175; impaired parents 53, 64–5; parental bond 174, 175, 243; triadic relationship 243; *see also* father; mother
pathogenic beliefs 181
perfectionism 32, 53, 64–5, 151; accepting imperfection 64, 65, 67; anxiety and 155; lack of provision and 155
persecutory anxiety 78–9, 155, 156, 165, 166, 168; persecutory fantasies 28; *see also* paranoia/paranoid
perversion 106, 237
Pick, Irma Brenman 17, 80–2
play therapy 60, 207–219; analyst's participation in play 5, 201, 204, 214–17; benefits of 5, 9, 201, 204, 211, 213, 219; displacement 214–15, 216, 217; enactment 211, 217; function of 213; play scenario 211; play sequence 5, 209, 213; reconstruction 218; trauma and 5; *see also* child/childhood
polarized roles 256
primal scene 174, 183, 184
projection 8, 67, 99, 169; anxiety 166; child 165, 209, 210, 233; enactment and 113–14, 122; guilt, projection of 66, 171; integration 156; projecting split-off aspects of oneself 156; sense of lack of provision and 156; turning intrapsychic conflict into interpersonal conflict 156
projective identification 9–10, 13, 81–2, 113, 132n2, 156, 262; analyst and 264; child 233; countertransference enactment as projective identification 263–4, 265; definition 160; enactment/projective identification distinction 91; provision and 156, 157, 175
provision 20, 172–7; analyst as *le sujet suppose savoir* 157; analyst as withholding provision/ineffectual parent 155, 160, 175; anxiety, sense of lack of provision and 155–6; conflict resolution and 156; lack of early environmental provision 155; perfectionism and 155; 'problem-solving mode' 177; projection and 156; projective identification 156, 157, 175; provision model of therapeutic action 7, 154, 155, 157, 175; wish for 157; *see also* analyst
psychic change 4, 5, 7, 9, 64
psychic reality 202
psychoanalytic frame *see* analytic frame
psychoanalytic societies and institutes 20
psychoanalytic technique 8, 35, 38, 59, 60, 100, 150; adaptability/flexibility 75, 105, 110; backing off 73; rethinking the clinical approach 74; shifts in 73, 213; staying the course 75–6; *see also* therapeutic action
psychosis/psychotic 81; transference psychosis 83

Racker, Heinrich 89, 110n1, 163, 209
reconstruction 16, 49, 218
reflective thought 243
regression 72, 80, 84, 85, 154, 244; countertransference enactment 91; extra-analytic encounter and regressive feelings/wishes 92, 93, 181, 183; integration 156; regressive behavior and manipulation 21n7
Reich, Annie 224
Reik, Theodor 255
rejection 95, 99, 107, 109, 112, 166, 191–2; fear of 94, 121, 159
relational perspective/school 6, 9, 39, 41; advantages of 42–3; anxiety 42; countertransference enactment 114; patient/

analyst co-construction of relational field 38; relational field 38, 39–40; relational model 40; relational scenario 99; relational self psychology 39

religiosity 68

religious belief 49, 52–9, 69; as adaptation 51; countertransference enactment and 52; Freud's legacy on 50; as 'illusion' 50, 51; intrapsychic conflict 52, 54; place in analysis 50–2, 67–8; religious observance 53; spiritual/mystical dimension of religion 51; *see also* God; Judaism/Jewish

Renik, Owen 265

repetition 98; not all repetition is perverse or addictive 107; repetitive behavior 118, 120, 125; repetitive relational experience 39, 40, 41, 176; repetitive resistance 166

repression 7, 155; enactment and 113–14; slip of the tongue 39, 43; trailing edge 45n6

resistance 29–30, 32, 34, 39, 40, 43, 83; repetitive resistance 166

role responsiveness 262, 264–5; analyst's reactivity/responsivity 122, 124, 264–5

Roughton, Ralph E. 224

Russell, Paul 257

sadism 20, 96, 106, 185, 255, 259, 260; analyst 94, 97, 108, 258; child 208, 211, 216; dominance-submission pattern 255–6; ego-syntonic sadism 255–6; sadistic pleasure 94, 245; sadistic superego 216

sado-masochism 99, 151, 152; child 202, 208

Sampson, Harold 2, 188; *see also* Control Mastery theory

Sandler, Joseph 264–5

Scarfone, Dominique 5, 17, 167, 170, 171, 174–5, 176–7, 178

screen memories 202

secret/secret-keeping 223, 225–6, 232; child 223, 225; clinical management of 224; corrosive effects of 223; countertransference reaction 224, 225, 231, 234, 237, 239–40; disclosure of 230–1, 236, 240; a form of acting out 224; fundamental rule 223, 231, 232, 236–7; 'partial saying' 235–6, 239

Segal, Hanna 106

self-esteem 147, 151, 170, 212, 277, 279; low self-esteem 159, 160, 168, 222

self-loathing 31, 53, 62, 267

self-object 52, 178n1, 182; self-object needs 7; self-object transference 61; self-selfobject matrix 41

self-protective measure 9, 40–1, 118–19, 173

self psychology 2, 6, 41, 52, 61, 73, 74, 144; empathic failure 60; idealization of 74–5; provision model 178n1; relational self psychology 39

self-reflective/reflective awareness 29, 40, 42, 43, 112, 132, 138

self-regulation 96, 212

self-representation 9, 52

self-righting 8, 138, 145, 149

sexuality 36, 106, 107, 228, 229, 240, 247–8, 266–7, 275; erotic transference 96, 150; intimate love relations 243–4; libidinal wish 8; sexual abuse 180, 185; sexual trauma 185; transference 186; *see also* gender issues

shame 25, 37, 267; associated with being wrong 30, 36, 39, 40, 41, 42; 'not me' aspect 126–7; shame-sensitivity 33, 39

Shaw, Daniel 52

slip of the tongue 25, 32, 33–4, 35, 42, 44; repression 39, 43

Slochower, Joyce 49, 157

Smith, Janet 7, 154–62, 167–9, 170, 172, 175–6, 177–8

Sorenson, Randall 50, 52

speaking up 19–20, 25, 34, 39, 42, 43; defense analysis 35; transference interpretation 48–9, 58, 63, 64, 66–7, 85; *see also* analyst

Spero, Moshe Halevi 51

split off aspects 5–6, 79, 100, 156, 232, 234; enactment and 113–14; projecting split-off aspects of oneself 156; reintegration of 5, 9, 64, 156, 235; retrieving of 9

splitting 166, 234

Steiner, John 82, 147, 156, 169

Stern, Daniel 10, 15, 145

Stern, Donnel 3, 7, 9–10, 125–30; dissociation 9–10, 113, 114, 115, 125

Stolorow, Robert 263, 264

Stone, Leo 50

Strachey, James 49

Strean, Herbert S. 93, 183

Sugarman, Alan 3, 5, 9, 213–17

suicidal patient 75, 170, 177, 244, 257, 276, 277; analyst's proviso 258; anxiety 164–5; countertransference reaction and 271–3, 277–8, 280, 281; suicidal acting out 280, 281
Sullivan, Harry Stack 255
supervision 18, 117, 126, 145, 149, 245; in-training psychoanalyst 119, 120, 123
symbolization 7, 96, 106, 126, 217, 228, 236; screen memories/material realities symbolic linking 202; symbolic function 90; un-symbolized experience 9, 114, 126

Target, Mary 212
Tarnower, William 93, 183, 184
therapeutic action 5, 130, 156; negative therapeutic reaction 166; theories about 8–9, 150; *see also* psychoanalytic technique
therapeutic alliance 19–20, 25, 157, 282; challenged 74, 75, 85; practical implications of 28; as prerequisite for interpretation 28–9, 44; *see also* working alliance
therapeutic frame *see* analytic frame
therapeutic zeal 37
third party 242, 247–8, 256, 258, 261; analyst, being tested by the patient 243, 256; cruelty report 245–6, 248, 249–50; cruelty report and countertransference 248, 249–50; exclusive allegiance 243, 244–5
'time' aspect of analytic frame 138–9; analyst, early ending of the session by 137, 138, 139, 142; extended time 137, 139, 142, 146, 152; patient's anger at being cut short of time 139, 142, 146; patient's attention to 137, 138, 139; *see also* analytic frame
transference 64, 81, 83; actualization of 90, 125, 125; affect and 16; definition 60, 254; erotic transference 96, 150; healing effect of 7–8, 104; negative transference 61, 74, 83, 85, 94, 99, 138, 147, 217; 'now moment' 15; positive transference 54; risks of 50; sexuality 186; total transference 60; transference gratification 182; transference love 12, 21n6; transference neurosis 49, 96; transference reaction 5; transferential/extra-transferential distinction 59–60

transference interpretation 5, 59; as curative agent 6, 64; intolerance to 49, 72; as mainstay of psychoanalysis 49, 60; speaking up 48–9, 58, 63, 64, 66–7, 85; *see also* extra-transference interpretation; interpretation
transitional object 107
transitional phenomenon/space 50, 51, 201
transmuting internalization 69n2, 144
trauma/traumatic experience 61–2, 100–101, 202, 251, 260; analyst 258; analyst as persecutor or victim 256; body-ego trauma 96–7, 106; child 202, 203, 206, 213, 240; environmental trauma 202, 213; iatrogenic trauma 103; mother, traumatic experience with 75–6, 76–8, 105, 120, 125, 131, 132, 166; patient's identification with the aggressor 251, 260; play therapy and 5; sexual trauma 185; transgenerational trauma 235
treatment: aim of 156; defense against anxiety 166; 'dose effect' 26; exclusivity 243; not showing up for the session 268, 271–2; not treatable patient/ 'unanalyzable' 255, 280; reasons for seeking help 25–6, 32; reasons for staying under treatment 26–7, 29; threat to quit 72, 80, 81–2, 83, 116, 268, 269, 271, 272
triadic relationship 243
Tuch, Richard 3, 18, 21, 25–34, 43–4, 50–1, 72–6, 112–16, 137–40, 180–4, 189, 223–6, 242–6, 262–8, 272–4, 276–8

unformulated experience/content 9, 113, 114, 122, 125–6

wearing the attribution 115–16, 264; refusal/failing to 115, 116; *see also* countertransference enactment
Weiss, Joseph 2, 188; *see also* Control Mastery theory
Westin, D. 113
Wilson, Mitchell 3, 10, 235–40
Winnicott, Donald 2, 6, 50, 51, 106–107, 144
working alliance 27, 158, 185, 191; conflict-free 27–8, 44n1; *see also* therapeutic alliance